The History of Jazz

Volume I Early Jazz: Its Roots and Musical Development

Early Jazz

ITS ROOTS AND MUSICAL DEVELOPMENT

GUNTHER SCHULLER

OXFORD UNIVERSITY PRESS
New York Oxford

Oxford University Press
Oxford New York Toronto
Delhi Bombay Calcutta Madras Karachi
Petaling Jaya Singapore Hong Kong Tokyo
Nairobi Dar es Salaam Cape Town
Melbourne Auckland

and associated companies in
Beirut Berlin Ibadan Nicosia

First published in 1968 by Oxford University Press, Inc., 200 Madison Avenue,
New York, New York 10016
First issued as an Oxford University Press paperback, 1986

For permission to reprint passages and examples from the books and music indicated, grateful acknowledgment is made to the following:

School of Oriental and African Studies, University of London, for excerpts and musical examples from *Studies in African Music* by A. M. Jones, published by Oxford University Press, London, 1959.

Mayfair Music Corporation for *Skip the Gutter*, instrumental by Spencer Williams, © 1928 by Mayfair Music Corporation, renewed and assigned to Mayfair Music Corporation. Used by permission.

MCA Music for *West End Blues* by Clarence Williams and Joe Oliver, © 1928 by MCA Music, a division of MCA, Inc. Copyright renewed 1955 and assigned to MCA Music, a division of MCA, Inc. Used by permission. All rights reserved.

Melrose Music Corporation for *Froggie Moore*, words by Benjamin and John C. Spikes, music by Ferd "Jelly Roll" Morton, © 1923 by Spikes Brothers; copyright renewed and assigned to Melrose Music Corporation. Used by permission. *New Orleans Blues*, instrumental by Ferd "Jelly Roll" Morton, © 1925 by Melrose Music Corporation; copyright renewed; used by permission. *Black Bottom Stomp*, instrumental by Ferd "Jelly Roll" Morton, © 1926 by Melrose Music Corporation, renewed and assigned to Melrose Music Corporation. Used by permission. *The Chant*, © 1926 by Melrose Music Corporation; copyright renewed; used by permission. *Beau Koo Jack*, words by Walter Melrose, music by Alex Hill and Louis Armstrong, © 1928 by Melrose Music Corporation, renewed and assigned to Melrose Music Corporation. Used by permission.

Mills Music, Inc., for *East St. Louis Toodle-Oo* by Duke Ellington and Bub Miley, © 1927 by Mills Music, Inc. Used by permission. *Black and Tan Fantasy* by Duke Ellington and Bub Miley, © 1927 by Mills Music, Inc. Used by permission. *Mood Indigo* by Duke Ellington, Irving Mills, and Albany Bigard, © 1931 by Mills Music, Inc. Used by permission. *Choo-Choo* by Andy Rasaf, Eugene Sedric, and Thomas Fats Waller, © 1939 by American Academy of Music. Used by permission.

Morley Music Company, Inc., for *After You've Gone*, words by Cresmer and Layton, © 1918 by Morley Music Company, Inc., renewed by Morley Music Company, Inc. Used by permission.

Library of Congress Cataloging-in-Publication Data
Schuller, Gunther.
The history of jazz.
Reprint. Originally published: New York: Oxford
University Press, 1968.
Includes index.
Contents: v. 1. Early jazz : its roots and musical development.
1. Jazz music. I. Title.
ML3506.S36 1986 781'.57 86-2403
ISBN 0-19-504043-0 (pbk.)

Printing (last digit): 9 8 7 6
Printed in the United States of America

To Duke Ellington

whose music has brought so much happiness
and beauty into the lives of all of us

Preface

Although there is no dearth of books on jazz, very few of them have attempted to deal with the music itself in anything more than general descriptive or impressionistic terms. The majority of books have concentrated on the legendry of jazz, and over the years a body of writing has accumulated which is little more than an amalgam of well-meaning amateur criticism and fascinated opinion. That this was allowed to pass for scholarship and serious analysis is attributable not only to the humble, socially "unacceptable" origin of jazz, but also to the widely held notion that a music improvised by self-taught, often musically illiterate musicians did not warrant genuine musicological research. Despite the fact that many "serious" composers and performers had indicated their high regard for jazz as early as the 1920s, the academic credentials of jazz were hardly sufficient to produce a serious interest in the analysis of its techniques and actual musical content.

Even the early writings of sympathetic composers like Aaron Copland, Edward Burlingame Hill, Constant Lambert, Darius Milhaud, and Virgil Thomson and of critics like Alfred Frankenstein and Massimo Mila failed to capture the elusive essentials of jazz, or they fell prey to basic misconceptions. For the rest there was an avalanche of derogatory articles and pamphlets by popular writers who fantasized relentlessly over the pernicious influence of jazz on music and morals. Moreover, the statements of many jazz musicians themselves in the early years of jazz encouraged others to treat the subject lightly.

After 1930, however, there appeared a number of books that were not only sympathetic and serious in intent but revealed an understanding of the essential nature of jazz: Robert Goffin's *Aux Frontières du Jazz* (1932), Wilder Hobson's *American Jazz Music* (1939), Frederic Ramsey's and Charles Edward Smith's *Jazzmen* (1939), and Hugues Panassié's *The Real Jazz* (1942). But even in these books, a musician interested in learning about jazz as a *musical language* could learn very little about its harmonic and rhythmic syntax, its structural organization, its textures and sonorities, or what in technical terms made one performance better than another. In addition, these authors were so heavily committed to propagating the absolute primacy of New Orleans jazz that their books were anything but comprehensive.

The first book to look closely at the materials and grammar of jazz was Winthrop Sargeant's *Jazz: Hot and Hybrid* (1946). Dissatisfied with the speculative or impressionistic approach of his predecessors, Sargeant used the tools of theoretical analysis to define jazz and to describe its musical anatomy. The standards Sargeant set were not met again until ten years later when the French writer and composer André Hodeir published *Jazz: Its Evolution and Essence,* in which the analytical screws were tightened once more, taking full advantage of the perspective provided by the innovations of Charlie Parker and the whole modern jazz movement. Apart from the intrinsic value of Sargeant's and Hodeir's books, they helped to stimulate new standards of excellence in jazz criticism. Their influence on Martin Williams, Nat Hentoff, Max Harrison, the present author, and a host of other writers contributing to magazines like the *Jazz Review,* is undeniable.

But by the early 1960s, jazz still did not have a systematic, comprehensive history dealing with the specifics of the music. On the one hand, there was Marshall Stearns's *The Story of Jazz* (1956), an astute and well-documented compilation of historical data and generalized opinion. Of course, as the title "the *Story* of Jazz" suggests very clearly, it did not claim to be more than that. It was directed to the layman and general reader, and as a historian and professor of English Literature Dr. Stearns could hardly have been expected to apply the analytic techniques used by Sargeant and Hodeir. Their books, in turn, were not comprehensive histories like Stearns's. Highly selective in the kind and amount of material analyzed, their books contained a particular perspective that led to critical gaps or misjudgments. The complex topography of jazz in all its vastness and myriad individualities still remained mostly unexplored.

This history, the first of two volumes, attempts among other things to fill some of those gaps, to explore, as it were, the foothills as well as the peaks of jazz. In fact, this volume has been written on the assumption that virtually every record made, from the advent of jazz recordings through the early 1930s, has been listened to, analyzed, and if necessary discussed. A true assessment of an artist (or a particular musical development) cannot be made without reference to the totality of his work and its relation to his contemporaries. An *analysis* of Beethoven's *Eroica* or Armstrong's *West End Blues* without reference to musical history or the development of musical style could yield a certain amount of factual information, but a full *evaluation* would obviously be impossible without considering the authors' total *oeuvre* and that of their immediate predecessors, contemporaries, and successors. The work of Johnny Dodds, for example, cannot be properly assessed without comparative listening to at least Sidney Bechet or Jimmy Noone. Similarly, jazz historians who write about the Original Dixieland Jazz Band without having listened to James Reese Europe or Earl Fuller recordings can hardly arrive at a reasonable evaluation of the ODJB.

Another approach employed here is to concentrate on those moments, those performances, and those musicians who in one way or another represent innovational landmarks in the development of jazz. In a sense this book is an answer in terms of specific musical detail to a series of interrelated questions: What makes jazz work? What makes jazz different from other music? Why do so many people find jazz exciting? How did it get that way? It is as if I were sitting down with a friend not as yet initiated into the mysteries of jazz, listening to records, responding to the kind of questions a musician might ask, and sharing with him the excitement and beauty of this music. Thus the book attempts to combine the objective research of the historian-musicologist with the subjectivism of an engaged listener and performer-composer. In this respect the book is directed particularly to the "classically" trained musician or composer, who may never have concerned himself with jazz and who cannot respond to the in-group jargon and glossy enthusiasm of most writing on jazz. Implicit in the perspective governing this history is the view that jazz is but one of many musical languages and cultures available to us in mid-twentieth century, and whether explicitly stating it or not, the book places jazz in that larger context.

Verbal explication and notated musical examples are of course no substitute for the music itself. If this is true of histories of "classical" music, it is even truer of jazz, a basically improvised music defying notation and in which recourse to the written score is both impossible and—if scores existed—irrelevant. Despite the limitations of musical notation, a score by Beethoven or Schoenberg is a definitive document, a blueprint from which various slightly differing interpretations can be derived. A jazz recording of an improvised performance on the other hand is a one-time thing, in many instances the only available and therefore "definitive" version of something that was never meant to be definitive. That it is and can only be definitive—whether inspired or not is, of course, another question—is inherent in the very nature and definition of improvisation. The jazz historian therefore is forced to evaluate the only thing that is available to him: the recording. Whereas we are interested primarily in the *Eroica* and only secondarily in someone's performance of it, in jazz the relationship is reversed. We are only minimally interested in *West End Blues* as a tune or a composition, but primarily interested in Armstrong's rendition of it. Moreover, we are obliged to evaluate it on the basis of a single performance that happened to be recorded in 1928 and are left to speculate on the hundreds of other performances he played of the same tune, none exactly alike, some inferior to the recording, others perhaps even more inspired. Jazz improvisation constitutes "work in progress"; and it ought to give the jazz historian pause for thought that certain artists never played their best performance of a given piece in the recording studio.

Still in an improvised art the recording is all we can go by. If he is to gain anything from this book, the reader is urged to listen to the records discussed as he reads. Neither the description and analysis of musical events nor the notation of excerpts from recordings can present the full experience. The reader must also listen.

The task of listening to and analyzing the hundreds of thousands of jazz recordings made since 1917 is, of course, a monumental one. Indeed it may be a lifetime occupation. It must be remembered that aural analysis—particularly of recordings of poor quality or ancient vintage—is a laborious, time-consuming process. A page of written score is after all a concrete object; like a painting it can be studied at leisure; it will not pass away. Performed music, however, even when recorded, exists only in time; it passes in an instant; it is in motion and cannot be frozen in time, as even the motion picture frame can. Thus the musical analysis of jazz brings with it very special problems, particularly in regard to aural perception, problems which do not necessarily arise, for example, in an analysis of Bach fugues.

The amount of material to be covered and heard in what purports to be a comprehensive history of jazz music soon made it apparent that this study would have to be divided into two volumes. A natural breaking point suggested itself in the stylistic and social changes that occurred in the early 1930s, the era of the Depression and the transitional period just prior to the Swing Era. Thus Volume I begins with the pre-history of jazz, its musical antecedents and sources, and takes the various stylistic and conceptual developments and the individual contributions up to 1932 approximately—the exact cut-off point depending on a variety of factors, such as availability of recordings or the quality of the contribution made by certain musicians by that time. Thus, for example, Fletcher Henderson's career is taken through the middle and late 1930s (the latter period very sketchily), while other stylistic lineages (like "Chicago-style" jazz) are cut off before the turn of the decade, in most cases to be dealt with in Volume II. If the preponderance of activity of a particular group or soloist falls into the post-1932 period, then he (or it) will be taken up in the sequel. This accounts, for example, for the virtual omission in Volume I of important figures like Jack Teagarden, Jimmie Lunceford, Chick Webb, and many others whose careers actually began in the late 1920s. No cut-off point, no matter how flexibly treated, can dispense neatly with all left-over or overlapping historical strands.

An undertaking of this magnitude can not be accomplished without assistance from friends, acquaintances, and fellow jazz enthusiasts. I owe particular thanks to Frank Driggs, Martin Williams, and Nat Hentoff who generously lent me recordings not in my own collection, many of them extremely rare. I am also grateful to Martin Williams for many helpful suggestions and to the many musicians and writers who have offered me encouragement in my work on this book. To the secretaries who labored valiantly with my illegible manuscript—particularly Maureen Meloy—I owe a special debt of gratitude.

To George Morrison I send my thanks for offering the hospitality of his home and granting me the interview found in the Appendix. The story told therein, intersecting so many areas of jazz and non-jazz music, underscores effectively the premise of this history: that jazz ought to be viewed not as the private domain of a collection of jazz aficionados, but rather in the larger context of the entire world of music. Lastly, I want to thank Ed Beach and station WRVR in New York City for providing endless hours of superb listening, for his indefatigable enthusiasm, incorruptible taste, and unpretentious, accurate comments.

This book would not exist without the original impetus given to it by Sheldon Meyer of Oxford University Press, nor without his watchful patience and editorial assistance over a period of far too many years. And if this book is grammatically and stylistically presentable, it is due to the sharp eye and conscientiousness of Mary O. Rohde, copy editor at Oxford University Press.

Boston, Massachusetts G.S.
November 27, 1967

Contents

Early Jazz

1

The Origins

During the second decade of our century, while the world was engaged in its first "global" war, and European music was being thoroughly revitalized by the innovations of Arnold Schoenberg and Igor Stravinsky and the radical experiments of the musical "futurists" and "dadaists," America was quietly, almost surreptitiously, developing a distinctly separate musical language it had just christened with a decidedly unmusical name: jazz. The developments in Europe, following a centuries-old pattern in "art music," were generated by the visions of single individuals—what the romantic century liked to call the inspirations of "creative genius." Jazz, on the other hand, was at this point not the product of a handful of stylistic innovators, but a relatively unsophisticated quasi-folk music—more sociological manifestation than music—which had just recently coalesced from half a dozen tributary sources into a still largely anonymous, but nevertheless distinct, idiom.

This new music developed from a multi-colored variety of musical traditions brought to the new world in part from Africa, in part from Europe. It seems in retrospect almost inevitable that America, the great ethnic melting pot, would procreate a music compounded of African rhythmic, formal, sonoric, and expressive elements and European rhythmic and harmonic practices. Up to the present time these jazz antecedents have been discussed and documented (in so far as documentation has been possible) only in sociological and historical terms. The main events, leading from the importation of Negro slaves into the United States through the rituals of the Place Congo in New Orleans to the spread of "jazz" as a new American music, have been well substantiated, but the details of this historical development must await much more research and documentation. Our knowledge of the links between certain important events—such as the dances at the Place Congo in the mid-nineteenth century and the emergence of the generation of jazz musicians after Buddy Bolden following the turn of the century—is largely dependent upon educated guessing rather than the sifting of factual data.

While further historical information may or may not be forthcoming, we can now define quite accurately the relationship of jazz to its antecedents on the basis of *musical analysis*. Through such studies it is possible to establish the musical links between earliest jazz and the various tributary African and European musical sources.

It is tempting to categorize this or that aspect of jazz as deriving exclusively from either the African or the European tradition, and many a jazz historian has found such temptation irresistible. Jazz writing abounds with such oversimplifications as that jazz rhythm came by way of Africa, while jazz harmonies are exclusively based on European practices; and each new book perpetuates the old myths and inaccuracies. From writing based on well-meant enthusiasm and amateur research, as much jazz criticism has been, more accurate analysis cannot be expected. But it now is possible to look at the music seriously and to put jazz's antecedents into much sharper focus. In the process the African and European lineages will become somewhat entangled, as is inevitable in the study of a hybrid that evolved through many stages of cross-fertilization over a period of more than a century.

African native music and early American jazz both originate in a total vision of life, in which music, unlike the "art music" of Europe, is not a separate, autonomous social domain. African music, like its sister arts—sculpture, mural drawing, and so forth—is conditioned by the same stimuli that animate not only African philosophy and religion, but the entire social structure. In so far as it has not been influenced by European or American customs, African music even today has no separate abstracted function. It is not surprising that the word "art" does not even exist in African languages. Nor does the African divide art into separate categories. Folklore, music, dance, sculpture, and painting operate as a total generic unit, serving not only religion but all phases of daily life, encompassing birth, death, work, and play.

The analogy to early jazz, even in the most general terms, goes still deeper. In the African Negro's way of life, words and their meanings are related to musical sound. Instrumental music independent of verbal functions in the sense of European "absolute" music is almost totally unknown to the African native; it exists only in the form of brief subsidiary preludes and postludes. (Even in such cases, there is considerable evidence of relatively recent European or American influences.) Basically, language functions only in conjunction with rhythm. All verbal activity, whether quotidian social life or religion and magic, is rhythmicized. And it is no mere coincidence that the languages and dialects of the African Negro are in themselves a form of music, often to the extent that certain syllables possess specific intensities, durations, and even pitch levels.[1] The close parallel relationships between words and pitch in African songs has been dealt with exhaustively by A. M. Jones[2] and will be discussed later in greater detail.

The extraordinary sonoric and timbral richness of these languages has an intrinsic musicality, which we are not surprised to find in a lesser form in the scat and bop lyrics of American jazz. The reciprocal relationship between African language and music is further emphasized by the fact that such purely functional forms as hunting calls, whistled marching songs, and instrumental love serenades (the latter European-influenced) are without exception translatable into words.[3] It is common knowledge that African drumming was originally a form of sign language. But beyond this, drum patterns, which in African music are thought of not as mere rhythms but as "tunes," are identified by so-called nonsense syllables. In jazz a similar reciprocal relationship between language and music survives in several manifestations, such as instruments imitating words in answering the vocal lines in blues or the "talking" technique of someone like Joe "Tricky Sam" Nanton, the great Duke Ellington trombonist. Conversely, we hear the instru-

1. It is fascinating to ponder the parallels to present-day serial techniques and experiments abstracting syllables and phonemes as purely acoustical musical elements.

2. A. M. Jones, *Studies in African Music,* 2 vols. (London: Oxford University Press, 1959).

3. See *Anthologie de la vie africaine,* Ducretet-Thomson 320 C 126 (disc 1), side 1, seq. 16; side 2, seq. 7 and 10; C 127 (disc 2), side 1, seq. 1-4.

mentalization of vocal jazz in almost every note ever sung by Billie Holiday, who more or less consciously incorporated the instrumental concepts of Lester Young and others into her style; it also survives as a kind of commercialized distant cousin in Jon Hendricks's verbal versions of improvised instrumental solos.

Thus, in certain fundamental musico-sociological aspects, jazz represents a transplanted continuation of indigenous African musical traditions. But, more important, these African traditions survive in an astonishing array of musical detail, covering all elements and aspects of music, including to some extent even harmony, which has generally been associated with the European branch of jazz ancestry.

RHYTHM

Since rhythm and inflection are the elements that most obviously distinguish jazz from the rest of Western music, it is highly revealing to study them in relation to African ancestry. In examining the nature of jazz rhythm we discover that its uniqueness derives from two primary sources: a quality jazz musicians call "swing," and the consistent "democratization" of rhythmic values. Both characteristics derive exclusively from African musical antecedents.[4]

Before we can discuss these qualities we must define our terms. "Swing"[5] is an aspect of rhythm that has for many years defied definition. While there is much truth to the often quoted Louis Armstrong comment on swing, that if you don't feel it, you'll never know what it is, such a remark really offers little help in making us understand what swing is. Admittedly, a definition of swing has about the same sketchy relationship to swing itself as jazz notation has to performed jazz. Like the description of a primary color or the taste of an orange, the definition takes on full meaning only when the thing defined is also experienced.

Swing in its most general sense means a regular steady pulse, "as of

4. See *Anthologie de la vie africaine,* Ducretet-Thomson 320 C 126 (disc 1), side 1, seq. 11, 16; and *History of Classic Jazz,* Riverside Records SDP11, Vol. 7, track 1.

5. In the context used here, "swing" is not the loosely named, semi-commercial style of the 1930s associated primarily with bands like Benny Goodman's and Tommy Dorsey's, but a rhythmic feeling.

a pendulum," as one Webster definition puts it. On a more specific level, it signifies the accurate timing of a note in its proper place. If this were the entire definition, however, most "classical" music[6] could be said to swing. In analyzing the swing element in jazz, we find that there are two characteristics which do not generally occur in "classical" music: (1) a specific type of accentuation and inflection with which notes are played or sung, and (2) the continuity—the forward-propelling directionality—with which individual notes are linked together. Seen another way, "swing" is a force in music that maintains the perfect equilibrium between the horizontal and vertical[7] relationships of musical sounds; that is, it is a condition that pertains when both the verticality and horizontality of a given musical moment are represented in perfect equivalence and oneness. These two swing qualities are present in all great jazz; they are attributes, on the other hand, that do not necessarily exist in great "classical" music.

In the performance of "classical" music, for example, there is a hierarchy of elemental relationships in which pitch is considered more important than rhythm. A "classical" musician can, and is frequently asked to, play a given series of notes mindful only of vertical accuracy, while paying no particular attention to its propulsive flow. It is often sufficient to play the notes at exactly the right time (the vertical aspect) *without* becoming involved in the horizontal demands of the passage. The good "classical" musician will, of course, connect notes so as to produce a phrase; this is a minimum requirement of all music. But to phrase is not yet to swing; and even a minimal amount of comparative listening will confirm the fact that in ordinary "classical" phrasing the rhythmic impetus is often relegated to a secondary role.[8]

6. "Classical" music is used to define the European non-jazz tradition, as exemplified by composers like Bach, Beethoven, Brahms, Debussy, Schoenberg, etc. There is no really adequate general name for this body of music, "classical" being merely broader and less offensive than terms like "symphonic" or "serious" music, which are either too narrow or misleading.
7. These and other technical musical terms are explained in the Glossary.
8. This trait in European music is traceable precisely to the fact that it is no longer a socially functioning music (in the primary sense of being related to physical activities), and has therefore developed a broader and necessarily leveled-off approach to rhythmic feeling. In a culture in which music is not used *primarily* in conjunction with work, play, ritual, and recreation, there is no consistent need for a strongly identifiable rhythmic impulse.

The rhythmic articulation in jazz and "classical" music thus differs at least in degree, and often even in kind.

For the jazz musician, on the other hand, pitch is unthinkable without a rhythmic impulse at least as strong; rhythm is as much a part of musical expression as pitch or timbre—and possibly more important.[9] This extra dimension in the rhythmic impulse of a jazz phrase is what we call "swing."

By the "democratization" of rhythmic values, I mean very simply that in jazz so-called weak beats (or weak parts of rhythmic units) are *not* underplayed as in "classical" music. Instead, they are brought up to the level of strong beats, and very often even emphasized *beyond* the strong beat. The jazz musician does this not only by maintaining an equality of dynamics among "weak" and "strong" elements, but also by preserving the full sonority of notes, even though they may happen to fall on weak parts of a measure. (The only exception to this is the so-called ghost note, which is more implied than actually played.) This consciousness of attack and sonority makes the jazz "horn"[10] player tongue almost all notes, even in the fastest runs, though the effect may be that of slurring. A pure "legato" is foreign to him because he cannot then control as well the attack impulse or the sonority.[11] It is no mere accident that when jazz musicians imitate their playing by singing, they use syllables which have fairly strong, bouncy consonant beginnings, for example, djah bah bah dah bah___. In a similar situation the "classical" musician uses the syllables *da* and *di* enunciated with much softer *d*'s and less fullness in the vowels.

The difference between "classical" and jazz interpretations of weak notes can be seen clearly by comparing the following musical exam-

9. The difference in performance characteristics is brought home forcefully when jazz groups take an occasional "classical" work into their repertoire, especially when the players resist the obvious temptation to "jazz the classics." Two notable examples that come to mind were the performances of Bach Inventions by Lenny Tristano's group in the late 1940s, and a few years later, the Modern Jazz Quartet playing Bach and also an excerpt from Ravel's *Mother Goose Suite*.

10. The term "horn" when in quotation marks shall refer to all wind instruments (i.e., brass, saxophones, clarinets, etc.), as it is commonly used by jazz musicians.

11. This factor also presents us with a clue as to why it has proven so difficult to incorporate the bowed string instruments into jazz.

ples. Example 1A is a well-known Scottish tune, usually played in the indicated manner:

Example 1A "The Campbells Are Coming"

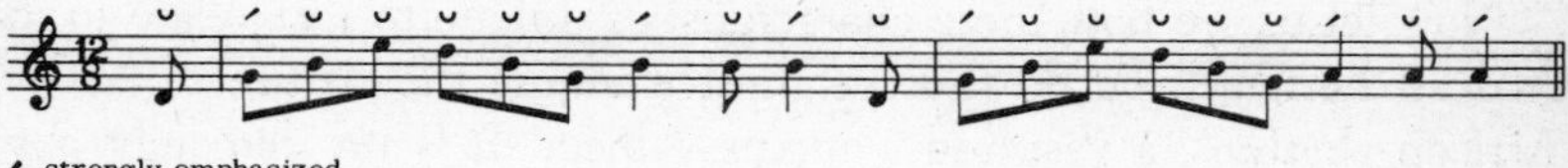

ʼ strongly emphasized
˘ relatively de-emphasized

In Example 1B, still more in the realm of absolute "classical" music, the sing-song emphasis of strong beats is hard to avoid; indeed, it can

Example 1B Mozart, Third Horn Concerto (last movement)

only be avoided by consciously emphasizing the eighth notes. So as not to give the impression that this problem exists only in music set in ternary time, Example 1C illustrates how binary time may have the sing-song effect, unless the musician compensates for the "weak" notes.

Example 1C Brahms, Fourth Symphony (first movement)

Played with a jazz feeling, all three examples would automatically appear with a more equalized inflection. In fact, as I have already stated, jazz inflection often leads to the other extreme (Ex. 2), in which the ostensibly weak notes are accentuated and further emphasized by elongation.

Example 2 Dizzy Gillespie, *One Bass Hit*

Another manifestation of the same principle is the so-called drum backbeat on the second and fourth beat of a bar, especially popular in

modern jazz drumming and rock and roll music. Similarly, the average jazz musician will count 1-2-3-4 but snap his fingers on 2 and 4, thus putting greater emphasis on these ordinarily weak beats than on 1 and
´ ˘ ˘ ˘ ´ ˘ ˘ ˘
3. (What a far cry from the 1-2-3-4, 1-2-3-4 of military marches!)

Now let us see how these characteristics unique to jazz relate to its African heritage. To do this we must examine the nature of native African rhythms, a vast and complex subject. It is not remotely possible to deal with the subject exhaustively within the confines of this chapter. It will, therefore, be necessary to limit our study to basic outlines, incorporating detail only in so far as it relates to jazz. Until the most recent years, African music was a source of mystification even to those musicologists and researchers who specialized in the field. The reason lies in the very nature of the music, for in respect to rhythm African music is unquestionably the world's most complex music. It was only within the last two decades that the non-African's understanding of this music reached a point where, by means of modern technological equipment, he could make an accurate analysis of it.

Great light has at last been shed on this subject by the uniquely qualified English musicologist, A. M. Jones, who in 1956 completed what is undoubtedly the most exhaustive and exacting study of African music extant, published as *Studies in African Music* in two volumes. Jones, who has lived in Africa a good part of his life, is by the evidence of this and other books a superior musicologist and writer. He alone among all researchers in the field realized that analyses based on field recordings by ordinary phonographic methods were inadequate. By the expediency of consulting with a "master" African musician, and by using more exacting and reliable recording methods, Jones has at last revealed to the world the extraordinary complexity and beauty of indigenous, non-Europeanized African music.

All previous attempts to comprehend African rhythmic usages had made two fatal mistakes: the African music was approached by way of European music, and no knowledgeable African was consulted who could, in one way or another, verify or refute the results of the findings. It is important to realize that the European point of view in this case does not merely lead to a wrong slant on the subject or to slight discrepancies in the facts, but, because the rhythmic organization of European music is totally different, it leads to "discoveries" diametrically *opposed* to the actual African musical practice. Prior to Jones's work, even the most careful notations of African rhythms were of little value, since their basic orientation was wrong. I recall somewhat shamefacedly my own efforts to transcribe African musical examples from recordings, in which I tried naïvely to harness the music within European-based time concepts, and I remember my bewilderment in the face of the enormity of the transcriptual problems.

The most salient feature of Jones's research work is unequivocal proof of what has long been suspected: African music, including its drumming, is wholly contrapuntal and basically conceived in terms of polymetric and polyrhythmic time relationships. But Jones also produces proof of a number of other features of African music that have not been recognized or have confounded musicologists: (1) African rhythm is based on additive rather than divisive principles; (2) African music is improvised, but only in a special sense of that word; and (3) it is improvised within a most complex and rigorous set of musical disciplines. Jones's two volumes develop these points both through musical scores and through their analyses.

When the European thinks of polyrhythm, he generally conceives of it as two or more rhythmic strands occurring simultaneously, retaining, however, vertical coincidence at phrase beginnings and endings, at bar lines, and at other focal points. The African, on the other hand, conceives his polyrhythms on a much more extended, more complex, polymetrically organized basis, where phrases rarely, and sometimes never, coincide vertically.[12] In fact, his overriding interest is in cross-rhythms, the more subtle and more complex the better.

The basic African ensemble consists of a solo cantor answered by a chorus, one or two bell players who beat out an unchanging basic pattern, hand-clappers (among the singers) who do likewise, and an ensemble of three or four drummers. Such an ensemble will produce a minimum of seven musical lines and very often a maximum of eleven lines. What is remarkable, however, is not the number of lines, but that—in the case of a seven-part ensemble—*six* of the seven lines may operate in different metric paterns which are, moreover, staggered in

12. In "classical" music until the 1950s, when significant experiments in this direction were made by such composers as Cage and Stockhausen, the lone precursor in the field was Charles Ives, who as early as 1906 composed polyrhythmic and polymetric structures which have long confounded "classical" performers, but which are naïve in comparison to the achievements of African musicians (for example, Ives's Fourth Symphony).

such a way that the downbeats of these patterns rarely coincide. Indeed, two of the drummers may play at cross-rhythms to each other for entire performances, which often continue for hours.

Two examples reproduced from the second volume of Jones's *Studies* will illustrate this approach dramatically:

Example 3 *Nyayito* Dance (bars 38-39)[13]

Example 3 occurs in what amounts to the fourth "chorus" of the *Nyayito* Dance, a funeral dance of the Ewe people in Ghana. The abbreviations and their meanings are as follows: GANK. = *Gankogui,* a bell-like instrument that lays down a fundamental background rhythm; AXAT. = *Axatse,* a rattle which accompanies *Gankogui;* CLAPS represent ordinary hand-clapping; ATSI. = *Atsimevu* and KAG. = *Kagaŋ,* both, in conjunction with *Sogo* and *Kidi,* constituting a four-part drum ensemble.

The top three lines of bars 38 and 39 (bell, rattle, and hand-claps)

13. Jones, II, 24.

comprise two measures of 12/8 time. Though the bar lines coincide, the three patterns vary enough to create in themselves a very rich rhythmic counterpoint, especially since *Axatse* breaks into the triple patterns of its partners with its phrase, consisting of 2 + 3 + 4 + 3 (the eighth note is the unit).

When we leave the top three lines, we also leave all vertical coincidence of bar lines and phrasing. Not only that; seen linearly, two of the lines—Song and *Atsimevu*—change meter frequently.[14] Song, at first in 3/4, switches to one bar of 3/8, three of 2/4, and another of 3/8; *Atsimevu*'s line begins with the last three eighth-beats of a 2/4 bar (left over from the previous page of score), is followed by two bars of 2/4, one 3/8 bar, then the beginning of an alternating 3/4 and 2/4 pattern. As can be seen at a glance, the vertical coincidence of bar lines is extremely rare, occurring only between bar four of *Atsimevu* and bar three of *Sogo,* bar three of *Atsimevu* and *Kidi*'s bar two, Song in bar five and *Sogo*'s bar four, and at two points between *Atsimevu* and *Kagaŋ*. Thus, out of a total of twenty-eight measures, vertical coincidence occurs only at five points. Another way of evaluating this remarkable feat is to realize that in a segment of music lasting only some six seconds, it is extremely difficult to avoid metric coincidence. When one remembers that this example of African music is improvised within a highly disciplined framework, one can only wonder at the connotation of "primitive" usually given to African music.

Turning to Example 4 (again from Ghana), we see that although the top five lines, comprising bell, rattle, and five hand-clapping patterns, are all in some way related, no two are exactly alike. Again, the result is a marvelous contrapuntal richness that simply does not exist in European music. As for the remaining four lines, the points made in respect to Example 3 apply as well.

We have been certain for many years that jazz inflection and syncopation did not come from Europe, because there is no precedent for them in European "art music." In fact, the few examples of syncopation we do encounter—and then only in the most rudimentary, if not primitive, forms, as in Dvořák's "New World" Symphony or Debussy's

14. It should be noted that the African does not think of meter in the European notated sense (he does not know printed music), but he does feel phrases in units that we Europeans call "measures" or "bars." Therefore Jones is thoroughly justified in notating the scores in this manner. Anyone doubting the relevance and efficacy of Jones's notational methods will find ample defense for them in Volume I of *Studies in African Music*.

Example 4 *Sovu* Dance (bars 32-35)[15]

15. Ibid., II, 86.

"Golliwog's Cakewalk"—were borrowed from simplifications of this very same African influence as found in American popular music in the late nineteenth century. But until now we have lacked musically documented proof of the fact that the syncopation of jazz is no more than an idiomatic corruption, a flattened-out mutation of what was once the true polyrhythmic character of African music.

Historians, ethnographers, and anthropologists have provided us with sufficient evidence of the fact that the African Negro, whether as a slave in America or as a native within the social structure of Islamic society (as in certain parts of West and Central Africa), is remarkably adept at accommodating his beliefs and customs to his new surroundings. In America over a period of some one hundred and fifty years, the African slave made many adjustments to the white man's social and cultural patterns, some by dint of force, others by a process of passive acculturation. Perhaps the most far-reaching changes in the early Afro-American's way of life occurred in religion and music; but even here, as has already been stated, it was not a matter simply of adopting the white man's conventions, but rather of infiltrating these, wherever possible, with features preserved from the Negro's own milieu.

Let us look once more at Examples 3 and 4. What we see here in notation, and what we can hear if we are capable of translating notation into sound, is the African's penchant for ensemble music in which many points of rhythmic emphasis coexist naturally and autonomously. The points marked * in Example 3 are felt by the performer of each part, indeed by all performers, as natural points of emphasis, that is, the feeling we "Europeans" associate with a downbeat. The African slave's adjustment to the white man's music consisted precisely of translating these polymetric and polyrhythmic points of emphasis into the monometric and monorhythmic structure of European music. Syncopation, preceding or following the main beats, was the American Negro's only workable compromise.[16] It left the Negro with a vestige of his love for cross-rhythms and cross-accentuation; at the same time

16. The Negro's concession to the white man's musical conception resides in the fact that syncopation substantiates the supremacy of the strong beat, for a syncopation is a modification, an embellishment of that beat; it is not independent of that beat. The African's polymetric designs, on the other hand, presume a basic equality and autonomy of all accented notes. It is also interesting to note that syncopation in the European sense is extremely rare in African music, and occurs only in the smallest rhythmic values (sixteenths).

it enabled him to carry on that tradition within the white man's musical structures.

Syncopation is the most direct way a musician has of emphasizing weak beats, other than outright accentuation. By transforming his natural gift for against-the-beat accentuation into syncopation, the Negro was able to accomplish three things: he reconfirmed the supremacy of rhythm in the hierarchy of musical elements; he found a way of retaining the equality or "democratization" of rhythmic impulses; and by combining these two features with his need to conceive all rhythms as "rhythmicized melodies," he maintained a basic, internally self-propelling continuum in his music. To the extent that they resisted other influences (which will be discussed later), all three qualities survived in jazz as "swing."

It is these "strange" rhythmic characteristics that confounded even sympathetic observers of Negro music in the nineteenth century. Although contemporary accounts and documentary evidence in this particular respect are rare indeed, those that exist, when studied in the light of the musical analysis we have offered above, are very revealing in that they substantiate in general descriptive terms the evidence of musicological research.

Both Fanny Kemble, the nineteenth-century actress and musician, and the three editors of *Slave Songs of the United States,* published as early as 1867, refer to these rhythmic characteristics, but not without considerable puzzlement and awe. Writing in her diary about a visit to a Georgia plantation in 1839, Fanny Kemble confirms both the functional work-song aspect of the slaves' music and its "perplexing" musical qualities. In describing her daily trips up and down the river to the plantation, she writes: "Our boatmen . . . accompany the stroke of their oars with the sound of their voices. I have been quite at a loss to discover any [familiar] foundation for many [of their songs] that I have heard lately, and which have appeared to me extraordinarily *wild and unaccountable*" (italics mine).[17] She goes on to praise "the admirable time and true accent" with which the slaves delivered the call-and-response patterns of these songs.

The introduction to *Slave Songs of the United States*[18] is a remark-

17. Frances A. Kemble, *Journal of a Residence on a Georgian Plantation (1838-1839)* (New York: Harper and Bros., 1864; reprinted, New York: Alfred Knopf, 1961), p. 218.
18. W. F. Allen, C. P. Ware, and L. M. Garrison, *Slave Songs of the United States* (New York: A. Simpson & Company, 1867; reprinted, New York: Oak Publications, 1965).

ably detailed and open-minded discussion of the nature of slave songs. The editors quite frankly admit their inability to cope with the strange rhythms of these songs in conventional notation. "The best we can do with paper and types . . . will convey but a faint shadow of the original. . . . The intonation and delicate variations of even one singer cannot be reproduced on paper." Again reference is made to "rowing tunes." Charles P. Ware, one of the editors, himself a plantation owner, indicates that as he has notated "these tunes, two measures are to be sung to each stroke, the first measure being accented by the beginning of the stroke, the second by the rattle of the oars in the row-locks." (Fanny Kemble also refers to "the rhythm of the row-locks" in her journal.) Ware goes on to say that on the "passenger boats" the boatmen do from "sixteen to thirty strokes a minute, twenty-four on the average."[19] However, "one noticeable thing about their boat songs was that they seemed often to be sung *just a trifle behind time* [italics mine]; in 'Rain Fall,' for instance, 'Believer cry holy' would seem to occupy more than its share of the stroke [see Ex. 5], the 'holy' being prolonged till the very beginning of the next stroke."

Example 5 "Rain Fall"

In a footnote to the song "God Got Plenty o' Room" (Ex. 6), F. W. Allen explains: "the above is given exactly as it was sung, some of the measures in 2/8, some in 3/8, and some in 2/4 time. The irregularity probably arises from the omission of rests, but it seemed a hopeless undertaking to *restore the correct time,* and it was thought best to give it in this shape as, at any rate, a characteristic specimen of Negro singing" (italics mine).

Allen's hesitation in notating the song in variable meters and his apology for doing so are perfectly understandable when we recall that changes of meter from measure to measure were virtually unheard of before the turn of the twentieth century, and we can appreciate Allen's dilemma in transcribing a musical language that even today can only be partially notated. In any event, what Allen had encountered was the Negro's love for irregular polyrhythmic metric patterns and poly-

19. This would indicate a tempo of about ♩ = 132.

rhythms, possibly by then already in a somewhat simplified form, although not necessarily so, since African music abounds with what to our Western ears appear to be relatively simple tunes. The point is that the slave continued to maintain the three basic canons of his musical tradition: (1) the foundation of a regular substructure, in other words, the beat (in the case of the boatmen, supplied by the sounds of rowing); (2) the superimposition thereon of improvised or semi-improvised melodies in variable meters and rhythms; and (3) a call-and-response format in which this musical material is set.

Example 6 "God Got Plenty o' Room"

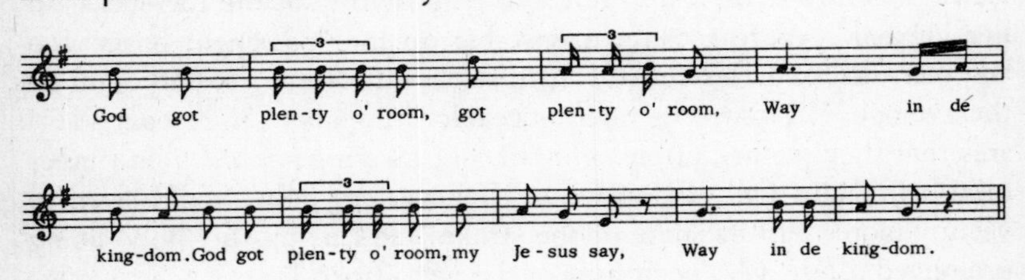

Ironically, it was the more charitable side of the white man's cultural attitudes that led to the corruption of African music in America, while at the same time the oppressive aspects helped the black man conserve the remnants of his African heritage. That is to say, since religion and, therefore, music, to a limited extent, were the first forms of expression allowed the Negro, his conversion both to Christianity and more gradually to European musical concepts was inevitable, given his natural talent for acculturation. At the same time the oppressive side of the white master's attitudes and the consequent social ostracization of the Negro from the white man's world caused the Negro to preserve those sanctioned forms of expression in his own characteristic ways.

Evolving in a steady process of musical assimilation, the Negro's rhythms were eventually transformed into the much simpler patterns of early jazz. Along this route, especially after Emancipation, various social reforms and corollary manifestations in social or religious rituals and in popular entertainment left their mark. The marching-band tradition of Italian and German immigrants blended readily with the funeral processions of the Negro; Anglo-American hymns blended with African monodic and diodic singing to become the spiritual and its secular counterpart, the blues. The development of the minstrel show provided the Negro with an outlet in the area of popular entertainment, absorbing in the process various popular musical forms from Europe—jigs, marches, polkas, quadrilles, etc.—and finally spawning a pianistic descendant: ragtime. All these forms contributed vitally to the development of jazz in its full-fledged form in the first decades of this century. To illustrate graphically how that historic moment relates to its African genesis via one hundred years of transformation and simplification, let us return to one of our previously cited examples of Ewe music.[20]

By the 1920s, the music of Example 4 would have been metamorphosed into something resembling Example 7, allowing, of course, for my conversion of the original African ensemble into a typical 1920s instrumentation. Although this transcription involved "jumping" not only from one continent to another, but also from one epoch to another, it can be seen at a glance that the basic content has remained the same and that very few changes were necessary to achieve this transformation. The instrumental conversion was accomplished as follows:

Ex. 4	Ex. 7	Ex. 4	Ex. 7
Gankogui	——	Clap 4	Tuba
Axatse	Banjo	Clap 5	——
Clap 1	Bass Drum and Piano	Song	Clarinet
Clap 2	——	*Atsimevu*	Trumpet
Clap 3	Woodblock	*Kidi*	Trombone
		Kagaŋ	——

Gankogui, Clap 2, and *Kagaŋ* were left out because they are already basically represented in the *Axatse*-banjo part and for reasons of stylistic purity. The *Gankogui* rhythm of Example 4 is none other than the South American samba rhythm; it also existed in many versions in American ragtime, and eventually appeared as the basic rhythmic

20. It is probably safe to say that by and large the simpler African rhythmic patterns survived in jazz, even in transformed cross-accents, because they could be adapted more readily to European rhythmic conceptions. Some survived, others were discarded as the Europeanization progressed. It also may account for the fact that a pattern such as ♪. ♪. ♪, so common as a ground pattern in African music, has remained one of the most useful and common syncopated patterns in jazz.

Example 7[21]

component of the Charleston of 1923. While both the samba and the Charleston existed in the jazz of the 1920s—the samba rhythm fitting into the category called "the Spanish tinge" by Jelly Roll Morton—neither pattern would have appeared concurrently with the straightforward two-beat "stride" rhythm, as played by the bass, piano, and drums. Clap 5 was eliminated because by 1920 American jazz was no longer capable of sustaining *both* rhythms of Claps 2 and 5, not to speak of the others. As I have already stated, I believe that over a period of many decades the original polyrhythmic complexity of African music became simplified in emulation of European practices. By the time jazz became known as such, rhythms such as in Claps 2 and 5 were no longer used simultaneously, for jazz rhythms evolved more or

21. All musical examples in this book are written at actual sounding pitch, i.e., non-transposing.

less on an "either-or" basis. Since the half-note triplets of Clap 5 were (and still are) least likely to appear in jazz, I have chosen to eliminate them in my musical metamorphosis. Song being the only part written in clearly definable pitches, I have tried to preserve its pitch outline as much as possible. But to accommodate the simple chord progression a 1920s band might have used, I had to alter some notes (parenthesized) in pitch but not rhythmically. The trumpet and trombone parts, being derived from drum patterns in which the notated pitches are not to be considered precise (in the sense of the vocal part), are for that reason free pitch transpositions of the *Atsimevu* and *Kidi* rhythms. In keeping with jazz practices of the 1920s the trombone part has been further simplified (from ♫♩ | 𝄾♪♪𝄾 to ♫♩|♫♩ ♪).

To gain an insight into the extraordinary time sense required to perform these African song-dances—a time sense that the best jazz musicians retain to some extent to this day—one need only compare the rhythm of the second and fifth clap patterns. I daresay that at the designated tempo of ♩ = 128, very few musicians could accurately play these two patterns concurrently. In my own experience as an instrumentalist I have noticed that far too many musicians in both the jazz and "classical" idioms are incapable of playing half-note triplets (3𝅗𝅥𝅗𝅥𝅗𝅥) accurately. The "classical" musicians take a good stab at it, generally by converting 3𝅗𝅥𝅗𝅥𝅗𝅥 mentally into 3♩♩♩ 3♩♩♩ (tied). But the jazz musician invariably translates 3𝅗𝅥𝅗𝅥𝅗𝅥 into ♩. ♩. ♩ . In any case the very slight difference between the third note of Clap 2 and the second note of Clap 5 would in virtually every case pull one musician into the rhythmic orbit of the other. Not so the African musician.

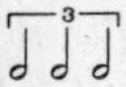

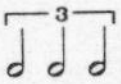

A. M. Jones came across many such infinitesimal time differentiations in his studies, but he was able to prove again and again that his African musician partner in these experiments *definitely* could feel and illustrate these subtle rhythmic deviations. When one realizes that the difference in elapsed time between the two notes in question is just over one-twelfth of a second, one must indeed marvel at the African's sense of timing. (Even more remarkable is the timed difference between the fifth note of Clap 2 and the third note of Clap 5; exactly one twenty-fifth of a second.) The African's sense of timing—at least in the case of the best native musicians—is evidently exact in an absolute way. No wonder that, as Jones puts it, "When we Europeans imagine we are beating strict time, the African will merely smile at the 'roughness' of our beating."[22]

Not being an African, I hesitate to make comparisons, but I would

22. Jones, I, 38. Later on (pp. 113-14) Jones, in analyzing *Sovu,* one of the Yeve cult dances, points out that his own European-influenced conception of a certain rhythmic pattern when checked against that of the master drummer was off at two points by one-sixteenth and one-thirty-second of a second respectively. Jones goes on to say: "Our version [was] almost exactly right, and yet when we [found] out what the African [was] really doing we [discovered] that it [was] totally wrong for it [was] based essentially on the wrong underlying conception. Whatever the pattern sounds like to us, we must always find out what he [the African musician] *intends* the rhythm to be."

hazard the guess that men like Charlie Parker, "Dizzy" Gillespie, Thelonious Monk, John Lewis, and Ray Brown have this sense of timing, or something very close to it. In any case, the point is not whether Charlie Parker's "time" was better than that of the "master drummer" in a Congolese village, but rather that this sense of time, to the extent that it does exist in jazz, is traceable to the African side of jazz heritage, while its debilitation has been the result of European influences.

Example 8 Stan Getz, *Early Autumn*

Polymetric ideas survive in abundance in jazz and indeed have become a commonplace in recent decades. Of the many striking examples I could cite, one of the most interesting and best-known is Stan Getz's famous tenor solo on the 1947 Woody Herman recording of *Early Autumn*, a composition by Ralph Burns. The entire solo (of which Ex. 8 represents only a brief excerpt) concerns itself with three approaches to polymetric organization: (1) the overlay of "irregular" meters upon the "regular" 4/4 beat; (2) the relocation of "regular" phrase patterns out of phase with the beat; and (3) the combination of the two approaches within one over-all phrase. Example 8, an instance of the latter, is taken from the final bars of Getz's solo. The original conception of the phrase is shown in 8A: two four-note groups followed by two five-note groups. Example 8B shows how the original phrase has been shifted one sixteenth beat later and accordingly regrouped within the basic 4/4 meter.

Finally example 8c is notated so as to preserve both the original phrase structure and its new disposition in relation to the 4/4 beat of the rhythm section.

A certain rhythmic pattern in ragtime can definitely be traced to African cross-rhythms. This pattern, in its simplest form or ,[23] appeared also in several variants, ; , for example, or . (All five patterns occur in Scott Joplin's *Maple Leaf Rag* of 1899, one of the first and most enduring of all "rag" compositions.) Once again we encounter the polymetric—or in this case—bimetric approach of the African native forced into the simple 2/4 pattern of European marches. Ernest Borneman states quite accurately that this 3+3+2 pattern[24] is "unmistakably African in origin and approach," "splitting the bar *metrically* rather than accentually" (italics mine).[25] This also connects with Jones's repeated substantiation of the theory that "African phrases are built up of the numbers 2 or 3 or of a combination of 2 and 3."[26] In this simple ragtime pattern the American Negro was again asserting an irrepressible urge to maintain two rhythms simultaneously *within* the white man's musical framework.

In addition, the African, by all available evidence, feels what we call an eighth note as his basic rhythmic unit, rather than the quarter-note division common in European music. Further research may contradict

23. Readers will recognize in this once again a close relative of the *Sovu Gankogui* pattern discussed earlier (pp. 13-14).

24. In *The Easy Winners* (1901) Scott Joplin used a pattern of 3+2+3: .

25. Ernest Borneman, as quoted in Marshall Stearns, *The Story of Jazz* (New York: Oxford University Press, 1956), p. 142.

26. Jones, I, 17. In a sense this can be said about all music, of course. The 5's and 7's of Stravinsky's music break down into components of 2 and 3, for example. Jones's distinction, however, while a subtle one, is crucial, since Indian music or Japanese ceremonial music, to name but two examples at random, do consist often of phrase lengths not of additive compilations of 2's and 3's, but of intrinsically larger units.

this evidence, but at the present time it is possible to say that he either thinks in eighth notes or, if he is momentarily thinking in quarter notes, is capable of feeling the eighth-note subdivisions just as strongly at any given moment in his music.[27] This fact, of course, leads to the interesting speculation whether the penchant in "modern jazz" to feel the eighth note as a basic time unit is in any way related to African music. It is certainly clear by now that one of Charlie Parker's most enduring innovations was precisely this splitting of the four beats in a bar into eight. Was this—like the emergence of some underground river—the musical reincarnation of impulses subconsciously remembered from generations earlier and produceable *only* when the carrier of this memory had developed his instrumental technique sufficiently to cope with it? Once again, the fact that no comparable trend has developed in European "art music" lends support to this theory.

Earlier I referred to the fact that one of the simplest examples of the Negro's inherent love for polyrhythmic organization is the custom of clapping to the weak beats of a bar. In fact, it is as complete a transformation of the African's polyrhythmic approach as is possible within the simple framework of the 4/4 bar. Both sets of beats compete with each other in attempting to dominate the rhythmic continuity. This antipodal approach is the very element that is missing in European art music, and at the same time is the element that sets up a basis for "swinging." The earlier, simpler, and rougher kind of jazz provides the best example of this basic bimetric approach. And a fair idea of what the Negro slaves may have felt in the early days of the transition of African rhythm to its Europeanized descendant can be gained, if one listens to such an early record, by mentally shifting the downbeat feeling we associate with beat 1 over to the second beat. This can be seen in a spirited rendition by four church singers from rural Alabama, providing their own clapping accompaniment, of the traditional "When the Saints Go Marchin' In."[28] Think our European 1 and 3 on their clapped 2 and 4, and you will feel the strong pull of the music, the pull that the African wants to feel in his music and that his Afro-

27. The designations eighth and quarter note are, of course, arbitrary terms, borrowed from European music, and applied here to African music only as a convenience.

28. *Been Here and Gone*, Folkways Records FA 2659 (*Music from the South*, Vol. 10), side 2, track 1, seq. B.

American cousins transformed in this ingenious way. As you conduct this experiment, you will feel the pull of these two rhythmic orbits so strongly that it will make you imagine you are two persons competing with each other in constant alternation. This feeling—exciting even in this primitive form—gives a pale reflection of what the African master drummer feels as he participates mentally in the many-stranded rhythmic lines of his music.[29]

If the reader wishes further aural evidence of the material thus far presented, it is best found in listening to the "swing" and rhythmic "equalization" of African music in certain recordings. Notable examples are Riverside's *History of Jazz Anthology,* Volume 1, track 1, sequence 4; and in the already mentioned Ducretet-Thomson *Anthologie,* disc 2, side 1, sequences 4B and 11.

FORM

In the minds of many a layman (and, for that matter, far too many musicians) form is thought to be largely an intellectual preoccupation. There is a widespread misconception—in itself based on the false notion of African music as "primitive" (ergo, non-intellectual)—that early jazz forms could not have derived from African backgrounds, and therefore must have developed in the "enlightened" environment of European civilization. The facts belie this oversimplified view. We shall find that in considering jazz form it is a formidable task to unravel the confusing tangle of influences leading back to *both* continents. For here we discover a problem not encountered in our investigation of rhythmic derivations: namely, forms are a much more transitory feature of musical language than rhythm. Whereas basic rhythmic practices persist, often, as we have seen, against almost overwhelming obstacles, forms are more fickle. In their most elemental aspects, form and structure are the natural by-products of harmonic and/or contrapuntal practices. But even at this level, pre-eminent forms like the sonata or the fugue have lost their validity in the music of our time because the harmonic tonal functions that originally generated them have vanished.

29. The scores transcribed by Jones offer incontrovertible proof that the master drummer not only feels his *own* rhythmic patterns, but is in close contact with the different patterns of every other member of the ensemble.

On a secondary level, less important forms are, of course, even more perishable, and often survive no longer than a generation or two. Such short-lived forms as quadrilles, marches, ragtime, and various dance forms figure prominently in the emergence of jazz and make the historian's job a complicated one.

The first misconception is that African musical forms are "primitive." African music—whether in large formal designs or small structural units within these designs—is replete with highly "civilized" concepts. Even a cursory glance at Jones's transcribed scores in his second volume or a casual listening to African ethnic recordings will confirm this fact. To be sure, these forms are not abstract artistic forms in the European sense, nor are they intellectually conceived. They are irrevocably linked to everyday work and play functions. Moreover, some observers have confused their very complexity with formlessness. As even our limited examination of rhythm has shown, nothing could be further from the truth.

African formal elements that interest us most in relationship to jazz are: (1) the so-called call-and-response pattern, (2) the repeated refrain concept, and (3) the chorus format of most recreational and cult dances. All three elements not only made the transition to early jazz but survive to this day in various extensions. The call-and-response pattern permeates all African music, and usually takes the form of a chorus responding to a leader or soloist. Even in those instances in which the formal scheme is not occasioned by an actual call with a specific response, African music is still basically antiphonal. This also applies to simple song-like material such as lullabies, in which the words are generally set in a kind of question and answer pattern, even though both question and answer are sung by the same individual. As a matter of fact, it would seem that the call-and-response pattern overlaps often with the refrain concept. Frequently the leader will improvise new lines, while the chorus reiterates the same phrases or very similar ones. Likewise in song material sung by a single individual,[30] the refrain has the effect of a recurring response, a concept we see perpetuated primarily in the blues and to some extent in spirituals (Ex. 9A and 9B).

30. The fact that such songs may in certain respects already reveal a European influence in no way affects the question of the refrain.

Example 9A Chant (the Vili tribe) and Free English translation[31]

Yé, yé. Mi unu kwina mayaka mami	Ye, ye. When I prepare my manioc,[32]
Bwal(a) bwa tiamuk(a) é,	All the village comes running.
Yé, yé, yé—Nzambi!	Ye, ye, ye—my God!
Bwal(a) bwa tiamuka.	All the village comes running.
Yé mi kana yanika bi kwango biami	When I prepare my manioc,
Bwal(a) bwa tiamuka.	All the village comes running.
Yé yé mwan(a) ma Delphine!	Ye, ye, and calls me little Delphine!
Bwal(a) bwa tiamuka.	All the village comes running.
Yé. Mi kwa mi unu ya nukina va ntoto yé.	Ye, they leave me alone, sleeping in the sun,
Bwal(a) bwa tiamuk(a) é	All the village comes running,
Yé. Mi mbasi be kala kwam(i)	Ye, and I am alone, without friends,
Bwal(a) bwa tiamuka.	All the village comes running.
Mi mvendu ami vana wu kala yi kala kwami.	I'm gonna leave this ungrateful place,
Bwal(a) bwa tiamuka,	All the village comes running,
Yé, yé. Nzambi!	Ye, ye—my God!
Bwal(a) bwa tiamuka.	All the village comes running.
Etc.	Etc.

The call-and-response pattern probably continues in its purest functional form in the religious services of the Baptist churches, especially in those astonishing "sermons" that are more music than oratory, and in the field hollers of the Southern sharecroppers that are gradually disappearing. The call-and-response format persists in jazz even today in much modified extensions. Combining with the repeated refrain structure of the blues, it found its way into the marching jazz of New Orleans, and in this form began to be known as a "riff." From there it infiltrated the entire spectrum of jazz from the improvised solo to the arranged ensemble. In the 1929 Okeh recording of *Mahogany Hall Stomp,* Louis Armstrong, for example, repeated a simple riff six times in one of his solo choruses. The riff became an integral structural

31. *Anthologie de la vie africaine,* Ducretet-Thomson 320 C 126 (disc 1), side 1, seq. 23. The English translation was freely adapted from H. Pepper's French translation, reprinted in the text accompanying the recording.

32. A plant, also called cassava, used for a variety of foods and drinks in the tropics.

Example 9B *How Long, How Long Blues*[33]

How long, how long, has that evening train been gone?
How long, how long, baby, how long?

Standing at the station, watch my baby leaving town,
Feeling disgusted, nowhere could she be found.
How long, how long, baby, how long?

I can hear the whistle blowing, but I cannot see no train,
And it's deep down in my heart, baby, that I have an aching pain.
How long, how long, baby, how long?

Sometimes I feel so disgusted, and I feel so blue,
That I hardly know what in the world just to do.
For how long, how long, baby, how long?

Etc.

device in the strongly rocking jazz of the Southwest, centering in Kansas City and fanning out from there through the Benny Moten band (see Ex. 10), and later through Count Basie, to become eventually an overworked cliché of the Swing Era. While Moten was incorporating the riff in his blues-based orchestral jazz, Fletcher Henderson in New York was attempting very much the same thing in the more

Example 10 *Toby*—Riff Pattern (Bennie Moten's Orchestra, 1932)

(The riff is repeated throughout the *A* sections of the *AABA* chorus structure.)

"sophisticated" area of the popular song. From there, the riff idea was taken over by Benny Goodman, who acquired the bulk of Henderson's library; and when Goodman discovered Basie in the mid-thirties, the two riff lineages converged and became a standard device in every stock band arrangement.

33. As sung by Leroy Carr, Vocalion 1191; reprinted from Samuel B. Charters, *The Country Blues* (New York: Holt, Rinehart & Winston, 1959), by permission.

Through over-use the riff soon lost its creative force as an orchestral device. But it survived in two other mutations: (1) the "riff tune," a tune consisting of nothing but short riffs altered only enough to accommodate changing chord patterns (the great guitarist Charlie Christian was undoubtedly the best riff-tune inventor), and (2) by way of Kansas City to bop, the modern jazz pattern known as "fours," whereby in the choruses preceding the final theme recapitulation the improvisers trade four-bar patterns in constant alternation or rotation. In the two conventional jazz forms, the thirty-two-bar song and the twelve-bar blues form, this device leads to interesting instrumental patterns if the number of improvisers does *not* correspond to the number of four-bar segments contained in the form. In such cases (as can be seen in Ex. 11A and 11B), the player finds himself improvising on a different part

Example 11A Distribution of "Fours" in Twelve-Bar Blues Form

12-Bar Chorus

Number of bars

4 4 4 4 4 4 4 4 4 4 4 4

Two improvisers Tpt. Sax. Tpt. Sax. Tpt. Sax. Tpt. Sax. Tpt. Sax. Tpt. Sax.

Four improvisers Tpt. Sax. Trb. Piano Tpt. Sax. Trb. Piano Tpt. Sax. Trb. Piano

Example 11B Distribution of "Fours" in Thirty-two Bar Song Form

(bridge)

A 8 *A* 8 *B* 8 *A* 8 ‖ *A* *A*

Number of bars

4 4 4 4 4 4 4 4

Three improvisers Tpt. Sax. Trb. Tpt. Sax. Trb. Tpt. Sax. ‖ Trb. Tpt. Sax. Trb.

B *A* ‖ *A* *A* *B* *A*

Tpt. Sax. Trb. Tpt. ‖ Sax. Trb. Tpt. Sax. Trb. Tpt. Sax. Trb.

of the structure in each chorus. In the blues form, consisting of a ternary pattern, two improvisers will hit the same pattern every *two* choruses, whereas four improvisers come full circle every *four* choruses. In the song form, a binary pattern, three soloists (a very common occurrence) will hit the same part of the song only after three full choruses. The "bridge" produces especially interesting combinations.

The saxophone, for instance, in our example plays the first half of the bridge in the first chorus, the second half in the second chorus, and misses the bridge altogether in the third chorus. Thereafter the pattern repeats itself. The interesting factor here is that this formal device corresponds closely to the love for cross-rhythms (in this manifestation, cross-patterns) that we encountered in African music. That is to say, the improviser in modern jazz fours finds himself in almost the same shifting relationship to the main structure as the African drummer achieves within his shifting polymetric structures.

The chorus pattern is prevalent in certain categories of African music. In this area, field recordings, usually considered the prime source for studying the music of remote regions, have been quite misleading, for the very simple reason that until A. M. Jones entered the field, such recordings almost never consisted of entire performances. The over-all structural pattern, therefore, could never be studied, since most recordings contained only short excerpts from much more extended forms. For centuries travelers have been telling us that African dances and ceremonies are apt to go on for hours and that they often consist of only one piece. Yet due to the misconception that such dances were all randomly improvised and therefore formless (as compared to the European notion of "closed forms"), no one discovered how the African was capable of sustaining his interest and his audience's for a single dance that may last an hour or more. Jones has found the answer. It is nothing more than the chorus pattern we accept so casually in jazz as *the* basic improvisational procedure.[34]

Jones analyzes seven dances employing the full African instrumental ensemble. These all have a common total structure divided into as many as five or six "master patterns," which are initiated by the master drummer, and whose length is determined (within certain very strict rules) by him.[35] Within each pattern a certain amount of variation may occur, but this is rare. Instead, each pattern is conceived as a variant of the previous pattern, with the understanding that all variants shall adhere to the basic rhythmic pattern peculiar to that dance.

34. Again, the "chorus" concept is conspicuously absent in European "art music," except for the passacaglia or chaconne form, which significantly originated as a dance form.

35. The close parallel to "extended form" techniques, as practised, for example, by Charlie Mingus when he dictates and controls the improvisations, is unmistakeable.

We have therefore an over-all structural pattern based on a principle of perpetual variation.

Actually three structural levels govern these dance forms. They reflect the fundamental cellular structuring of nature itself: the over-all form breaks down into still relatively long "master patterns," which in turn consist of repetitions of smaller phrase fragments, which in themselves may contain tiny cell-patterns (Ex. 12).

Example 12

Over-all form

Master patterns

Phrases

Motives

Since the African ceremonial dance in its pure form does not use harmony—at least in the European sense of vertical chordal structures based on "root" notes—the master drummer cannot arrange his choruses in terms of chord "changes," as the jazzman does. Instead, his guiding line is the vocal melody (Song), the structure of which the master drummer must know intimately so as not to violate its basic order. In this respect the strictures placed upon the master drummer in terms of *when* he may change patterns are so formidable as to stagger the European imagination. Indeed they throw into startling relief the naïve complaints of certain "jazz purists" that jazz is getting too complicated. The African's dances show how an almost unbelievable complexity can be achieved without sacrificing "swing."

Thus far we have examined African elements in jazz forms. What about the European influences? Jazz of today, and even the jazz of the early twenties, reveals almost no *specific,* direct European formal influences, for the simple reason that such European forms were already completely assimilated by 1920. These forms exerted more influence on the forerunners of jazz than on jazz itself. In this sense we can see, for example, how ragtime form, consisting of sometimes three-part, sometimes four-part structures (in contrast to the *single* forms of the thirty-two-bar song or the blues) was a direct continuation of march forms. It is misleading to say, as Marshall Stearns and others have said, that "ragtime had a pseudo-rondo pattern of its own." This comes from the mistaken notion that this pattern "more or less resembles the rondo form of the minuet and the scherzo."[36] Aside from the fact that the minuet is not a rondo form, ragtime form developed from the march or the quick step, not the minuet.

In a classical rondo the first strain returns before each new section, as in the schema *ABACA*-Coda. While a rag such as Scott Joplin's *Euphonic Sounds* has basically the same outline (*AABBACCAA*), it is dangerous to conclude therefrom that Joplin had this particular European model in mind. The confusion arises from the fact that both the minuet and the march have the same formal design; in fact the only basic difference between the two is that the minuet moves in triple time, the march in duple time. Both have a first part set in *ABA* form, followed by a Trio (*CD* in the minuet, *CD* or CDC^1 *in the march*[37]), and then a recapitulation of *AB*, making a grand total of *ABACDAB*. Out of some thirty-odd ragtime pieces by Joplin, only a handful employ the rondo *ABACA* format, and then probably only coincidentally. At he same time none correspond exactly to the march or minuet form outlined above. The most common ragtime form consists of an *AABBACCDD* schema (*Maple Leaf Rag, Fig Leaf Rag, The Easy Winner,* etc.) and occasionally the repeat of *A* after the *B* strain is eliminated completely, as in Joplin's famous *Cascades.*

Despite the fact that it is difficult to find much *exact* schematic correspondence between ragtime forms and those of the march, the evidence points overwhelmingly to the march as the formal progenitor of ragtime. In the first place, ragtime, like the march, has a duple time signature, and most of the rags, such as Joplin's *Maple Leaf Rag,* are marked "tempo di marcia" or "in slow march time." In fact, many of the early rag compositions were called "marches" outright: Joplin's *Combination March, March Majestic, Antoinette* (some of these in the manner of the French 6/8 quick step), James Scott's *The Fascinator* and *On the Pike,* and Charles Hunter's *Tickled to Death,* actually subtitled "Ragtime March and Two Step."[38] Furthermore, ragtime developed originally in the Midwest, a region where the march-playing

36. Stearns, p. 141.
37. C^1 is a variation of C.
38. Rudi Blesh and Harriet Janis, *They All Played Ragtime* (New York: Alfred A. Knopf, 1958), Appendix I.

band has always been—and is to this day—extremely popular. Inevitably, too, concert bands like John Philip Sousa's contributed heavily to the spread of ragtime, even if in a somewhat ponderous and diluted form. And if internal formal evidence is needed, we can find it in the fact that almost all rags modulated, like the march, to the subdominant in the so-called Trio (C section); and a large percentage of them, especially the early ones, retained the two- or four-bar modulation leading *into* the Trio. All these facts taken in conjunction would indicate rather conclusively that ragtime, as another form of American Negro music leading toward the full flowering of jazz, reveals a close structural affinity to the European march.

Exact proof of the origin of the blues has almost completely disappeared. We commonly find the very general statements that the blues is derived from the spiritual or the field holler or both; and that the spiritual is in itself a crossing of African melody with European (mostly English) hymns. All very well and good, but it has never been recorded exactly how and when these assimilations came about. We have already seen how the verbal or poetic aspects of the blues perpetuated the African call-and-response pattern. But what about the classic perfection of the twelve-bar or eight-bar blues and its chord progression and related three-part schema? How and when did the Negro adopt the I-IV-V progression (tonic, subdominant, dominant) that has become the formal and harmonic foundation of the blues—a foundation the Negro slave certainly did not bring with him from Africa?

To find the answer we have to go back to the beginning of Negro music on this continent. During the seventeenth and eighteenth centuries slave ships unloaded thousands of Negroes in the Southern waterfront cities. Tribal groups were separated, and individuals were shipped to different plantations. By so doing the white owners hoped to destroy whatever vestiges of cultural patterns the slaves had brought with them. The plantation owners could not have known that such close ties as existed between the Negro's musical traditions and his daily life were not to be broken so easily. Nor could they have guessed that the Negro would use his rich musical traditions—mainly singing—to communicate with his fellow slaves. Like the Negro's native drum languages, singing was a means of personal communication that was more or less private,[39] the exact nature of which not only baffled the white man but even amused him in a patronizing way. The Negro also began to appropriate some of the music he heard in his new surroundings: a fragment from a hymn, a few notes of a song whistled by an overseer, a scrap of music heard at a dance, and so on. Very gradually, Negroes all over the South, each in his own individual way and unaware of the totality of this process of musical acculturation, infused the white man's music with their own instinctual traits. In effect, this led to an astonishingly rich effusion of musical expressions. Although this music showed its common background, it was as diversified in detail as the varied tribal music on the African continent. Because of the Negro's necessarily hermetic social situation, and the limited means of large-scale communication, slaves in Texas, for example, had virtually no contact with their brethren in Georgia. Even in our own time the average Alabama sharecropper thinks he has traveled some, if he has left his own *county* some time in his life.[40]

Through the years and decades this marvelously rich accumulation began to crystallize into more specific modes of expression: the field holler, the spiritual, the country blues, the work song, the ring-shout—all of them strongly related and overlapping. The problem of tracing these developments is complicated enormously by the fact that they occurred on many levels of talent and, as I have indicated, in all manner of environments, ranging from rural to urban. Not all Negroes were (or are) equally gifted musically, and the Negro family living in some lonely cabin obviously would sing a different music than the Negro living in or close to a large urban center.

One thing, however, is clear from all available evidence: until the time of the Civil War all the forms of expression mentioned were performed either solo or in unison, *not* in harmony, and they were for the most part unaccompanied. We will return to the subject of blues harmonies later in this chapter; for the moment it interests us because in the blues, as it ultimately developed, form was determined by har-

39. It should be noted that to this day many Negroes—perhaps a majority—think of jazz as just such a medium of personal, if not secretive communication with their own race.

40. Folkways Records FA 2651-3 (*Music from the South*, Vols. 2-4), performed by Horace Sprott.

monic functions. Before that time, neither its phrases nor its harmonic patterns were fixed, and consequently the specific form remained discretionary. It must be remembered that the blues was not an "art music." It had very little to do with mere chords and melodies; it was an essential mode of expression, through which a minority could render its suffering.

The first harmonic accompaniments probably took place on crude homemade instruments like banjos, made by stretching dried raccoon skins over a gourd and using wire strings or even horse hair. They may have started immediately after the Revolutionary War, and have been inspired by use of the guitar as an accompaniment, which in all likelihood many of the slaves encountered in stopovers on the Caribbean islands,[41] on their way from Africa to the Southern United States. In any case, the first hint the white man had of these musical developments was the minstrel shows, a form of entertainment that sprang up in the 1830s. Although most of the minstrel music consisted of "thinly disguised Irish reels, hornpipes, and English country dances," there was also music "with strange modal harmonies and a sharply rhythmic dissonance, like *Ole Dan Tucker, Jonny Boker,*" and the famous minstrel solo dance, *Juba,* which is said to have come from the plantations.[42] Almost imperceptibly harmony infiltrated the Negro's music either in the form of simple banjo accompaniments or, under the influence of Anglo-American hymns, in part singing—the latter influencing the spirituals. By contrast, the blues, as a gradually emerging synthesis of field hollers, work songs, and prison songs, was best served by the banjo and guitar.

Spirituals and ring-shouts, as more or less fixed forms, undoubtedly developed earlier than the blues. After Emancipation, Negroes presumably could have established their music on an equal basis with that of the white man. In 1871 the Fisk Jubilee Singers, from Fisk University in Nashville, began a series of highly successful national and international tours, presenting spirituals in choral versions that were greatly influenced by white singing societies. In preparing these programs the choir director's primary task was to codify the previously

41. Some of these stopovers lasted long periods of time, very often several years, according to Ernest Borneman in "Creole Echoes," *Jazz Review,* II, 8 (September 1959), p. 15.
42. Charters, pp. 26-7.

improvised melodies and to provide them with set harmonizations. It was inevitable that he should turn for models to white religious hymns, with their simple forms and chord progressions.

But this sudden flowering of Negro music as an "art form" was not allowed to spread. As the Reconstruction era ground to its chaotic finale, and as, finally, the Northern "occupation" troops were withdrawn under Southern political pressures, the Negroes found their road to liberty blocked by a hardened core of white citizenry. As the harsh realities of segregation were felt, the field cries and work chants were revived. But "without overseers to force the musical outcry into 'nonsense' songs, the music took on a new intensity,"[43] and in the next decades a crude blues form developed, still largely unaccompanied, and linked together in irregular, freely improvised patterns. This blues was still more in the realm of *sung speech* rather than song per se. And it is significant that there is no recorded use of the term *blues*, either as a plain noun or as a title, until the turn of the century, by which time the blues had migrated to the cities in the wake of the great population shifts caused by Southern industrialization. In the cities the country blues acquired a rough harmonic form corresponding to the three-part stanza form, which, as Marshall Stearns points out, is a form "quite rare in English literature and may have originated with the American Negro."[44]

From this point on, the blues form, with its pianistic adjunct, boogie-woogie, became codified in three principal forms, an eight-bar pattern (considered by many to be the earliest version), a twelve-bar form, and a sixteen-bar form. In time the twelve-bar format predominated; for one thing it was used for the publication of blues, beginning with the years shortly before World War I. By the 1920s the blues had become a national craze and a permanent fixture of jazz language.

At this point it must be emphasized that the blues form and its relatives, the field hollers and work songs, survive today on many levels, from the most "primitive" country blues to the most "sophisticated," even commercialized, urban blues and rock and roll. Questions of intuitive talent and environment aside, one can say with certainty that the forms of these various shades of blues vary in exact proportion to their degree of urbanization.

43. Ibid., p. 29.
44. Stearns, p. 104.

What conclusions can we draw from these observations? The blues structure, like ragtime, was an admixture of African influence (the call-and-response pattern) and European harmonically derived functional form. But unlike ragtime, the blues were improvised and as such were more successful in preserving the original and melodic patterns of African music. The blues remain, even to this day, a less formalized expression than ragtime. They offered a simpler harmonic progression in a shorter form, whereas ragtime developed lengthy three-part forms including modulations, each part of which in itself consisted of a relatively sophisticated harmonic progression. Whereas the blues made five fundamental harmonic steps in the span of twelve bars, ragtime music generally changed root positions *every* measure, or at least every two measures. Moreover, the faster tempos of ragtime left little room for the rhythmic and inflective freedoms preserved in the blues. A blues singer had at least two bars to delineate a phrase, and all on one single chord. Thus, even when the blues became formalized as an eight- twelve-, or sixteen-bar structure in a European-derived 4/4 meter, its unique simplicity left enough room to preserve a number of African rhythmic-melodic characteristics.[45]

HARMONY

Harmony has already been mentioned as the basis of blues structure in its later stages of development. But harmony had a number of other functions in the pre-history of jazz. Once again, scanty musical documentation has hampered previous attempts to assess harmony's growing importance in the development of jazz. One thing is clear: any discussion of harmony in jazz and its antecedents must begin with the realization that in the beginning Afro-American music had no harmony. When harmony did occur it was accidental and, in any case, not functional diatonic harmony in the European sense. In the Fanny Kemble account of 1839 already cited, the boatmen slaves were singing "all in unison." And Charles P. Ware, writing on slave songs

45. In simple country blues sung by itinerant blues singers it is not unusual to find thirteen-bar, thirteen-and-a-half-bar, or other irregular structures (see the recording by Memphis Slim, *The Saddest Blues,* United Artists UAL 3050, side 2, track 2).

nearly thirty years later, says flatly, "there is no singing in parts, as we understand it."[46]

Indeed, why should it have been otherwise? European harmonic disciplines are totally unknown in traditional African music. It would, therefore, be easy to conclude, as most studies of jazz have, that the harmony of jazz derives exclusively from European practices. In one basic sense, this is true; but this conclusion seems to be another one of those over-simplifications in which historians indulge so readily when documentation is scanty. For in another sense—perhaps equally crucial—the *particular* harmonic choices Negroes made, once they adopted the European harmonic frame of reference, were dictated entirely by their African musical heritage. There is considerable evidence that the Negroes assimilated only those harmonic-melodic tendencies that permitted the integration of their African traditions. If this is so, we should be able to find a logical parallel to the assimilation process we have outlined in respect to rhythm.

In a very real sense, European traditional harmony and melody are merely two sides of the same coin. To put it another way, a melodic line contains certain definite implications about any possible harmonizations; and, of course, the reverse is also true. Melodies are very often horizontal projections of a harmonic substructure, and harmonies are often just verticalizations of melodic segments. By contrast, African music is unilaterally melodic, that is, not harmonic in structure. "Harmony," where it occurs, is merely a concomitant of the melodic line. Conversely, melodic lines are not conceived of as arising from a chord progression. In this respect, African music does not have the two-way cross-relationship between melody and harmony we have in European music. But this added latitude in European music played a very critical role in the Negro's early assimilation of harmony. Quite logically, he adopted those simpler harmonies that accommodated the types of melodies he brought with him from Africa. This African melodic repertoire, moreover, was predominantly pentatonic. It is self-evident that pentatonic melodies can easily be fitted into diatonic harmonic patterns, while the reverse is certainly not true. (It is, therefore, difficult to say with certainty that a given tune is purely pentatonic, since the omission of the fourth and seventh degrees of the scale does not in itself prove pentatonism. But this is ultimately irrelevant, since the African

46. Allen, Ware, and Garrison, p. v.

musician does not think in terms of either a pentatonic or diatonic framework.) Melodies which are not strictly pentatonic, of course, also exist in African music, although all evidence so far indicates that these are less frequent. In such cases, the subdominant and the leading tone are admitted into the scale. Interestingly enough, in the case of many West African tribes, the leading tone, when used, is sung flatter than in European music. This practice was undoubtedly perpetuated in the "blue note" in jazz, which shall be dealt with later (and see the Glossary). Except for its flatted leading tone, this non-pentatonic scale is, of course, the same as the European diatonic scale, and even contains the same voice-leading characteristic of sharpening the subdominant when used in conjunction with the dominant.[47] Melodies based on such scales were, of course, easily fitted into diatonic chord progressions. The result was that the Negro was able to retain a good part of his native melodic repertory *within* the harmonic framework of Western musical tradition.

We have already noted the fact that Western harmony is foreign to African music. A harmony of sorts, however, does exist, and again we must refer to A. M. Jones, who makes two major points in this connection. One is that African chorus singing is either unisonal or diodic, and in the case of the latter, sung in organum. That is to say, in the diodic category, some singers in the group produce "harmony" at what the Western ear calls consonant intervals, and such diody is performed in parallel intervals. Jones's second observation concerns the kinds of intervals used in parallel organum. "African harmony," he says, "is sung either in parallel fourths, parallel fifths, parallel octaves, or parallel thirds." "When the Africans sing in parallel fourths the lower voice always sharpens the subdominant, thus avoiding a tritone fourth."[48] In other words, the African making "harmony" in fourths is doing no more than singing the tune melody a perfect fourth lower. This is indeed not harmony in the Western sense but, as we have said, diody. Similarly, when doubling the melody in fifths, the African singing the lower of the two parallel lines will flatten the leading note to make a perfect fifth with the subdominant. However, "when we

47. It should be made clear that the terminology and indeed the relationships among tonic, dominant, subdominant, and the entire diatonic hierarchy are quite unknown in African music. These terms are used here only as a convenient means of identification for the reader trained in the European tradition.
48. Jones, I, 217.

consider parallel thirds," Jones points out, "we find the situation is, musically, totally different. When the African sings in parallel thirds the lower voice introduces no accidentals whatever."[49] Thus, in organum in thirds, "the lower voice is no longer singing the same tune as the higher" voice, because obviously some of the thirds will be major and some minor. It is even more remarkable that many tribes who sing in parallel thirds "do so to the total exclusion of any other interval." "Some tribes sing in continuous *organum* in fourths. These tribes never, by any chance, sing even an isolated third."[50] The same is true of tribes who sing in fifths and octaves. Jones concludes that African music in respect to harmony can be divided into two distinct ethnomusical groups: "Experience in listening makes it evident that the octaves-tribes, the fifths-tribes, and the fourths-tribes all belong to the same harmony family, which we dub the '8-5-4' tradition. The typology of harmony thus divides Africa[n music] into two distinct streams—the thirds-tribes and the 8-5-4 tribes." "We have a strong feeling that the 8-5-4 tradition is the main harmony tradition of Africa as a whole and is probably the older."[51]

It is evident that these harmonic practices were perpetuated by the Negro slaves in their new environment. Once again, one of our two primary American documentary sources provides commentary to this effect. In his reference to the absence of part singing in the slaves' music, Ware goes on to say, "and yet no two appear to be singing the same thing." The "basers" (a term for the chorus singers who answer the leader) often hit "some *other note than chords,* so as to produce the effect of a marvelous complication and variety, and yet with the most perfect time, and *rarely with any discord*" (italics mine).[52] Under the circumstances, this parallels remarkably the phenomenon A. M. Jones was observing in Africa some one hundred years later.

What do these findings of Mr. Jones tell the jazz musicologist and historian? Perhaps not enough to make any certain deductions, but his evidence suggests distinct possibilities as to why the adoption of Western harmony by the American Negro progressed relatively smoothly, leaving almost no trace of any drastic transformations.

49. Loc. cit.
50. Ibid., p. 218.
51. Ibid., pp. 219, 221.
52. Allen, Ware, and Garrison, p. v.

Marshall Stearns, in paraphrasing Richard Waterman, perpetuates a half-truth when he says, in *The Story of Jazz,* that European and West African music blended so easily because "unlike other musics of the world, they are very much alike."[53] It would be more precise to say that, while European and African harmony are based on two totally different conceptions, there are coincidental, superficial similarities which made the transition (in terms of harmonic practices) from Africa to the Southern United States virtually unbroken.

But the question goes even deeper, and here we return to the hypotheses posed earlier. One or both of the following seem reasonable possibilities. First, it seems to be of considerable significance that the tribes forming the bulk of the slave trade came from West Africa, primarily from the belt that stretches from Dakar through the Gold Coast and Dahomey to Nigeria.[54] A. M. Jones points out that the great majority of these West African tribes belonged to the unison- or thirds-tribes; almost none belonged to the fourths- and fifths-tribes. From this, one can assume that neither the unison nor the thirds group had much difficulty in integrating their melodies into Western harmony. In the case of the unison group there were, of course, no harmonic complications to begin with. Similarly, the thirds group which, we should recall, sang in what happens to coincide with the use of thirds in the diatonic system, found no basic "harmonic" discrepancy with their own music. This seems all the more inevitable if we bear in mind that the Western tradition between approximately 1700 and 1900 developed exclusively along the triadic principle of building harmonies in thirds.

An alternate theory could apply to those slaves who belonged to the "5-4" tradition: the Camerouns, certain sections of the Congo, as well as small pockets of tribes in West Africa. Although their organum "harmonizations" in fifths and fourths emphasized pentatonic elements, they nevertheless assimilated readily into diatonic harmonies. Even the African's use of the raised subdominant produced—quite coincidentally—a striking analogy to established usage in Western functional diatonism. Beyond this it is entirely conceivable that the

53. Stearns, p. 14. Stearns errs even more when he also implies that African harmony is similar to European, and that such similarities are not found in any other musics of the world.
54. See the map in Jones, I, facing p. 230.

blues chord progression of I-IV-I-V-I represented a horizontalized form of the primary intervals used by these fourths- and fifths-tribes. But the thirds-tribes also found the blues progression acceptable, because it preserved the diatonic alternation of major and minor thirds.

Summing up, we can say that harmonic elements in the prehistory of jazz were not so much *derived* from European musical sources as carried over by the Negro from African traditions. Coincidentally, the European and African traditions overlapped enough to offer no profound problems of synthesis.

MELODY

Previously we have indicated that in many respects melody and harmony can be thought of as two aspects of the same musical process. Therefore, much of what has been said in the section on harmony also applies to melody, especially as regards the superimposition of African melody on European harmony. But there are two added factors: the occurrence of the blues scale and the relationship between speech patterns and melodic shapes.

The question of the derivation of the blues scale has occupied many jazz historians, yet because of the insufficient documentation and the generally amateurish musicological approach of most writers on jazz, the origin and role of the blues scale in jazz prehistory have been barely touched upon. Almost every writer describes, sometimes even analyzes, the blues scale and how it is used. But almost no one has ventured to say anything about how and why it developed. The only author who probed this question in any depth was Winthrop Sargeant in his altogether remarkable book (especially for its time) *Jazz: Hot and Hybrid.*[55] In fact, Mr. Sargeant was entirely on the right track in his chapters "The Scalar Structure of Jazz" and "The Derivation of the Blues," but he was prevented from finding the final pieces of the puzzle by the absence at that time of the voluminous field-recording documentation and exhaustive scholarship (such as A. M. Jones's) that has taken place in the interim.

What Mr. Sargeant recognized with an uncanny assuredness was

55. (New York: E. P. Dutton & Company, 1946; reprinted, New York: McGraw-Hill, 1964).

that the blues scale as used in jazz really divides into two identical tetrachords (Ex. 13).

Example 13

He then points out that in the blues, especially in the least commercialized and earliest recorded ones (Bessie Smith's, for example), these two tetrachords are kept quite disjunct, that is to say, one or the other is used but generally not both. In more sophisticated and/or instrumental improvised jazz, both tetrachords were, of course, used even in the twenties, but in the majority of early or simple jazz the performer rarely strayed beyond the four-note limits of one of the tetrachords.

Mr. Sargeant also correctly analyzes the functions of the four pitches in relation to a central note, the tonic *c* in Example 13A, the dominant *g* in Example 13B, the arrows indicating the direction in which the pitches invariably move. Although Sargeant suspected the African derivation of the blues scale,[56] he could not have known at the time that its division into identical tetrachords stems directly from (1) the quartal and quintal "harmony" of African singing, and (2) the tendency of African melodies to shift around a central tone.

We have already dealt with the first point to some extent in the section devoted to harmony. We have also pointed out that while African melody tends to emphasize pentatonism, the use of the subdominant and the leading tone is by no means uncommon. Including these two tones, marked × in Example 14, we have, of course, the scale known in European music as the diatonic scale:

Example 14

When the African from what Jones calls an 8-5-4 tribe "harmonizes" the notes of this scale in parallel fourths and fifths, we get the following scales:

56. Ibid., p. 188.

Example 15

(Black note heads indicate "harmony" notes.)

which, when combined, will be seen to contain all the notes of the blues scale:

Example 16

(The square note head indicates a blue note, whose pitch may vary by more than a half tone, ranging between a sharp and a flat intonation of the designated pitch.)

It must be emphasized here that when the African sings in parallel fifths or fourths, he thinks of these alternate notes as equal in validity and function to the prime melody. A melody may be, for example, primarily in unison, but may break into quartal harmony at a cadential point (Ex. 17A), or the chorus may answer the cantor in harmony (Ex. 17B),

Example 17A Paddle Song[57]

Example 17B *Icila* Dance[58]

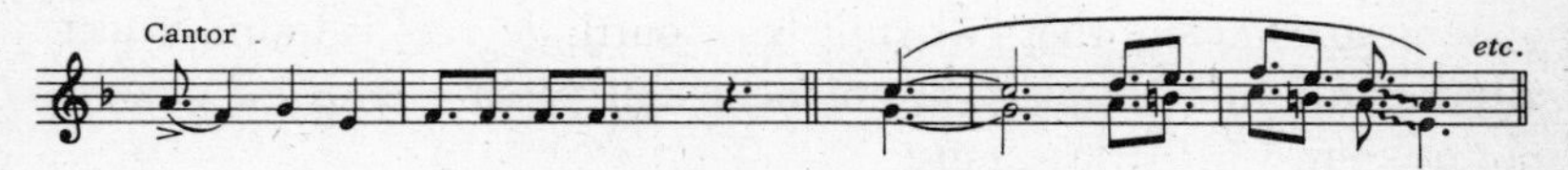

in which case the melody may actually progress for longer stretches in parallel intervals. But whatever the case may be, neither of the two alternative pitches has priority over the other at any given moment. One is simply an *equivalent* "harmonic" variant of the other.

The African also does not think in terms of a key center. Indeed, for notating African songs in Western notation, key signatures are not

57. Jones, II, 9.
58. Ibid., 220-21.

only incorrect but irrelevant (although their use is helpful to the Western reader). A tune that might be in the key of F could just as properly be notated in the key of C, since the African is not "aware of [European] organization of scales and keys."[59]

When the Negro made his first tentative attempts to combine his African melodic heritage with the European diatonic system, he found that he could readily do so by alternating, as equivalently as in his native land, the two seven-tone scales he already knew (see Ex. 15). At first these attempts must have been somewhat cautious, but by the latter part of the nineteenth century definite patterns in which blue notes were used became established. Still later, in the 1920s, in a slightly more codified but nevertheless free form, these blue-note inflections became a *sine qua non* of jazz, spreading through the recordings of urban and country blues singers like Bessie Smith, Blind Lemon Jefferson, and Big Bill Broonzy, and instrumentalists like King Oliver and Louis Armstrong.

In his analysis of blues recordings Winthrop Sargeant came upon other facts, the significance of which has been made clearer through subsequent studies of the Negro's African musical heritage. For example, Sargeant points out that "it is unusual for a sixth [degree] to move to a second."[60] This relates not only to the Negro's discrete use of the blues tetrachords, but also to the fact that skips of a fifth are rare in African melody, even as "harmonic" equivalents. Sargeant also observes that in the blues recordings he studied "the fourth degree [of the scale] is the least used tone of the tetrachord, and for that matter, the least used tone of the entire scale."[61] This corresponds entirely to a similar treatment of the subdominant in African melody. Sargeant goes on to comment that "when it [the fourth degree] is found it usually has the humble place of an incidental passing tone," a practice not unknown in African music.

It is well to remember that the recordings Sargeant analyzed were made in the 1920s; in other words, some fifty to seventy years after the time the first contacts between African melody and European harmony were made. It is logical to assume that in time the harmonic practices themselves began to influence melodic choices as well. Cer-

59. Jones, I, 48.
60. Sargeant, p. 165.
61. Ibid., p. 166.

tainly by the twenties, these two elements were so intimately interrelated that it would be impossible to say which of the two, harmony or melody, dictated to the other.

One of Sargeant's sharpest observations involves the use of the third- and seventh-degree blue notes. He says: "In the passages of hot jazz from which the above data were taken, the blue seventh had, if anything, a tendency toward slightly lower and slightly more stable intonation than the blue third."[62] Again this is corroborated in African melodic practices. We have already seen that it was the seventh (or leading tone) that was flatted. The third *could* be flatted, but only as a harmonic equivalent of the seventh; otherwise it was sung as an essentially pure major third. Naturally, as time passed, and as the whole concept of a blue tonality developed here in America, the initially strict vocal habits of the Africans were gradually loosened, and the practice of using the entire span of minor to major third and minor to major seventh developed.

In studying the field recordings of the famous Dennis-Roosevelt expedition to the Congo, Sargeant noted that "the blues scale, which we have found to be characteristic of so much American Negro music is lacking in the form in which it is used in America. There is frequent use of the flat seventh, however."[63] Sargeant could not have found the full blues scale in African recordings, since indeed it does not exist in that form in Africa, but developed out of melodic-harmonic practices peculiar to African music only, as we have shown, upon contact with European harmony.

We can easily see now how the blues scale, once it had settled into a more or less distinct form, led to the development of the standard blues chord progression. For it constituted a selection of certain harmonies and a certain progression from the European harmonic repertory, which not only suited the blues melos but was an exact harmonic corollary to it.

The harmonic ambiguity (in terms of European key centers) the American Negro brought with him from Africa also helps to explain the structure and nature of the riff. This device, is, of course, of a much later origin. But this should not lead one to conclude that it is of white origin or traceable to any European heritage. On the contrary,

62. Ibid., p. 168.
63. Ibid., p. 217.

there is no Western precedent for it. The riff incorporates several basic African elements.

Let us define a riff as a relatively short phrase that is repeated over a changing chord pattern, originally as a background device, although it later came to be used as foreground material in the so-called riff tunes of the Swing Era.

Example 18A

Example 18A shows a riff placed over the three root chords (I, IV, V) found in the blues. In true riff tradition, the riff itself remains unchanged while the underlying harmony shifts. Only in bars three and four is there a complete diatonic identity between the tonal centers of both the melody and harmony. In bars one and two, the melody coordinates with the harmony only by virtue of the *e* flat, which is the blue third of the underlying C chord. In bar five, the clash between melody and harmony is still more severe, producing in effect a primitive sort of bitonality. I hasten to reiterate that the African and the American Negro (at least initially) did not think of it in those diatonic terms. On the contrary, the Negro was simply perpetuating his unawareness of key centers in the European sense. His harmonic ambivalence allowed him to play a melody, such as the above riff, in any one of several key centers.

He was also perpetuating another of the basic characteristics that differentiate African music from most other "primitive" music cultures, including those of the whole Indo-Arabic bloc: namely, the fact that African music is based on repetition, whereas Indo-Arabic music is based on variation. The repetitiousness of the riff corresponds exactly to the repetitive structuring of African songs and dances, especially work and play songs. Lastly, the particular tonal relationship of a riff to its attendant harmony in a blues, for example, is traceable to the pre-eminence, harmonically, of fourths and fifths. We have seen that many African tribes can switch at will to fourth and fifth harmonic equivalents. But generally they will not use both within the same song, since songs are usually in one or the other tradition. But often tribes that sing in fourths in certain songs sing in fifths in others. In the hypothetical riff example the Negro could find equivalent "harmonic" notes as in Example 18B. In measures three and four he

Example 18B

could retain the same pitches as in one and two (repetition principle) and yet accommodate these pitches in the F chord by thinking of them as the upper parallel equivalents at a distance of a fifth (harmonization above being not unusual in Africa); or, alternately, as the lower parallel organum in fourths of the riff motive transposed to the key of F. In measure five the procedure is reversed; the riff can be thought of as the upper parallel (in fourths) or the lower parallel (in fifths) of its transposition. This may sound complicated in Western musical terminology, but it is easy to see how in actual practice the Negro could readily perform these transpositions, since it was a part of a centuries-old heritage. It is thus evident that the Negro, who was capable of remarkable dexterity and sophistication in rhythm, could clearly solve the less complex melodic and harmonic problems involved in transferring his African musical heritage to America.

Closely related to this problem is the tendency of African melodies to shift around a central tone. Jazz uses this device both in the blues and in the riff. Literally thousands of examples of blues and riffs substantiate the fact that these melodies revolve around a central tone, usually within the small range of a fourth or fifth. This does not necessarily mean that such a central tone becomes a key center. It is simply regarded as a central pitch around which the other pitches revolve, with none of the implications that a hierarchy of relations exists, as in European diatonic harmony. Thus in jazz melody another African tradition was preserved in that melodies tended to develop little "melodic whirlpools," in Sargeant's phrase, within tetrachordal groupings and around a central tone. This either coincided directly with or related indirectly to the European diatonic principle of the priority of the tonic. Once again an African tradition was perpetuated in a European musical framework.

Finally, the riff is also closely related to the whole concept of drum patterns, as practiced in African ensemble music. Drum patterns are repeated, as has already been explained, until the master drummer signals the change to another set of interrelated patterns. In the larger sections which result from such signal changes the several drum patterns may be interlocked and synchronized. But the drum patterns may not correspond metrically or durationally to the song or the bell (*Gankogui*) patterns. The total duration, for example, of all the small drum patterns may not equal the duration of the song or stanza segments. Thus the drum pattern on its various repeats shifts in its relationship vis-à-vis the song and bell patterns.[64] The riff functions essentially the same way, although in most jazz contexts in a less complex structural relationship.

The answer to the question when the blues developed is obviously much more difficult. By the nature of things, a suppressed, largely illiterate minority group is not in a position to leave behind much documentation. We are therefore resigned to gleaning tiny particles of evidence from the few inquisitive and sympathetic white sources that have come down to us. Many of the tunes in the aforementioned collection of *Slave Songs of the United States* contain examples of flat sevenths. The editors, however, make only one veiled reference to this melodic characteristic. In the Introduction one reads: "and what makes it all the harder to unravel a thread of melody out of this strange network is that, like birds, they seem not infrequently to strike sounds that cannot be precisely represented by the gamut" (diatonic scale). Those sentences were written in 1867, and the reference is obviously to "blue notes." In his first edition of *The Cabin and Plantation Songs as Sung by the Hampton Students* in 1874, Thomas Fenner writes in the Introduction: "another obstacle to its [the slaves' music's] rendering [on paper] is the fact that tones are frequently employed which we have no musical characters to represent. Such, for example, is that

64. See numerous examples of this procedure in Jones, Vol. II.

which I have indicated as nearly as possible by the flat seventh in *Great Camp Meetin', Hard Trials,* and others." Fenner goes on to say that "these tones . . . are rarely discordant and often add a charm to the performance," an opinion shared by virtually all writers on jazz, past and present. These two references alone would tend to confirm the widely held opinion that the blues scale was in existence for some time before the Civil War. And in fact, my own position as delineated above, is that the blues scale *always* existed—potentially—in American Negro music; it was simply one of the heritages brought along from Africa.

So far we have discussed only the blue seventh and third. What about the fifth, what jazz musicians have been calling the "flatted fifth"? Curiously, Sargeant discounts its very existence: "I have even heard the theory of a 'blue fifth' advanced, though I have never been able to find any consistent evidence to support such a theory."[65] The fact is that the flatted fifth exists in numerous recordings as early as the twenties.[66] As for its relationship to the Negro's African musical heritage, any conclusions would be premature. But there are several possible hypotheses, which incidentally might constitute a fruitful area for future research.

There are two possibilities. One is based on the fact that the raised subdominant, as we have already noted, exists under certain conditions in African music. It was therefore not entirely foreign to the American Negro's aural sensibilities. The question of the difference between a raised subdominant and a flatted dominant, or fifth, is irrelevant, since the African does not think in terms of internal key relationships. And unless there were clearly established microtonal differences between the two enharmonic degrees, the Negro would have no problem in treating both as one and the same, especially since blue notes in general are treated with considerable variability in pitch.

It is also possible that the development of the flatted fifth is entirely twentieth century in origin. It could be the result of two trends combining. One would be the increased sophistication and freedom with which the Negro used the Western diatonic system and the development of chromaticism in Western art music—although the latter seems

65. Sargeant, pp. 169-70.
66. For example, Bubber Miley with Duke Ellington's orchestra on *Animal Crackers* and *Black and Tan Fantasy* (see Chapter 7, Ex. 2 and 6).

a less likely possibility. The other trend relates to the use by many African tribes, especially West African, of the "harmonic" third. The flatted fifth may have been an unconscious attempt to use thirds equivalents.

It is of great significance that the blue fifth is used in jazz almost always in conjunction with the blue third. If we construct a tetrachord that includes these two tones (black notes in Ex. 19) and is otherwise identical to the two other common tetrachords (whole notes), we see that the blue-fifth tetrachord is in a parallel relationship of a *major*

Example 19

third to the upper (blue seventh) tetrachord, and in a parallel relationship of a *minor* third to the lower (blue third) tetrachord. Since the African, like the European, recognizes "both major and minor thirds as partaking of a quality of 'third-ness,' " as Jones puts it,[67] then it may be that this introduction of equivalent patterns involving the blue fifth answered a feeling the Negro brought from Africa.

There is still the question of the relationship of speech patterns to melodic shapes. When writers on jazz have occasionally referred to this relationship, especially in regard to the blues,[68] it has invariably been in very generalized terms. In recent years, however, attempts have been made to study the relationships between speech and melody patterns among African natives.[69] While these findings do not always agree in all particulars, they generally agree on one important fact: African melodies employ a device that has been called a "shift of center." A segment of melody will revolve around a "mean center" in a manner that correlates closely with the extremely "melodic-tonal" features of African speech. In usual practice this segment may be followed by another whose "mean center" shifts to a higher or lower

67. Jones, I, 218.
68. Bernard Heuvelmans, *De la bamboula au be-bop; Esquisse de l'evolution de la musique de jazz* (Paris: Editions de la Main Jetée, 1951), pp. 123-4.
69. Marius Schneider, "Phonetische und metrische Korrelationen bei gesprochenen und gesungenen Ewe Texten," in *Archiv für Vergleichende Phonetik*, VII, 1 (1943-44). Also Jones, I, Ch. 10, "Tone and Tune."

position, but in which the melody is consistently faithful to speech contours.

Is this not what we have in the vocal blues, and by implication in its instrumental derivatives? It is hardly necessary to belabor the point that the vocal blues are more sung speech than outright song, and as such follow speech contours very closely. The African "shift of center" occurs quite naturally at the fifth and ninth measures of a twelve-bar blues. It need not do so, of course, as some blues will attest; on the other hand, such a shift of center does occur in most blues. This may not be immediately apparent to the casual listener, for the actual melody may, like the riff in Example 18A, remain in the same pitch area. The shift of center occurs in terms of the harmonic relationship of the melody to the harmony. If the melody, as in the final chorus of Bessie Smith's *Cold in Hand Blues* (see Ex. 19 in Chapter 5), hovers around the dominant of the basic key—in this case the key of B flat—then the melody will revolve around the super tonic (second degree of the scale) in bars five and six, and around the tonic in bars nine and ten. Example 20 shows the relationship in musical notation. By making this shift, the Negro was able to preserve African elements, which, seen superficially, might appear to be completely European-determined.

Example 20

Mr. Jones thoroughly analyzes the relationship between speech and melody in respect to certain Ewe tribe songs, and the reader is referred to this study. It deals in painstaking detail with the norms and exceptions to what otherwise seems to be a very close parallel relationship between spoken speech and sung melody, and, parenthetically, it discusses the widespread use of elision in African speech.

Elision is, of course, a common feature of the American Negro's use of English, and aside from its interesting musicality, these speech habits seem to be closely related to melodic patterns. In this connection it is interesting to read W. F. Allen in the Introduction to *Slave Songs of the United States:* "The Negroes keep exquisite time in singing, and do not suffer themselves to be daunted by any obstacle in the words. The most obstinate Scripture phrases or snatches from hymns they will force to duty with any tune they please, and will dash heroically through a trochaic tune at the head of a column of iambs with wonderful skill."[70] The songs reproduced in that book confirm this observation in manifold ways. In general, one can conclude that the close relationship between speech and song observed by Schneider and Jones in Africa is perpetuated in jazz, at least until the intrusion of Tin Pan Alley and commercial popular music.

TIMBRE

Timbre is generally the least discussed musical element in jazz, and yet it is probably the characteristic more than any other that identifies something as jazz or non-jazz for the uninitiated. This fact, indeed, has been a principal cause of the confusion in the public's mind between real jazz and commercial derivatives of jazz that happen to use a jazz instrumentation and jazz timbre. Even composers like Stravinsky, Milhaud, and Ravel in the 1920s made the error of regarding jazz instrumentation and jazz sonority as the *primary* ingredients, and they completely disregarded such aspects as improvisation or the inflection and swing of jazz. Even today when, for example, the average symphony trumpet player plays with a cup mute in a symphonic work, he will almost automatically start playing with what he assumes to be a "jazz vibrato." These and similar oversimplifications and misconceptions regarding jazz timbre are probably inevitable, for most new art forms attract popular attention through their most external aspects.

Jazz instrumentation, and its resultant sonority, has been generally considered to be derived from its African background, although there has been no satisfactory explanation of this connection. Jazz sound has also been misconstrued, for not entirely explicable reasons, as being "strident," "harsh," even "tinny." Comments such as Sargeant's that early jazz "must have produced a rather raw, brassy and harmonically thin type of music"[71] abound in jazz literature, critical as well

70. Allen, Ware, and Garrison, p. iv.
71. Sargeant, p. 225.

as fictional. Conversely, the sweet or commercial bands of the twenties and thirties were often characterized as rich and full-sounding. There may be a grain of truth in both positions, but on the whole such reactions seemed to represent illusion more than fact. For instance, the Paul Whiteman orchestra may have given many people the illusion of rich, smooth quality by virtue of its extremely efficient and virtuosic, not to say slick, ensemble work, and indeed, at certain periods, by the very size of the ensemble. On the other hand, a smaller jazz group with a New Orleans instrumentation that played not quite so smoothly would surely have sounded "raw, brassy and harmonically thin" to the same listeners. The poor acoustical conditions under which jazz was performed and recorded may also have contributed to such slanted impressions. For imaginative and sensitive ears, however, even in an old acoustical recording, the sound of the King Oliver band, for example, in its heyday was an extraordinarily beautiful, rich, and full one, mellow in timbre like a fine wine. All the great players from Louis Armstrong through Coleman Hawkins, Ben Webster, Charlie Parker, Dizzy Gillespie, to Sonny Rollins and beyond—yes, even Lester Young—are characterized by a larger-than-life sound and projection; not to mention such ensembles as the Duke Ellington orchestra of the thirties and forties and the Count Basie band of the last thirty years. Conversely, the individual sounds of Art Hickman's or Guy Lombardo's musicians of the twenties, or even the majority of Stan Kenton's players in the forties and fifties, could hardly be considered strong and full, for smoothness or loudness of performance can not necessarily be equated with opulence of sound.

The sonority of real jazz is traceable directly to African singing and indirectly to African speech and language. The more we depart from the core of this African tradition, through whatever influence, European or otherwise, the more we depart from the original sonority conception of jazz. (This, incidentally, does not mean that the intrinsic *compositional* worth of such a jazz work is necessarily inferior; we are referring at the moment only to *timbral* and *sonoric* considerations.)

African speech, singing, and playing are all marked by an open tone and natural quality. In this they are closer to European and Western tradition than to the Islamic, which is indeed characterized by a thin, nasal, wavering quality. The Islamic tradition is recognizable by a nasal and stringy quality of voice, and its instrumentation is accordingly dominated by double-reed and string instruments. Here again, we find not only a refutation of Ernest Borneman's previously mentioned theories on the Hispano-Arabic-Mediterranean origin of jazz, but also clearly at least one fundamental reason why instruments like the oboe, the bassoon, and the higher strings have not readily found a place in jazz.

African instrumentation reflects the vocal quality of African speech. We can hear this in the deep ringing tones of African ivory horns, in the penterating timbres of the xylophone and marimba, even in the relatively dark quality of African flute playing, and above all in the multi-voiced drum ensemble, without which most African music could not function. The typical ensemble has a rich variety of drums carefully tuned prior to each performance according to strictly predetermined pitch associations. An ensemble of four drums, therefore, does not produce only the rich polyrhythmic structures we have discussed earlier in this chapter but also a pantonal low-register pitch polyphony. The sound of this ensemble does not, of course, "strike the ear as a series of chords: their [the drums'] notes are not sufficiently precise to produce this effect."[72] It is, nevertheless, as any recording of African drumming will attest, a rich percussive substructure that is more than mere noise, and is preserved in a simpler form in the sonority concepts of the best jazz drummers (for example, Sid Catlett, Kenny Clarke, Elvin Jones, Max Roach, and Dannie Richmond.)

We have already referred to the vocal-syllabic identification of drum patterns, an obvious corollary to the drum languages of African tribal communication. We have also seen that in many African languages each syllable and word has a specific pitch association, and accordingly word meaning changes with pitch variations. And we noticed how the correlation between pitch and word content was preserved in a fairly unadulterated form in the blues, despite the transfer to the English language. One of jazz's great attractions is that it has preserved the typically African open tone and natural quality. Some would refer to this quality as "earthiness," others as "beauty of sound," while still others have seen it as raw and vulgar, since it lacked the "polite" sounds of European art music. But in purely acoustical terms of purity and amplitude, the open-toned, natural quality of African speech and song appears in the playing of all the great jazz stylistic

72. Jones, II, viii (Note).

innovators, in the singing of Bessie Smith, Billy Eckstine, Sarah Vaughan, even Frank Sinatra, or in the tone and touch of pianists like Art Tatum, Erroll Garner, Thelonious Monk, or a bassist like Ray Brown; and it must have been that quality, too, that helped to make Buddy Bolden legendary around 1900. The African quality of jazz sonority can be heard, moreover, in the individuality and personal inflection of the jazz musician's tone. His is not basically the cultivated and studied tone of Western art music, nor a tone that is bought in the music store along with the instrument. Jazz's strength and communicative power lie in this individuality, which comes from inside the man; indeed a jazz musician without this individual quality is not a jazz musician in the strictest sense.

By contrast, a symphony orchestra player performs a different function in which great individuality is not a prerequisite. Indeed, it is more likely to be a liability, except in the case of certain solo players and then only in moderation, since improvisation and creative involvement are not part of the symphonic orchestral picture. Under the circumstances, qualities of extreme individuality must be curbed and subjugated to the style of the composer being performed. The jazz musician, by contrast, must control his individual approach only in terms of his own conception, not that of another composer. This crucial difference between the two idioms is frequently misunderstood on both sides.

This element of individuality is then another African characteristic carried over into jazz. It is so strong in quality that it has survived despite the fact that jazz developed almost entirely on instruments that came out of the tradition of European art music. This is one of the miracles of jazz, and it is never sufficiently emphasized.

IMPROVISATION

Improvisation is one element of jazz that does not fit into any of the aspects of jazz music so far discussed, although of course it is involved with all of them. The improvisation of many lines at the same time is a typically African concept, and is perpetuated in most forms of early jazz, a music marked above all by "collective improvisation." With the advent of the arrangement (a decidedly "white" influence) and the incorporation of the solo in an otherwise arranged or at least partially prearranged context, the multi-linearity of early jazz was abandoned until the late 1950s. The juxtaposition of solo and ensemble music is also a basic characteristic of African music; it manifests itself in the entire call-and-response typology and specifically in the cantor-to-chorus relationship. But the ensemble or choral sections of such African music are based on very strict organizational principles, largely founded on repetition. Variational techniques do exist, but they occur only in certain categories of music, and even then are reserved almost entirely for the leading performer, the master drummer.

Improvisation is the heart and soul of jazz. But this could also be said of countless other folk and popular musics. It is therefore somewhat reckless to imply, as some jazz writers have done, that the Negro found something of his own heritage in Spanish music in the Southern United States, especially in *improvised flamenco music*. First of all, flamenco music was probably the least exportable of all Spanish regional styles, and it is not likely that it was prevalent in New Orleans, for example. Furthermore, even in such other Spanish idioms that did transfer to the New World, the underlying structural conceptions were so different from African music that no easy assimilation could possibly have taken place. One need only point out that, while *some* Spanish music and *some* African music are both improvised, the nature of these improvisations is entirely different. Spanish improvisational techniques involve elaboration and embellishment more than they do strict variation. These elaborations may contain variational ingredients, but their primary purpose is one of adorning, embellishing, and making more complex a given and simpler melody. Compare this with African variational concepts. In a variation by an African master drummer, for example, what may already be relatively complex expositional material (what Jones calls a "seed-pattern") is varied, manipulated, augmented, diminished, fragmented, regrouped into new variants. All of this is done, moreover, without any sense of embellishing. On the contrary, the drummer's skill as an improviser will be judged by his ability to use with a maximum of variety the essential motivic material of a given pattern, all within, we reiterate, exceedingly strict rules and traditions.[73] It should also be noted that African music, unlike Arabic, is basically not microtonal in structure.

73. Jones, I, 174 ff.

By contrast Arabic (North African and Spanish) music is basically a homophonic, variational, microtonal music, and does not feature the solo-to-ensemble juxtaposition. This fact would tend to refute the importance Ernest Borneman attaches to the influence of Hispano-Arabic culture on jazz.[74] It is true that the former had considerable effect on Creole music, which is certainly a part of the prehistory of jazz. The variational and solo-determined character of Creole music cannot be disputed, but its role in the development of jazz is demonstrably a limited one, as will be shown in succeeding chapters.

There is another theory most vigorously championed by Ernest Borneman to the effect that American jazz developed primarily from the Creole music of New Orleans, which in turn was a "Latin American music," spawned out of a mixture of African and Spanish influences in the West Indies and Caribbean islands. The Caribbean was used by slave traders as a stopover between Africa and the American South. Although Borneman's theory leads him to the untenable position that the only true jazz is Spanish- or Latin American-influenced jazz, there are certain points in his theory that are worth further investigation. It is true, of course, that many of the slaves came in contact with Spanish music in their stay of weeks or months or years in the Caribbean. It is also likely that the slaves found in the music of "Spanish and Portuguese settlers similarities [to African music] in the handling of rhythm and timbre."[75] But I suspect that these were mostly superficial, coincidental similarities, for it is a fairly undisputed fact that African and Arabic-Islamic-Spanish rhythms are two entirely different disciplines, the former polyrhythmic, the latter monorhythmic in essence. Mr. Borneman thus seems too hasty when he concludes that "Creole music had a head start over the development of spirituals, blues and other forms of Anglo-African music."[76]

Borneman is also on shaky ground when he attempts to develop a theory that, as early as the Middle Ages, African music had a strong influence on Arabic music, even though musicological research, to our knowledge, in no way substantiates this.[77] According to Borneman's neat theory, there were all kinds of African strains in the music of Spain,

74. Ernest Borneman, "Creole Echoes," *The Jazz Review,* II, 8 (September 1959), 13-15; II, 10 (November 1959), 26-7.
75. Ibid., II, 8, 14.
76. Loc. cit.
77. See, for example, Jones, I, 207, 208.

which the Negro slaves upon arrival in the Caribbean recognized immediately as a sort of musical second cousin. Borneman, for example, makes the mistake of construing the coincidental similarity between the familiar Spanish-Portuguese rhythm ♩. ♩. ♩ and the identical pattern in African songs and dances[78] as a generic identity. The fact is that in Spanish music this rhythm is used in terms of a divisive metric conception, while in African music it is felt as an additive pattern—a crucial and fundamental difference.

It might be fruitful, nevertheless, to investigate further the notion that, with the nearly eight-hundred-year domination of Northern Africa and Spain by the Arabs, certain Islamic influences eventually found their way to the New World via the Spanish and Portuguese settlers, and there found acceptance among the African slaves, not because they recognized any African strains therein but because specific musical elements were discovered to be identical with those in their own tradition.

On the subject of Spanish music and its relation to jazz, the theory has been advanced—seemingly without any reasonable foundation—that there is some mysterious relationship between Andalusian flamenco music, especially the *cante hondo,* and the blues. There is very little besides certain peripheral, coincidental evidence to support this theory. It is interesting but not necessarily productive, for example, to contemplate the fact that *hondo* (or *jondo*) is said by some philologists to mean "soul" in Sindhi language, one of the languages of Mohammedan people of India. Visions of a tieup between *cante hondo* (in other words, "soul song") and the recent proliferation of so-called soul music in jazz immediately comes to mind. But the jump from one culture to another, five thousand miles and two thousand years apart, is not made that easily. There is still continuing speculation that Hindu music is the "mother of European music." This in turn leads to even grander theories that link Hindu music with jazz through ancient India's influence on Islamic-Spanish and perhaps even African cultures. Some have read significance into the fact, observed by, among others, the noted Spanish composer Manuel de Falla,[79] that certain kinds of Hindu and most flamenco music are accompanied by clapping hands, stamping feet, tapping sticks or canes,

78. See also Borneman, II, 8, 14.
79. As quoted by Aziz Balouch in *Cante Hondo* (Madrid: Ediciones Ensayos, 1955).

and snapping fingers, which the gypsies are said to prefer to the use of castanets. But these are superficial similarities, outweighed by other more fundamental differences. First, flamenco music is based on a quite variable chord progression *totally* different from that of the blues; and, second, in its declamation, it uses a combination of recitative and variational techniques that are not a consistent essential feature of the blues, in any case the early un-Europeanized, unsophisticated, uncommercialized blues.

In this connection it is worth mentioning that Indo-Pakistani music is divided into six principal modes, three of which—afternoon modes—are nothing but the blues scale. To establish a possible historic link between these modes and the American Negro's blues scale might be an interesting project for a future student of jazz.

A. M. Jones has pointed out that *all* drum patterns in African music are equipped with "nonsense syllables." In fact, this is how drum patterns are notated when and if this becomes necessary (Ex. 21, also

Example 21 *Nyayito* Dance (bars 47-8)[80]

80. Jones, II, 27.

Ex. 3 and 4). This is also the means by which these patterns are taught. Another subject for further research would be the connection in the Negro's remembered background between these nonsense syllables and jazz scat-singing, another phenomenon virtually without precedent in European music.[81]

It is thus evident that many more aspects of jazz derive directly from African musical-social traditions than has been assumed. Very few discussions of the prehistory of jazz have gone beyond the simplistic generalizations that jazz rhythm came from Africa but jazz melody and harmony from Europe. The analytic study in this chapter shows that *every* musical element—rhythm, harmony, melody, timbre, and the basic forms of jazz—is essentially African in background and derivation. And why should it have been otherwise? After all, centuries-old traditions that are not merely artistic cultivations but an inseparable part of everyday life are not abandoned so easily. Acculturation took place, but only to the limited extent that the Negro allowed European elements to become integrated into his African heritage. Until the 1920s, he took only those European ingredients that were necessary for his own music's survival. Thus one can say that within the loose framework of European tradition, the American Negro was able to preserve a significant nucleus of his African heritage. And it is that nucleus that has made jazz the uniquely captivating language that it is.

81. In this connection the reader is referred to Jones, I, 183-7, where is reprinted a "poem" made up of eleven stanzas of nonsense syllables that correspond to the notation of the drum variations on a standard pattern, as improvised and then written down by the master drummer, Mr. Tay, with whom Mr. Jones consulted on his book. As Jones says, the result is "a spontaneous yet closely organized poem in pure sound," in which astonishingly enough each variation—though improvised—is constructed in couplets.

2

The Beginnings

It is impossible to establish the exact beginnings of jazz as a distinct, self-contained music. Some historians use the year 1895 as a working date; others prefer 1917, the year that the word *jazz* seems to have become current and the year that the Original Dixieland Jazz Band made what are generally considered the first jazz recordings; still others prefer dates in between. But whatever date is picked, it is safe to say that in purely musical terms the earliest jazz represents a primitive reduction of the complexity, richness, and perfection of its African and, for that matter, European antecedents. Once we get past the fascinating stories and legends of early jazz, once we penetrate beyond jazz as a reflection of certain crucial changes in the social evolution of the American Negro, we are left with a music which in most instances can hold the musician's attention only as a museum relic. The purely musical qualities, heard without regard to their historical and social trappings, have lost their particular, almost topical meaning for us; and as musical structures, in performance and conception, much of the earliest jazz sounds naïve or crude or dated.

This is not to say that we cannot or should not listen to early jazz in the context and aura of its historical past. Indeed, if we as individuals can be conscious of the historic interest, we surely can enjoy early jazz more than its purely musical qualities warrant. Objective discussion of early jazz is made more difficult because no large body of recordings exists. The problem of assessing the quality of early jazz is compounded further by the fact that the pre-1923 recordings that do exist (or even those that are presumed to exist) cannot all be considered jazz in the strictest sense. Most of these recordings were made by society orchestras, novelty bands, or jazz groups who were forced by the companies recording them to play novelty or polite dance music.

The beginnings of film coincide roughly with those of jazz. Yet by 1915 the cinema had already produced its first great artist, D. W. Griffith. In jazz—as far as recorded proof goes—we have to await the recordings of King Oliver and Louis Armstrong for comparable achievement. We may assume, of course, that King Oliver was playing nearly as well in 1916 as in 1923, and that players such as Jelly Roll Morton, Freddie Keppard, Bunk Johnson, and Buddy Petit were producing above-average jazz in the decade before jazz recording began in earnest. But we lack proof. The unfortunate circumstances that placed a social barrier between a colored performer and the white recording companies have robbed us of the evidence forever.

But even if we could find isolated examples of great enduring jazz in this formative period, we would still have to admit that early jazz represents, speaking strictly musically, a relatively low point in the Negro's musical history. Indeed, how could it have been otherwise? Circumstances such as segregation and extreme race prejudice forced the music to be what it was. That it was as much as it was, and that it had enough strength to survive and eventually grow into a world music, is abundant proof of its potential strength and beauty.

From this nadir, jazz gradually developed not only in quality but also in basic conception and intent. The musicians who produced it were undergoing some very profound social changes, and their music obviously had to reflect this. Many jazz followers accept the necessity of these social changes but are unwilling to accept the corollary changes in the music itself. Such a contradiction in position, is, needless to say, untenable. In the succeeding chapters we will trace the musical developments that led from the humble beginnings of jazz in the first decades of our century to the 1930s.

Let us begin by acknowledging how difficult it is to know how the earliest jazz really sounded. Nevertheless, we can make some fairly positive assumptions about it. Much valuable research has been done since *Jazzmen* was first published in 1939.[1] Such research has confirmed that much of this early music was either not jazz or not even intended to be jazz. It may have incorporated into its style certain jazz characteristics, but the fact that these had developed in Negro music did not automatically make this music jazz (to say so would be tantamount to saying that *all* Negro music is jazz). The research has also shown that early jazz in both its essential and its peripheral manifestations sprang up in many parts of the United States, not only in New Orleans.

In his publisher's foreword to Samuel Charters's monograph on early New Orleans Negro musicians, Walter C. Allen writes: "Many of these men were not jazz musicians; many had strict classical or legitimate training."[2] Charters substantiates this statement a hundred times in the body of the text.

Leonard Feather, in *The Book of Jazz*,[3] publishes an interview with W. C. Handy, composer of *St. Louis Blues* and other important jazz songs, during which, despite the interviewer's somewhat slanted questions, nothing is said by Handy to prove that either he or the musicians he knew were *jazz* musicians. Indeed, the words *novelty* and *minstrel* figure more prominently and are used more consistently than the word *jazz*. When questioned as to his interpretation of the word *jazz*, Handy skirts the issue and states instead: "I've played with many novelty musicians. Even in the minstrel days we played music similar to jazz, but we didn't call it jazz." Nor was it jazz. Minstrel music was at most a tributary source of jazz, and Handy was primarily a minstrel musician, cornet soloist, and band director. In his own *Father of the Blues: An Autobiography*[4] Handy says that when he was doing much traveling with his band in 1896, often hiring musicians in the various

1. Edited by Frederic Ramsey, Jr., and Charles Edward Smith (New York: Harcourt, Brace and Company, 1939; available as Harvest Book HB-30, paperback). Valuable books published later include Samuel B. Charters, *Jazz: New Orleans, 1885-1957*, Jazz Monographs No. 2 (Belleville, N.J.: Walter C. Allen, 1958); Samuel B. Charters and Leonard Kunstadt, *Jazz: A History of the New York Scene* (Garden City, N.Y.: Doubleday & Company, 1962); Nat Shapiro and Nat Hentoff, eds., *Hear Me Talkin' to Ya* (New York: Rinehart & Company, 1955); Leonard Feather, *The Book of Jazz* (New York: Horizon Press, 1957).
2. Charters, p. iii.
3. Feather, pp. 23-25.
4. New York: The Macmillan Company, 1941.

cities visited, "the New Orleans musicians were scholarly and played classics." In Denver he had an English clarinet player in his band, and at other times it included Mexicans and Germans. He also claimed he "couldn't get a good Negro clarinet player." It is also significant that when Handy, who was from Alabama, traveled constantly all over the South as a young man, he never heard of Bunk Johnson or Buddy Bolden. Feather interprets this to mean that Bolden and Johnson were not as famous as claimed by historians who have supported the idea that jazz went up the river from New Orleans to Chicago; but it may also mean that the wide social gulf that separated the world of New Orleans honkey-tonks and that of minstrel circus bands would have made it unlikely for Handy to have known about Bolden. Handy's pedigree as a *jazz* musician can also be questioned on the basis that the blues which he published as *Memphis Blues* in 1912 was not a blues at all; it was closer to the cakewalk than to anything else.

In other parts of Feather's chapter jazz is frequently equated with ragtime. But when Eubie Blake, for example, tells Feather that he was playing ragtime before 1898, he is simply saying that he was playing ragtime, not jazz. The guitarist Danny Barker recalls that "the most exciting form of musical entertainment [in New Orleans] was not the jazz bands but the brass bands."[5] Alphonse Picou, the veteran New Orleans clarinetist, stated flatly that the music he heard around the turn of the century was not ragtime, "it was nothing but marches they was playing—brass marches—parade music."[6] And Edmond Hall, his colleague, who started playing in New Orleans around 1915 as a youngster, adds that "in the very early days of brass bands, in the 90's and even before, the music was mostly written—I mean in the kind of band my father played in. As time went on, there was more improvising."[7] And to this can be added Buster Bailey's interesting comment on his clarinet playing in 1917 and 1918: "I . . . was embellishing around the melody. At that time I wouldn't have known what they meant by improvisation. But embellishment was a phrase I understood."[8]

5. Shapiro and Hentoff, p. 15.
6. Ibid., p. 18.
7. Ibid., p. 22.
8. Ibid., p. 78.

The excellent *They All Played Ragtime* by Rudi Blesh and the late Harriet Janis attempts to prove that ragtime was a distinct music separate from jazz. In a summary "Postlude" we read that "ragtime . . . is *in* Negro song and Negro jazz."[9] In due time ragtime piano became instrumentalized, and its even-note, slightly stiff syncopations and unimprovised, formalized patterns gradually loosened up and were absorbed into the main current of jazz.

Garvin Bushell, living in his hometown of Springfield, Ohio, until 1919, recalls that "ragtime piano was the major influence in that section of the country. . . . The change [to jazz] began to come around 1912 to 1915, when the four-string banjo and saxophone came in. The players began to elaborate on the melodic lines; the harmony and rhythm remained the same." Bushell adds: "The parade music in Springfield was played by strictly march bands, but there was instrumental ragtime—and improvisation—in the dance halls." Still on the same subject, Bushell says in speaking of music in New York in the early 1920's, "You could only hear the blues and real jazz in the gut-bucket cabarets where the lower class went. You usually weren't allowed to play blues and boogie-woogie in the average Negro middle-class home. That music supposedly suggested a low element."[10]

In those years of vast changes, as several musical styles coalesced into the one that finally came to be known as jazz, the only tributary source of jazz that seemed to remain constant was the blues. It is unlikely that the blues changed basically between the 1880s and the early 1920s. And one can be sure that when Bunk Johnson says that as a kid he "used to play nuthin' but the blues"[11] in New Orleans barrelhouses, he was playing essentially the same instrumental blues that spread like wildfire in 1920s race recordings, or—going back in time—that he had heard Buddy Bolden play in the 1890s. The permanence of the blues is substantiated in a statement made by the important Denver musician and band leader George Morrison. In a lengthy taped interview with the author in 1962, Morrison said without any prompting, "Oh, the blues, they *never* changed." (See Appendix, p. 359.)

9. (New York: Alfred A. Knopf, 1950), p. 269.
10. Nat Hentoff, "Garvin Bushell and New York Jazz in the 1920's," *The Jazz Review,* II, 1 (January 1959), 11-12.
11. Shapiro and Hentoff, p. 7.

Morrison's interview as a whole supplies much the same kind of information we have so far submitted; and, in fact, his life's story is so typical of his generation of Negro musicians that it is worth describing. By so doing it is also possible to repair the undue neglect of a fine musician. Although Morrison's father and grandfather had been square-dance and coon-song fiddlers, young George set out to be a concert violinist. He developed into such a fine violinist that no less a master than Fritz Kreisler, upon hearing him play Kreisler's *Tambourin Chinois* in 1920 at the Carlton Terrace on Broadway and 100th Street in New York, introduced himself to Morrison and offered to give him six free lessons on certain technical and bowing matters. Despite such a talent, however, a career as a symphony or concert violinist was not then possible for a Negro. Morrison turned to those areas in which he could earn a living as a violinist, but first he played guitar in a string band in the mining camps near Boulder, Colorado—a band similar to the famous Six and Seven-Eighths band of New Orleans and hundreds of similar string combinations around the country at that time. Then about 1911 Morrison became violinist-leader of various trio combinations in the parlor houses of Denver, jobbing around in hotels, studying in Chicago while playing at the famous Panama Cabaret and with Dave Peyton's orchestra at the Grand Theatre, eventually returning to Denver to form another trio, which within a few years grew into an eleven-piece orchestra that became the most popular orchestra of the Denver area. During his eleven years at the Albany Hotel, Denver's second largest hotel, Morrison had in his band at one time or another such famous jazz musicians as Andy Kirk, Jimmie Lunceford, Jelly Roll Morton, and Alphonse Trent. In 1920 scouts from the Columbia Record Company heard Morrison, invited him to New York, and recorded him on the opposite side of a Ted Lewis number in material not of Morrison's own choosing. For reasons not entirely clear, Morrison did not get to record again, but while in New York he helped Perry Bradford to launch Mamie Smith's career and recommended his white Denver colleague Paul Whiteman to the Victor Company. Even this capsule biography discloses a pattern that was typical of hundreds of fine Negro musicians' careers: a series of near-misses caused largely by his skin color.

Morrison's recollections of the music he played in the early decades of the century corroborate what we have been saying. Between about

1901 and 1911, when he was playing in a five-piece string band formed with his brother and brother-in-law, his repertory consisted of waltzes like "After the Ball," sentimental popular ballads like "Darling, I Am Growing Old," and marches like the famous "Double Eagle." Furthermore, according to Morrison, they played these "just straight; we couldn't improvise. We were lucky to play them straight!" When he was old enough to play in the red-light district of Denver, the situation was more or less the same, for the finer houses did not tolerate any rough or vulgar music. Gentility was the key word, and accordingly Dvorak's "Humoresque" or two choruses of a popular tune played on the violin, doubled on the cornet, and accompanied by sentimental piano arpeggios was the typical fare. Fast tunes seem also to have been avoided.

When Morrison's trio grew to a quintet, to a septet, and finally to an eleven-piece band playing for dancing at the Albany Hotel, Morrison emulated the style of the most famous white orchestra in the West, Art Hickman's. Although the tunes by now were closer to jazz ("Dardanella," "Ja-Da," "Royal Garden Blues"), Morrison says that his men played more or less straight, while he "improvised" on the violin.

When the jazz age began in earnest, Morrison naturally turned to jazz as well, but his orchestra, playing primarily for white society dances, never abandoned entirely the "sweet" side of the music. The band played only in a two-beat style, and Morrison recalls laughingly that he did not like the four-beat style of jazz when it became current. He felt that "it was hurrying the rhythm" too much. Where there had been two leisurely beats, there were now four frantic ones, played twice as fast.

Morrison today in his seventies can still play in all the styles his career demanded. He demonstrated this for the author on tape, playing in succession short improvisations on "Sweet Sue," "Darktown Strutters' Ball," and an extemporized blues, as well as his own "classical" and spiritual-influenced violin and piano compositions.

The story of George Morrison and his musical development could, as we have said, be duplicated a hundred times. We cite the careers of Wilbur Sweatman, Noble Sissle, Will Marion Cook, W. C. Handy, Erskine Tate, Eddie Heywood, Sr., Garvin Bushell, countless Creole New Orleans musicians, as well as many unnamed others like Morrison whom jazz history has overlooked. The picture that emerges from these careers is that the music played depended almost entirely on for whom it was played. The music of a Negro playing for white society dances was different from that required at a rough southwestern honky-tonk; and both were different from that of the novelty bands of New York, like Earl Fuller's, or the slick dance orchestras, like Art Hickman's and Paul Whiteman's. The city of New Orleans itself sported two kinds of jazz: the rougher, blues-colored music of Uptown and the more polite Creole music of Downtown.

Buster Smith, who influenced Charlie Parker, confirms this diversity of styles: "Of course most of us played that sweet stuff once in a while. It was all according to the kind of audience you had. You couldn't play our kind of music in some of the big places, the 'high collar' dances. No, they wanted that hotel music. We found out our stuff was too rough."[12]

There are many indications that as the jazz age approached and jazz styles narrowed down to a kind of early mainstream, the more polite bands became hotter and the hotter bands more polished. Edmond Souchon's words ring true when he compares King Oliver's early playing at the Big 25 in Storyville, the red-light district of New Orleans, with two subsequent periods in Oliver's career: "By the time Oliver was playing at the Tulane gymnasium [for dances], he had acquired a technique that was much more smooth, and . . . his band was adapting itself to the white dances more and more. At Big 25 it was hard-hitting, rough and ready, full of fire and drive. He subdued this to please the different patrons at the gym dances. . . . By the time Oliver had reached Chicago and the peak of his popularity, his sound was not the same. It was a different band, a different and more polished Oliver, an Oliver who had completely lost his New Orleans sound."[13]

Sifting through these remembrances and hundreds of others that are sometimes contradictory, we soon realize that not *all* the music played by Negro musicians in New Orleans or elsewhere was jazz.

12. Don Gazzaway, "Conversations with Buster Smith, Part II," *The Jazz Review,* III, 1 (January 1960), p. 12.

13. Edmond Suchon, M. D., "King Oliver: A Very Personal Memoir," *The Jazz Review,* III, 4 (May 1960), p. 11. Mutt Carey substantiates this (as quoted in Shapiro and Hentoff, p. 42): "I'll tell you something about Joe's records. I haven't heard a single one that comes close to sounding like Joe's playing in person."

Some of it was; some of it contained elements that at later stages of development became an essential ingredient of jazz; and some of it was not jazz at all. A great part of it was a kind of borderline music that was on the verge of becoming jazz. But to ferret out which was which, especially without sufficient recorded documentation, is as useless as trying to determine at which point rain becomes sleet and sleet becomes snow.

The only generalization we can permit ourselves is that the music that became known as jazz existed for many years as a multi-faceted music whose character depended largely on geographical disposition and the social and racial constitution of its audience. But since, until the race record boom of the early 1920s, the main consumer was the white man, and since even most middle-class Negroes shunned the blues and other rougher but more authentic forms of jazz, it is not difficult to see where the emphasis in style and conception lay.

In any other period in jazz we could now isolate the important innovational recordings and appraise them objectively in terms of their contribution. This is clearly not possible in the pre-1923 era. Almost all the great musicans who played authentic jazz before the 1920s made their first recordings years later. King Oliver, Freddie Keppard, Louis Armstrong, Jelly Roll Morton, Sidney Bechet, Bennie Moten's orchestra—all started recording in 1923, the year also that Bessie Smith cut her first blues sides (after Mamie Smith had started the blues rush in 1921). It would be rash to assume that all these musicians played the same way in 1923 as they did in 1915 (or, in applicable cases, before); at least not in terms of quality, and probably not even in general style. Once jazz had become a distinctive entertainment commodity in cities like Chicago, New York, Los Angeles, Kansas City, and once the Original Dixieland Jazz Band's records began to sell widely, events moved rapidly. Players reached sudden success and then as rapidly declined, sometimes all within a very few years. Many of the New Orleans musicians loved the money and fame they earned in Chicago, but at heart they were homesick. In many cases they did not know how to cope with the frenetic pace of life in a Prohibition-era Chicago. The occasionally violent ups and downs in careers were reflected in the music. Therefore, one cannot assume that the King Oliver of 1923, for example, was the same man and played the same music that first thrilled the customers at Big 25 eight years earlier. On the contrary, it would be safer to assume (with Dr. Souchon) that the character and quality of Oliver's music had changed, as it did again even more drastically in the later 1920s.

Under the circumstances the best we can offer is an educated guess that the *general stylistic* outlines of Oliver's playing in 1923 were probably the same, but the fire and drive, the "wonderfully joyous New Orleans sound,"[14] were carried forward not so much by Oliver himself as by his disciple Louis Armstrong. When we listen to such early recorded Armstrong as his rare solos with Oliver's Creole Jazz Band or *Railroad Blues* (1924) with Trixie Smith, the easy elegance of *Mandy, Make Up Your Mind* (1924), the blue-noted wah-wah cynicism on Ma Rainey's *Countin' Blues* (1924) and *I Ain't Gonna Play No Second Fiddle* (1925) with Perry Bradford, we are probably hearing a slightly more spirited and advanced version of what King Oliver, Bunk Johnson, and others were playing during the war years.

Except for riverboat jobs, Armstrong stayed in New Orleans until 1923. The pace there was more leisurely; musical traditions were well entrenched and not likely to change as rapidly as up north. In 1923, the peak years of the jazz recording craze, which was to contribute so significantly to the rapid dissemination and growth of jazz, were still several years in the future. Even without recorded proof of Louis's work as second-cornet player with Oliver's Creole Jazz Band, one could assume that the Armstrong of the years 1923-25, that is, just prior to his first maturation in the Hot Five period, still retained a great deal of the pure New Orleans style of his immediate predecessors. We are told that during the war, when Armstrong was still in his teens, older New Orleans trumpet men like Chris Kelly, Buddy Petit, and Kid Rena could still "cut" Louis,[15] but probably by 1923 or 1924 he was beginning to equal or better them. They were on their way down, or in any case their abilities remained constant, while Louis was definitely on his way up. Somewhere in those years their stylistic paths intersected.

But Armstrong's was a very special talent, and even in its earliest stages its innovative quality and originality shone through. Armstrong in this sense is therefore less reliable as an illustration of the classic New Orleans style. A more trustworthy example of the early pure

14. Suchon, p. 11.
15. Charters, p. 62.

cornet style can be heard in the recording of Bunk Johnson's reminiscences and demonstration of Buddy Bolden's playing. By talking, whistling, and playing, Bunk attempts to bring back to reality the exact conception of Bolden's style some thirty-five years earlier. No one can judge with absolute certainty the accuracy of Bunk's re-creation. Memory patterns and unconscious influences during the interim years could have played tricks on his mind. Nevertheless, a detailed analysis of this demonstration suggests that Bunk was indeed very close to Bolden's conception, or at least very close to his *own* early style, which was by Bunk's own admission influenced directly by Bolden. Some divergencies may exist, but these would seem to be infinitesimal. This is suggested by the fact that Bunk's several variations on one of Bolden's "make-up" tunes stay close not only to the tune but to a very specific style and strict tradition.[16] Such stylistic cohesiveness, of course, was an essential feature of pure New Orleans playing. That Bunk's variations are very close to Bolden's way of playing is further demonstrated by the *rhythmic* characteristics of his style; there are notably few excursions into a more modern rhythmic conception. The rhythms swing lightly, almost joggingly, in typically happy, even-note patterns.

This style was also very close to ragtime. In fact, those figures that remain most constant during Bunk's numerous variants of the tune are a fine synthesis of both ragtime and march phrasings, two genres which, as we have already seen, were very closely allied. The ragtime heritage in Bunk's Bolden imitation is made even clearer by comparing his playing with that of his accompanist, the New Orleans pianist Bertha Gonsoulin. Many of the figures are the same, although differences between the basically percussive touch of a piano and the legato phrasing possible on a brass instrument, plus the fact that ragtime was a piano-conceived music, make the tune flow more smoothly on Bunk's cornet. This affords us a perfect glimpse of how piano ragtime became instrumentalized, and how "ragging a tune" in the particular relaxed manner favored in New Orleans led to the classic New Orleans style. Bunk's demonstration also reminds us that this style did not permit

16. In this remarkably informative demonstration, Bunk plays altogether five versions of the tune: two of them whistled, three played on the cornet, and all five with several choruses each, thus offering excellent possibilities for comparison and verification. *This Is Bunk Johnson Talking*, American Music 643.

improvisation in the strictest sense of that term. It consisted more of embellishment of a melody than improvisation on chords, and much outright repetition. Here, of course, we have the crucial difference between New Orleans and later styles. Bunk's playing certainly demonstrates how strict were the canons of that New Orleans tradition. It is perhaps a reflection of a typically New Orleans clannishness, often cited by musicians and historians.[17] The highly disciplined nature of this music was the most important factor in holding it together for so long. It was only the genius of a Louis Armstrong, erupting coincidentally with a major social revolution (brought on by the post-war industrial boom), that was able to break through these bonds.

Another reliable reference to the early New Orleans style is the recordings made by Kid Ory in San Francisco in 1921 on the Sunshine label, among them *Ory's Creole Trombone* and *Society Blues*. The former title is a clear, albeit naïve example of the kind of ragtime-plus-march-plus-minstrel hokum that made up much of the early jazz repertoire. The piece is dated, repetitious, and corny, and Ory never really makes any of the breaks that are the whole point of the piece. But the recording interests us because of the consummate artistry of Mutt Carey, a remarkable cornetist who has never received his due, probably because he recorded only once in his prime.[18] His performance here lends credence to the opinion voiced by Armstrong, Bunk Johnson, Danny Barker, and others that there were many fine trumpet players in New Orleans besides the famous names that have survived on recordings and in the history books. Carey's playing in 1921 was extraordinarily secure, elegant, and imaginative. His tone was full, his rhythmic conception relaxed and modern for its time, and his technique flawless, or at any rate commensurate with his ideas, which were far from ordinary. On these recordings he sounds almost like Rex Stewart from Duke Ellington's famous band of the 1930s. They cer-

17. See, for example, Garvin Bushell in *The Jazz Review*, II, 3 (April 1959), 17. Accounts of this clannishness thread throughout Alan Lomax's *Mister Jelly Roll: The Fortunes of Jelly Roll Morton, New Orleans Creole and "Inventor of Jazz"* (New York: Duell, Sloan and Pearce, 1950; reprinted, New York: Grove Press, 1956).

18. The 1921 Sunshine date is, except for one side (*Ory's Creole Trombone*) reissued on Folkways FJ2811A, a rare collector's item. Carey did record frequently in the 1940s, but he was then over fifty, past his prime, and had been inactive in music for nearly twenty years.

tainly confirm New Orleans trombonist Preston Jackson's opinion of Carey: "Mutt had a very mellow tone and a terrific swing . . . Mutt wasn't a high note player; he wasn't as strong as Louis Armstrong or Joe Oliver."[19] All the recorded evidence substantiates this and indicates further that Carey was happiest when playing as part of a collectively improvising ensemble. He was not the driving virtuoso player that Armstrong was. There is no question, however, that Carey represents the pre-1920 New Orleans style at its purest and most eloquent.

Still another sadly neglected example of the early New Orleans manner can be heard on recordings made in 1927 by the Sam Morgan Jazz Band. This was a marvelous-sounding nine-piece group made up mostly of men who had stayed on in New Orleans after the great exodus to Chicago earlier in the decade. The band was led at the time of recording by Sam Morgan, one of the better jazz trumpet players in New Orleans, and it listed among its personnel two of his brothers, Isaiah and Andrew, trumpet and saxophone respectively. Samuel Charters states in his monograph on New Orleans jazz that the eight sides made by this band "are the only recordings of a first-rate [New Orleans] band playing anywhere near its prime" made during the 1920s.[20] And hearing these recordings, one can heartily agree. *Bogalousa Strut,* one of the band's best recordings, is not only well played but exudes that warm and joyous feeling that marks the best of the New Orleans instrumental music of the period. Yet Sam Morgan's Jazz Band is barely mentioned in the well-known books on jazz, and is not even listed in Charles Delaunay's famous discography.[21]

In 1927 there was probably no big city other than New Orleans—except perhaps Kansas City—where this style still flourished. Chicago and New York were already pushing jazz in quite different directions. But the men of Morgan's generation (b. 1895) who stayed on in the New Orleans area had not lost the spirit and style of the music of their own youth, and either could not or chose not to change. By a mere chance, Columbia Records captured this marvelous anachronism, happily in post-acoustical recordings.

19. Shapiro and Hentoff, p. 40.
20. Charters, p. 134.
21. Charles Delaunay, *New Hot Discography: The Standard Directory of Recorded Jazz,* ed. Walter E. Schaap and George Avakian (New York: Criterion, 1948).

The first thing one hears in this band is its old-time swing and a feeling one might characterize as "quiet and uncomplicated exuberance." Much of this is generated by the rhythm section, swinging along in a happy, bouncy 4/4 rhythm. Above this substructure, an interesting polyphonic web is woven by the rest of the band, two cornets, muted trombone, and two saxophones. Although the saxophones represent a departure from the classic clarinet-trumpet-trombone tradition, both players are completely imbued with its style and feeling. Through the use of saxophones, however, an interesting shift of emphasis occurs: unlike the clarinet's, the saxophone's range does not permit the invention of obbligato lines *above* the lead cornet. Therefore, in the first two choruses alto and cornet double the melody, and in subsequent full-ensemble choruses both saxophones weave flowing arpeggiated lines which crisscross the more stationary trumpet lines. Since the recording balance favors one of the saxophones—Earl Fouché's alto—putting his lines very much in the foreground, the effect is almost three-dimensional and lovely, rather as if one is looking at a distant view through a trellis. Notable too are Sam Morgan's simple but hard-driving cornet lines in the outside choruses, some with growls and wah-wahs, and the extra ensemble intensity of the last chorus, with the rhythm section moving up a notch dynamically and the drummer, "Shine" Nolan Williams, beating out a rocking two and four on the ride cymbal.

Some of the other seven sides are almost as good. *Steppin' on the Gas* features a rich, dense ensemble polyphony. It is a woven tapestry of sound, in which individual voices, momentarily cresting an ensemble line, project unexpectedly and unpredictably, only to recede again into the over-all polyphonic weave. The beat is completely 4/4, and the way the players listened to each other is a joy to behold. The band recorded three hymns during the two sessions, interesting examples of how Negro sacred music blended and overlapped naturally with the secular. Structurally, they are not remarkable since the hymn tunes are never really fused effectively with the jazz rhythmic substructure; they are simply two musics occurring simultaneously. But *Over in the Gloryland* is at least interesting for the devotional fervor of the band's playing and for its twenty-four-bar harmonic structure, which is very close to the classic blues (Ex. 1):

Example 1 *Over in the Gloryland*

Degree of chord	I	IV	I	I	V	I	IV	I	I	V	I
Number of bars	4	2	2	2	2	4	2	2	1	1	2

We have previously suggested that the King Oliver band of 1923, great though it was, already reflected a certain loss in the intensity of expression of earlier days. This was not only the result of gradually changing conceptions occasioned by the rise of younger men and the eruption of jazz as a nation-wide craze, but also by King Oliver's own highly disciplined, very personal and strict interpretation of what the New Orleans style meant to him. The extraordinary unity of the Creole Jazz Band was exacted at the price of renouncing all stylistic progress. It represents the New Orleans style's last-ditch stand before the world and at the same time its finest full flowering. But the handwriting was already on the wall. Within a few years, the clarity of Oliver's conception was to become completely dissipated, never to be revived in such a pure form again. The glory of the Creole Jazz Band is that it sums up—in Oliver's somewhat personal terms, to be sure—all that went into the New Orleans way of making music: its joy, its warmth of expression, its Old World pre-war charm, its polyphonic complexity, its easy relaxed swing, as heady as a hot summer night in New Orleans, its lovely instrumental textures, and its discipline and logic. Thus Oliver's musical vision contained the seeds of its own demise: in perfecting and ritualizing the ideals of a just bygone era, it wrote its own death sentence. Louis Armstrong, fifteen years younger than his mentor, was to take the same elements and, seeing them through an entirely different personality, was to use them to precipitate the first major revolution of jazz.

Oliver's Creole Jazz Band represents one of jazz's great achievements. It is worthy of our close attention, not only for its own merits, but for the lessons it can still teach us. It proved, for example, that planning, organization, and discipline are not incompatible with jazz expression; but that at the same time, they must not become autocratic and rigid procedures incapable of assimilating new ideas.

It is not mere coincidence that Louis Armstrong left Joe Oliver's band in 1924. As second cornet in an organization dominated by its leader's personality, Louis had too little scope for his daring new ideas.

Besides, was not Oliver "the King" and Armstrong's mentor to boot? It was obvious that Louis had to leave and make his own way, because Oliver's way was restricting the twenty-four-year-old protégé. Oliver for his part tried in vain to cling to his musical reign in the only way that he could: in terms of the collective disciplines of the New Orleans style. Jazz had to wait another few years to discover (in Jelly Roll Morton's Red Hot Peppers and Duke Ellington's early recordings) that the dominating leadership of a single individual need not be incompatible with collective participation.

As Oliver's recordings of 1923 recede further into the historical past, each succeeding generation will undoubtedly find it harder to relate to them. Forty years or so of solo-oriented jazz make it difficult for people to understand the collective music-making conception the Creole Jazz Band represented, and of course the antique sound of the old acoustical Gennett, Okeh, and Paramount recordings is strange to modern ears. For me they have a lovely sound all their own, as nostalgic and personal as the sound of a Model T. On the other hand there is no denying that the sound is acoustically unfaithful, and that recording techniques of the day were inadequate to cope with the polyphonic intricacies of that music.

Even the average ear, however, can adjust with repeated hearings to this acoustical misrepresentation. But the capacity to grasp in its totality a multi-linear sound structure, as opposed to picking out isolated strands from it, is a more specialized ability not given to all people. The particular beauty of the New Orleans conception, however, lies precisely in its polyphony, and one can view with some misgivings the imposition of stereo-separation techniques upon contemporary examples of collective improvisation, New Orleans revival or otherwise. The multi-faceted texture of the Creole Band generates a special beauty all its own that the solo concept, so fundamentally different, can never achieve. The whole philosophy behind Oliver's approach is based on the perfect rendition of a completely predictable result. Performance excitement derives from the perfected rendition of certain traditional devices and patterns. At its worst this approach leads to a kind of circus-stunt psychology, and it ages rapidly: either the stunt has to be made even more staggering, or else an entirely new act has to be created. And certainly Oliver would not have any of that. On the other hand, at its best it results in moments of musical greatness within certain prescribed disciplines and limits. The only real surprises tolerated in the New Orleans style were the breaks,[22] especially the two-cornet breaks of Oliver and his young protégé. Long a tradition in the New Orleans style, these breaks were what every interested listener waited for. There can be no question that the popularity of the break and the excitement it generated were a strong contributing factor in eventually expanding the solo break into the solo.

For the player Oliver's tightly controlled concept of the New Orleans style meant a maximum of freedom within an over-all format designed by the leader. This still worked in 1923 because none of the players—not even Armstrong or Johnny Dodds, and certainly not Honoré Dutrey or Kid Ory—were sufficiently skilled to carry the full load, either in musical, technical, or emotional terms, that a jazz solo required. Being one cog of a larger wheel perfectly suited their limited talents. In fact, the simplicity—and often naïveté—of their individual lines made the relative complexity of a four-part polyphony feasible. Greater individuality, forcefulness, and individual complexity would have resulted in chaos. If nothing else, the various lines would have cancelled each other out. On the other hand greater fluency and instrumental skill were inevitable, and for this reason alone the polyphonic collective style was doomed to extinction. Once a single player could hold the listener's attention, the collective ensemble became unnecessary. While we may regret the virtual extinction of the collective ideal in jazz, it was inevitable and inherent in the highly individualistic nature of jazz expression.

Still we can marvel today at the steady, controlled, rocking 4/4 beat of performances like *Canal Street Blues, Froggie Moore,* and *London Café Blues.* It is not a sensational kind of excitement we experience here; on the contrary it is quiet and consistent, and it moves us because of the unanimity of conception reflected in the rhythmic feeling of the musicians.

We can also marvel at the way the individuals' roles are integrated into Oliver's concept of the band as a single instrument. The players rarely get in each other's way, and each in his particular register and function adds to a rich over-all harmonic-melodic fabric. But let us not assume that such unanimity was a foregone conclusion. We need only compare the Creole Band with any number of other contempo-

22. See Glossary.

rary groups. In Clarence Williams's Blue Five, for example, also recorded in 1923, there is constant superfluous duplication of notes and lines, even though that band had one less horn to contend with. It is as if in Oliver's band we hear a latter-day expression of the ensemble disciplines of the African drum ensemble, with Oliver as the leader or master-drummer, and Armstrong, Dodds, and Dutrey the subordinate musicians who function only to complement the leader. In this connection it is a mark both of Armstrong's talent and of the ingrained dominance of the ensemble style that one of the most explosive soloists jazz has ever known fitted into the structure of such a band.

We must also marvel at the sense of form and progression that we encounter in all the best Creole Jazz Band recordings. The vertical integration we have spoken of is matched by a sense of horizontal progression, all the more wonderful because it is a four-part polyphonic progression. Not only does each chorus develop out of variations or embellishments of the composition's theme, but from chorus to chorus there is a real sense of progression within an over-all pattern. This is especially true of Oliver's own playing, as Martin Williams has shown in his excellent monograph on King Oliver.[23] The key word here is theme. In all the early New Orleans performances the original composition played a predominant role in "improvisation." The younger men like Armstrong, Sidney Bechet, and Johnny Dodds gradually broke away from the theme-improvisation concept, and after the mid-twenties solo improvisation, with few exceptions, came to mean extemporizing on chords rather than melodies. Yet even Armstrong, in his occasional solos with Oliver, often stayed close to the melody, as, for example, in his solo on *Froggie Moore* (Jelly Roll Morton's composition).

Oliver was a master of this referential kind of improvisation.[24] Example 2 represents the three last choruses of *Mabel's Dream* (in the Paramount version, matrix no. 1622/1). Letter *A* is a fairly literal statement of the Trio theme. But at letter *B* Oliver "wants to swing this theme," as Martin Williams puts it, and to do this he has to "recast its melodic line." Comparing *A* and *B*, we see that nine out of sixteen

23. Martin Williams, *King Oliver,* Kings of Jazz series (New York: A. S. Barnes and Company, 1961).

24. André Hodeir in his book *Jazz: Its Evolution and Essence,* tr. David Noakes (New York: Grove Press, 1956) has called this "paraphrase" improvisation.

measures are identical; the other seven represent various degrees of embellishments or fill-ins. These changes have one purpose: to introduce more swing to the melody. In measure three of *B*, a blues-ish phrase adds to the effect, anticipating an even more blues-like interpretation for the third chorus (letter C). In the final chorus, only six measures remain identical with the original Trio tune. Five blue notes

Example 2 *Mabel's Dream*—Paramount Version

—there were none in the theme—are introduced (indicated by × in the example), and to "deliver this final and most drastic departure, he [Oliver] uses his wah-wah mute," thus transforming the original naïve tune "into a plaintive yet dignified blues."[25]

Yet Oliver is not playing a solo in the strict sense. With the exception of Dodds's clarinet, the full ensemble is accompanying Oliver. Recording balance is so poor that one cannot hear all of Louis's second-cornet counter-melodies, or Dodds's obbligatos when he enters for the last two choruses. But one can hear enough to say that Armstrong faultlessly matches Oliver's lead in style and character throughout. At letter *A* Armstrong shadows Oliver in sixths and thirds, providing the proper harmony notes. As Oliver becomes freer, so does Louis. The latter's uncanny ability to compose logical lines with the inner harmonies—no mean task in the severely restrictive patterns of diatonic voice-leading—can be clearly heard on the differently balanced Okeh version of *Mabel's Dream,* recorded a half-year later than the Paramount version.

25. Williams, p. 47.

Was Louis's reputation such that the Okeh recording engineers wanted to hear him as clearly as (or more clearly than) Oliver, or was it mere chance that caused Louis to overbalance the lead voice? Or was it simply Louis's tremendous intensity and drive that, as Lil Hardin claims,[26] projected beyond King Oliver? In any event, this circumstance affords us a chance to hear clearly Armstrong's second-cornet work. We can almost feel the lines bursting at the seams, so to speak, barely content to be confined to their secondary role (Ex. 3, page 84). In its simplicity—required and fulfilled—it is an amazing performance. As Oliver follows the same three-chorus pattern of gradual departure from the tune, Louis also becomes correspondingly more rambunctious, his vibrato flaring, swinging hard—almost as if *he* wanted to drive the band, not from the lead line but from the "inside" voices. And one almost wants to believe that Louis set the faster (dance?) tempo of this Okeh version.

Oliver occasionally gave Louis solo spots. These indicate that though he could not yet (or chose not to) shed entirely the ensemble style of his mentor, Armstrong's own personality began to assert itself, and differences between the styles of the two men began to emerge. Louis's first recorded "solo" with Oliver occurred in the 1923 *Chimes Blues*. It was unusual for the Creole Jazz Band in that it was accompanied only by the rhythm section. Yet it is a solo only in the sense that it takes place alone; it is not yet fully a solo in character and conception. It might easily have been one part of a collectively improvised chorus lifted from its background. But it is clearly headed in the solo direction, and it is *not* a thematic variation. It is worth noting too that only in Armstrong's two choruses is the harmonic change in the sixth bar performed correctly. Louis moves to an F sharp diminished chord, where previously the ensemble had stubbornly tried an F minor chord, with pianist Lil Hardin blithely continuing in F *major!* Of course, early jazz is filled with thousands of such harmonic discrepancies, and Oliver's band certainly was no exception. There are other flaws, too, such as the badly played two-cornet breaks on the Gennett *Snake Rag,* perfected two months later when it was recorded again on the Okeh label; Dutrey's out-of-tune trombone on *Southern Stomps;* or Lil Hardin's frequent problems with the chord changes (for example, in *Snake Rag, Chimes Blues, Just Gone*); the dull tempo and barber-

26. *Satchmo and Me,* Riverside 12-120.

Example 3 *Mabel's Dream*—Okeh Version

shop harmonies of *Sweet Baby Doll;* the ragged rhythm section of *Camp Meeting Blues;* or Dodds's faltering rendition of the famous clarinet obbligato on *High Society*.

But such deficiencies must be balanced against the many delights these recordings offer. Take the wondrous luminous quality and voicing of the parallel seventh-chord progression in the opening to *Froggie Moore* (Ex. 4).

Example 4 *Froggie Moore*

It looks innocuous on paper, but Dodds's and Dutrey's warm quality adds just the right sheen, while the fact that the most important interval in the chords, the seventh, occurs only in the lower middle-register piano gives a fascinating disembodied quality to the ascending progression.

Then there are Oliver's and Armstrong's successful duet breaks on *Riverside Blues;* the textural and dynamic variety of *Chimes Blues* and *London Café Blues;* Bill Johnson's walking bass lines on the banjo in *Canal Street Blues;* the driving swing and excitement of most of the Okeh sides and the Gennett *Alligator Hop;* and lastly Oliver's own justly famous solo on both *Dipper Mouth Blues* recordings. Here the Okeh performance especially has a remarkably dense and well-balanced texture, perfectly captured by the engineers; and its great swing must have had an overwhelming effect in person in 1923.

Since that year jazz has experienced a prodigious development in terms of instrumental virtuosity, dynamic and timbral variety. It is, therefore, all the more amazing that we can still listen with interest to the Creole Jazz Band, since these features are virtually nonexistent on its recordings. With a few already cited exceptions, the polyphonic density remains the same throughout each piece and each instrument remains in its prescribed range: Dodds ; Oliver ; Armstrong ; Dutrey .

Thus the total range remains inexorably the same: . Each piece is like a solid, horizontally spun-out block of sound, maintained at an unswervingly steady pace and density. And yet we are fascinated because the linear and vertical details *within* this sound-block are, for the most part, continually varied in kaleidoscopic fashion. Occasionally, the linear complexity borders on the chaotic; it may only be saved by the fact that all the lines are operating over a very simple harmonic substructure. The accidental intertwining and crossing of instrumental lines makes out of these innocuous tunes and chord progressions a piquant listening experience, one that is enhanced precisely by the accidents of voice-leading that might easily be considered wrong in another (especially a "classical") context: such as the "wrong" notes, the chance parallelisms and convergence of lines, and their heterometric placement. The capacity of the New Orleans collective improvisational style to contain such chance results is one of its most endearing qualities, a main source of its fascination and effectiveness. But it is well to note again that as the harmonies and rhythms in themselves became more complex, the polyphonic or heterophonic approach became infeasible. Only with the advent of atonality in jazz has the re-investigation of true polyphony become possible again.

As a mainstream tradition, the New Orleans style in its pure early form did not survive the 1920's. Even King Oliver and Jelly Roll Morton succumbed to the pressures of changing styles, and their great recordings of that decade represent both the end of an era and the beginnings of a new one. A few orchestras stayed on in New Orleans and fought to maintain the pure style. They managed to survive economically until the end of the 1920s. But by then the inroads of the new solo style and influence of sweet and commercial bands had taken their toll, so that the large New Orleans-style ensemble had become a relic by 1930.

Of course, Oliver's influence pervades jazz history not only in terms of the New Orleans ensemble his orchestra exemplified, but also in his personal influence on two important trumpet players through whom both main lineages of trumpet playing have come down to us in our time. The chart on the next page illustrates this influence graphically.

As Chicago and New York became the centers of jazz activity, New Orleans was virtually forgotten. A few men like Oscar Celestin, Kid Shots Madison, the Marrero brothers, A. J. Piron, Sam Morgan, Chris Kelly, Punch Miller, and a host of lesser players strove to maintain the true tradition; and a few were fortunate enough to be recorded.

But by the mid-twenties the scouts from the big New York record companies were no longer looking for the "hotter" New Orleans bands. When by accident some of these orchestras were recorded, they were more often than not asked to present their more genteel repertoire. Moreover, the real focus and momentum of New Orleans ensemble playing was gone, and many of the players, performing for white audiences for reasons of economic survival, were forced to emphasize the more tawdry and dated clichés of the style. But examples such as *Careless Love, Original Tuxedo Rag* (1925) by Celestin's Tuxedo Jazz Orchestra, and the eight sides cut by Sam Morgan's band are representative of the essence of the style, even though they may not in all cases constitute its highest performance achievements.

TRUMPET LINEAGE

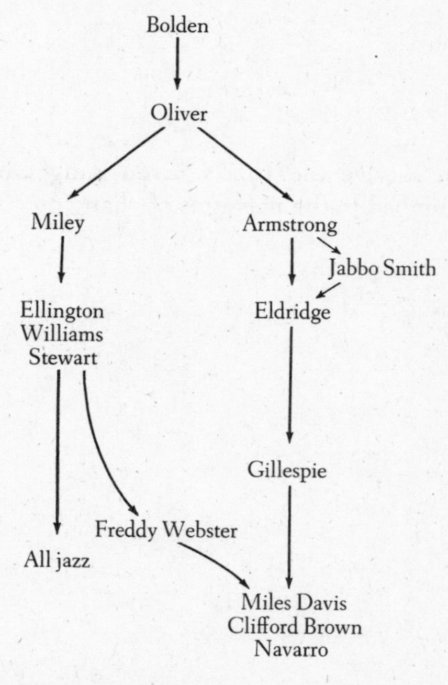

It was inevitable that a music as young and vigorous as jazz would develop rapidly and positively. Even without Louis Armstrong, a rapidly changing world would probably have exacted its changes in the music. The New Orleans elders tried to preserve what was basically a nineteenth-century "romantic" musical tradition in the face of enormous musical and stylistic changes. But one of their own was to cut these ties with finality. Through Louis Armstrong and his influence jazz became a truly twentieth-century language. And it no longer belonged to New Orleans, but to the world.

3

The First Great Soloist

When on June 28, 1928, Louis Armstrong unleashed the spectacular cascading phrases of the introduction to *West End Blues,* he established the general stylistic direction of jazz for several decades to come. Beyond that, this performance also made quite clear that jazz could never again revert to being solely an entertainment or folk music. The clarion call of *West End Blues* served notice that jazz had the potential capacity to compete with the highest order of previously known musical expression. Though nurtured by the crass entertainment and night-club world of the Prohibition era, Armstrong's music transcended this context and its implications. This was music for music's sake, not for the first time in jazz, to be sure, but never before in such a brilliant and unequivocal form. The beauties of this music were those of any great, compelling musical experience: expressive fervor, intense artistic commitment, and an intuitive sense for structural logic, combined with superior instrumental skill. By whatever definition of art—be it abstract, sophisticated, virtuosic, emotionally expressive, structurally perfect—Armstrong's music qualified. Like any profoundly creative innovation, *West End Blues* summarized the past and predicted the future. But such moments in the history of music by their very brilliance also tend to push into the background the many preparatory steps that lead up to the masterpiece. Certainly, *West End Blues* was not without its antecedents. It did not suddenly spring fullblown from Armstrong's head. Its conception was assembled, bit by bit, over a period of four or five years, and it is extremely instructive to study the process by which Armstrong accumulated his personal style, his "bag" as the jazz musician would put it.

Armstrong's recording activity in the years 1926-29 was so prolific that the jazz analyst's task is both easy and difficult. On the one hand, the recordings give an exhaustive, almost day-by-day documentation of Louis's progress. On the other hand, he recorded so much, under so many varying circumstances and pressures, recorded such a variety of material with the indiscriminate abandon in which only a genius can afford to indulge, that the task of gaining a comprehensive view, in purely statistical terms, is formidable. The wonder of it all is that Armstrong, irrespective of what or with whom he recorded, maintained an astonishingly high degree of inventiveness and musical integrity, at least until the early 1930s, when he did succumb to the sheer weight of his success and its attendant commercial pressures.

In Oliver's Creole Jazz Band we have already observed the twenty-three-year-old cornet player skillfully treading the fine line between the functional requirements of second cornet to King Oliver and his own burgeoning solo tendencies. In even these earliest Armstrong recordings, tiny phrase-cells began to appear and recur, which seen in retrospect, became the stand-by devices of his solos. This is not to say that they were mere mechanically delivered clichés. They were for the most part original with Louis (a few seem to have come from Bunk Johnson and Oliver), and they were fundamental manifestations of Armstrong's particular brand of lyricism. They became the pivotal points upon which a solo was constructed, and through the years they were expanded in expressive scope and function until entire solos could be constructed from them.[1]

Armstrong's emergence as a soloist coincides with his joining the Fletcher Henderson band in New York. Here Louis could test his creative and instrumental abilities in a less fettered context than that provided by Oliver's orchestra. In fact, Henderson—who was already one of the leaders in setting the post–New Orleans jazz style, through his emphasis on soloists and arrangements, sometimes of a fairly sophisticated nature—hired young Louis specifically to be his featured

1. The process of developing a few motivic traits into a personal style can be observed in every great jazz artist, whether it be Armstrong, Parker, Monk, or Lester Young. I also refer the reader to Chapter 7, on Ellington.

soloist. This provided the perfect opportunity for Louis to develop his musical identity, to eliminate that which was of secondary quality or imitative, and to refine the personal ingredients of his maturing style.

In listening to the Henderson band recordings made between October 1924 and October 1925, one is amazed at the disparity in quality between Armstrong's superior work and that of his colleagues in the band. Even Louis's most conservative solos are comparative triumphs of style and conception. This fact is the more impressive when we consider that his colleagues included such men as Coleman Hawkins, Charlie Green, and Buster Bailey, and the entire band consisted of the best jazz musicians money could buy. And yet the level of inspiration jumps when Armstrong enters with a solo and drops when the ensemble returns. This is especially painful when Louis's solos are juxtaposed abruptly with the trumpet lead-work of Elmer Chambers or Howard Scott (as, for example, in *Mandy, Make Up Your Mind*). The light, airy, open quality of Louis's solos, the elegance of tone, and the easy swing of his beat, freeze suddenly into stiff, stodgy, jerky rhythms and a grey undistinguished tone quality.

What is it that distinguishes Louis from the rest? Why does an Armstrong solo stand out like a mountain peak over its neighboring foothills? There are four salient features, none of which, to my mind, take priority, but which are instead inseparable elements of a single total conception: (1) his superior choice of notes and the resultant shape of his lines; (2) his incomparable basic quality of tone; (3) his equally incomparable sense of swing, that is, the sureness with which notes are placed in the time continuum and the remarkably varied attack and release properties of his phrasing; (4) and, perhaps his most individual contribution, the subtly varied repertory of vibratos and shakes with which Armstrong colors and embellishes individual notes. The importance of the last fact cannot be emphasized enough, since it gives an Armstrong solo that peculiar sense of inner drive and forward momentum. Armstrong was incapable of not swinging. Even if we isolate a single quarter note from the context of a phrase, we can clearly hear the forward thrust of that note, and in it we recognize the unmistakable Armstrong personality. It is as if such notes wish to burst out of the confines of their rhythmic placement. They wish to do more than a single note can do; they wish to express the exuberance of an entire phrase. Again, it is most revealing to compare the pulsating life of an Armstrong note and the lifelessness of a similarly placed note played by his Henderson colleagues.

What is amazing is that the four ingredients of Armstrong's stylistic conception are already so clearly formed in even the earliest solos with the Henderson band. These are simple, unaffected solos that today are not particularly startling. And yet in the degree by which they surpass the other players' performances, in terms of their simple, impeccable design, though frequently they were based on the most sentimental, banal Tin Pan Alley material, they command our attention. Two solos from late 1924 illustrate the point. *Mandy, Make Up Your Mind,* an Irving Berlin tune typical of the period, is transformed by Armstrong into an infectious jazz solo. If we compare the original tune and Armstrong's improvisation on it, we can learn much about his methods at that time (Ex. 1).[2]

Armstrong's entrance already leaves no doubt that this is going to be a jazz solo. The contrast to the preceding prissy ensemble is startling as Louis attacks and sails across the first measure in swinging syncopation. In measures four and seven, he manages to avoid the dated eighth-note pattern of the original, and when we look further into how he managed this, we come upon an interesting fact: Armstrong's phrases are shifted ahead by one bar. Berlin's song, subdivided into two-bar segments, falls into a pattern of measures one and two, three and four, five and six, etc. But Armstrong shifts his phrases so as to straddle the tune's natural phrase divisions, grouping measures a and one, two and three, four and five, six and seven. At measure eight tune and improvisation more or less coincide (although Armstrong insists on loosening up the jerky tightness of the original). Armstrong immediately returns in measures nine and ten to the task of reshaping the tune, and once again he shifts phrase-emphasis. This time the shift is by one beat, not by one bar. The syncopated accented notes (*a* natural, *b* flat, *a* flat, *d* flat) receive the strongest weight. This was evidently quite unexpected and, in fact, upset the rhythm section playing its simple stride accompaniment. Apart from shifting the beat,

2. In notation, jazz solos tend to look misleadingly rigid. Notation cannot capture the subtle nuances of tone, rhythm, attack, and phrase inflection. The notated examples must therefore be considered in conjunction with the recorded performances.

Example 1 *Mandy, Make Up Your Mind* *

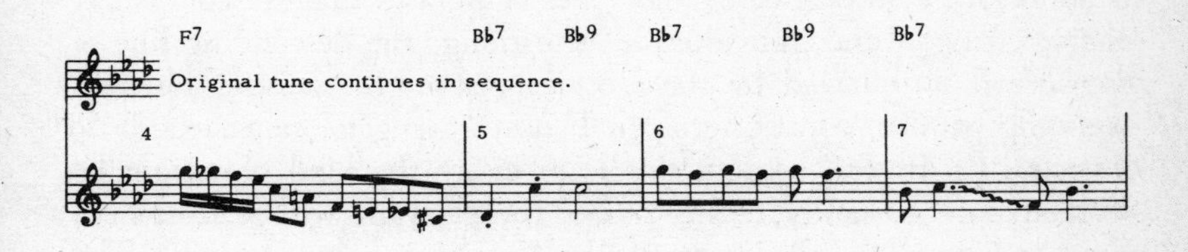

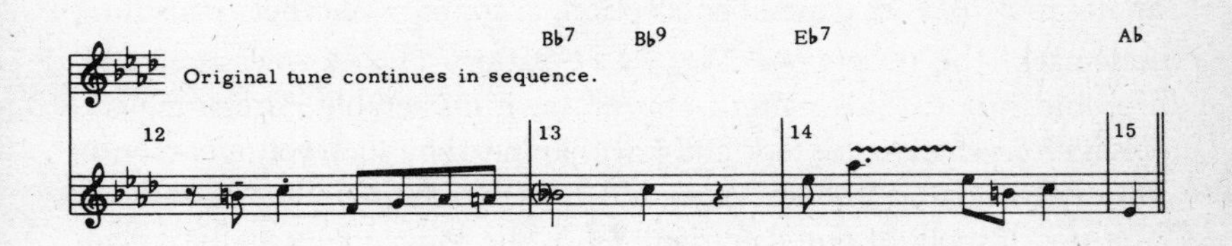

Armstrong's bars nine and ten are subtly dissonant. Since each of the accented notes, as Louis plays them, extends by a hair into the first and third beats (indicated by the ties into the eighth-note rests in the example), tiny dissonances by suspension are set up. Louis's *a* natural clashes with the E flat chord, his *b* flat with the A flat chord, his *a* flat and *d* flat with the G flat and F chords, respectively. At this point, the improvisation connects again with the tune, departing from it once more only in the final measure.

It is interesting to note that Armstrong's range in this piece and in other solos of that period is extended at its upper end. No longer required to stay in the instrument's middle register, Louis could roam over the entire trumpet range, and in the next decade he would extend his upper range gradually to high *e* flat. The *Mandy* solo also contains one of the three or four types of phrases that are completely characteristic of and individual to Armstrong: the descending line of measure four followed by the ascending seventh interval. This descending pattern, consisting of an F ninth arpeggio, came readily to Armstrong's fingers, because this is precisely the kind of phrase he worked out constantly in his second-cornet work with Oliver (see Ex. 3 in Ch. 2, *Mabel's Dream*—Okeh Version, measure twelve). The solo in *Mandy* is outstanding also in that it contained no blue notes. This was not mere happenstance. There is considerable evidence to the effect that Armstrong, especially in those years, intuitively separated song material into two distinct categories: Tin Pan Alley songs, where blue notes were not mandatory and were probably out of place; and blues and New Orleans standards, where blue notes would be very much at home.

The second solo from this particular period, *Go 'long Mule*, is very similar to *Mandy* in general conception. It contains another Armstrong trademark: the simple ♩♩𝅗𝅥 or ♩♩♩𝄽 pattern (Ex. 2, measures one, five, and nine). This pattern appears in innumerable Armstrong improvisations even to this day, and it was imitated by such younger men as Johnny Dunn and Bubber Miley. With its two shortened notes and one long note (spelling out *daht-daht-dah*), the long note usually embellished with a light shake, it was an effective pattern for establishing an easy, relaxed swing feeling. This same three-note pattern occurs again in *How Come You Do Me Like You Do* (Ex. 3, measure two), a solo that contains still another Armstrong trademark: the  pattern, with its characteristic "rip" to the high note (measures four and sixteen in the solo). This, too, occurs in literally dozens of Arm-

Example 2 *Go 'long Mule*

(〰 designates a slight shake.)

Example 3 *How Come You Do Me Like You Do*

(The *f* in m. 7 should by rights have been an *f*♯.)

strong solos, and some of his most effective breaks were based primarily on this little motive or ones very similar to it (for example, *Potato Head Blues, Muggles, The Last Time*).

In *Texas Moaner*, a blues recorded with Clarence Williams's Blue Five, we have not only one of the descending arpeggio runs (Ex. 4, measure three, note how they always head for the seventh of the chords), but also one of Armstrong's first double-time breaks (Ex. 4, measures seven and eight), including the characteristic opening "rip." Here the implied beat is felt in eighth notes, double the time of the

Example 4 *Texas Moaner*

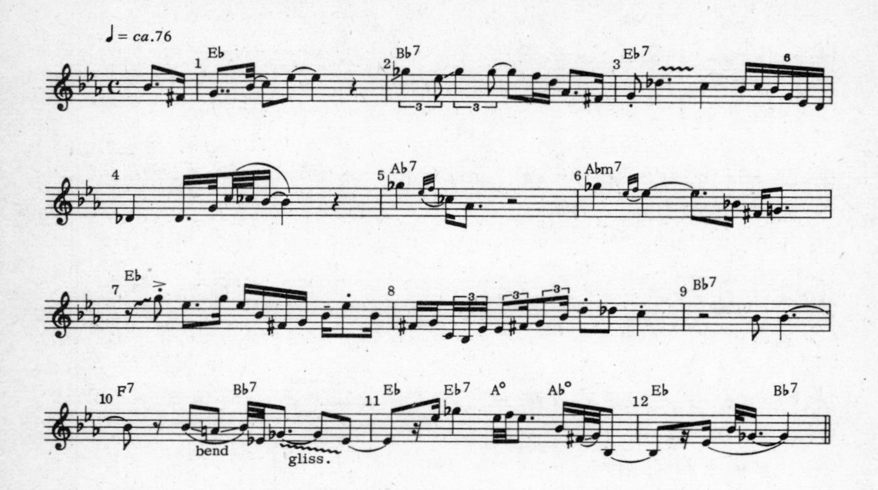

usual quarter notes. The rhythmic freedom and variety of this solo as actually played by Louis defy exact notation, as does his slight rushing in the middle of the break.

One of Armstrong's most brilliant and driving solos from this period is *I Ain't Gonna Play No Second Fiddle* on a little-known record by Perry Bradford's Jazz Phools (Ex. 5). The blistering drive of Louis's playing, the imperious, almost cocky way in which his trumpet rises out

Example 5 *I Ain't Gonna Play No Second Fiddle*

of the previous ensemble, was unique in its time (late 1925). Here the tempo is quite fast (♩ = 184), with measure seven (once again a descending arpeggio going to the seventh) about as fast as any trumpet player, except Jabbo Smith, could play before Roy Eldridge and Dizzy Gillespie.

It was during this period that Armstrong began to work out one of the most important technical components of his conception and tone: his vibrato. He recognized early that vibrato could be an essential ingredient in giving rhythmic momentum to his playing. Instinctively he realized that a vibrato—its speed, its intensity, its degree of pitch oscillation—is a highly personal element, and that it is not something we add *to* the tone, something we superimpose *on* it, but an "internal element in the tone that gives it motion. It should be something that makes the tone go *forward,* not *up and down.*"[3] Armstrong's vibrato was the kind that imparted movement. In fact, one can say that because of his particular vibrato even a single note in an Armstrong solo swings. It was a personal touch he undoubtedly acquired initially from his (or others') vocal techniques.

To the vibrato were soon added two other Armstrong trademarks, the "shake" and the "terminal vibrato."[4] The shake was simply a more extreme way of enlivening and swinging the tone. The terminal vibrato was frequently used on longer notes, which started relatively "straight," and gradually "loosened up" to end in a wide vibrato or shake or, in its most extreme form, in a "rip." Example 6 illustrates the terminal vibrato graphically.

Example 6

In the ensuing years Armstrong made an increasing and, in the thirties, often excessive use of these devices. Through him they became an integral technique of trumpet and, by extension, brass playing.

3. Gunther Schuller, *Horn Technique* (London: Oxford University Press, 1962), p. 71.

4. The term was first used by André Hodeir in *Jazz: Its Evolution and Essence,* tr. David Noakes (New York: Grove Press, 1956), pp. 66-7, in a chapter on the trombonist Dickie Wells.

In November 1925 Armstrong left Henderson and went back to Chicago. His wife, Lil, had stayed there, leading a band at the Dreamland; and Chicago was then still the center of jazz, where work for a jazz musician was more varied and lucrative. These circumstances led indirectly to one of the most remarkable long-term recording projects in the history of jazz: Louis Armstrong's famous Hot Five and Hot Seven. The recordings made under these names not only made Armstrong an international name but probably contributed more than any other single group of recordings to making jazz famous and a music to be taken seriously.

The remarkable thing is that the Hot Five never existed as a band outside the recording studios. Its personnel, however, did play together in the band at the Dreamland and other clubs and ballrooms. As Kid Ory has put it, "We all knew each other's musical styles so well from years of working together."[5] Indeed, Armstrong had known Ory since 1918 when he had played in the latter's Brownskin Band. He had probably known Johnny Dodds in New Orleans as a boy, but in any case had worked with him in Oliver's band for two years; so also had Johnny St. Cyr and Lilian Hardin, who was now Armstrong's wife. The musical and personal rapport of the Hot Five was very close to begin with, and it grew even closer under Armstrong's leadership and growing fame.

Louis was a famous musical personality by the time he started the Hot Five recordings, at least in the eyes of the Negro public, virtually the only buyers of jazz records in those days. The Hot Five recordings were, therefore, an almost predictable success. Although Armstrong in 1925 and 1926 was not yet at the zenith of his powers, and although the playing of his four colleagues often left very much to be desired and never equaled Armstrong's own high standard, the Hot Fives were far above average. The group instantly became the talk of musicians and the Negro public.

The first date on November 12, 1925, produced no earthshaking jazz, although Armstrong was certainly in excellent form, his tone lithe and well-centered, his ideas well-shaped, his rhythm secure and varied. The band played in a greatly modified New Orleans style, halfway between a partly discarded and half-heartedly maintained

5. Nat Shapiro and Nat Hentoff, eds., *Hear Me Talkin' to Ya* (New York: Rinehart and Company, 1955), p. 110.

ensemble style and a not yet fully crystallized solo style. Except for Armstrong's, the individual solos were not strong enough to sustain the new conception. Though in some sense more "advanced" than Oliver's, the music was less complex and had not yet coalesced into a unified style. A similar situation existed in the middle 1700s between the truly complex music of Bach and its presumably more sophisticated and "advanced" successors. The supporters of Telemann, Christoph Graupner, Michael Haydn, and others, who misconstrued Bach's polyphonic masterpieces as "old-fashioned" when compared to the new homophonic forms, failed to hear and see the daring inventiveness of Bach's music. Similarly, viewed in objective retrospect, the early Hot Five recordings did not compare favorably with the best of Oliver's Creole Jazz Band. But they represented the "new thing"; they celebrated the new dance crazes that followed in the wake of the Charleston's phenomenal success; and, in general, they corresponded to the optimistic, uninhibited view of life prevalent in the Jazz Age of the mid-twenties.

The second group of dates three months later was somewhat more successful musically and in addition produced the Hot Five's first hit record, *Heebie Jeebies*. Generally, however, the group was still finding itself. Apart from a number of embarrassing solos—especially those of Lil Hardin (*Cornet Chop Suey,* for example)—and the intrusion of ideas more related to vaudeville and the movie-houses than to jazz (Ory in *Oriental Strut,* Lil Hardin in her own *You're Next*), the quintet was at least striving for a greater expressive range, always impelled forward by Louis's driving, "never quit" horn. But the strain involved in these efforts shows, even in Louis's playing. In listening to these sides one can hear him reaching out for the surprise note, the unusual shape of line, the extra bit of punch, sometimes making it, sometimes not quite. The frequent "clinkers," the occasional inferior choice of note (including the completely wrong harmonic change in the thirteenth bar of his chorus on *Muskrat Ramble*), the evidence of not quite knowing the material well enough (as in *Oriental Strut*), the slight extra edge of tension—all attest to the growing pains of the group. On the other hand, there are the innovational, extended stop-time choruses and breaks of *Cornet Chop Suey,* which foreshadow *West End Blues* and *Weather Bird.*

In connection with the above-mentioned *Heebie Jeebies,* Armstrong's famous scat vocal, a word must be said about Louis's singing. To the listener oriented to "classical" singing, Louis's voice, with its rasp and totally unorthodox technique, usually comes as a complete shock. The reaction is often to set the voice aside as primitive and uncouth. Actually, Louis's singing is but a vocal counterpart of his playing, just as natural and as inspired. In his singing we can hear all the nuances, inflections, and natural ease of his trumpet playing, including even the bends and scoops, vibrato and shakes. Louis's singing is unique and its own justification. It has added a new school or technique of singing to Western music, notwithstanding the fact that its orientation is completely African in origin.

On May 28, 1926, Armstrong was involved in two recording dates under two different leaders, Erskine Tate and Lil Hardin Armstrong. The fact that these two sides were not recorded under Louis's leadership undoubtedly accounts for their general neglect by jazz critics and historians. But they are worthy of our attention, not only because they provide interesting comparisons to the Hot Five recordings, but also because the Tate sides are the only example of Armstrong operating in a big-band context in 1926.

The importance of Erskine Tate's Vendome Theatre Orchestra has never been properly assessed, in terms either of its own intrinsic merits or of the role it played in Armstrong's life. It is too often overlooked that Armstrong left New York and Henderson to play with two Chicago orchestras, Erskine Tate and Carroll Dickerson at the Dreamland. Tate's ten-piece orchestra was the best large group in Chicago, in many respects Henderson's Chicago counterpart. Armstrong stayed with Tate several years, and always spoke glowingly of the association, referring to the highly skilled pit band as "Professor Erskine Tate's Symphony Orchestra." Other musicians, too, spoke with the utmost respect and admiration of this singular group, and there were few who did not aspire to play in it.

A violinist, like many theater orchestra leaders, Tate received a fairly comprehensive musical training at various Chicago conservatories. His first big orchestra at the Vendome in 1918 accompanied dance and vaudeville acts, evidently played mostly light classics, and gave hour-long concerts nightly in the pit. With the emergence of jazz, Tate's repertory expanded to include jazz, however without dropping the classics. Forming an early "Third Stream" orchestra, in potential if not in fact, Tate's musicians all had to read very well. Some indeed were legitimate musicians. At the same time the list of jazz names that one time or another played with Tate includes Earl Hines, Teddy Weatherford, Fats Waller, Freddie Keppard, Jabbo Smith, Buster Bailey, Darnell Howard, and Omer Simeon, besides Armstrong. And it was a formidable band, judging by the only two sides it recorded, as well as by contemporary accounts: "[Tate] had collected the best musicians and was able to interpret to perfection any kind of music . . . from classical . . . to jazz."[6] Several men doubled in the reeds, including one Alvin Fernandez, who played oboe in the "classical" overtures and clarinet and saxophone on the jazz pieces.

The two sides recorded in 1926, *Static Strut* and *Stomp Off*, are jazz and feature outstanding solos by Armstrong and Teddy Weatherford, the legendary pianist who left Chicago in the late twenties and spent the rest of his life in the Far East. Since Weatherford was probably the single most important influence on Earl Hines, and since he recorded only four other sides with a band,[7] his solos with Tate are of considerable historic interest. They are more than just that, however, for they display a strong rhythmic style, caught halfway between its ragtime ancestry and the later "trumpet piano style," a cross between James P. Johnson and Earl Hines. Because of his absence from the American jazz scene, Weatherford is one of the many neglected men of jazz, and one is not surprised to hear from the contemporary account just quoted that Weatherford "was ahead of all pianists contemporary to him. He was truly sensational then and all the pianists, Earl Hines included, copied him."

Armstrong was also in fine form on this date, especially on *Static Strut*, contributing a long, bursting, exuberant solo that includes a modulating break and a spectacular leap of a ninth in the break before the bridge. It is altogether Louis's flashiest and most inventive recorded solo to that point. The band and the arrangement are sharp and up to date, centered upon a very strong and—for the day—hard-swinging rhythm section (piano, banjo, tuba, and drums). Both sides

6. Ibid., p. 107.
7. Some solo and trio sides were recorded in the thirties in Paris and Calcutta, by which time the advanced style of other pianists had bypassed Weatherford. His isolation from the competitive American jazz scene had evidently kept him from developing.

featured the new Northern big-city style: a "hot" rhythm that was thoroughly danceable. Even the wild, all-out collective ensemble on the out-chorus of *Stomp Off*, New Orleans in principle, had a sharp, hard Chicago edge to it that King Oliver would have deplored—and undoubtedly did.

The other two recordings referred to were labeled Lil's Hot Shots, though the personnel was exactly that of the Hot Five. It is therefore surprising that the two sides, *Georgia BoBo* and *Drop That Sack*, sounded completely different from those of the Hot Five. Not knowing the exact circumstances and personal relationships attendant to that date, we find difficulty in explaining why the ensembles have much more of an older New Orleans feeling, why Louis plays generally inferior solos (or none as on *Georgia Bo Bo*), and why Ory and Dodds on the other hand turn in simple but effective solos, certainly superior to their work under Armstrong's leadership. This would tend to substantiate the often-advanced theory that for some personal or musical reasons Ory and especially Dodds were intimidated on the Hot Five dates.

We can quickly pass over the next Hot Five date, which featured for the most part quasi-novelty numbers by Lil Hardin Armstrong. They added nothing to the group's stature, and are mildly interesting in that they constitute (along with *King of the Zulus*) the nadir of Hot Five recording activity. By the following two dates, June 23 and November 16, however, the Hot Five records were beginning to swing more consistently. The sheer force and rhythmic drive of Armstrong's playing—if not yet his inventiveness—were beginning to exert their influence on the other four players. When Louis is playing, ideas, swing, and rhythm seem to fall automatically in place. When he stops, it is as if the engine of a motor had been cut out. And at such time, with amazing consistency, Lil Hardin Armstrong's watery piano invariably emerges.

Armstrong is by now effectively consolidating his experiments of the preceding years. Compare, if you will, his playing on *Sweet Little Papa* with any of the solos with Henderson (like *Mandy* or *Copenhagen*). Where the earlier solos had a kind of straightforward linear-horizontal shape, *Sweet Little Papa* roams over the entire trumpet range, in great arching descending and ascending lines, occasionally abruptly changing course. The smooth rhythms of the earlier improvisations give way to stronger, contrasting, harder swinging rhythms. Double-time breaks abound. Melodic line and rhythm combine to produce more striking contours. This was, of course, the result not only of Armstrong's increasing technical skill, but also of his maturing musicality, which saw the jazz solo in terms not of a pop-tune more or less embellished, but of a chord progression generating a maximum of creative originality. Louis's solo conception developed in exact proportion to the degree his solos departed from the original tune. His later solos all but ignored the original tune and started with only the chord changes given. As already noted, the details of these improvisations made use of a number of smaller ideas or devices that were original with or peculiar to Armstrong. His choruses on *Sweet Little Papa* contain the ♩♩𝅗𝅥 pattern, the descending arpeggios, the flutter-tongued lead-in note (a device not unknown to Oliver) before a new chorus or an eight-bar segment thereof, the breaks starting with the "ripped" upper note (see final chorus and coda), the embellishing shakes, and so on. But in contrast to the earlier solos, where these phrase-turns stood out amid otherwise bland playing, they now become part of a total, unified conception.

The way these personal trademarks have now pervaded the entire improvisation can be clearly seen in Armstrong's most remarkable recorded solo of 1926, *Big Butter and Egg Man*. His entire performance on this dated tune is superior. His solo chorus is especially notable and has already been singled out for praise by André Hodeir.[8] It is worth reviewing once again, as it summarizes perfectly Armstrong's creative capacity at this particular stage. It displays his intuitive grasp of musical logic and continuity, coupled with an imaginative sense of variation.[9] Note, to begin with, the subtle pitch and rhythm alterations in the triple call of measures one through five (Ex. 7). Hodeir comments: "This entry by itself is a masterpiece; it is impossible to imagine anything more sober and balanced."[10] One could add that no

8. Hodeir, pp. 56-8.
9. Armstrong's capacities in this respect ought to lay to rest the strange notion held by many jazz musicians and jazz buffs that structural logic, a conscious sense of variation and development, is an intellectual preoccupation incompatible with true jazz creativity. Louis Armstrong never was and never will be an intellect. Yet there is no question that his music comes not *only* "from the belly," but also from a mind that *thinks* in musical terms and ideas.
10. Hodeir, p. 57.

Example 7 *Big Butter and Egg Man*

composer, not even a Mozart or a Schubert, composed anything more natural and simply inspired. Notice also the repeated use of the melodic-rhythmic component ♪♩. (usually moving from the second degree to the tonic) in measures seven, nine, fifteen, and nineteen and its rhythmic variant in measure ten. What is interesting is that in each instance the phrase is completed in a different manner. Diversity is combined with identity and repetition.

The bridge is certainly the imaginative climax of the solo. First there are the repeated *c*'s (measure sixteen), making use initially of the alternate-fingering effect available to brass players, then elongating this into quarter-note triplets. The chord progression shifts to B flat, but in measure twenty Louis returns unexpectedly to the *c* with which he started the bridge, now the ninth of the chord, initiating a superbly syncopated descending chromatic line. This in turn leads to the high point of the solo, the connecting phrase that straddles the traditional break between the end of the bridge and the final eight bars. In the astonishing swing of this ♫ phrase, with its "ghosted" sixteenths, Louis "seems to have foreseen what modern conceptions of rhythm would be like," as Hodeir so perceptively suggests.[11] Of course, there are the indescribable elements of Louis's playing, the utter purity and sumptuousness of his tone and the easy perfection of his swing, floating effortlessly in time while being nevertheless the acme of rhythmic accuracy.

On the same date Armstrong also recorded a bit of scat-nonsense written by his wife and himself called *Skit-Dat-De-Dat*. It is an interesting performance since it consists to a large extent of two-bar breaks, affording us an excellent opportunity to compare the three soloists of the group. The contrast between Louis on the one hand and Dodds and Ory on the other is startling; *Skit-Dat-De-Dat* confirms incontestably that they were no match for Louis. As in dozens of other recordings, in their *Skit-Dat-De-Dat* solos their time and intonation are bad, and their ideas tawdry.[12] Out of a nostalgia and loyalty for the grand old men of New Orleans one may wish to ignore these faults, but a musical evaluation that is not based on an objective analysis is invalid or irrelevant. Can there be any serious question regarding the difference in quality of Dodds's and Ory's breaks here as compared to Louis's, especially in view of the ingenious introductory break with which Louis starts the side? Does this look like a break for a piece in C major (Ex 8)? If the key of C had already been established prior to the break, the *b* flat, *e* flat, and *a* flat would simply be heard as blue notes or lowered altered notes. But since the break starts the piece un-

11. Loc. cit.
12. Nevertheless, André Hodeir was unfair to Dodds because his rather negative evaluation was based on a small, inferior segment of Dodds's recording activity (pp. 59-61).

accompanied, our ear perceives this as some kind of E flat (or possibly C minor) melody, and it is therefore the tonic key of C *major* that sounds strange in bar three. There is, to my knowledge, no compara-

Example 8 *Skit-Dat-De-Dat*—Introductory Break

ble example of such tonal ambivalence in jazz until Dizzy Gillespie's famous "out-of-key" break on *I Can't Get Started* (rather mild on the recording but frequently roaming far afield in Dizzy's live performances).

Armstrong participated as a "sideman" in two sessions in April 1927.[13] Both dates were rather subdued in spirit, as if Louis were biding his time, harnessing his creative energies for the future, while Dodds once again played better under his own leadership than on an Armstrong record date. The Dodds date, however, is notable for two developments that in their diverse ways were to play an increasingly important part in Louis's life. One was Earl Hines's first appearance on records with Louis; the other was Louis's first encounter—on his own dates—with the sentimental, sugar-coated world of Tin Pan Alley in the form of Rube Bloom's hit tune *Melancholy*. Here we can hear the first signs in Armstrong of a sweet, crooning trumpet style, that was to become his bread and butter only a few years later.

For the next date under his own leadership, Armstrong expanded to seven men, adding tuba and drums, and within a span of eight days recorded the famous Hot Seven sides. Though they were far above average and added to Armstrong's fame, they produced only one truly remarkable performance (out of eleven) and have generally been somewhat over-estimated. Was the strain of Armstrong's phenomenal personal success beginning to show? Was he pushing himself beyond what he could cope with? Did he take less care in preparing the numbers? These are questions that come persistently to mind in listening critically to these sides. In some respects the performances were an improvement over previous ones. The addition of drums and tuba certainly helped to de-emphasize Lil Armstrong's role, and Johnny Dodds

13. The first, Jimmy Bertrand's Washboard Wizards; the other, Johnny Dodds's Black Bottom Stompers.

played noticeably better than before. But as the band moved further away from its New Orleans background and reached out for more sophisticated formats and longer solos, the strain was beginning to show. This is natural in a pioneer effort, and such an evaluation is not meant merely deprecatingly.

Armstrong is indeed reaching for much more on these recordings, and occasionally over-reaches. The solos tend to be longer; his upper range is now stretching for the occasional *c* and *d* flat; the ideas are more complex; the breaks are almost without exception in fast double-time, sometimes nervously so. Louis's last break on *Keyhole Blues* attempts to be too clever and does not really come off. On *Alligator Crawl,* an interesting attempt to jump octaves in the chromatic phrase (bar seventeen of Louis's solo) is muffed, and the end of Louis's break can only be described as lame. His solo on *Weary Blues* gets off to a poor start, as he badly muffs a chromatic line (in any case a cliché not worthy of him). He recovers, but then in desperation starts quoting *Twelfth Street Rag,* which happened also to be recorded the same day.

On *S. O. L. Blues* Louis is more successful and produces an interesting forerunner of *West End Blues.* The five descending phrases, each starting on high *b* flat, already have the impassioned quality and conviction of the later piece. When the same blues was re-recorded at a faster tempo the next day, under the title of *Gully Low Blues,* some of the luster of inspiration was already gone. Louis's solo is a touch more mechanical, and his vocal perfunctory. (The corny ensemble tag-ending, muffed badly the previous day, had in the interim been carefully rehearsed!) Comparing the quite different results on the same tune, recorded only twenty-four hours apart, serves to remind us of the transitoriness of jazz. How many great solos were played by Louis outside the recording studio, perhaps only a few hours earlier or later?

The one remarkable Armstrong performance, already alluded to, is his famous stop-time chorus on *Potato Head Blues.* In contrast to many of the Hot Seven sides, the tempo here is just right, and Louis was evidently really ready for this chorus. Nothing could be more balanced and perfect than the first phrase with its move to the sixth in measure two (not counting the anacrusis measure)—incidentally, on the familiar ♩♩𝅗𝅥 pattern—followed by the daring syncopation of measure three. Later (in measure twelve) there is a surprise *d* flat, over a D-seventh chord, resolving to *c*. And then, in measure twenty-five, occurs one of Armstrong's most memorable phrases (Ex. 9) made even more memorable by the throbbing poignancy of his tone and vibrato.[14] These are but the high points of a solo that shows in its totality the extravagant richness of Armstrong's fertile imagination.

Example 9 *Potato Head Blues*

But as great as this stop-time solo is, it too suffers to a small degree from the conflicts present in the other ten Hot Seven sides. At moments in this solo a slight tension appears, in contrast to the utter relaxation of *Big Butter and Egg Man;* there is a feeling of "is he going to make it?," especially from measure seventeen on. One can feel that Armstrong is just barely keeping up with the changes of the bridge, and at several places in the last sixteen bars there are moments of slight hesitation (to which the band adjusts). Fingers and mind were not quite as one in several places, and it is only in the final two bars of the chorus that Louis seems to relax. In view of the daring of this solo some such uneasiness is quite understandable.

Curiously, Dodds fares much better on the Hot Seven sides. Undoubtedly he felt more at home in the blues material that predominated, and perhaps the additional rhythm section helped him in his time (not to speak of the fact that the drummer was his own brother, Baby Dodds). In any case his playing is much more controlled, and the solos on *Wild Man Blues* and *S. O. L. Blues* (and its remake *Gully Low Blues*) are quite good, though certainly conservative compared to Louis's. One becomes painfully aware at times, however, of the trombonist's poor taste, sloppy intonation, and bad timing. (Until recently it was assumed the trombonist was Kid Ory, but it has become clear that this was not the case. Lacking confirmation, I would guess the trombonist to be Honoré Dutrey, who was working with Louis's regular ten-piece band at the Sunset Café.)

14. It has always seemed to me that Hoagy Carmichael must have been familiar with this passage. Bars three and four of *Stardust* contain exactly the same notes and chord (at a ballad tempo, of course) as the first bars of the Armstrong example (Ex. 9). *Stardust* was written in 1927, and Hoagy Carmichael was an intimate of Bix Beiderbecke's circle, whose hero was Louis Armstrong.

During the days of the Hot Seven recordings, Armstrong recorded Morton's *Chicago Breakdown* with this ten-piece band. The performance contrasts markedly with the Hot Five and Hot Seven recordings in that it returns in part to the older New Orleans big-band ensemble style. In fact, in its ensembles it closely resembles 1920s recordings made in New Orleans by Sam Morgan, the New Orleans Owls, and Celestin's Original Tuxedo Orchestra, particularly the latter's *Original Tuxedo Rag*. Since the Hot Seven and Red Hot Peppers were recorded within days of each other, it is evident that Louis played a more traditional music for dancing at the Sunset, and used the small-group recordings to experiment with a more advanced style and a more soloistic conception.

Chicago Breakdown also interests us because it features an early Earl Hines solo. As a consequence of Hines's revolutionary "trumpet style" piano, so directly allied to Armstrong, the entire band gets a rhythmic lift it could never get from Lil Armstrong's soggy piano. Hines's style was certainly not entirely worked out at this time, but it was there in all of its essential characteristics. The record also affords —once again—interesting comparisons between Louis and his colleagues of the day, in this case soprano saxophonist Boyd Atkins (who was famous as the composer of *Heebie Jeebies,* Armstrong's first big commercial hit) and Stomp Evans on bass saxophone. The jerky, unswinging playing of these two men is far removed from Louis's modern conception.

By the end of 1927, some seven months later, Armstrong's style had coalesced into a near-perfect blend of relaxation and tension, as demonstrated on six spectacular sides, all using the Hot Five format, recorded in December. Four sides had the great guitarist Lonnie Johnson as an added starter. And what a difference he makes! Armstrong is now no longer outnumbered four to one but has a strong ally. Johnson's swinging, rhythmic backing and his remarkable two-bar exchanges with Armstrong are certainly one of the highlights of classic jazz. Johnson's influence also affects Dodds and Ory, who contribute their best playing to date with Armstrong, and even Lil Armstrong is improved. This plus the fact that the bass register of the piano is for some reason much better recorded (giving the Hot Five *some* kind of bass for the first time) makes these recordings more consistently successful, musically, than any of the previous dates.

Put 'Em Down Blues and *Ory's Creole Trombone,* recorded in September, had already maintained a light ensemble swing that the earlier sides rarely found and never sustained. And Ory—in that delightfully punchy, leathery style of his—plays his own composition well, although he still had not mastered its traditional figures, especially in the bridge. Armstrong fakes his way through his break, but is otherwise in top form. In *The Last Time,* also in September, while Ory slips back into the stiff routines, replete with wrong notes, from which he had momentarily emerged for his own piece, Armstrong delivers one of his most spectacular breaks.

In the December dates things are still better. *Struttin' with Some Barbecue* contains a brilliant Armstrong solo with extravagantly shaped lines and bursting vitality. The several breaks, a device traditionally requiring note values shorter than the rest of a solo to achieve a sense of speed and virtuosity, roll off at lightning speed in triplets. (Armstrong seems to have been in a "triplet" phase, as almost all his breaks during this period attest.) The opening of this solo is based on essentially the same notes with which Ory had just finished; it is full of brilliant high notes, and the swinging cross-rhythms and ghost notes of measures twenty-five and twenty-six are especially good. On *Got No Blues* we hear a good example of Armstrong's sense of motivic continuity. The triplet figure at the end of his first break is used again in the next break, which ends his solo, to modulate to a new key—both the repetition of a motive and the modulation were unusual procedures for that day. With *Hotter Than That* and *I'm Not Rough* we have nearly reached the apex of Armstrong's development as an esthetic and technical innovator. Here for the first time we also encounter a highly developed sense of form and textural variety almost on the level of Jelly Roll Morton's work.

Hotter Than That is a remarkable performance, in which the addition of Lonnie Johnson plays a vital part. The ensembles and solos swing in a manner that makes it quite clear why the term "hot jazz" was coined. Apart from that, the formal scheme is interesting in that it presents a greater degree of variety in the over-all structure as well as within its thirty-two-bar subdivisions (Ex. 10). Obviously the constant two-bar breaks add much to the textural variety of the performance. Armstrong's break (in A^1) incidentally is the first instance, to my recollection, of a trumpet break that is not a phrase ending, but a

Example 10 *Hotter Than That*

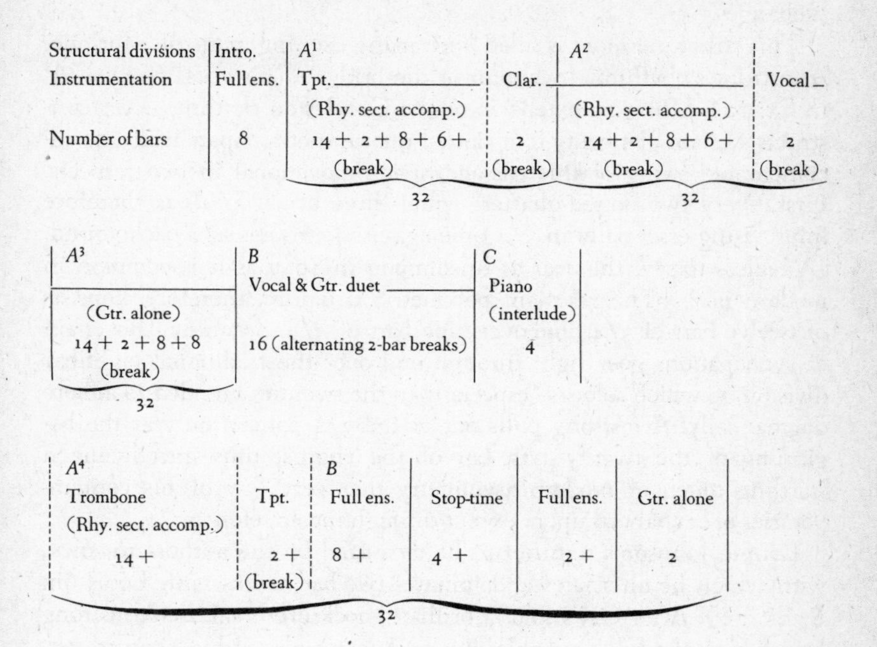

connection to the next improvised segment. As the instrumentation is reduced from the introductory full ensemble through two solo choruses (with only rhythm accompaniment) to only voice and guitar, the two-bar breaks of the first three choruses lead quite logically to a half-chorus consisting of a whole chain of these two-bar breaks. From here and the succeeding piano interlude, the instrumentation builds up again to full ensemble and the interestingly segmented final chorus, ending with a reminiscence of the earlier two-bar trumpet and guitar exchanges.

This structural mold is filled with many exciting moments: for one, Armstrong's rhythmic invention in the bridge of his vocal chorus (A^3 in Ex. 10). Using an extension of the Charleston rhythm, Louis constructs a chain of twenty-four dotted quarter-notes. Apart from the incomparable swing of this passage, it is innovational in two respects. First, every two dotted-quarters equal three beats. Louis is therefore improvising essentially in 3/4 time against Johnson's 4/4 background. (Needless to say, this was as uncommon in 1927 as it is common in modern jazz.) The resultant polymetric structure, therefore, consists of twelve bars of 3/4 time over nine bars of 4/4. Secondly, this chain of syncopations goes right through and over the traditional eight-bar division, to which soloists (especially in the twenties) tended to adhere dogmatically. Armstrong pulls out of the 3/4 pattern only at the beginning of the twenty-sixth bar of the chorus, thus introducing a startling touch of modern asymmetry that very few of his contemporaries ever chanced upon, except through incompetence.

Lonnie Johnson's stature can be measured by the authoritativeness with which he alternates and imitates two-bar breaks with Louis (in *B*, Ex. 10). After Ory's solo, a brilliant, cocksure break by Armstrong brings back the full ensemble. But he has not played his last card yet. Listen to how magnificently Louis strides across the four bars of stop-time (measure twenty-five to twenty-eight of the final chorus), recalling momentarily the 3/4 dotted-quarter pattern of his vocal chorus.

I'm Not Rough, a slow blues, is just as successful. Again an interesting formal scheme is developed (Ex. 11). Lonnie Johnson sets the unusual tone of the performance by introducing (in A^1) a zither-like guitar tremolo that adds tremendous intensity as well as sonoric interest and variety. A^2 differs from A^1 in that it is conceived by all participants in a more sustained manner, including Dodds's two-bar "long note" break right in the middle. In general, the ensembles dominate this performance, not only numerically but in quality. They recapture —rather unexpectedly, it would seem, in the midst of what was after all a stylistic revolution in full force—the true spirit of the New Orleans ensemble, that remarkable feeling than can only be described as half laughing, half crying. An astonishing moment occurs in the middle four bars of the last chorus. Just at the moment where Armstrong takes the ensemble into a bouncy double-time, Ory decides to play a two-bar ascending glissando, the very antithesis of rhythm. The resultant contrast here is one of those fortunate accidents of intuition that can happen in inspired ensemble improvisation.

Example 11 *I'm Not Rough*

Structural divisions	Intro.	A^1	A^2	A^3	A^4
Instrumentation	Piano (alone)	Full ens.	Full ens. (Clar. break in 7, 8)	Tpt.——— (Full ens. accomp.)	Gtr.——— (Banjo alone accomp.)
Number of bars	4	12	12	12	12

A^5	A^6			Coda
Vocal——— (Gtr. counter line) (Banjo accomp.)	Clar.——— (Full rhy. sect.)	Full ens.——— (dble. time)	(norm. time)	
12	4	4	4	2

It is interesting to note too that the miniature call-and-response pattern embedded in the first four bars of the piece (between trumpet and trombone at A^1) is preserved in two of the three succeeding ensemble choruses: A^3, trumpet and guitar; A^6, clarinet and trombone. It is also significant that the September and December Hot Five dates included more ensemble work than any of the previous sessions. For the lesser players it shifted the emphasis away from the long solo, and left it in the hands of the two men who could best handle it: Armstrong and Johnson.

The two remaining sides are lesser achievements. Ory's *Savoy Blues* is primarily a series of solos with Louis sparkling. Of the three ensembles, two are arranged (rather naïvely at that), leaving only one improvised ensemble. *Once in a While* has an interesting final stop-time chorus by Louis. It is set over a two-bar pattern of ♩ 𝄽 𝄽 ♩ | 𝄼 ♩ 𝄽 | an augmentation of the Charleston rhythm which in turn comes from the first four bars of the tune (Ex. 12). Louis does not feel entirely comfortable over this uneven pattern—neither does Ory, who makes the wrong entrance once—and his chorus shows signs of strain, ending rather abruptly, as if he had suddenly realized that the three minutes were up. This and similar weak endings, fluffs, and other flaws, lend support to Ory's statement that the Hot Five and Seven made very few retakes.[15]

Example 12 *Once in a While*

Half a year later (June 27 and 28, 1928) Louis again took a Hot Five group into the recording studio, but this time with a completely revamped personnel. The reasons for this change have never been stated unequivocally by any of the principals involved. Certainly one important reason must have been that the extraordinary stylistic changes of those years, initiated in large part by Armstrong himself, now necessitated changes in personnel that would reflect these newer conceptions. The period 1926-29 marked not only the greatest surge of recording activity up to that time, but also saw the formation of hundreds of small and big bands, all of which made jazz a highly competitive field. Whatever personal factors may have entered into his decision to scrap the old Hot Five band, Armstrong undoubtedly also felt that the men he was working with in Carroll Dickerson's band were much closer to his current conception. This conception was by now far removed from the old New Orleans ensemble style, and already a host of disciples, imitators, competitors—as well as innovators already completely removed from any New Orleans influences (Duke Ellington, for example)—were crowding the field. And Louis must have felt that Dodds, Ory, and St. Cyr were too steeped in the older tradition to make the change. More than that, Armstrong knew or sensed that more and more arrangements would be required in order to set off his solos, and he must have realized that Ory's and Dodds's reading abilities were too limited. This is not to say that these musicians could not read, but that they could not read well enough to cope with more complex arrangements; and in any case they did not really feel at home in these sophisticated surroundings. Dickerson's "large" ten-piece band espoused the new "arranged" style, with its overtones

15. Shapiro and Hentoff, p. 110.

of show business, its Tin Pan Alley popular tunes (as opposed to real jazz or New Orleans material), and its general aura of commercial sophistication. Armstrong's fame was such that he had to keep up with the changing times, a lesson that King Oliver, for one, had failed to learn.

Armstrong's decision was historically correct; however, that is not to say that the actual personnel changes constituted an immediate improvement. They certainly did in the case of Earl Hines, and probably in the case of Zutty Singleton, the drummer. But the first efforts of Fred Robinson (trombone), Jimmy Strong (clarinet), and Mancy Cara (banjo) were no better than the uneven work of their predecessors, and frequently even worse. If Dodds and Ory played out-of-tune, hit wrong notes, or did not swing, they at least were strong musical personalities, and something of this always survived. Not so with their replacements. When they were bad, there were no saving qualifications. As a consequence, the June 1928 Hot Five dates are quite uneven in over-all quality, ranging from Armstrong's masterpiece *West End Blues* to an inept rendition of Fats Waller's 1919 *Squeeze Me*. These sides are analogous to the May 27 recordings in that, once more, the band tries for too much—in this instance often too much exterior effect.

West End Blues is certainly the crowning achievement of this date, and perhaps of Armstrong's recorded output. Part of the reason is that it is almost entirely Louis's vehicle. The simple King Oliver blues tune is left uncluttered by any of the arranger's dated clichés that mar the other recordings of this period. His introductory free-tempo cadenza was for a time one of the most widely imitated of all jazz solos. It made Armstrong a household name, and to many Europeans it epitomized jazz.

Louis's introduction (Ex. 13) was, of course, a startling breakthrough, for it combines two ideas—the occasionally used opening break (for example, *Skit-Dat-De-Dat*) and the extended stop-time chorus—into a cadenza that is free in tempo. Yet despite its rubato freedoms, the introduction is, in retrospect, clearly in double time to the main tempo of the piece.

Louis had found the perfect jazz counterpart to the hundreds of popular cornet cadenzas that were such an integral aspect of the American musical tradition. In this particular respect, the jazz trumpet had come full circle back to its origins as the star of those outdoor brass and marching bands that contributed in the first place toward making jazz an instrumental music.

Example 13 *West End Blues*—Introduction

Louis's *West End Blues* introduction consists of only two phrases (*A* and *B*). As has already been intimated, these two phrases alone almost summarize Louis's entire style and his contribution to jazz language. The first phrase startles us with the powerful thrust and punch of its first four notes. We are immediately aware of their terrific swing, despite the fact that these four notes occur *on* the beat, that is, are not syncopated, and no rhythmic frame of reference is set (the solo being unaccompanied). These four notes should be heard by all people who do not understand the difference between jazz and other music, or those who question the uniqueness of the element of swing. These notes as played by Louis—not as they appear in notation—are as instructive a lesson in what constitutes swing as jazz has to offer. The way Louis attacks each note, the quality and exact duration of each pitch, the manner in which he releases the note, and the subsequent split-second silence before the next note—in other words the entire acoustical pattern—present in capsule form all the essential characteristics of jazz inflection. In this connection it is interesting to note that the *f* sharp of measure one is held a fraction longer than the previous three notes. This is not accidental, for this *f* sharp serves a triple function: (1) in conjunction with the next two notes (g and *b* flat) it is the beginning of Oliver's theme; (2) as the "blue" lower neighbor of *g*, it definitely establishes the key of E flat (these notes are unaccompanied and on paper, for example, could belong to the key of C minor); and (3) it is the most pungent and striking note in the entire first phrase (one need only substitute any other harmonically possible note—*b* flat, *e* flat, *g*, *c*, or even *a* flat—to appreciate the excellence of this pitch choice). In measure three Armstrong does a remarkable thing rhythmically, something we have come to call "metric modulation" in recent years:[16] the tempo changes. However, it does not change haphazardly, but in fact in a precise rhythmic relationship to the previous tempo: the triplet eighth-notes of measure three equal the duple eighth-notes of measure two. Triplets in the tempo of the first and second measures would be, of course, much faster, and the next order of triplets would be slower than what Armstrong actually plays. Intuitively, he realized that the one would be too fast—even for his advanced technical powers—the other a little too leisurely.

The first and third notes of measure three are very interesting in this connection. Armstrong seems not yet to have made up his mind whether he would continue in eighths or not. There is no emphasis of any kind to indicate triplets in the *e* flat, *f*, and *f* sharp, and since the rhythm, as already explained, corresponded to the eighth notes of the previous measure, it would seem that Armstrong was at first intending to proceed in ordinary eighth notes. Here we have an example of how the implied harmonic context (E flat major) influenced and determined Armstrong's rhythmic choice. As Louis moved to the *g* (fourth note in measure three), the triplet pattern emerged in his mind, along with the E flat arpeggio moving to C minor. But since the speed of the already-played first three notes of measure three did not correspond to any triplets in the tempo of the opening measures, Armstrong faced two choices: either to continue in a slower out-of-tempo triplet pattern or to abandon the idea of triplet arpeggios altogether. His choice was unquestionably the right one, even though it involved an unorthodox procedure in jazz: a change of tempo. The daring and, at the same

16. "Metric modulation" is a term first associated with certain compositions by Elliot Carter in which specific relationships common to diverse tempos are exploited. See Glossary.

time, simplicity of this intuitive decision is remarkable. It is typical of how a great jazz improviser finds a positive solution to something that started out originally as a mistake or a moment of indecision.

The second phrase (*B*) is one of the descending lines ending on the seventh that we have seen many times previously in Armstrong's work. In *West End Blues* it is a brilliantly expanded version of this idea, elongated by means of sequence and near repetition (brackets C^1-C^2 and D^1-D^2). Again the blistering drive and swing of the phrase-opening relaxes gradually into a state of repose, this time to set up the quiet statement of the theme itself.

After the spectacular introduction to *West End Blues,* the theme (Ex. 14), harmonized in the simplest fashion, is doubly haunting in its utter simplicity. But from measure seven it begins to build up again,

Example 14 *West End Blues*—Theme

expanding in its contours and intensity, until—in the last two bars of that chorus—Louis is ready for the spiraling triplet arpeggio, a variant of measure three of the introduction. Louis's next entrance is as vocalist. Here he improvises alternating phrases with the clarinet (initially canonically, later more freely) in a pattern which, except for minute details, seems to have been clearly outlined by Armstrong and Strong before recording.

As remarkable as the performance is thus far, Louis's final chorus (Ex. 15) is the perfect climax, structurally and emotionally. It can only be described as ecstatic. Beginning with a long high *b* flat, held for almost four measures, Louis builds up an extraordinary sustained tension. All the pent-up tension of this long note finds release in an impassioned, almost stammering repetitive phrase that seems to float, completely unencumbered rhythmically, above the accompaniment.

Example 15 *West End Blues*—Final Chorus

This chorus fulfills the structural conditions of climax with a sense of inevitability that is truly astonishing in an improvised work. Louis's four choruses for this piece by themselves make a perfect structural line, from the brilliant introduction through the more subdued inner chorus to the impassioned finale. The interspersed solos by Robinson and Hines (even though the latter's is excellent) are not on Louis's exalted level, and detract from the over-all caliber of the performance.

For the remainder of these sides Louis does not fare nearly as well. *Skip the Gutter* is uneven, containing one corny break not worthy of Louis (in the middle of the clarinet solo), a number of fluffs, but also a brilliant exchange of two-bar phrases between piano and trumpet. *Fireworks* is a lively number that sounds like an imitation of Chicago-style jazz. Robinson comes alive for a brief solo, and Hines—after a shaky first solo—manages to sneak in a very smart "bitonal" break at the end of his second solo. On *Sugar Foot Strut,* despite a generally happy, bouncy feeling, Louis's stop-time solo does not quite come off. Here, as in *Two Deuces* and *Squeeze Me,* Louis and the band are trying to be too flashy, too hip. They are seeking the striking effect, and more often than not it is a nearly empty gesture. This leads to all kinds of pitfalls: the quite unjustified double-time ensemble in the middle of *Two Deuces;* the shaky vocal business, imitating Bing Crosby and the Rhythm Boys, on *Squeeze Me* (one of the rare examples of Louis's singing out of tune); the stiffly arranged "let's-wow-the-public" ensembles of *Don't Jive Me;* and the fancy endings on nearly all the pieces. At an even lower level, the total lack of harmonic co-ordination between banjo and piano on *Skip the Gutter* and *Don't Jive Me* can only be explained by the incompetence of Cara or a lack of preparation prior to recording time. Strong's clarinet solos are inevitably out of tune and not particularly inspired, while Robinson plays so many wrong notes and puts himself in impossible positions so often that one begins to wonder how Louis could have tolerated him. Perhaps he did not care. The work of his sidemen—once the music had moved away from the collective ensemble—was in many ways less critical; it reflected not on Louis nor on the ensemble (since there was very little of it left), but only on the individual himself.

There remains the remarkable Earl Hines. Apart from Johnny Dodd's Black Bottom Stompers recordings (in effect a Hot Seven group) and the "big-band" *Chicago Breakdown,* the June 1928 Hot Five sides were Hines's first major recordings. With his radically new piano conception and his clear, light, linear style, Hines brought a whole new texture to the ensemble, and a greater sense of swing. His playing is remarkably consistent and leaves no doubt that, for the first time, Armstrong had met a colleague who understood him and was almost his equal.

The contrast with most other pianists of the period is striking, and there is no question that Hines's childhood training in classical piano had an enduring influence on his technical capacity and on the originality of his conception. Hines was more than a proficient two-handed pianist. He was one of the very first[17] to develop a style that assigned different functions to the left and right hands. He was aided in this by his formidable command of the keyboard and his varied touch. In essence his conception of the piano unified the striding left-hand of ragtime pianists and their successors (James P. Johnson, Luckey Roberts, etc.) with a new melodic-linear conception in the right hand. Evolving nost notably in the context of various Armstrong-led groups, and revealing many parallels to Louis's style—an almost trumpet-like attack and brilliance, the frequent double-time excursions, a similarity in the shape of melodic lines—Hines's piano playing would inevitably be characterized as "the trumpet piano style." These basic Hines characteristics can be heard already in his first solos with

17. The aforementioned Teddy Weatherford (1903-45) was probably the first to have thought of the piano in these non-orchestral terms, and in fact he was one of Hines's few early influences.

the Hot Five, especially in *West End Blues,* a solo with an astonishing over-all fluency, considering that it vacillates in the right hand between the "trumpet style" and certain pianistic arpeggio figures, which are prevented from becoming mere clichés by Hines's superior control of touch and timing.

Skip the Gutter features a remarkable Hines and Armstrong duet (to be surpassed only by their famous *Weather Bird,* recorded six months later.) Since Louis follows Hines in these breaks, Hines is the challenger, Louis the challenged. The over-all continuity that results is astonishingly varied and at the same time logical. The formal plan divides into the following pattern: $\left\Vert: \begin{matrix} 2 & - & 2 & - & 6 & - \\ - & 2 & - & 2 & - & 2 \end{matrix} :\right\Vert$. Hines starts with a two-bar phrase that just hovers on the brink of double time, an urge that Armstrong fulfills in his answer. Hines then settles into a relaxed triplet swing, which Armstrong imitates perfectly, although with a totally different yet complimentary choice of notes. Knowing Louis will not be imitating him in his next six bars, Hines launches into a real pianistic two-bar run which would have made no sense on the trumpet. He then straightens out into a more horn-like passage that meets Armstrong half-way, so that Louis can finish the phrase (Hines's six bars as well as the sixteen-bar chorus). Louis does so with a beautifully swinging single repeated note, replete with half-valve bends and triplet cross-accents. As Louis finishes, Hines enters with a diminished-chord arpeggio, but he makes a surprise entry on the fourth beat, so that it appears momentarily as if Hines has skipped a beat. A one-beat extension of the arpeggio (thus producing in effect a five-beat phrase) pulls him back into line with the 4/4 meter, not without throwing in a syncopated dissonance on the first beat of the next measure (measure eighten of the thirty-two-bar duet). After Louis answers this in kind, Hines creates two double-time passages that Louis has no chance of topping. These two Hines breaks are essentially alike, but one is a variant of the other. Though the variation consists merely of shifting the left-hand walking tenths from the beat to between-the-beat syncopations, the result is startling. In fact, it is upsetting to the unaware listener, since it seems that again Hines has somehow lost half a beat. Only when the listener *thinks* in double time during this break does Hines's rhythmic accuracy become apparent. These two measures (Ex. 16) are characteristic of Hines's

Example 16 *Skip the Gutter*

work and frequently appear in similar form. In its rhythmic counterpoint, Hines's style attained a complexity and independence of the two hands that had probably never been heard in jazz before. As Hines returns to "single" time, he hesitates momentarily in his right hand—the only flaw in his playing on the entire side. But he rights himself quickly, and Louis ends the duet with a chromatically descending triplet run that is in character and inflection a corollary to his pedal-point break in measure sixteen. This amazing tour de force is a striking example of how the improvisatory spirit of jazz challenges the creative impulse and makes possible a dialogue in musical terms as natural as normal conversation.

The other Hines solos are of a uniformly high level. He rarely gets caught off-guard. When he does (as in *Don't Jive Me,* right after a *seven*-bar ensemble passage) it is in the more over-arranged routines of the band. Of passing interest, too, are the two tremolo barroom style accompaniments Hines provides on *West End Blues* (for Robinson) and on *Two Deuces* (for Louis). Here again, Hines's superb dynamic and touch control raises a tawdry device to a level of classic refinement.

From here on Armstrong and Hines share equal honors on most sides. A week after the *West End Blues* date, Louis recorded three more pieces, one with his Hot Five personnel, the other two with Carroll Dickerson's eleven-piece band. Hines and Armstrong dominate these Hot Five sides completely, as comparison with the other soloists, Robinson and Strong (on tenor saxophone), makes painfully clear. It is perhaps not entirely fair to blame Strong for the aimlessness of his solos, the uninspired choice of notes, and the total lack of swing—in short, their utter banality. This was simply the way the jazz saxophone was played in those days. Even Coleman Hawkins was caught up in these narrow stylistic confines at this time. The two Dickerson big-band sides are typically "sophisticated" and "clever," featuring the latest fancy whole-tone modulations and surprise endings. Armstrong and Hines are equal to the situation. Consider, for example, the absolute authority with which Louis starts his solo on *Symphonic Raps* (Ex. 17):

Example 17 *Symphonic Raps*

Or consider the rhythmic variety of Hines's solo on *Savoyager's Stomp* (Ex. 18):

Example 18 *Savoyager's Stomp*

Note its quarter triplets in bars one and two, the very sparse third and fourth bars, his elimination of the stride left-hand until the middle of the sixth bar, the amazing ascending left-hand chromatic run against the leaping, syncopated right hand (bars nine and ten, not in Ex.)—compare all this with any other pianist of the day, and Hines's superiority becomes obvious.

The next spate of recordings took place in December of 1928. Once again they produced two or three outstanding sides, but in over-all quality they were uneven, albeit this time for a different reason. While the band's playing was generally improved technically and more cohesive in conception, many of the sides suffered from stiff arrangements (or arrangements stiffly played), touches of sentimentality, and poor material. Commercialism was beginning to exert its subtle pressures, forecasting the decline of Louis Armstrong as an innovative force.

The outstanding sides are *Weather Bird* and *Muggles,* which are considered by many aficionados to be the zenith of Armstrong's early career. *Weather Bird,* King Oliver's famous composition, becomes a bravura piece for Hines and Armstrong alone without accompaniment. There is extraordinary rapport between them. Hines is not a mere accompanist to Louis; he participates fully in the improvisatory give and take. As the two players challenge each other, try to outflank each other, they alternate between complete unanimity rhythmically and melodically, and complete independence. In extreme cases of the latter—with both players involved in independent syncopated lines and cross-accents—the explicit beat is momentarily suspended. Here the two masters are years ahead of all other jazz musicians, and Armstrong in particular provided a fund of phrase turns that trumpet players were still borrowing and making into clichés ten years later (as in Ex. 19).

Example 19 *Weather Bird*—Trumpet

Both musicians here anticipate for a moment the future of jazz; they are unencumbered by the incessant "chomping" of a rhythm section and project strong linear shapes that propel the music forward—airy, jagged lines and rhythms that even then pointed toward the bop lines of the forties. Basically Armstrong and Hines adhere to the original three-part ragtime format of the piece as recorded by Oliver's Creole Jazz Band in 1923 (with Louis on second cornet), merely expanding Oliver's $A^1BA^2C^1C^2C^3$ form to $A^1B^1B^2A^2C^1C^2C^3$-Coda. But the content is transformed fundamentally. The block-like polyphonic structures of Oliver's performance, which were broken only by two-bar built-in breaks and revealed no organic development from chorus to chorus, are translated by Armstrong and Hines into an over-all new form in which each chorus builds and feeds upon the preceding one. The means are twofold: variation technique combined with gradual dissolution into splinter subdivisions of the original sixteen-bar structures.

Both procedures are handled in terms of a gradual progression. A^1 and B^1 are expositional in character, stating the theme material in long lines and unbroken continuity. Hines is the first to hint at the gradual breakdown of rhythmic continuity. In B^2 and A^2 he departs more and more from the regular stride rhythm. The resultant accents and syncopations are taken up—but only sporadically—by Armstrong. The interlude (before C^1), with its free rhythms and undermining of the beat (Ex. 20), announces in effect how the C choruses will be treated.

Example 20 *Weather Bird*—Interlude

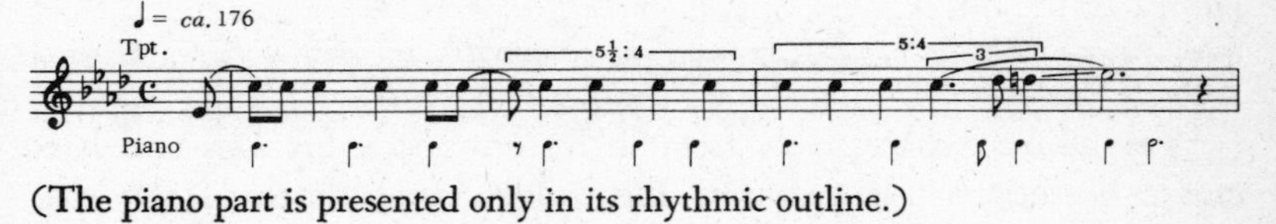

(The piano part is presented only in its rhythmic outline.)

Hines's solo (C^1) is followed by three more choruses in which the original two-bar break of the composition becomes the element through which the form is gradually broken down. Example 21 shows this development in schematic form, ending with the final one-bar exchanges of the coda.

A necessary corollary to this structural progression was an analogous breakdown of the thematic material. This meant that in order to arrive at the short two- and one-bar phrases of the last choruses, some short motivic fragment of the original had to be extracted. For this purpose Armstrong used a combination of the original chromatic duet-

Example 21 *Weather Bird*—Scheme of Ending

Structural divisions	C^1	C^2				C^3	
Instrumentation	Piano solo	Tpt. (break)	Duet	Tpt. (break)	Duet	Piano (break)	Duet
Number of bars	16	2	6	2	6	2	6

		Coda								
Piano (break) (E♮)	Duet	Tpt.	Piano	Tpt.	Piano	Tpt.	Piano	Tpt.	Piano	Tpt. Piano
2	6	2	2	2	2	1	1	1	1	ritard.

break he had played in Oliver's band and variants of the opening notes of the *A* and *C* themes (Ex. 22 A, B, C, D, E, F).

Example 22 *Weather Bird*—Theme Variants

With Hines progressively freer in his cross-accentuations and harmonic deviations—for example, the sudden appearance of the sustained *e*-natural unison (in the key of A flat) in bar nine of C^3 (see Ex. 21)—the logical outcome of this musical dialogue was the freer tempo of the one-bar exchanges in the coda and the final act of dissolution, Armstrong's *ritardando* climb to the high *c*.

The cohesiveness of this performance is at a level we usually attribute to consciously premeditated composition. When we realize that it is the result of spontaneous creation born of the passing moment, we can only marvel at the musicianship displayed. And it reminds us again that jazz in the hands of such masters is an art and at such times far removed from the arbitrary, purely visceral view of jazz many enthusiasts hold.

If *Weather Bird* results in a draw between the two men, *Muggles* definitely goes to Armstrong, and is, in fact, one of his greatest flights of imagination. His solo, which occupies the entire last third of the performance, is especially striking coming as it does after two dreary solos by Robinson and Strong. As Louis enters on the last two bars of Strong's slow blues chorus, going abruptly into double time, the phrase soars out like a bird suddenly routed from its nest. The impact of Louis's entrance constitutes one of the great joyful moments of jazz, and even young players who have no particular affinity for Armstrong's style are impressed by the daring and modernity of this passage.[18] This is undoubtedly due to its strong rhythmic articulation, again bop-like in character. In fact, this solo is almost entirely rhythmic, with virtually no melody. Its first twenty measures revolve entirely around the central tone, *c*, and eight of these contain literally no note other than *c*. All this is done with only one direct rhythmic repetition. The first part of Louis's *Muggles* solo moves away completely from the idea of a collectively improvised background. In fact, part of the overwhelming dramatic effect of the solo is that it is placed over a sustained chordal background. The held notes of trombone and clarinet, Hines's tremolos, Cara's reiterated 4/4 strokes, all combine to create a static background which is the perfect foil for Armstrong's rhythmic punctuations. These also contrast superbly with the rest of his solo. As he returns to the original tempo, Louis delivers himself of one of his most impassioned statements. Earthy, plaintive, expansively declamatory, weighted down with blue notes—it is the epitome of sophisticated, urban instrumental blues.

Almost as outstanding was the Alex Hill–Armstrong collaboration, *Beau Koo Jack*. The group was enlarged to seven by the addition of Louis's erstwhile Henderson colleague, Don Redman, who had in the intervening four years established a major reputation as an arranger. *Beau Koo Jack* was, however, written by Alex Hill and, therefore, arranged by the composer. Hill was one of the very best early arrangers in jazz, but he has been strangely underrated by critics and historians, possibly because—as Hugues Panassié suggests—his best work was never recorded. Be that as it may, the arrangement of *Beau*

18. This solo exists in notation in Leonard Feather's *The Book of Jazz* (New York, Horizon Press, 1957), p. 217; also in the same author's *Encyclopedia of Jazz* (New York, Horizon Press, 1960 edition), p. 70.

Koo Jack reveals a high degree of skill and imagination, and is one of the best arrangements ever made for Armstrong. Understandably it results in one of Louis's most perfect solos (Ex. 23), economically structured and superbly executed despite the bright tempo. Judging by the comparatively clear ensemble and the fullness of its sound, Hill was the kind of arranger who made musicians feel at ease and

Example 23 *Beau Koo Jack*—Trumpet Solo

made them sound good.[19] It is also an interesting arrangement from the point of view of the relationship of the improvised solo to the arranged background. Hill explores several degrees or proportions of interrelation:

a. fully arranged ensemble
b. arranged ensemble with one player improvising (or embellishing melodic line) *within* the ensemble, that is, not an outright solo
c. arranged ensemble as background for soloist
d. alternating fully arranged ensembles with solo breaks, two bars apiece
e. collectively improvised full ensemble
f. solos with only rhythm accompaniment (unarranged)

Moreover, these various associations are not applied merely in a chorus-to-chorus pattern. On the contrary, very seldom does a chorus use only one of the six combinative approaches, one chorus may successively use a, b, and e, or a, c, and b. In view of the complexity of the resulting over-all form, the performance represents a minor miracle. A large part of the credit must go to Redman, who as an arranger-colleague probably felt challenged by Hill's schematic context: in addition to contributing a fine solo, he also walked the fine line between solo and ensemble improvisation with consummate skill.

Indeed, in his association with Armstrong, Redman comes off better as a player than as an arranger. On *Save it, Pretty Mama,* Redman is both composer and arranger, but except for a flashily virtuosic piano solo that Hines tosses off as if it were a C major scale, the performance is listless. Its pretty opening mood (in character not unlike that of Ellington's *Mood Indigo* of two years later) is unfortunately not sustained past the first twelve bars. The piece *Hear Me Talkin to Ya',* not particularly distinguished Redman, does not compare with his arranging work for Henderson and McKinney's Cotton Pickers.

No, Papa, No and *Basin Street Blues* are both good, although not without qualifications. On *No,* again a blues, Armstrong is in fine form, playing around (in the fourth chorus) with phrase repetitions like a cat with a mouse. But clarinet and trombone are weak and

19. The strong similarity of the tune's opening idea to a certain phrase in Gershwin's 1925 Piano Concerto leads one to speculate whether Hill, who probably knew Gershwin in Hollywood, also knew the Concerto.

floundering, while Hines's good solo is marred by an out-of-tune piano. *Basin Street Blues,* full of arranged passages, is spoiled by another badly balanced, slightly out-of-tune vocal ensemble, also a celesta introduction and coda which, though sophisticated and clever, are out of place on the blues-ish tune. On the credit side, Armstrong makes an indescribably surging entrance (as in *Muggles,* over a sustained background) that has all the more effect for following the insipid vocal. Louis is reaching for the sky again, with bold stabs into the high register and headlong double-time runs. The level of intensity rises in his second chorus and reaches its peak in a break of reiterated high *b* flats that are literally bursting with swing. At this point for the first time the whole band catches fire. For about four or five bars, that poignant New Orleans mixture of sad and happy music comes back. The phrase then subsides into a quieter mood, and Louis deftly simplifies his improvisation until it links up with the final "evaporating" two-bar coda on the celesta.

Both *St. James Infirmary* and *Tight Like This* are comparatively inferior and suffer from a variety of weaknesses. Both pieces are in minor keys with very little harmonic variety, and therefore lend themselves poorly to solos, at least with these soloists.[20] Don Redman's arrangements, which sound like nightclub production numbers, do not help matters. Finally on *Tight Like This,* we hear the already-noted tendency toward commercialism, now at a more advanced stage, manifesting itself in an increasingly saccharine sentimentalism and a grandstanding, high-note final chorus.

By early 1929, Armstrong and his manager Joe Glaser had found the successful commercial formula to exploit Louis's talents: from now on he was to play in front of various big bands (Carroll Dickerson, Luis Russell, Les Hite, Chick Webb) who would exploit the commercial tunes of the day and provide backgrounds for his display pieces. Such recordings fall into sterotypes and need not detain us very much. There is, however, one exception: *Mahogany Hall Stomp.* It is one of Armstrong's best, but beyond that is unique in several respects. It is the first recording Armstrong made with a pizzicato

20. There is a fascinating correlation between the quality of jazz solos and the "feeding capacity" of the chord changes, especially in earlier jazz. In any event, solutions for playing on little-varied "changes" or in minor keys were not developed consistently until the late thirties and in the "extended" improvisations of Miles Davis in the late fifties.

string bass, and as such displays a more advanced "swing" feeling than any of his previous recordings, all made either without a bass instrument or else with a tuba. Paradoxically, Pops Foster's bass lines, in conjunction with the semi-improvised backgrounds of the first two sixteen-bar choruses, recapture completely the warm feeling and texture of the bigger New Orleans bands of the twenties (particularly certain Sam Morgan recordings like *Bogalousa Strut*). One cannot help wondering whether the orchestra, which had just recorded an insipid rendering of *I Can't Give You Anything but Love,* was relieved to get into an old New Orleans standard. Furthermore, *Mahogany Hall Stomp* probably had more than a touch of nostalgia for at least six of the players who came from New Orleans: Armstrong, Albert Nicholas, Pops Foster, Paul Barbarin, Lonnie Johnson, and Luis Russell—including four-fifths of the rhythm section. More than that Armstrong, Nicholas, Barbarin, and Russell had all played together in the same band back in New Orleans at Anderson's Annex. Thus the New York date in 1929 was in the nature of a reunion, and the band captured perfectly the true New Orleans spirit—perhaps one of the last such attempts before the New Orleans revival a decade later.

Records like *West End Blues, Muggles, Weather Bird, Potato Head Blues, and Beau Koo Jack* showed Louis Armstrong at the full extent of his mature powers. It would have been beyond even his genius to develop past this point, even if the temptations of commercial success had not been as strong as they now were. That Armstrong was not completely suffocated by these commercial constraints is a measure of his greatness. He survived the thirties much better than most of his generation, much better for example than his mentor Joe Oliver survived even the twenties. In fact the resilience of Armstrong's genius is such that even past sixty his playing and singing were technically unimpaired. And despite years of showmanship, lipsplitting grandstanding, mugging and clowning, his art was indestructible. In his most recent comeback (early 1964) he revealed a new depth and poignancy in even the most uninspired musical material.

The years of the Hot Five represented, nevertheless, a peak activity that could hardly be surpassed. The records of the next decade, though numerous and commercially successful, added nothing to

Armstrong's stature as one of jazz's greatest innovators and musical giants. They did, however, add to his reputation as a trumpet player. His conceptions, exploratory in the twenties, became set and firmly embedded in his mind and lip, so to speak, through constant repetition and the elimination of all but sure-fire formulas. From a purely instrumental point of view, Armstrong's trumpet playing remained immune to ravages of both commercialism and time.

In the first two or three years of this period (1929-31) Louis extended the range of his solos upward by still another notch, the high *d*'s in *Some of These Days* and the *e* flats in *My Sweet* and others. No matter how tawdry the material, his tone was firm and glowing with an incandescent quality that shone through even the old recording techniques. While his ideas were by then formula-ridden and to a large extent repetitions from the Hot Five period, they are securely executed. The breaks at the end of *Ain't Misbehavin'*, for example, are well played but occur almost note for note as early as 1926. The upward rip on the first note of a break, the subsequent descending arpeggio, the ascending return ending on the ♩♩𝅗𝅥 pattern—all the phrasing idiosyncrasies peculiar to Armstrong that we have noted since his earliest records—now became the formulas, the clichés by which a public could easily recognize him. How formula-ridden Louis's tailor-made arrangements were is shown by the fact that virtually *every* recording made with the Dickerson band is patterned after the same formal outline, as academic as a textbook sonata form—trumpet solo, vocal, short alto-saxophone break (allowing Louis to pick up his horn), and trumpet out-choruses. Despite this, there are many memorable moments on the sides made in the early thirties, with Louis soaring expansively above the ossified arrangements. He really led these various bands as a true trumpet (and vocalist) leader, thereby setting the stage for all the Harry Jameses and Ziggy Elmans to come. But even fifteen years later none of them caught the "true tone" and depth of Louis's playing on *Some of These Days, Ding Dong Daddy, Lazy River,* the second *Stardust* master recording, *Between the Devil and the Deep Blue Sea,* his wild break on *Shine*—to name a few. Nor can one say less regarding his magnificent scat vocals on *Lazy River* and *Ding Dong Daddy*. These sides, listenable virtually only when Louis is playing, make one forget the lesser efforts like the vaudevillian *Dear Old Southland,* one step removed from an *Eli Eli* interpretation of the kind made famous by Ziggy Elman in dozens of trumpet solos in the 1930s, or *My Sweet,* where the arrangement closes in on Louis so that even he cannot extricate himself.

For the rest there is a wasteland of whimpering Lombardo-style saxophones, vibraphones and Hawaiian guitars, saccharine violins, dated Tin Pan Alley tunes and hackneyed arrangements. Once in a while the elegant trombone of a Lawrence Brown (then with the Les Hite band) penetrates the labyrinth of commercialism. Occasionally, the accompanying band swings, as in *Shine* or *Ding Dong Daddy,* but these are the exceptions. Armstrong had made his contribution, he had "paid his dues," and, as one of his friends put it to me once, he now wanted to enjoy the returns. It is a choice not unknown in the annals of the arts.

4

The First Great Composer

Jazz is primarily a player's and improviser's art; it has produced preciously few composers (in the strictest sense of that term). In the light of recent developments in jazz, the emphasis may shift more and more to composition, but this is still a matter of conjecture. If the emphasis on original composition were to continue, as presently exemplified by the compositions of, let's say, Charles Mingus or George Russell,[1] it would nevertheless be safe to predict that such composing would have very little direct stylistic influence on the players of the future. For it is virtually axiomatic that each succeeding jazz style has been nurtured on the conceptions of the immediately preceding generation of players, and not its composers. (It is, of course, quite the contrary in "classical" music.)

In jazz, the dividing line between composer and performer is a fine one, subject to considerable overlapping in the sense that *all* jazz players can be considered composers since they are in effect composing extempore. However, the large majority of jazz musicians are composers only in this very general sense, and their composing is intimately related to and determined by their role as instrumentalists and performers. Even when they compose a piece in a more premeditated sense, most musicians are hardly more than composers of tunes based on standard chord progressions and forms. This is not to denigrate this

1. At the time of writing, this is a reasonable question due to the enormous influx of musical conceptions originating outside of jazz, such as aleatory procedures, the influence of John Cage, and even Third Stream.

type of compositional activity; it constitutes, after all, the bulk of the jazz repertoire. The point is that it represents a different *category* of composition, and composition in the stricter sense has until now played a curiously minor role in the development of jazz.

It is manifest that the basic stylistic and conceptual advances in jazz have been determined by its great instrumentalist-improvisers—Louis Armstrong, Earl Hines, Coleman Hawkins, Lester Young, Charlie Parker, Dizzy Gillespie, Miles Davis, John Coltrane, Ornette Coleman—not by Jelly Roll Morton, Duke Ellington, Thelonious Monk, John Lewis, George Russell, and Charlie Mingus. Players may admire and respect the latters' work, may even be influenced by them in some secondary ways, but these are not the men they emulate on their instruments. The reasons are obvious: An instrumentalist cannot emulate in totality a compositional conception which is in itself based on the collective efforts of a number of players (as in the case of Ellington and Mingus[2]). Secondly, the majority of the composers mentioned are either not virtuoso musicans in the sense of a Parker or an Armstrong, or are so unorthodox instrumentally as to preclude emulation, since in such cases the result could only lead to *imitation*. In emulating a Parker or Armstrong, the musician has a much simplified problem. Although there is a quasi-compositional conception at the root of these players' styles, the emphasis is clearly on the instrument and the performance.

These thoughts bring us to the legendary Ferdinand Joseph ("Jelly Roll") Morton, pianist, gambler, pimp, self-proclaimed "inventor of jazz," but above all the first of that precious jazz elite: composer. Morton actually represents both of the composer categories just mentioned. He certainly composed an impressive number of "tunes" that became staples of early jazz repertory, numbers such as *King Porter Stomp, Wolverine Blues, Milenburg Joys, Georgia Swing, Chicago Breakdown,* and *Wild Man Blues*. But most of these were more than mere thirty-two bar tunes or twelve-bar blues. They were original multi-thematic structures which embodied (like most ragtime) a definite, detailed compositional conception, which had to be retained in

2. To appreciate the problem fully, the reader need only project the notion of a trumpet player, for example, attempting to imitate Ellington and all the compositional, stylistic variety that name stands for.

performance to a much greater extent than is usually required in jazz.

But Morton was also a remarkably creative arranger. His best arrangements were not mere orchestrations, but carefully organized structures in which all the details of instrumentation, of timbral relationship, of rhythmic and harmonic counterpoint were realized as integral compositional elements. His "arrangements" were more like re-compositions, and in their "composed" elements were as finite as the formal outlines on which they were based. These were the ingredients which, when coupled with Jelly Roll's unique abilities as a band leader—at least with those New Orleans men who respected him—resulted in 1926 in a series of recordings under the name of Jelly Roll Morton and His Red Hot Peppers which many consider to be "the finest recordings of New Orleans music ever made."[3]

In trying to separate fact from fiction in Jelly Roll Morton's life, the historian faces a virtually insurmountable task. One of the most flamboyant extroverts jazz has ever known, Morton was led by his musical and personal frustrations to exaggerate and embellish the truth as freely as the occasion seemed to demand—at least in his public utterances. However, his many unquestionable talents, his real contributions to jazz as a performer and composer, and the statements of many of his fellow musicians produce a total picture which tends to make even his most hyperbolic assertions seem plausible. When, for example, Jelly Roll said that he wrote his first jazz tunes in 1902, or that he used scat-singing as far back as 1907, there is not only no proof to the contrary, but Jelly's own considerable accomplishments in themselves provide reasonable substantiation. As Omer Simeon, his clarinetist, once put it, "he could back up everything he *said* by what he could *do*."[4] And this Jelly Roll proved rather conclusively in his playing on the Library of Congress recordings.

If one is to believe Morton's own accounts, his career as a composer began in the early years of the century, with the composing of *New Orleans Blues* (1902 or 1903), *King Porter Stomp* (the date variously given as 1902 or 1905), *Jelly Roll Blues* (1905), and *Wolverines,*

3. Alan Lomax, *Mister Jelly Roll: The Fortunes of Jelly Roll Morton, New Orleans Creole and "Inventor of Jazz"* (New York: Duell, Sloan and Pearce, 1950; reprinted, New York: Grove Press, 1956), p. 193 (paperback edition). This book, based on recordings Morton made at the Library of Congress, is a moving, sympathetic, and definitive account of Morton's life.
4. Lomax, p. 220.

which Johnny St. Cyr remembers hearing as early as 1906. Morton also recalled writing *Alabama Bound* and *Indian Blues* around 1905, but these pieces apparently never achieved much currency.[5] Morton left New Orleans in 1907, never to return, and seems to have covered most of the United States in his various careers as pool-shark, parlor-house "professor," gambler, vaudeville comedian, and night club owner. He *always,* however, played the piano as part of these occupations or as a means of tiding him over between jobs and moves to another city. In 1922 he finally settled down for a period in Chicago. Bunk Johnson recalls running into Morton "in Gulfport, Mississippi, 'round in 1903 and 1904."[6] In 1911 James P. Johnson heard him in New York, playing *Jelly Roll Blues.* Morton's publisher friend Reb Spikes met him in 1912 in Tulsa, Oklahoma, and later that year he stayed in St. Louis for a short period, where he apparently made his first written arrangements. Eventually, according to Jelly, his arrangement of *Jelly Roll Blues* was published in Chicago in 1915, which probably makes it one of the first, if not the first, jazz orchestration ever published. Still later, in the mid-twenties after the immense success of *Wolverines,* which to Morton's annoyance was renamed *Wolverine Blues* by the publishers ("it is not a blues"), more than a dozen Morton orchestrations were published in simplified form by the Melrose Brothers Music Company of Chicago.

It should be evident that Morton had as varied a career as he claimed, even though, like all men who suffer from feelings of inferiority and frustration, he was given to enlarging the facts when attacked or ridiculed. Especially in purely musical matters, though, he possessed not only an accurate memory (as his performances on the Library of Congress records certainly demonstrate) but a composer's ability to make discriminating distinctions. For this reason his statements about other musicians and early jazz in general are extremely valuable. They not only tell us a great deal about his contemporaries, but they tell us much about Morton and his music. As a Creole, he had an obvious disdain for the "black Negroes" and their music, which spills over into his musical commentaries. This is worth noting because, paradoxically, it

5. In any case *Alabama Bound* is, like many of the blues Handy used to write down and publish, hardly attributable to any one single composer, this type of song being in fairly common use all over the South.
6. Lomax, p. 113n.

provides one of the background clues to the greatness of the Hot Peppers recordings; in fact his unequivocal prejudices against the black Uptown Negroes and their music were responsible for both Morton's most successful achievements and his ultimate decline as a force in jazz. For Morton's uncompromising pride in the music he stood for (and indeed claimed to have originated) led him to create the finest recorded tribute to New Orleans music ever achieved. But it also induced the stubborn arrogance of his later years which kept him from realizing that New Orleans music and his own innovations, now thirty-five years old, had long been superseded.

As we separate Jelly Roll's musical comments from their general context, the picture of what kind of musician Morton was unfolds in considerable clarity and detail. His mentor and earliest musician friend was Tony Jackson, the legendary pianist who was, even according to Morton, "the greatest single-handed entertainer in the world," a statement confirmed unanimously by other musicians of the period. Undoubtedly part of Morton's admiration stems from the fact that Jackson was a "man of a thousand songs": "There was no [music] from any opera or any show of any kind or anything that was *wrote on paper* that Tony couldn't play" (italics mine).[7] More explicitly Jackson was evidently capable of singing anything from operatic selections to blues, perhaps not an unusual condition in the polyglot musical climate of New Orleans. But it is clear that in all these respects Tony Jackson was Jelly's idol, and his emphasis on notating his music, planning his recording dates in advance, and publishing his orchestrations, and his love of opera excerpts and ragtime music are all largely attributable to the influence of Tony Jackson.

Significantly, Jackson was almost the only "real dark" musician Morton revered. His prejudices on this score were painfully clear, and unquestionably influenced his opinions of other musicians. It certainly explains why he rated Freddie Keppard much higher than Armstrong and Oliver,[8] why he surrounded himself with Creole musicians in

7. Ibid., p. 43.
8. The possibility that Keppard was perhaps really superior to Louis Armstrong can never be entirely denied since Keppard's recordings were all made in his years of decline when he was rapidly drinking himself to death with "half a gallon to three quarts [of white lightning] a day." It is, of course, one of the tragic ironies of jazz history—and again a result of the clannish attitudes

Chicago, and why, in fact, he was considered very much an outsider by the majority of New Orleans musicians in Chicago. Morton's prejudices were implanted at an early age and rigorously maintained throughout his life. In all fairness, however, it must be pointed out that his was not so much a case of individual prejudice as of class distinctions rigidly maintained by both the Downtown Creoles and the Uptown black Negroes. Alan Lomax's interviews in the 1940s with old-time New Orleans musicians, as reported and evaluated in *Mister Jelly Roll,* are unequivocally clear on this point. Morton was born early enough (probably 1885) to have grown up in an atmosphere in which these social and ethnic distinctions had not yet been broken down by the confluence of Creole and black music in Storyville, the New Orleans red-light district.

But in the first decade of the century, Morton was still able to make very clear musical distinctions between jazz and ragtime.[9] "Ragtime is a certain type of syncopation and only certain tunes can be played in that idea. But jazz is a style that can be applied to any type of tune."[10] Morton added that he started using the word *jazz* in 1902, specifically to "show people the difference between jazz and ragtime." To prove his point, Morton did in fact "jazz" any type of tune: ragtime pieces, operatic excerpts like the "Miserere" from *Il Trovatore,* French quadrilles, one of which Morton claimed to have transformed into *Tiger Rag,* French tunes like *C'été 'n aut' can-can, payé donc,* the famous Mexican standard *La Paloma,* or even Sousa marches. It is clear throughout Morton's biographical narrative that jazz, ragtime, and the blues were at that time still three distinctly separate musical categories. Of these, he apparently felt that ragtime and blues were unalterable

---

of Creoles like Keppard—that he refused an offer in 1917 to make what would have been the first jazz recording. Keppard turned down the offer for fear that other trumpet players would steal "his stuff," with the result that a white band, the Original Dixieland Jazz Band, became the first to record. Lomax, pp. 154n, 155n.

9. See Chapter 2, pp. 66, 67.

10. Lomax, p. 62. Another "reason for trying to adopt something truly different from ragtime," Morton wrote to his friend Roy J. Carew, "was that all my fellow musicians were much faster in manipulations . . . than I and I did not feel as though I was in their class"—a rare moment of modesty for Morton. From a letter partially reproduced in Orrin Keepnews and Bill Grauer, Jr., *A Pictorial History of Jazz: People and Places from New Orleans to Modern Jazz,* rev. ed. (New York: Crown Publishers, 1955), p. 60.

traditions of long standing (neither of which, significantly, he claimed to have invented). To Morton the composer, ragtime and blues were not just musical styles, but specific musical forms: the one a multi-thematic structure, the other an eight- twelve- or sixteen-bar single-theme form with a predetermined chord progression. These were forms as well-defined as the sonata form was to a "classical" composer, and Morton accepted them as active, continuing traditions.

At this point Morton's claims to be the "originator of jazz" begin to take on a degree of plausibility. In his mind and perhaps in actual fact Morton had isolated as "jazz" an area not covered by the blues or rag-time. Since he applied a smoother, more swinging syncopation and a greater degree of improvisational license to a variety of musical materials, such as ragtime, opera, and French and Spanish popular songs and dances, Morton's claim to have invented jazz no longer seems quite so rash. As he put it so succinctly in regard to his transformation of *La Paloma,* "The difference comes in the right hand—in the syncopation, which . . . changes the color from *red to blue*" (italics mine). [11]

To the annoyance of unsympathetic musicians, Jelly Roll never tired of emphasizing his nonpareil ability as a pianist and, in all but the last ten years, his virtually continuous employment in the better entertainment establishments of the country. But here, too, confirmation by musicians and other contemporaries exists. Bunk Johnson, for instance, told Alan Lomax: "[Morton] was a really good piano man. Had lots of work at the Great Southern Hotel playing waltzes and rags for the white people."[12] Louis "Big Eye" Nelson, one of Sidney Bechet's mentors who certainly had no great love for Jelly Roll, begrudgingly admitted that Morton "come to be a real good piano player."[13] In Nelson's interview with Lomax, he also confirmed in many details Morton's analysis of jazz and its distinctness from rag-time. Yet he made it clear that his own sympathies were more on the side of jazz as an "all head music." His final word—clearly delineating the dividing line between Downtown and Uptown music, and presumably between men like Morton and himself—isolated what to him was a crucial difference: "You've got to play with the heart. Picou,

11. Lomax, p. 62.
12. Ibid., p. 113n.
13. Ibid., p. 88.

. . . he's a good enough musician, but they"—and here he was referring to the note-reading Downtown musicians—"*They* don't play with the *heart*."[14] Dr. Leonard Bechet echoed these sentiments. "Picou's a very good clarinet, but he ain't hot."[15] Musicians like his brother Sidney Bechet and like Morton saw this difference and blended the more technically controlled playing of Downtown with the hot, unabashedly emotional playing of Uptown Negroes.

An equally extreme disparity of conceptions is revealed in Jelly Roll's first encounter with W. C. Handy. When Morton met Handy in 1908 in Memphis, he requested the latter's band to play a blues, but Handy replied that "blues couldn't be played by a band."[16] This is not surprising since Handy's band was more in the nature of a concert or circus band. According to Jelly, Handy and (for that matter) Memphis heard instrumental orchestral blues the first time when Freddie Keppard and his band came there on an excursion and played Morton's *New Orleans Blues*.

Recalling a later period, probably in 1912, the then leading piano player in Texas, George W. Smith, frankly admitted that Morton "in those days could carve everybody," including himself. And what Smith remembered most was Jelly's playing of the blues, above all his specialty, *Jelly Roll Blues*.[17] Corroboration of the quality and nature of Jelly Roll's early piano playing was also tendered years later by another master pianist, James P. Johnson. He told Alan Lomax: "First time I saw Jelly was in 1911. He came through New York playing that *Jelly Roll Blues* of his. . . . Of course, Jelly Roll wasn't a piano player like some of us down here. We bordered more on the classical theory of music."[18] This statement confirms what Morton said all along: that he did not play regular ragtime, but played "jazz." What Johnson did not know was that Morton could play in any of the styles of the day, including those bordering "more on the classical theory of music," as Morton's Library of Congress recordings demonstrate beyond a doubt.

Perhaps Morton's brother-in-law, Bill Johnson, a bass player, confirmed most succinctly that Jelly Roll was playing "something differ-

14. Ibid., p. 93.
15. Ibid., p. 98.
16. Ibid., p. 141.
17. *Downbeat*, April 1938; quoted in Lomax, p. 145n.
18. Lomax, pp. 143-4n.

ent" in those early New Orleans days: "You could go by a house where Jelly Roll would be playing and you'd know it was him because nobody did . . . play just like him."[19]

Of course, one need not depend solely on his contemporaries' accounts to find out what Jelly's music was like. Aside from his own re-creations and rather explicit statements on this subject, his comments on his fellow musicians round out the picture. Again we are struck by the perception of his statements, the fine distinctions that only a superior musician would make. "George Baquet was the earliest *jazz* clarinetist"[20] (the italics are Morton's), or "Buddy Bolden, the great *ragtime* trumpet man" (italics mine).[21] "Bud Scott was, no doubt, the great guitarist, although Gigs Williams and Buddy Christian could fake *when the music wasn't too hard*" (italics mine).[22] Or about Keppard, a very revealing remark reflecting Morton's own penchant for using a great number of ideas: "there was no end to his ideas; he could play one chorus eight or ten different ways."[23] [He had] "great imagination. . . Any little place in the music that didn't have any notes on, he would fill right up."[24] Or in speaking about later big-band jazz, Morton lamented: "It is great to have ability from extreme to extreme, but it is terrible to have this kind of ability without the correct knowledge of how to use it."[25] But Morton's most florid and, in a way, most touching comment was prompted by Albert Cahill, his Storyville piano player colleague: "Cahill, with his so soft, sweet, non-exciting, perfect perfection of passing tones, and strange harmonies, cool and collective [did he mean collected?] style."

The Harlem musicians who derided Jelly Roll in the thirties did so partly because he antagonized them with his bragging about the past, and partly because they thought he was an old-fashioned "corn-ball." But they failed to realize that in some ways Morton was still way ahead of them. He had a total conception of jazz that transcended

19. Ibid., p. 160n.
20. Ibid., p. 124.
21. Ibid., p. 60.
22. Ibid., p. 125.
23. Ibid., p. 126.
24. Nat Shapiro and Nat Hentoff, eds., *Hear Me Talkin' to Ya: The Story of Jazz by the Men Who Made It* (New York: Rinehart & Company, 1955), p. 90.
25. Lomax, p. 181.

the external details of style. If a music was going to be "loud and blatant" and if it was going to lack contrast and variety, Morton considered it simply bad music and poor jazz no matter how advanced in style. But what hurt most of all was that his detractors did not even seem to know what he was talking about. The one musician who by rights should have understood him was Duke Ellington; however, a long-standing feud of unknown origin between the two men evidently precluded any mutual rapport, at least in public. As for the rest, very few understood Morton's fine qualitative distinctions. For Morton was the first theorist, the first intellectual, that jazz produced. And jazz has never been sympathetic to the intellectual.[26]

Morton's vision of jazz entailed contrast and variety—instrumental, timbral, textural; in short, structural. In his finest recordings he realized this vision, embracing all the pertinent essentials of the art of composition. Jelly Roll Morton's conception of jazz as a music different from ragtime was unveiled in his very first compositions, *Jelly Roll Blues* and *New Orleans Blues*. The question immediately arises whether the 1923-24 recordings of these pieces and his later Library of Congress re-creations of them can be considered representative of their *original* conception twenty and thirty-five years earlier. Morton stubbornly maintained his highly individual views on jazz to his final days, stylistic advances and the ridicule of younger musicians notwithstanding. But perhaps the most striking proof is provided by the Library of Congress recordings themselves. They not only resemble the twenties recordings in all essential aspects; but the entire series is proof of Morton's extraordinary ability in distinguishing the various kinds of music and styles of his youthful years.

It takes only a few moments of comparative listening to any early ragtime recording to hear the marked difference between Jelly Roll's

26. The neat catalogue of opposing opinions Leonard Feather has compiled in his *The Book of Jazz* (New York: Horizon Press, 1957), pp. 31-5, setting up "the critics'" pro-Morton views against a solid phalanx of "musicians'" counter-opinions, could be just as easily reversed. Such statistical polemics serve only to fan the flames of controversy surrounding Morton, and such tactics have never been a valid substitute for objective scholarship and analysis. For instance, Martin Williams's brilliant, definitive essay does present Morton in the proper light ("Jelly Roll Morton," in Nat Hentoff and Albert J. McCarthy, eds., *Jazz* [New York: Rinehart & Company, 1959], pp. 59-81).

jazz style and the more rigid, conservative ragtime. At even the most superficial level of listening it is clear that Morton has moved away from the stiff, "classically"-oriented right hand and the march-like left hand.[27] Even James P. Johnson, who was certainly one of the more advanced ragtime pianists, always retained the original square 2/4 feeling, a rhythmic tightness that Jelly loosened up and smoothed out early in his career. Morton accomplished this innovation by making improvisation, especially in the right hand, the keynote of his piano style, thus directly opposing it to ragtime, a music largely written down. By means of his improvisational methods, Morton was able to horizontalize the music, as it were, and to suppress the vertical, harmonic emphasis of ragtime and other musical forms. This horizontalization was a crucial addition without which, either in Morton's or subsequent players' terms, there could be no jazz. It made possible a rhythmic forward momentum, the *sine qua non* of swing. (Again Morton's several transformations into jazz or ragtime, quadrilles, tangos, marches, and opera excerpts on the Library of Congress recordings make this difference strikingly clear.) But those improvisations of Morton's that still retain a close tie to ragtime were either based on the composition's theme or were embellishments of it. They were not improvisations over merely a chord structure, as in later jazz. These improvised right-hand "manipulations" were Jelly's pride and joy, and by means of them he was able to give his melodic lines a much freer, looser feeling than ragtime had ever known.[28] But they also provided a whole new sense of continuity, and a formal conception that involved the elimination of ragtime's strict repetitions and imitations, and substituted instead variational procedures stretched over chorus-like patterns, with several strains combining into larger complete ideas. This was a radical innovation, one that even the early ragtime instrumentalists like Bolden and Bunk Johnson never adopted in quite that way. It was, moreover, an innovation only a composer, thinking in larger structural terms, would make.

27. A graphic illustration of this difference is offered by Morton himself in his two recorded versions of Joplin's *Maple Leaf Rag,* the first in pure ragtime style, the second "along the lines of jazz creation." (The Library of Congress Recordings, *Jelly Roll Morton,* Vol. 3: *Discourse on Jazz,* Riverside RLP 9003, side 2, seq. 1, 2.)

28. How free these could get at times is shown by the seventh chorus of *New Orleans Joys* (see Ex. 8 in this chapter).

Out of his concern for a more extended, freer continuity, Morton developed—apparently at a very early date—an over-all structural scheme in which the final rocking stomp was always contrasted with a more delicate and quiet preceding section. The latter was, of course, more often than not the old ragtime Trio, or at least derived from it. The point is that Morton, with his keen sense of structural and dynamic contrast, retained precisely that aspect of ragtime or the old quadrilles that gave variety to his compositions. It was the lack of contrast within a given piece that annoyed Morton so much in later jazz styles, a lack of contrast that was in fact a virtual fixation of jazz until comparatively recent years. It is very much worth noting that the man who was considered to be such an egotist realized that an unrelievedly loud or otherwise relentless performance is likely to be more ostentation than artistry.

While the schematic framework and syncopated rhythmic patterns of ragtime provided one point of departure for most of Morton's music, the blues was an equally important element. In fact, to state it in a somewhat generalized, schematicized form, Morton, in combining ragtime and blues, combined two sets of opposites: conventional ragtime was based on strict repetition of phrases and was basically unimprovised, whereas the blues, especially at the turn of the century, was essentially improvised[29] and as such featured no exact repetition, at most a sort of near- or half-remembered repetition. This form provided the improvisational freedom and emotional expressiveness that one side of his nature demanded. Here he learned to apply to basically diatonic material—"unbending" its tempered intonation in the process—the intonational and expressive freedom of the blue notes. This was not just a matter of flatting thirds and sevenths. It meant re-thinking the music he played in terms of a melodic-harmonic language that did not exist in Western music, a language in which the blue notes, like the embellishing microtones of Indian and other Asian music, gave the music its expressive latitude, subject nevertheless to relatively strict habits of voice-leading, harmonic functions, and rhythmic associations. In the blues he found the melodic leavening with which to loosen up the music's linear flow. And the liberating inducements of improvisation he characteristically equated, not with the free-form extemporiza-

29. The first "blues" was not notated and published until 1912 when W. C. Handy published *Memphis Blues*.

tions of early blues, but with the somewhat restrictive disciplines of variation. It was improvisation as the eighteenth-century baroque musician understood the term: embellishment of or improvisation on a given thematic material over a relatively fixed harmonic background.

It is not likely that Morton heard "baroque" improvisations, but he did hear the vestiges of this technique as they survived in Italian and French opera. We know that Morton attended performances at the French Opera House in his youth, but actual attendance would not even have been necessary for him to have become familiar with popular operatic standards; they were known to all well-trained Creole musicians and the white society for whom they played. From this source young Ferdinand absorbed much of what later found its way into his own music. He learned to appreciate the unity of form that characterized the great opera arias, many of which, significantly, were simple two- or three-part forms, not unlike ragtime pieces schematically. Morton also heard how Verdi, Massenet, and Donizetti varied or embellished their melodies upon repetition and how they introduced new material in the form of countermelodies, contrasting figures in the accompaniment, and "descant" lines. Morton learned to value the sense of enrichment and complexity contributed by such counterlines, which he was to emphasize in theory and in practice all his life. Many a highpoint in a Hot Peppers recording can be traced to Morton's uncanny ability to weave the right kind of secondary line or idea—very often a riff—into the fabric of a solo improvisation.

Although not motivic variation in a strict sense, a riff did provide an alternative melodic variant for a given harmonic context. As such, Morton's use of riffs was still another means of providing contrast and variety, as was his almost obsessive exploitation of the "break." He was fond of saying that "without a break you haven't got jazz," and that the break "didn't come in until he originated the idea of jazz." It will probably never be possible to pinpoint exactly when the break came into use, but it existed in an embryonic form in some early rags (Joplin's 1901 *Easy Winner*). Something like it also exists in traditional opera when singers, taking advantage of the fermatas composers often provided on high notes or at phrase endings, hold the note out *ad libitum* or interpolate short cadenzas. The latter practice differs from the break in that it distorts and adds to the total duration of a phrase, whereas a break takes place *within* an eight- or sixteen-bar phrase. Similarly, though time is suspended in a break, the underlying beat is implied, while in an operatic fermata or in a cadenza no beat or tempo is felt. Also, since the operatic "break" is composed, it does not have the element of surprise that the improvised jazz break always has. Despite these differences, I have always been struck by the fact that the two-bar break in earliest New Orleans jazz most often consisted of a single note or contained one note held almost long enough to fill the entire two bars. Morton's music is full of such breaks (*Kansas City Stomps, Big Fat Ham*), and they were a characteristic feature of Dodds's and Bechet's early clarinet breaks, as well as those of many other New Orleans players, before Armstrong made the double-time break a permanent virtuoso feature of jazz. Morton's long- or single-note breaks are especially effective in the faster, raggy pieces, where the sudden "suspension" of time comes as a complete surprise and contrast. Whether Morton invented the break or merely adapted it from opera or another source, he is "probably the only man, musician or critic" who has made it a "principle."[30] It might be added that he also made it an art, since he used it as a subtle climax, not a mere gimmick that had no relation to what preceded and followed. Morton peppered all his piano and orchestra performances with breaks, but he went even beyond this by writing them directly into his compositions, so that their retention became mandatory in performance. This was again the kind of consequent step only a composer would take, and Morton was certainly the first jazz musician to insist upon the inclusion of particular compositional details in an otherwise improvised performance. The early *Jelly Roll Blues* already has two such breaks composed into the piece, as well as a six-bar stop-time section.

Another early piece, *New Orleans Blues*, contains an example of melodic bass writing in the second strain co-incidentally in the form of a break (Ex. 1). Again Morton's need for variegated continuity is the

Example 1 *New Orleans Blues*

source of his inspiration. Similar trombone-like figures abound in his music and remind us that even in his piano pieces his bass lines are constantly striving for linear, contrapuntal relief from the striding left

30. Williams, in Hentoff and McCarthy, p. 68.

hand (for example, the chromatic-step bass lines of *King Porter Stomp*). We are indebted to Alan Lomax for first pointing out that these bass figures are attributable not only to Morton's own occasional "fooling around" with the trombone, but to the fact that his father, Ed La Menthe, "played a slidin' trombone" and "could cooperate pretty well in a band."[31] Lomax inferred that "in almost every line of his compositions Jelly Roll wrote bass figures in tailgate style and sonorous bursting melodies; trombone phrasing is the Jelly Roll trademark." It should also explain why Morton's compositions contain so many built-in trombone breaks.

This penchant for trombone lines is one indication of Jelly Roll's basically orchestral approach to both the piano and composition in general. And again it serves to differentiate Morton's jazz from the others' ragtime. For a pianist, his pieces contain relatively few pianistic breaks and quite a few instrumental ones. The trills in the first break of *Jelly Roll Blues* are definitely clarinet-inspired, and were always orchestrated as such by Morton. The first part of *Chicago Breakdown* contains two unpianistic breaks, one definitely for trombone, the other for clarinet or cornet; the high-register breaks in *Big Fat Ham* are for clarinet. The C minor section of *Wild Man Blues* has what can only be a trombone break, while the Trio of *Grandpa's Spells* contains a series of non-pitched accents obviously intended for the drums.[32] The list could easily be enlarged, but these examples indicate the wide gulf between Morton's instrumental conceptions and the strictly pianistic approach of his ragtime contemporaries. Jelly Roll carried this orchestral conception to the point where it permeated his playing, and it is obvious that he was really trying to emulate the sound of an entire band in the richly sonorous stomp choruses with which he always ended his piano renditions.

I think that Morton must have been greatly impressed by the way opera composers like Verdi and Donizetti managed to organize their larger ensemble pieces. And many of them are indeed marvels of ingenuity, satisfying both the dramatic demands of the plot and the exigency of keeping a multi-layered vocal ensemble and orchestra musi-

31. Lomax, p. 34.
32. One is reminded of another great American "original," Charles Ives, who also, inspired by the marching bands of his native Danbury, Connecticut, incorporated imitations of bass drum and cymbal accents in his piano works.

cally intelligible. In point of fact, ensemble pieces like the Sextet from *Lucia di Lammermoor* or the Quartet from *Rigoletto,* in which each voice is assigned a clearly delineated function, are not as far removed from New Orleans ensemble jazz as one might think. The structural parallels are obvious. We have seen how an identical disposition of "voices" occurred in Oliver's Creole Jazz Band (with Armstrong's improvised second-cornet lines not dissimilar to the role assigned by Verdi to the contralto Maddalena). But the most perfect examples of this kind of improvised-ensemble organization were produced by Jelly Roll and his Red Hot Peppers, where contrasting individual lines attain a degree of complexity and unity that jazz had not experienced before.

Perhaps Morton's unique quality as a jazz musician, however, was his continued investigations in musical form, investigations intimately related to his innate desire to provide for the greatest possible variety in musical content. Here he combined two principal ideas: the two- or three-part form with its modulations and interludes inherited from ragtime, and the concept of perpetual variation. Within this general framework, applied in nearly every Morton performance that has come down to us, he introduced further levels of variety and contrast—imaginative juxtaposition within a single piece of polyphony, harmony, solo, counter-melodies, and stop-time rhythm—all used as individual structural elements.

It is instructive to place Morton's views of these matters in their historical context. Jazz went through many changes in the 1920s. It became synthesized into a single, recognizably different musical language; it also proliferated and split into at least two major directions by the end of the decade; it produced several major artists, and was thus elevated to a burgeoning, if still somewhat erratic, art form. But the significant fact for our discussion of Morton is that in this period jazz went through fundamental transitions in style, in social position, in geographical relocation (from New Orleans to Chicago and thence to New York and Kansas City), and, finally, in compositional material.

The twenties also saw the first inroads of popular music into jazz, and it is significant that this occurred early in the history of jazz. It was as if pop music and commercial interests had been standing by in the wings, ready to move in on the fledgeling music. One by one, the major jazz artists—even those with a direct connection to the more integral, purer jazz materials evolved in New Orleans—succumbed to the influence of thirty-two bar popular songs and increasingly put them into their repertoires. Even the blues as a form was threatened, although enough of the major soloists and ensembles (especially Negro) maintained a close contact with the true form. It can probably be said that, had this contact not been maintained, jazz as a distinct musical form would not have survived the thirties. Nor was the influence of pop material entirely destructive. Jazz was not only able to absorb the intruder—as it had absorbed many divergent elements even in its earliest formative periods—but it actually was challenged to new heights by this material, something we can see as early as the work of Louis Armstrong in the late 1920s.

Seen in this context, Morton's hold-out, not only in the twenties but throughout his life, for the earlier ragtime-*cum*-blues admixture ran straight against the main current. In this we find the most telling answer to the dual question of why Morton became an anachronistic figure in mid-career and why his music and conceptions had very little direct influence on any of his major contemporaries or successors. Morton's music represents the end of a line (apart from later attempts at revival). Some of the ingredients of Morton's conception were to reappear again—slightly altered, of course—in Ellington's varied and extended forms, in the Kansas City riff tradition, in the classic (and I do not mean "classical") cohesion of the Modern Jazz Quartet, and so on. But in none of these cases can we speak of a direct influence back to Morton. The fact remains that by the time Morton hit his peak in the Red Hot Peppers recordings, the kind of material he used and many of the ways in which he used it had become old-fashioned and no longer interested the young avant-gardists of the twenties.[33]

33. Martin Williams, in his searching essay on Morton (in Hentoff and McCarthy) tries to make a case for a wider Morton influence and cites Andy Kirk, Jimmy Rushing, Don Redman, and other Southwestern musicians as having admitted being "inspired" by Morton's music. But surely, even these few men did not fully comprehend the implications suggested by Morton's scores. In any case none of these men were major performers, and performers have always been the main seed carriers in jazz. Williams is closer to the point when he says that Morton's *King Porter Stomp* survived unaltered as a jazz standard into the early 1940s and, through the famous Henderson arrangement, influenced the entire Swing Era generation of arrangers. But even so, this does not yet constitute a major influence such as that of Armstrong or Parker.

For Morton one of the prerequisites of good music was a strong, interestingly varied form. The theme-solo-theme format of later jazz bored him, perhaps not so much as a performer but certainly as a composer. Innovators like Armstrong and Hawkins were not composers in Morton's sense, and tended to look upon any material, new or old, for its potential to them as performers. Morton was a purist in this respect.

Though Morton was thus unable to spread his gospel of form, that is, variety and contrast, we can still enjoy in retrospect the formal splendors of his work as a last great flowering of an already dying and superseded tradition. In any event, one cannot study and appreciate Morton's work without recognizing the uniqueness of his ideas on form and the variation principle. They are deeply embedded in all his work. Uni-thematic pieces are a great rarity (*Jungle Blues, Hyena Stomp*), while bi- and tri-thematic pieces abound; and when the composition did not already contain sufficient formal contrast, Morton would intersperse blues choruses at just the proper moments. Through an effective balance between repetition, near-repetition, and variation, Morton was able to achieve sophisticated forms, which often came close to the rondo form and occasionally even surpassed it in complexity. Outright repetition of entire themes is extremely rare, appearing mainly in his earliest ensemble recordings like *Big Fat Ham*. But contrast this with the orchestral version of *Grandpa's Spells*, which even in its broadest outlines looks formidable: Introduction A A^1 B B^1 A^2 C^3 C^1 C^2 C^3 "tag" ending, and we gain an idea not only of Morton's range, but also of the great extent to which he diverged from his contemporaries.

The best examples of how the variegated influences described earlier were transmuted into Morton's own highly individual jazz conception are the Victor Red Hot Peppers recordings of the later twenties. We have seen how Armstrong's Hot Five and Hot Seven recordings matured over a period of several years, marked by trial and error, by various commercial diversions, but ultimately resolving into the remarkable achievements which were to influence the course of jazz for several decades. Similarly, Morton's 1926 Victor recordings did not suddenly spring full blown from his head. They were likewise developed over a period of time and based on an already venerable and well-understood tradition. In comparison to Armstrong's, Morton's development is not nearly as well documented. His recording career was much more erratic than Armstrong's, precluding the almost day-by-day experimentation, luxuriating in both failure and success, that Armstrong was able to enjoy. More than that, I suspect strongly that Morton's orchestral conception was well articulated—although not yet matured—several years *before* he made his first ensemble recordings in 1923. This is clearly demonstrated by the early Paramount and Gennett sides, the former with a pick-up group, the latter with the New Orleans Rhythm Kings (NORK). To be sure, the two Paramount sides, *Big Fat Ham* and *Muddy Water Blues,* do not display the extraordinary structural, rhythmic, and sonoric variety of the later Victor recordings. In fact, they are formally rather repetitious for Morton, but they do show a number of his musical and stylistic trademarks, particularly in the kind of relaxed, loping, triplet rhythms in *Muddy Water* and in Morton's own remarkably melodic and linearly cohesive piano accompaniments behind the three solo choruses. Not until the sensitive melodic accompaniments of John Lewis for the modern jazz quartet is there anything comparable in jazz history. Morton was certainly not satisfied with the typical "oom-pah" accompaniments of ragtime and early jazz. But he went further than any of his contemporaries, even the exceptional ones, by daring to accompany a solo or even an ensemble with right-hand countermelodies that were finely-structured themes in their own right, sometimes even with variations. Indeed, often these improvised backgrounds have a haunting beauty far beyond that of the solo they are ostensibly accompanying. In the old acoustical recordings, Morton's backgrounds are hard to pick out, but they are worth listening for, as they almost always support, embellish, fill out, and feed the main soloist.

His accompaniments in *Muddy Water* interest us particularly because these are Morton's first recordings. There is no trace of uncertainty or experimentation in his playing here, but rather the work of a seasoned musician, in full command technically and sure of his functions as ensemble pianist and leader. Of particular interest is the way Morton uses one of his favorite right-hand devices, one that in a lesser pianist with a weaker sense of form we would call a cliché. It is nothing more than a frilly grace-note embellishment , which Morton used to add sparkle and bounce to his upper register lines. In *Muddy Water* this little trifle is used as an element in building continuity. After scattered appearances in the earlier choruses, it finally accumulates into a chain of sixteen direct repetitions, in other words a kind of upper-register pedal point, during the trumpet's solo chorus, and so effectively prepares and signals the return of the collective ensemble.

These sides also reveal Morton's ability to get the best from his players. The three improvised blues choruses that form the middle section of *Muddy Water* are certainly above-average solos for the period. They are unpretentious and all cut from the same stylistic cloth, which is no mean achievement when one realizes that the three soloists in question—Arville Harris, alto sax; Wilson Townes, clarinet; and (presumably) Natty Dominique, cornet—were relatively obscure youngsters in 1923.

Morton departs from the typical New Orleans format of a three-man front line by adding a saxophone. Although the saxophone had begun to be used extensively in jazz by 1920, many of the New Orleans-trained musicians were still opposed to it. Morton experimented with putting the saxophone into the New Orleans ensemble conception from time to time throughout the twenties with mixed success. Here the player, Arville Harris, was well chosen, and his tone and swing blended in surprisingly well.

In July 1923, both Morton and the New Orleans Rhythm Kings—whether by accident or design we shall probably never know—found themselves in Richmond at the Gennett studios. They teamed up for five titles, in which Morton's influence on what was an often rhythmically stiff, esthetically erratic, and formally unsophisticated group can be clearly discerned through even casual comparison between the NORK's own dates and those with Jelly Roll.[34] Morton managed to unbend the group enough to produce something close to an easy swing feeling. This is particularly notable on *Clarinet Marmalade,* a ragtime-y march-derived piece made famous by the Original Dixieland Jazz Band, which lent itself rather easily to a jerky two-beat treatment. Morton loosened up the rhythmic continuity and texture by introducing numerous two-bar breaks, by varying the instrumentation in

34. A comparison easily made on Riverside RLP 12-102.

successive choruses, and by his own imaginative piano backgrounds. Morton also used one of his favorite ending devices: kicking off the final out-chorus with a preparatory two-bar lead-in phrase, and then driving the final chorus home with a strong drum back-beat.

Mr. Jelly Lord is distinguished by another Morton device, which he was to perfect on such later recordings as *Smoke House Blues:* going into double time. As yet Morton does not entrust double time to the entire ensemble without first initiating it himself in his own piano background behind Leon Rappolo's normal-time clarinet solo. Morton's structuring of the phrase is interesting because it is asymmetrically built. In the two eight-bar phrases under discussion, Morton lopes along in triplets ♩♪ for five bars, then in the sixth bar breaks into a double-time rhythm ♫♩ , setting up perfectly the lumbering tuba break in bars seven and eight, then returning to double time for two more bars, and finally slipping back into the original triplet pattern. The way is thus prepared for the ensuing ensemble double time, which in turn is the perfect foil for the next surprise: a long sustained-note clarinet break. By very simple means Morton moves abruptly between two rhythmic extremes: the ultimate in rhythmic enlivenment (double time), and the almost complete suspension of time (a long held note).

Having indicated the potential of orchestral jazz, Morton disappointingly produced nothing worthy of comment in his next thirteen ensemble sides (if we exclude for the moment the two 1925 trio sides on the obscure Autograph label), all under various names and for various recording companies. Though we can describe today how these sides fail, not only on Morton's high terms but even comparatively on those of much lesser jazzmen, it is probably too late to say what personal and practical circumstances contributed to these failures. Suffice it to say that some of them are abominably bad (like the four sides cut as Jelly Roll Morton's Kings of Jazz in September 1924), some are merely fair, and a few are honest failures, as when Morton misjudges the structural pacing in the Paramount version of *Mr. Jelly Roll* (or *Mr. Jelly Lord*) by arriving much too late (and after much bland noodling by a kazoo) with what was clearly intended to be a side-saving climactic double-time stomp. Coming too late, and being unrelated to anything previously on the record, it merely sounds tacked on.

If there is one success in the thirteen foregoing sides, it must be the Gennett version of *Mr. Jelly Lord,* which has at least a scintillating piano solo with an ingeniously distorted quotation of one of Morton's favorite melodic motives, and some delightfully clashing blue notes, elevated to the level of "dissonance" by being shifted rhythmically into unexpected anticipations. But the instrumental ensembles are marred by two watery saxophones[35] and some poor voice-leading. In fact, the band is obviously reading the Melrose stock arrangement, made not by Morton but by one F. Alexander. But Morton surely could have avoided the bad balance in the orchestration of the final chorus where the trumpet plays the third part *under* the two saxophones. All of these various failures point to the fact that Morton was for one reason or another unable to schedule rehearsals or fashion better arrangements.

In the Red Hot Peppers recordings, in contrast, his work was much more careful. Several of the musicians who worked with Morton on these sides have described his methods as a leader. These statements are quoted in a number of sources,[36] but they all attest to the fact that Morton rehearsed carefully—he even paid for rehearsals; that he shaped the arrangements either in written-out or dictated form; that he discussed with his players where breaks and solos would fit best, although he retained a final veto; that he rarely if ever interfered with the solo work; that he knew what he wanted over-all and often worked until he got it. The results of these painstaking methods are to be found on roughly a dozen sides made under the Red Hot Peppers banner for Victor, starting in September 1926, a time when Armstrong's Hot Five recordings had produced only one or two outstanding sides and Armstrong's musical peak lay a year or so ahead.

With the very first side, *Black Bottom Stomp,* Morton seems to be putting the world on notice about his claims as a jazz musician. First of all, the piece, like most of the Victor sides, is superbly recorded. There are none of the problems of listening through the tinny surface

35. Incidentally, there is no clarinet on this recording, as all discographies claim. Other discographical errors in the Morton catalogue I have found are (1) that Gennett 5219 and 5220 have two saxophones; (2) I am reasonably certain that Morton is the pianist on Gennett 5219; and (3) there is only one trumpet on the September 21, 1926, Red Hot Peppers date, and that, I suspect, is Lee Collins, not George Mitchell.

36. For instance, clarinetist Omer Simeon in Shapiro and Hentoff, pp. 181-2.

of earlier acoustical recordings. The tremendous exuberance and vitality of this performance are captured perfectly with a live, roomy acoustical presence. *Black Bottom Stomp,* one of Morton's finest compositions, was probably written expressly for this recording date. Although in two parts, it actually sports at least four different themes and one variant that one cannot quite elevate to the status of "theme." It has all the Morton ingredients: built-in breaks, stop-time phrases, rhythmically lively themes, frequent contrasts of sustained whole-note phrases with bouncily syncopated eighth-note patter, and a brilliantly stomping Trio. But beyond this, it offers a special dividend, perhaps unique in diatonic music, "classical" or otherwise: the first part, with its three separate themes, is in B flat, and yet no B flat chord (with the single exception of a passing-tone second inversion) ever appears; it is avoided and delayed until the ninety-sixth bar of the piece (Ex. 2). This gives

Example 2 *Black Bottom Stomp*—Chord Progression[37]

$$\mathrm{VI} \;\Big|\; \mathrm{IV}^{\mathrm{dim}} \;\Big|\; \mathrm{VI}^{7\,(+3)}_{2} \;\Big|\; \mathrm{VI}^{7\,(+3)}_{1} \;\Big|\; \mathrm{II} \;\Big|\; \mathrm{I}_{2} \quad \mathrm{V}^{7}_{3} \;\Big|\; \mathrm{I}^{\mathrm{dim}} \;\Big|\; \mathrm{V}^{9} \;\Big\|$$

the whole first part a curiously suspended and unresolved feeling and imparts a unique forward momentum, since the ear craves for the resolution to B flat. When it finally does come, Morton charges right on, via a short quadrille-derived interlude, to the Trio in E flat.

The formal timbral and textural scheme, one of Morton's richest, is given in Example 3.[38]

37. The superscripts refer to degrees of the chord beyond those of the basic triad, 1, 3, and 5 (which are assumed). The subscripts refer to the inversion of the chord, first, second, or third. The superscripts in parentheses refer to additional alterations of the chord required by the key signature.

38. Martin Williams in his monograph *Jelly Roll Morton* in the Kings of Jazz series (New York: A. S. Barnes and Company, 1963), allows his enthusiasm for Morton and for *Black Bottom Stomp* in particular to exaggerate its formal cohesion beyond the call of duty. His paragraph on page 67 presents a well-meaning but garbled version of what happens in *Black Bottom Stomp*. Williams ascribes a call-and-response pattern to the eight-bar introduction. This is far-fetched and probably the result of hearing the introduction as consisting of a sustained chord answered by a chattering eighth-note figure. This impression, however, is erroneous and probably based on the unintended prominence of the sustained note in trumpet and trombone. The acoustically weaker clarinet actually has in the first bar an eighth-note figure of which the "chattering" figure in bar two is simply a continuation. Furthermore, if Williams insists on calling the chord-to-moving-figure pattern a call-and-response pattern, then by the same logic he would have to call the first theme—four bars of sustained

Example 3 *Black Bottom Stomp*—Scheme

Structural divisions	Intro. vamp	A^1	A^2				A^3	
Instrumentation	Full ens.	Full ens. (arr.)	Tpt.	Full	Tpt.	Full	Clar. (Banjo)	Interlude (modulation)
Number of bars	[4]	[8]	4	4	4	4	16	4

B^1			B^2		B^3		B^4	B^5
Full	Tpt.-Trb. (break)	Full	Clar.	Full	Piano (no rhy.)	Full (as in B^2)	Tpt. (stop-time)	Banjo (partly 4-beat)
6	2	12	18	2	18	2	20	20
20			20		20			

B^6			B^7			Coda
Full (2-beat)	Drums	Full	(Tom-tom)	Trb. (break)	Full	
6 *mp*	2	12	6 *ff*	2	12	2

A^1 is a written-out ensemble in harmony, repeated exactly. A^2 alternates trumpet solos with ensembles, all of them written out and in four-bar phrases. A^3 features a clarinet sticking close to the written theme with only banjo accompaniment. B^1 is a twenty-bar structure for full ensemble, improvised, while B^2 initiates a string of solos: clarinet,

---

chords followed by four bars of moving figures—a call-and-response theme as well.

Williams hears another call-and-response pattern in connection with the first theme when he says: "The first theme (actually almost a series of chords) is given in harmony, then in solo 'call' by the trumpet and in variational 'response' by the clarinet and trombone, then back to harmony." The trumpet does not "call" nor does the clarinet "respond"; they merely play Morton's composed thematic variants over the same underlying chord progression. The trombone does not play at all in this particular sequence except in the harmony passages.

The confusion continues when Williams calls the Trio the "second B theme" after having stated that the entire piece consists of "three themes" (p. 66). The banjo chorus can hardly be said to contain a "break"; the final "stomp" chorus features a tom-tom or Indian drum, not a bass drum; the bass is not very "audible"; and there is only one trombone break in that chorus.

There remains the question of how many "themes" *Black Bottom Stomp* has. I cannot blame Martin Williams for being confused. Actually in multithematic ragtime pieces each theme had its own chord progression. In this

Omer Simeon (B^2); piano, Morton (B^3); trumpet, George Mitchell (B^4); banjo, Johnny St. Cyr (B^5). Many an arranger would now have followed with the final out-chorus, but Morton has another card up his sleeve. B^6 although for full ensemble, is kept to a light, transparent *mezzo piano* (perfectly complemented by the cymbal break in bars seven and eight), and only then (B^7) is Morton ready for the *fortissimo* home-stretch chorus with strong tom-tom back-beats. What Morton has done here is to create six different timbre combinations with only seven instruments in the total ensemble: trumpet and rhythm, clarinet and banjo and rhythm, clarinet and rhythm, piano (*no* rhythm), banjo and rhythm, full ensemble. Similarly, four varieties of rhythm make their appearance: two-beat, four-beat, the Charleston (or Spanish tinge), and a strong back-beat. Let us remember that all this happens in less than three minutes, and nevertheless shows no signs of being merely jumbled and arbitrary. Morton's instinct for structural cohesiveness is operating perfectly. Note how the clarinet's Charleston rhythm in A^3 links up with the two-bar turnback phrases (bars nineteen and twenty) in the *B* strains: and the stop-time accompaniment of B^4. Note too how the rhythmic components in A^2 and B^1 are related (see Ex. 4A and 4B).

Example 4 *Black Bottom Stomp*—Motivic Fragments

sense *Black Bottom Stomp* has only two main sections. However, part one—as composed by Morton and as played by the Red Hot Peppers—has three sixteen-bar variants on the same chord progression which are *in effect* new themes. The second of these (for trumpet) even has its own little variation in that bars nine through twelve are a variation of bars one through four. In the Trio section the situation is clearer. There is a single theme to which the cornet, despite occasional embellishments and slight deviations, adheres in all the ensemble choruses of part two (choruses one, six, and seven). Even the cornet's solo chorus refers frequently to the melody and rhythmic elements of the theme. The clarinet, piano, and banjo present new "variations," not on the theme but freely on the chord progression.

Similarly, in segment A^1 there is also an augmentation (Ex. 4C) of the basic rhythmic components shown in Example 4A.

The rhythmic substructure is equally interesting. If we follow the bass of John Lindsay, we can hear how perfectly he alternates the basic two-beat rhythm (2/2) with hard-driving 4/4's on one hand and whole-note single-beat passages on the other. These changes of pace do not occur at phrase junctures, but are apt to break in at any point in the sixteen- and twenty-bar phrases, balancing with and reacting to the soloists and ensembles.

It is this kind of structural cohesion, in the small and in the large, and the control of these elements in a format combining improvisation and pre-arranged outlines, without losing an iota of swing, that make Morton the master of the pure New Orleans style.

Above all, though, it is the playing, the remarkable swing and drive (at a good clip of ♩ = 276), the superb instrumental balances, that ultimately captivate and excite us. Morton contributes a stunning fingers-flying solo, which in that day probably only Hines could have equaled. The three front-liners—Mitchell, Simeon, and Ory—contribute excellent work, following Morton's recipe: "Always give 'em melody with plenty rhythm."

I think a very special lift is given to these 1926 Victor recordings by the string bass of John Lindsay. This raises the question of the bass instruments in early jazz, a problem that has not been dealt with as far as I know. The following remarks are based on the premise that the best bass instrument for swinging is the pizzicato string bass. It has precisely the acoustical "attack and decay" pattern that provides the essence of swing.[39] If we picture the production of a bass pizzicato in

39. We must differentiate here between the way in which a jazz player plucks a bass and the way the average "classical" player does. The latter usually produces a kind of lifeless short thump, while the jazz player, especially today—one need only think of Ray Brown—can produce long "melodic" pizzicato notes in which the decay of tone is prolonged often as much as a whole note in a slow tempo. This is produced by a slightly different playing technique, involving a different right-hand position and (frequently) a change in the height of the bridge.

graphic terms as ⊿⎯⎯ or ⊿⎯⎯ , we see that it contains a sharp rise in tone, a nearly immediate impact that is a prerequisite of precise rhythm and swing. The decay's relation to swing is more complex. A plucked note can not be sustained at the level of its attack; there is bound to be a more or less rapid decay in volume of sound. Given this acoustical fact, the jazz bass player has a much different problem than a "horn" player. In order to fulfill one of the conditions of jazz inflection and jazz swing—namely the full sustaining of pitches (or at least the illusion thereof)—he must perforce create the *illusion* of sustaining the note. The natural, gradual decay pattern of a plucked note helps him to do this, for it *fades* into silence, that is, it does not stop abruptly (graphically: ⊿⎯⎯⎯⎯). It therefore creates the illusion, particularly in long durations, of sustaining through what may in fact be silence. And so it fulfills both the vertical and horizontal prerequisites of swing (as discussed in an earlier chapter), vertical through precise impact, horizontal by sustaining into the next notes and thus providing a forward momentum.

The tuba cannot really duplicate the swing conditions of a bass pizzicato. At best, in the hands of an exceptional player it can create the illusion of a pizzicato. But then we have an illusion of what is already an illusion. In any event tuba players of such extraordinary sensitivity were rare in early jazz. Bass Edwards, Walter Page, and John Kirby came close to producing the kind of rhythmic life a pizzicato gives quite automatically.

I do not wish to discuss at length when and to what extent the string bass was used in New Orleans in pre-recording days. Suffice it to say that photographs of most of the early non-marching ensembles, including even the rare photograph of Buddy Bolden's band, picture a string bass. We also know that both in outdoor functions and in early recordings the tuba was used because of its greater carrying power. And, of course, a number of groups, including Armstrong's Hot Five and Oliver's Creole Jazz Band, frequently used no bass at all, wind or string.

In any event, the string bass in *Black Bottom Stomp* strikes the listener as a revelation. And John Lindsay, a contemporary of Morton and a very experienced player, was one of the best and most advanced players Morton could have employed. Lindsay had a full, centered tone, and a springy strongly swinging beat that combined beautifully with Johnny St. Cyr's banjo. If we add to this well co-ordinated, well-balanced team, the discreet drumming of Andrew Hilaire and, floating above, the lacy melodic descant lines of Morton, we have a rhythm section beautifully integrated in respect not only to rhythm but also to timbre and registral placement. The section provided an airy, subtly swinging rhythmic substructure that contrasted sharply with the often turgid, cumbersome tuba-led rhythm sections of the period.

Black Bottom Stomp would have been a perfect recording but for the ensemble confusion in chorus B^4. Here, evidently, some signals got crossed, for most of the chorus is over by the time the players remember what Morton had rehearsed—not enough, obviously—and what was wanted of them. Despite this flaw *Black Bottom Stomp* was a remarkable beginning.

The other two sides recorded on the same day maintain this standard, or nearly so. *Smoke House Blues* (incidentally, not a blues) is a beautifully planned performance in slow tempo. Although it is probably the extraordinarily warm and moving playing above all that captivates us forty years later, there are many other features worth mentioning. Its improvised ensemble polyphony in the opening and closing choruses is beautifully realized. The players stay out of each other's way and compliment each other perfectly. In fact, these ensembles are as good an example as one can find of how the New Orleans collective improvisation worked. Each of its three registral layers was assigned a specific function. The trumpet, in its middle register, lined out the melody and had the option of embellishing it in rhythms essentially equivalent to the main tempo of the piece. Roughly an octave above, the clarinet provided slightly faster-paced descant embroideries, while below, the trombone functioned in a slower-moving time continuum, participating (at the player's discretion) in either the bass line or tenor counter-lines. Graphically we can depict this structure as

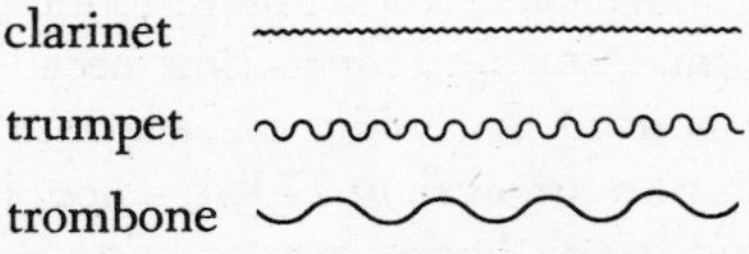

clarinet

trumpet

trombone

But the side's most unusual moment comes when Morton combines his favorite texture-loosening devices: double-time and the break.

Without warning, in the clarinet's solo chorus, Morton doubles the tempo for two bars. Since the basic beat is a leisurely 2/2, the double-time eighth notes of those measures have the real effect of a *doubled* double-time. But Morton tops even this by playing a sixteenth-note line, thereby doubling the tempo once more. Simeon then follows with his two-bar solo break (in double time), easing the tempo back into the slow two-beat feeling. It is a master stroke of rhythmic contrast, and comes precisely at the right moment in the over-all performance.

Morton himself contributes a half-chorus solo which has seemed out of place rhythmically to some observers. But he in fact continues in the already-established rhythmic-melodic vein, and it is the piano's relative lack of presence acoustically and the fact that the rhythm section is quiet that create the impression of inadequacy. This solo contains one of Morton's most imaginative breaks  followed by his exultant shout of self-approbation: "Ah, Mister Jelly." Few moments capture the essentially unpretentious nature and the bitter-sweet humor of jazz so creatively and spontaneously.

Smoke House Blues closes with a coda of three improvised tag-endings which surely must be the prototype *par excellence* of this much-abused device. Remarkably, almost mysteriously, this tag-ending is so perfectly timed and incorporates dead silence so effectively that we are surprised when yet another tag appears, even when we know the recording and are expecting it.

The third side from this date, *The Chant,* was written by the Chicago pianist-arranger Mel Stitzel, but could not be better suited to Morton's conception. As a composition it contained most of Morton's cherished devices: a multithematic form, sudden and interesting harmonic shifts, and riff-like melodies. In addition, these devices were contained in perhaps a more "modernistic," more "hip" form than Morton himself could have conceived. The introduction (Ex. 5) is in a call-and-response format, startling for its time because the call in the clarinet and trumpet is in D flat, while the response is in D natural. At that the call's key is an ambivalent D flat, since, harmonically unaccompanied, it has no strong D flat roots, while on the contrary the trumpet's strong repeated *c*'s tend to emphasize the key of A flat with a curiously "minor" feeling, a diminished fifth away from the succeeding D major phrase. The tonal ambivalence is complemented rhythmically by the syncopated anticipations which obscure the feeling of strong and weak beats, so that only in retrospect do we realize where the first beat of the measure was located (Ex. 5).

Example 5 *The Chant*—Introduction

These rather startling harmonic textural contrasts are precipitously followed by an eight-bar phrase in B flat which, however, continually veers off toward E flat ninth chords or G flat major seventh chords. Thus an interesting over-all harmonic progression evolves (Ex. 6):

Example 6 *The Chant*—Introduction

Key	D♭-D	B♭	E♭9	B♭	G♭maj 7	B♭	E♭9	B♭	D♭	D
Bars	4 - 4	1	1	1	1	1	1	2	4	4

It is only then that the piece settles into its main tonality of A flat, emphasized by a very stationary riff melody and by Morton's use of a pedal-point *a* flat in the bass. But in the third theme the A flat tonality is again disturbed by a sliding chromatic harmonization which was all the rage in the mid-twenties as employed in the popular piano hits of people like Zez Confrey, Rube Bloom, and Louis Alter.

The melodic motive at this point is common property, a phrase we encounter in hundreds of jazz solos and sung blues.[40]

After the third theme has been stated, there follow some well-played solos, including a brilliant Simeon break, his "smeary," blues-y

40. The motive is undoubtedly one of those basic melodic turns whose origins reside in the dim past of early Southern blues, and which, therefore, everyone considered common property. The phrase was not only used consistently by Oliver, Armstrong, and Sidney Bechet in their solos—it appears on the Henderson recording of Oliver's *Snag It*—but also is one of the main themes of James P. Johnson's extended "symphonic poem" *Yamekraw*, composed in 1927, and of the popular 1920s standard *Copenhagen*.

solo, and a rare tenor banjo solo by St. Cyr. Ory comes to grief in his solo, evidently misreading his part by skipping two bars in the changes. But Morton more than recovers in the succeeding piano solo and the closing high-flying ensemble choruses.

Everyone, including the Victor Company, evidently thought these three sides were a great success, because six days later we find Morton with an enlarged crew back in the studio. But this time it was agreed to do three "hokum" sides, which meant spoken introductions from old minstrel or vaudeville routines, funny sound effects like automobile horns, steamboat whistles, church bells, and the like. In saying that these three sides do not come up to the level of the previous date I do not wish to imply that they are less good because of the "hokum" trappings, although it is quite possible that Morton, his publisher Melrose, and the recording director were somewhat distracted by these extramusical considerations. In any event, though the sides are superior and perhaps even better-than-average Morton, none go beyond what Morton had already accomplished six days earlier.

Dead Man Blues is certainly the best of the three, although I think it has been overrated by some writers. As in *Smoke House Blues,* its opening and closing choruses are excellent improvised polyphony.[41] But the high point of the side is undoubtedly the clarinet trio, a quiet, simple riff-like melody scored in close harmony for three clarinets—Morton's bow to Don Redman (the "inventor" of the clarinet trio) and to a non–New Orleans "modern" idea. When repeated, an almost tender, blues-y trombone obbligato slides in underneath the clarinets. It results in the kind of quiet beauty Ellington used to such advantage a few years later.

In December 1926 Morton cut five more sides, of very mixed quality, ranging all the way from an insipidly banal *Someday Sweetheart* to the highly successful *Grandpa's Spells,* one of Morton's most original ragtime-*cum*-stomp pieces. In its orchestrational variety *Grandpa's Spells* surpasses even *Black Bottom Stomp*. Again, with only seven instruments at his disposal, Morton squeezes out eight instrumental-timbral combinations: full septet; open trumpet and rhythm; muted

41. Incidentally, it may be a small point but in his monograph *Jelly Roll Morton* Martin Williams errs when he calls the closing chorus the "third appearance of the third theme" when in reality it is a varied "recapitulation" of the first theme (p. 69).

trumpet and rhythm; clarinet and rhythm (three times); trombone and bass; bass alone; guitar alone; piano, banjo, drums (without bass). In the outline (Ex. 7) we can see how these combinations do not occur merely in chorus-by-chorus alternation but are broken down into two- and four-bar phrases.

Example 7 *Grandpa's Spells*—Scheme

Structural divisions	Intro.	A^1				A^2	
Instrumentation	Full	Gtr. (low. reg.)	Full (impr.)	Gtr. (Piano embell.)	Full (impr.)	Tpt.	Full (impr.)
Number of bars	4	4	4	4	4	4	4

		B^1			B^2			A^3					
Tpt.	Full (impr.)	Full	Piano (break)	Full	Clar.	Clar. (break)	Clar.	Trb.	Bass	Full	Trb.	Bass (Piano)	Full
4	4	6	2	8	6	2	8	2	2	4	2	2	4

C^1	C^2	C^3		C^4	Coda
Tpt.	Clar. (2-beat, partly 4-beat)	Piano (2-beat)	Clar.	Full	Gtr. (like A^1)
		no bass	no bass		
16	16	8	8	16	2
p		*mp*		*f*	

Further interest and variety are provided by Morton's piano interpolations—little runs, embellishments, and single chords—as behind the guitar and trumpet in A^1 and A^2. Note how, also in A^2, Mitchell in his second solo entrance inverts the phrase he played the first time. Morton also dares to contrast strong dynamics played by a few instruments with soft dynamics played by many. This we can hear in the hard-swinging trombone and bass exchange of A^3 relieved by the soft muted solo of C^1. The reverse dynamic contrast occurs at C^3 and C^4, where the former acts as a "set-up" for the final out-chorus. Furthermore, C^3 has a curiously suspended feeling, in that Lindsay's bass does not play behind either the piano or the clarinet. This, of course, heightens the contrast when Lindsay does return in a strong, swinging final collective improvisation.

Almost as successful is *Original Jelly Roll Blues,* which receives a well-integrated, happily jogging performance. *Doctor Jazz* is notable for its breaks, some of them duet and some of them ensemble. *Cannon Ball Blues,* somewhat uneven, may have been insufficiently rehearsed, as it was the last side cut that day.

To discuss the remaining *Peppers* recordings in detail would be to repeat much of the foregoing, and this in connection with performances that are rarely up to Morton's previous standards. In 1927 another "hokum" date, with laughing hyena and goat imitations, as well as a *Jungle Blues* which even Morton could not save; and then some half a dozen dates followed between 1927 and 1929. All in all, twenty-odd sides were produced, but none of these ever attained the perfection of the 1926 recordings. There are partial successes like *Kansas City Stomps* or *Georgia Swing,* but for the most part Morton seems to have lost his touch. Many of the records are corn-laden curiosities and period pieces. For reasons no longer discernible, Morton chose to go back to the tuba in 1927, and, as I have implied earlier, this factor negatively influences the potential or actual swing of all the succeeding sides. This despite the fact that the tuba players were excellent; indeed on one of the later New York dates the tuba player, Harry Prather, is clearly the best musician on the date. Still there are distinctions to be made in tracing the pattern of the *Red Hot Peppers'* demise. The first New York date in 1928 (*Kansas City Stomps, Georgia Swing*) retains much of the New Orleans-transposed-to-Chicago feeling. But the next three dates in July 1929 show a marked deterioration as Morton succumbs to a "more modern" band instrumentation and conception: three brass, four saxophones, and rhythm, usually scored in harmony and unimprovised, with a personnel that was very uneven and that in any case had a different orientation from Morton's. Clearly this was not Morton's cup of tea. But he obviously felt that he must keep up with the new trends, with the "solo" approach, with the just developing "big band" era of Henderson and Ellington. Symptomatic of his change are the publicity photographs which show Morton with a baton in hand, fronting the band à la Paul Whiteman, with one Rod Rodriguez substituting as pianist. (Almost all the inept piano solos on these sides are, of course, by Rodriguez, not Morton. It is both sad and funny to hear Rodriguez trying several times to imitate one of Morton's right-hand breaks, which the latter had obviously taught his protégé.) In any case the results on the Camden sides mark the nadir of Morton's recording activity.

The next date (November 1929) produced much better results, for Morton returned to a smaller, conventional New Orleans instrumentation and a string bass. The three "horns" (Red Allen, J. C. Higginbotham, and Albert Nicholas), however, were young Turks weaned on Louis Armstrong's more "up-to-date" stylings, and the result is at best a kind of compromise Dixieland, at worst a real discrepancy between Morton's rhythmic conception and theirs. Such stylistic discrepancies also riddle the still later recordings (1930). Occasionally, on particular sides, where Morton has more or less given up the polyphonic approach for a string-of-solos conception, a soloist's individual talents will provide a ray of light, as do Bubber Miley's two solos on *Little Lawrence* and *Pontchartrain Blues,* Sandy Williams's almost "boppish" trombone on *Fickle Fay Creep,* Morton's playing on *Harmony Blues,* which suggests the rhythmic freedom of Erroll Garner of nearly twenty years later, and the bass clarinet solo of Eddie Barefield on *If Someone Would Only Love Me.* And when the soloists understood each other, as on the July 14, 1930, date with a front line of Ward Pinkett, Geechy Fields, and Albert Nicholas, the result could be as good as on *Blue Blood Blues,* which in its quiet way anticipates the style and quality of many a small-band date of the later thirties.

Fickle Fay Creep, the last of the Red Hot Peppers recordings, marked the beginning of a nine-year hiatus in Morton's recording activity (leaving aside the 1938 Library of Congress records). The almost straight decline from the heyday recordings of *Black Bottom Stomp* to *Fickle* can only be understood against the background of rapidly changing styles and the relocation of jazz in New York that was taking place in the late twenties. And perhaps Martin Williams is right when he says that Morton "had too much taste and insight merely to repeat and decorate, to reiterate and complicate what he had already done. It was time to try other things."[42] But, now in his mid-forties, these "other things" were evidently beyond his reach. Like many before and after, Morton had to cede the field to others. But before he did so entirely, he left us at least two great monuments to himself and the particular kind of jazz he loved and preached: his

42. Hentoff and McCarthy, p. 79.

Library of Congress memoirs and the best of the Red Hot Peppers recordings.

We cannot pass over Morton's trio and quartet sides, for they contain at least one gem, the 1928 *Mournful Serenade,* and several other pieces worthy of Morton's name. While still in Chicago and during the hey-day of the kazoo, Morton was impelled to use this unfortunate "instrument," and it all but mars the 1924 and 1925 small-group sides. However, beneath the out-of-tune hooting, we can pick out some worthy musical moments. The kazoo on *My Gal* is particularly obnoxious since it operates in the same register as the clarinet, totally obscuring Volly de Faut's excellent pre-Benny Goodman style of playing. De Faut's talents are heard to better advantage on *Wolverine Blues,* where the kazoo is mercifully absent. In fact, this duet side is surprisingly good for its time (1925). Morton and de Faut respond well to each other, displaying a fairly high level of harmonic and rhythmic rapport. De Faut's three choruses are each confined to a different register, and Morton, who could rarely be satisfied with merely bland "accompaniments," shows his empathy to the clarinetist's relatively sophisticated and disciplined approach. In the final moments, the two players achieve a degree of unity without sacrificing individual freedom—the essence of heterophony—that clearly foreshadows the celebrated Hines-Armstrong duets of 1928.

No kazoos mar the later small-group recordings. A trio date with the Dodds brothers produced some lovely, intimate music (*Wolverine Blues* and *Mr. Jelly Lord*), with Johnny Dodds in his best form. He is rhythmically relaxed, and plays with a dark, sandy tone that contrasts strikingly with the bright, harder-driving clarinet of Omer Simeon, usually heard on Morton recordings. The small instrumentation of these sides also provides us with an acoustically uncluttered opportunity to study Morton's approach to accompaniment, with its long melodic lines, its unerring sense of where to back up or fill in, its striving to emulate the orchestra, and its unusual ability to find the balance between what is accompaniment and what at the same time is soloistically independent.[43]

But the crowning achievement of the small-group recordings is the

43. On the negative side, these small-group recordings also expose Morton's tendency to rush tempos, and both drummers, Baby Dodds and Tommy Benford, can be heard valiantly trying to hold the tempo, not always successfully.

Mournful Serenade date of 1928. Simeon is back on clarinet, and delivers the kind of disciplined stylistically flexible playing Morton knew how to deal with so well. Two sides (*Shreveport Stomp* and *Mournful Serenade*) were recorded at the end of one of the Red Hot Peppers dates, which up to that point had not produced anything really outstanding. Both titles show how wide Morton's stylistic range was, and how well he could produce within the total breadth of this range. *Shreveport Stomp* harks back to the march-like ragtime music of an earlier era, whereas *Mournful Serenade* is the kind of blues-y piece Ellington was to perfect a few years later with *Mood Indigo*. (It is even possible that Ellington may have known *Mournful Serenade* and expanded on one of its ideas.) *Shreveport Stomp* was flashy for its time, and part of its "hipness" came from a chorus in which both players modulate wildly in abrupt measure-to-measure harmonic shifts: D^7 | G min | E^7 | A | $G^\flat$ | $D^\flat$ etc. (The piece is in B flat.) This is the kind of playing around with key centers jazz musicians started to do in the twenties, mostly as a novelty, and they still do today on tunes like *Tea for Two*.

For *Mournful Serenade* the trio was augmented to a quartet by the addition of Geechy Fields, a trombonist with a minor reputation who was, however, in excellent form that day. Just a simple blues, the piece is planned out and carried off in a manner on a level with the best of the Red Hot Peppers recordings. Morton—not the full ensemble—sets the mood, accompanied only by drums. There follow clarinet and trombone choruses which perfectly sustain the established mood. Morton now turns back the clock a few years by paying tribute to Oliver's *Chimes Blues* and a *fin de siècle* nostalgia, which in turn becomes the perfect foil for the next chorus in which clarinet and trombone accompany Morton with sustained organ-like sounds. The final chorus breaks out into polyphony, and the interplay of the four musicians, the placing and timing of double-time suggestions and of Morton's sudden brilliant right-hand run in thirds, the wonderful clarity of the polyphony—all these make *Mournful Serenade* a minor masterpiece.

A discussion of Jelly Roll Morton would be incomplete without some mention of his solo piano recordings. Some of these were piano rolls and, therefore, quite inaccurate representations, since they blur one of Morton's unique qualities, his pianistic touch. Fortunately he recorded a great deal as piano soloist, and most of his pieces exist in several versions, even aside from the Library of Congress recordings.

Jazz being primarily an instrumental *ensemble* music, few people realize that the unaccompanied solo piano as it exists in the classical field is an extreme rarity in jazz; and jazz pianists who qualify in this category are, even today, limited to a select few. Nor are the reasons for this generally understood. A jazz pianist who is going to perform unaccompanied must in effect fulfill three functions simultaneously: he must play a melody or some form of a leading line; he must provide an underlying harmony; and he must also be his own rhythm section and bass line. This is not as easy as it may sound, and it explains why there always have been many piano-bass-drums trios in jazz. In the early days particularly, this pianistic triple-function was even more difficult to achieve because the roles of melody, harmony, and bass were more conventionally standardized and specified in respect to register. A melody had to be in the upper register, harmony had to be in the middle register, and the bass roots had not only to be in the bass register but, because of the simplicity of harmonic thinking, had to be very clearly stated. It is obvious that to encompass all these functions, three hands would be a lot better than two. One may ask why the "classical" piano tradition did not encounter this same problem. There are at least three basic reasons: first, one of the major traditions in "classical" piano adhered to an essentially polyphonic conception (inventions, fugues, canons). Secondly, the homophonic branch of the "classical" tradition never confined itself to rigid conventions in respect to range and contours. And perhaps the most important reason is that "classical" piano was never as concerned with stating the steady, explicit "beat" of the music as was jazz. The beat in "classical" music, even in strict tempo pieces—and leaving aside the whole question of rubato in the romantic literature—was and is much more implied than explicitly stated. This removed the necessity for at least one of the three above-mentioned functions, and hence for one of the three hands.

The jazz pianist, given two hands and the rather rigorous allocation of the three functions, must perforce combine all three or compromise in some way. The left-hand stride piano 

brought into jazz from ragtime was the earliest compromise answer. It was also a translation into pianistic terms of the down-beat after-beat rhythms of march music. This left-hand technique produced the bass roots (X in the musical example), the harmony (Y), and both combined, providing the rhythmic structure against which the right hand could now play, embellish, and improvise. Obviously a trio which uses bass and drums relieves the pianist of having to plunk out the chord roots and to line out the rhythmic beat. As will be seen in Volume II, the whole development of jazz piano reflects a gradual realignment and liberation of the three functions described above.

The old ragtime pianists, of course, grew up with that particular discipline and, within the stylistic confines of ragtime, developed it to a high order of sophistication and virtuosity. Morton was no exception, and in so far as he rhythmically rounded off the edges of ragtime to produce jazz (to oversimplify momentarily), he carried the triple-level function of ten fingers to a temporary zenith. There is no better proof than the piano solos Morton recorded for the Gennett label in Richmond, Indiana, in 1923 and 1924.

Today it is difficult to get musicians, especially young people, to listen to older jazz, particularly piano music. It is easy to see that they are put off by the unrelieved "oom-pah" of the left hand, the rigid ragtime syncopations, and the frequent melodic clichés. This is understandable in view of the stereotyped image of ragtime as a zany, cornball novelty music, an inaccurate image perpetuated by the silent films, by vaudeville and, to be sure, by certain mediocre ragtime practitioners who capitalized on its show-business aspects. But at its best, the early jazz piano of Morton, Hines, and Weatherford is well worth listening to, especially if one is willing to dig below the stylistic (and acoustic) exterior, and is prepared to listen critically and analytically. The treasures in these recordings do not reveal themselves in a once-over superficial listening.

The six solo sides Morton recorded in 1923 are of unerringly high quality, technically as well as conceptually. In them Morton is the complete master of the three structural levels already discussed. Morton's playing is clean and swings well. And anyone who doubts Morton's role as catalyst in the metamorphosis from ragtime piano to jazz should compare his 1923 recordings of *King Porter Stomp* and *New Orleans Joys* to those of most other pianists of the day or to the best of the ragtime players. The difference in swing content is striking.

These 1923 sides are notable too for the richness of Morton's harmonic voicings. As one listens one has the impression that Morton was hearing big brass chords or full-voiced ensembles, and was stretching his fingers to emulate this orchestral vision. Compared to his contemporaries, Morton had an uncommonly sensitive ear to chord balances as they relate to register, tempo, and, of course, the melody they accompany. Related to this is Morton's sensitive touch, which never is forced, even in the strong final choruses. These qualities can be heard to best advantage in the lovely sustained chords of the Trio of *Kansas City Stomps*.

Morton generally keeps good time on these solo recordings. There is very little of the tempo-rushing we encounter occasionally on the ensemble sides. And on one piece, *New Orleans Joys,* Morton experiments with a bimetric and birhythmic independence of the two hands that has confounded many a jazz critic, and is, I dare say, the first recorded example of the kind of "between-the-cracks" rhythm that Erroll Garner has exploited so masterfully since the mid-forties.

An absolutely precise notation of the passage in question is probably not possible, or if possible, so complex in notation as to be virtually unreadable. However, a very close translation which reflects Morton's intentions is given below (Ex. 8):

Example 8. *New Orleans Joys*

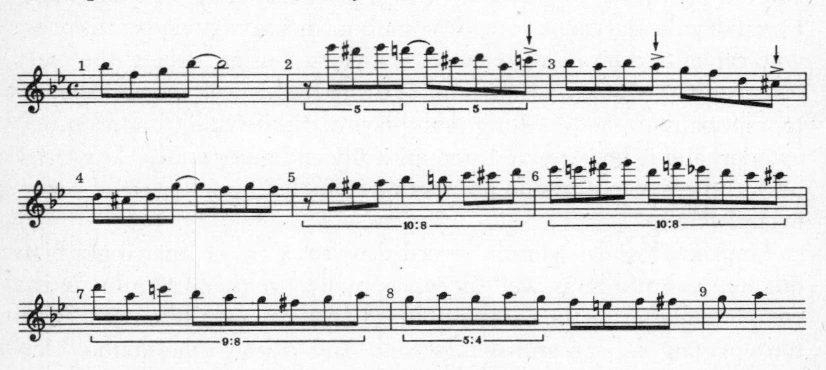

Obviously Morton was not floundering rhythmically,[44] as some critics

44. We must rule out the possibility of Morton faltering, since his left hand retains the steady "Spanish tinge" Habañera beat, and after eight bars the two hands meet again in musical confluence.

have vaguely suggested. He is simply trying to bifurcate the music into separate tempo levels, the kind of idea Morton's contemporary Charles Ives explored so thoroughly in dozens of works. In the second measure of the passage in question, Morton contracts the tempo of the right hand in such a way as to be roughly 1/10 (or one quintuplet eighth) ahead of the left hand. The melody if played conventionally would read as follows (Ex. 9):

Example 9

Shifted rhythmically ahead it falls between the beats. It is interesting to note that within the contracted right-hand tempo Morton tried to preserve the loping triplet feeling inherent in the New Orleans style. This we see in the durationally longer *f* natural (in measure two, Ex. 8) and in the extra length (not reflected in the notation) of the eighth-note rest at the beginning of the measure. Thus, what Morton was really trying to play within the 10-over-8 contraction was:

Example 10

That the result is not accidental is borne out clearly by Morton's accentuation of the line. The accents at ↓ in Example 8 are displaced down beats, which the reader may recognize as being distant relatives of the African cross-rhythms discussed in Chapter 1.

In measure five (Ex. 8) Morton starts a second out-of-tempo phrase, a long, arching line which takes four measures to complete and hitches up again with the main tempo and melody in measure nine. What makes this entire passage even more remarkable is that Morton's left hand is not playing a straight 4/4, but the Habañera (or Charleston) rhythm, which is in itself an unequal-beat pattern. Morton was on to something here which, except for Erroll Garner, was not again seriously explored by jazz musicians until the sixties, and then in a more arhythmic than polyrhythmic sense.

Jelly Roll Morton's place in jazz is still a matter of controversy. It is the same kind of controversy jazz itself has generated within the world of the arts. For it feeds on the confrontation of Morton the man, the "character," with Morton the musician; just as the social origin of jazz and its consistently anti-establishmentarian position in our society (unsolicited, to be sure) have sustained the various prejudices regarding jazz, while its musical virtues have been largely ignored or misunderstood. If we can forget the legend and concentrate on the music, it becomes clear that Morton's role in the development of jazz is a crucial one. And the evidence for this we can still find today in the musical record he left us, incomplete though it is, since it excludes the first twenty years of his career.

His importance can perhaps best be measured by criteria applicable to every great artist: the balance between his failures and his successes. For Morton's failures are interesting and minor failures, based as they were not on errors of conception, but rather on errors of circumstance. His successes, however, were profound and unique within the context of pre-1930s jazz. Morton's misfortune was that his successes came too late. Because of circumstances, Morton's contribution to jazz was disseminated at a time when a new generation was already converting an entertainment music into an art music. This step would not have happened—or at least not in quite the same way—without Jelly Roll Morton's superior groundwork.

5

Virtuoso Performers of the Twenties

With the rapid spread of jazz in the 1920s, many minor and major figures were drawn to the new jazz idiom and its lucrative opportunities. The musicians and groups discussed in this chapter have in most cases very little in common except that they represented, in one way or another, the performer elite of their time. As the lesser "major" figures of the twenties, they were, along with Armstrong and Morton, the musicians who influenced the future course of jazz or produced music of such enduring beauty and power that they still warrant our attention today. While not on the level of Armstrong or Morton, they were nevertheless influential leaders on their instruments or influential in spreading new ensemble conceptions.

The inclusion of the Original Dixieland Jazz Band may surprise some readers. But in my view this group has rarely been properly evaluated. It has been exaggeratedly denigrated, and because the ODJB was a white group, many have found it difficult to accord it the recognition it deserves. Others have, of course, wildly overrated the group and have tried to give the impression that it developed without benefit of any Negro influence, entirely out of its own creative resources.[1] Neither faction seems to have taken the trouble to listen dis-

1. Such is the case in H. O. Brunn's book, *The Story of the Original Dixieland Jazz Band* (Baton Rouge: Louisiana State University Press, 1960). Although it is excellently researched in some respects, particularly those that emphasize the absolute primacy of the group, it consistently avoids mention of Negro New Orleans musicians. Bunk Johnson and Freddie Keppard or the

passionately to the ODJB recordings. Their historic importance as the "first jazz recordings ever" makes objective listening understandably difficult. But beneath all the controversy regarding the band's musical pre-eminence, their historical primacy, and the color of their skin, there lies a purely acoustical factual record.

The career of the ODJB was both as fantastic and as typical as any that jazz has had to offer. Its story features the inevitable high points: the gradual grouping together of basically self-taught musicians, their sudden catapulting to world-wide fame, their equally sudden demise, and, in between, the million dollar law suits over copyrights and the petty jealousies, alcoholism, premature deaths, and all the rest.[2]

The controversy over the music of the ODJB in its heyday—the only recent parallel that comes to mind is the initial controversy over the Beatles—was nurtured by many extra-musical factors. There was to begin with the very term *jazz,* only a few years earlier an obscene expression current in red-light districts. Then there was the novelty of the music, its unprecedented exuberance and unabashed vulgarity (certainly as compared to the polite music that was played in Northern cabarets and dance halls prior to the appearance of the ODJB). Another factor was the rapid changes in the social scene resulting from the First World War, for it seems that the ODJB, rather than having precipitated those changes by its music, came along at precisely the right moment to benefit from and to articulate them. Finally we must understand that American musical sophistication in 1917 was sufficiently low to allow the ODJB's trombonist Edward B. Edwards to make, unchallenged, statements to reporters such as: "None of us know music." (This was not true, particularly of Edwards, who read music and was well-trained on his instrument.) "Jazz, I think, means jumble." Jazz is "the untuneful harmony of rhythm."[3] In an age when

---

Excelsior and Onward brass bands are not mentioned once. Armstrong makes only one appearance and then only to be quoted out of context in order to underscore the illusion that the ODJB was almost the only band in New Orleans and the "first great jazz orchestra." In Nick La Rocca's formative years, 1910 to 1912, the Eagle Band, Oscar Celestin, cornetists Bunk Johnson, King Oliver, Freddie Keppard, Tig Chambers, and Manuel Perez were all playing in Storyville, and it is hardly possible that La Rocca never heard any of these early jazz greats.

2. See ibid.

3. *Ragtime Review,* June 1917.

music, even jazz music, was taken seriously by only a very small minority, La Rocca's description of "how jazz works," namely, "I cut the material, Shields puts on the lace, and Edwards sews it up,"[4] hit just the right non-intellectual mark. It was an age when "public relations" was just coming into its own, and "jazz" was a press agent's dream come true. Journalists, eagerly aided by the members of the ODJB, outdid each other in describing the virtues and hazards of listening to the band, often stretching poetic license and "musical criticism" to the breaking point, as when a cub reporter claimed to have heard "violins snicker and shriek" and likened the band to "a chorus of hunting hounds on the scent, with an occasional explosion in the subway thrown in for good measure."[5]

Before we deal with the ODJB's recordings, we must explore the musical background of the group. It is safe to say that Nick La Rocca was its leader and musical spark, although clarinetist Larry Shields was in some ways its most sensitive musician. La Rocca, born into an Italian immigrant family, was initially reared on the light fare of the Old French Opera and on Sousa marches. His first "professional" jobs as a teenager were, however, not with brass bands, as one might expect, but with neighborhood groups featuring mostly a violin or two, guitar, and string bass. His first band (in 1908) consisted of the basic small-band group already prevalent in New Orleans: cornet, clarinet, trombone, and rhythm. What this band played was, of course, ragtime. La Rocca was then a part-time musician and a non-reading "faker." It wasn't until some years later that he was skilled enough to join some of the larger brass bands, like Braun's Military Band and, in 1914, Jack "Papa" Laine's various parade bands.

Laine, a drummer, was the most popular white musician in New Orleans, and many brass players of La Rocca's generation passed through the bands (marching, concert, circus, ragtime) that Laine led or hired out. By 1910 these bands had converted almost entirely from French and German marching music to ragtime pieces like Joplin's *Shadow Rag, Maple Leaf Rag,* and old stand-bys like *Praline* (or *No. 2 Rag*) and *Meat Ball.* The latter two when later appropriated by the ODJB became known as *Tiger Rag* and *Livery Stable Blues* (or *Barnyard Blues*) respectively, and there is no question that La Rocca

4. As quoted variously in numerous sources, including Brunn, p. 23.
5. Ibid., p. 55.

and other white musicians picked these tunes up in their apprenticeship with Laine[6] and through listening to the dozens of Negro bands that paraded in New Orleans at every opportunity.

By 1915 New Orleans was bursting with so much jazz music (although it was not yet called jazz) that inevitably out-of-town promoters discovered it and imported it to cities like Chicago. Actually the new music was not unknown in Chicago, for Bill Johnson's Original Creole Band (with Freddie Keppard), cornetist Tig Chambers and Sugar Johnny Smith, trombonist Roy Palmer, not to mention pianists Tony Jackson and Jelly Roll Morton—New Orleans musicians to a man—had all been through Chicago at one time or another. In fact, it is reported that Tom Brown's Band from Dixieland was imported to Chicago to replace Johnson's Creoles. In any event, New Orleans was overflowing with musicians, and the extreme competition made a musical living precarious. Chicago, on the other hand, offered a new territory. Within a few years many New Orleans groups, including the white imitators of Creole and Negro jazz like Tom Brown's Band and in 1916 the ODJB, replaced the sedate string ensembles in the Loop and South Side entertainment palaces of Chicago.

In New York Keppard and the Creoles had not been a real success. Since the ODJB played a music similar to that of Keppard's or Sugar Johnny's aggregations, what made this group such a sensation in New York in 1917? And why did the ODJB not make a comparable splash in Chicago one year earlier? In the first place, the ODJB was a more than average success in Chicago, so much so that word of the group reached New York entertainment circles through visiting show-business personalities such as Al Jolson. It succeeded, after all, where Tom

6. Both Bunk Johnson and Arnold Loyacano, a white guitarist and bass player in Tom Brown's Band, the first white New Orleans band to travel to Chicago (in 1915), confirmed that *No. 2* was a staple of the white bands' repertoire (see Nat Shapiro and Nat Hentoff, eds., *Hear Me Talkin' to Ya: The Story of Jazz by the Men Who Made It* [New York: Rinehart & Company, 1955], pp. 36, 81). It is one of the sad stories of jazz history that a few years later, several of these white musicians would be engaged in legal squabbles over copyrights to these anonymous tunes, whose ownership, if any could be claimed at all, could have been contested by any number of older Negro musicians like Buddy Bolden and Bunk Johnson. Another irony that might give pause to the white supremacy theorists in jazz was the fact that two of Jack Laine's regular musicians, Achille Baquet and trombone player Dave Perkins, were very light-colored Negroes.

Brown's Band had not. On the other hand, one can be certain that the ODJB was still developing—during the Chicago year the clarinetist Alcide Nunez was replaced by Larry Shields—and that the band did not hit its full stride until the end of the year. In other words, the qualities which set it apart from other groups were worked out during the Chicago period when it was able to work consistently, to rehearse and to play to an increasingly demanding audience. I am certain that the initially rather rough polyphony of the group was refined during the Chicago period[7] and that the one element that set the ODJB apart from all other groups, namely its frenetic drive and capacity for playing pieces at much faster tempos than was then common, was developed during this time.

This in turn provides the answer for at least part of the first question above. James Reese Europe's group and others had provided New York with exciting music. But it had never heard anything quite as frantic and lively as the music of the ODJB at Reisenweber's. Nor had New York made as much contact with other New Orleans musicians, white or black, as Chicago had. The seemingly uncontrolled polyphony of the ODJB was a radically new phenomenon in New York music after years of concentration on simple melodies and even simpler accompaniments. Furthermore, the barnyard hokum the band sometimes used attracted much extra-musical attention. In fact, the arrival of the ODJB in New York coincided with a "shift in popular dancing away . . . from gentility, ballroom decorum and elegance of motion to a franker, jerkier, faster and snappier kind of dance; and in cabarets and on the vaudeville circuits . . . a persistent vogue for 'barnyard hokum' "[8] and "novelty" sounds. Finally, the color lines were undoubtedly still drawn so clearly as to make a similar success for a comparable Negro group impossible.

The ODJB reduced New Orleans Negro music to a simplified for-

7. In this connection it is worth quoting Brunn's outrageous claim that "at this time" (1916) the ODJB's "distinctive brand of counterpoint that was to be a distinguishing feature of jazz was unfamiliar to New Orleans musicians" (p. 24).

8. From album notes for Jazz Odyssey, Vol. 1, *The Sound of New Orleans,* Columbia Records C3L 30, by Frederic Ramsey, Jr., and Frank Driggs. Farmyard imitations were not new, having been popular "musical" fare for many years. The vogue was initiated by an opus called *Farmyard Caprice* in which the musicians were required to imitate literally every farmyard animal. The piece was a tremendous hit and was recorded by every big concert band in 1912.

mula. It took a new idea, an innovation, and reduced it to the kind of compressed, rigid format that could appeal to a mass audience. As such it had a number of sure-fire ingredients, the foremost being a rhythmic momentum that had a physical, even visceral, appeal. Moreover, this rhythmic drive was cast in the most unsubtle terms, as was the ODJB's melodic and harmonic language, with none of the flexibility and occasional subtlety shown by the best Negro bands of the period. But in its rigid substitution of sheer energy for expressive power, of rigid formula for inspiration, the ODJB had found the key to mass appeal.

It is typical of the kind of nonsense perpetrated in the name of jazz in those early days that La Rocca and the other members of the ODJB could claim they could not read music and that therefore their playing was *ipso facto* freshly improvised and inspired during each performance, when in truth their recordings show without exception exact repetitions of choruses and a great deal of memorization. On the one hand La Rocca and Edwards kept bombarding the public with such provocative statements as, "I don't know how many pianists we tried before we found one who couldn't read music."[9] On the other hand their playing belied the myth of total anarchy such statements were designed to create. Contrary to being improvised, these choruses were set and rehearsed, and they were unchanged for years, as the recordings of *Sensation Rag* and *Tiger Rag* made in 1919 in England prove beyond a doubt. In the former piece, in both the New York and London recordings, the format is exactly the same: *AABBCCBABCB,* with each second and third *A, B,* or *C* section being an exact repetition.

The ODJB thus did not actually improvise. In fact, the only player who tried to vary his playing was the drummer, Tony Sbarbaro. Not only did he vary his choruses from performance to performance, but within a piece he achieved considerable variety by the clever use of a large collegtion of drums, cowbells, woodblocks, and cymbals. Sbarbaro's versatility contrasts notably with the other players' limitations. For example, La Rocca's range was only about an octave and his rhythmic ideas were also limited. On the other hand, in his simple way he showed more rhythmic drive than any of his colleagues except Sbarbaro. Occasionally La Rocca even swings a phrase, especially synco-

9. As quoted in Frederic Ramsey, Jr., and Charles Edward Smith, eds., *Jazzmen* (New York: Harcourt, Brace and Company, 1939), p. 51.

pated "lead-in" phrases, and it must be said that he and Sbarbaro together constituted the motor power of the band. Edwards was comparatively rigid in his melodic and rhythmic ideas, although it is doubtful that other trombonists of the period were much better. And Edwards could on occasion produce some fairly snappy counterlines, as on *Clarinet Marmalade*. The latter was, of course, Larry Shields's famous vehicle, and shows his liquid, lithe tone to particularly good advantage. Henry Ragas, the pianist, died just before the band left for London in 1918. It is hard to evaluate his work because of poor presence on the 1917-18 acoustical recordings, but he seems to have been a clean and sensitive player.

The ODJB's most famous recording, their legendary million-dollar record—it outsold even Sousa and Caruso—was *Livery Stable Blues,* also known as *Barnyard Blues.*[10] William Russell and Stephen W. Smith, in their chapter on New Orleans music in *Jazzmen,* claimed that Freddie Keppard first played *Barnyard Blues,* although they offered no substantiation.[11] Beyond the authorship of the tune proper, there is, of course, a similar question in regard to the barnyard breaks which really made that piece the enormous hit it was. Again the ODJB claimed the three animal effects—the whinnying horse, the crowing rooster, and the braying donkey—to be their own invention. Preston Jackson, however, recounted that Joe Oliver used to take breaks "imitating a rooster and a baby. . . . The La Rocca boys of the Dixieland Jazz Band used to hang around and got a lot of ideas from his gang."[12] Furthermore, any brass player knows that half-valve or three-quarter-valve sounds on a piston instrument will readily produce a great variety of animal onomatopoeia. These sounds are discovered by every beginning student when he fails to press the valve-keys down fully, or when a valve gets stuck. It is therefore presumptuous of La Rocca to claim that he was the first to produce such sounds and incorporate them in a tune.

The barnyard hokum sounds were, as already stated, one of the main attractions for the ODJB's audiences in Chicago and New York. Nevertheless, many critics have exaggerated the place these effects

10. See the story of the lawsuit regarding this tune in Brunn, pp. 75-87. Brunn compounds the confusion by stating flatly that La Rocca composed *Livery Stable Blues* in 1912.

11. Ramsey and Smith, p. 30.

12. Shapiro and Hentoff, p. 42.

occupied in the music of the ODJB. Actually, it was the band's imitators, like Earl Fuller or the Louisiana Five, who made a fetish out of these corny effects and thereby stigmatized the new "jazz" in a particularly unfortunate manner. The ODJB was comparatively moderate in its use of barnyard sounds, again partly because the players' instrumental techniques were too limited to work out more than two or three of these effects, which they were content to repeat exactly within a performance or indeed from performance to performance.

The ODJB rose quickly, and fell almost as fast; by 1924 the group had passed into history. But even before that the thin veneer of its musical content had begun to wear away. Unlike jazz in general and many Negro musicans in particular, the ODJB was not able to absorb into its style the new popular songs coming out of Tin Pan Alley *en masse* in the early twenties. This is clearly shown by its very first record date for Columbia in 1917.[13] and the later 1920 to 1922 recordings, in which, under the pressure of recording executives, the group was forced to record songs foreign to its limited repertory. The result was a music caught between Dixieland and dance music. The players were unable to cope with the ensemble problem of stating and adhering to the published melody. The collisions of "contrapuntal" lines in the later recordings are embarrassing, especially when the group was forced to add an alto saxophone, although there really was no place for it in the ODJB's simple polyphonic structure. The beat, the drive, the almost immature nervous energy—in other words, the very ingredients that distinguished the playing of the band—were suppressed in the later records. These were hardly more than commercial fox-trot renditions.

Still, in a balanced assessment of the ODJB, its best recordings, like *Sensation Rag, Clarinet Marmalade, Dixie Jazz One Step,* and *Livery Stable Blues,* were an infuriating mixture of bad and good, of tasteless vulgarity and good musical intuitions. But beyond the music the ODJB left behind, it held, for better and for worse, a crucial place in the formative period of jazz. It fulfilled the role in a manner that was not altogether unworthy.

Parenthetically, it would not be fair to leave the ODJB without brief mention of some of the group's competitors. Perhaps the closest

13. One side, *At the Darktown Strutters' Ball,* was reissued in Columbia's Jazz Odyssey, Vol. 1, *The Sound of New Orleans,* C3L 30, side 1, track 7.

of these in some respects was Jimmy Durante's Original New Orleans Jazz Band. In 1917 Durante was a ragtime piano player and, as an enthusiastic admirer of the ODJB, was determined also to—in his own famous words—"get into the act." Upon La Rocca's advice he imported from New Orleans two of the better players still left there, Frank Christian (cornet) and the light-skinned Negro clarinetist Achille Baquet. To complete the personnel Durante added Johnny Stein (drums) and Frank Lotak (trombone). All except Lotak had been prominent members of the white New Orleans tradition. Stein, Baquet, and Christian all had come out of the Jack Laine school, and Stein and Christian had led their own bands. Baquet was the brother of George Baquet, the clarinetist who is credited with being the first to play the classic piccolo obbligato in *High Society* on the clarinet.[14] Achille Baquet had been playing professionally in New Orleans since 1908, often with future ODJB members like Edwards and Sbarbaro. Stein had been the titular head of the band that later became the ODJB.

With these musical backgrounds, the group Durante assembled was bound to produce authentic Dixieland. Like the ODJB, whom they imitated closely, the members of NOJB did not really improvise. Their outstanding musician, as can be heard on their early 1919 Gennett recording (*Ja-Da Medley*), was Baquet. With his big, almost vibratoless tone and good control of the entire range, Baquet blended better with the cornet than most other clarinetists did. He avoided the squeaks and squeals of the other Dixieland clarinetists (particularly Ted Lewis), and his syncopations often have a rudimentary sort of swing.

The most successful competitor and imitator of the ODJB was Earl Fuller's Famous Jazz Band. Fuller was one of the more successful novelty-band drummers who sprang up around 1915 and 1916. He originally came out of the James Reese Europe school and, like most drummers of the day, imitated Europe's star drummer Buddy Gilmore, often called "the first jazz drummer" in the modern sense of the word. After the phenomenal success of the ODJB, Fuller, who had in the meantime become a leader himself, reduced his Deluxe Orchestra at

14. Though highly regarded in the legendry that surrounds early New Orleans jazz, George Baquet is less than impressive on his few appearances on records. With Bessie Smith in 1923 (*Whoa Tillie* and *My Sweetie Went Away*), his playing is unmitigatingly stiff and yelping in the Ted Lewis manner.

Rector's Restaurant to a five-piece band with the same instrumentation.

Fuller's band began recording in May 1917, four months after the ODJB's first date. Though strictly commercial in intent, Fuller's recordings, which are almost always overlooked by jazz historians, are of considerable historical interest in that they combine the New York styles of James Europe and the popular concert bands (like Conway's and Pryor's) with the New Orleans style of the ODJB. In other words, Fuller's band was an important transitional group.

Its versatility was based on the widest commercial appeal. Thus it had three basic kinds of repertory: (1) the ODJB-type of numbers, (2) the marches and one steps, and (3) popular tunes like *The Old Gray Mare* and *Li'l Liza Jane.* These categories often overlapped in performance. A piece like W. C. Handy's *Beale Street Blues* would be played in a combination of circus-band style and New Orleans polyphony. Other recordings simply grafted the three "horns" of the New Orleans manner onto the rhythmic substructure of Europe's style. The band's ricky-tick rhythms and cornetist Walter Kahn are very hard to take today. Moreover, its performances are structurally monotonous in their exact repetitions. Nevertheless, the band had a crude sort of excitement similar to that of Europe's orchestras, an excitement generated mostly by the drummer, Dusty Rhoades. Playing primarily on snare drum and (alternatively) woodblocks, he was the only member of the group who varied his playing. An interesting example of this occurs in the last chorus of *Li'l Liza Jane.* At a fast tempo Rhoades breaks into the following variation (Ex. 1)[15]:

Example 1 *Li'l Liza Jane*

Another ODJB competitor was the Louisiana Five. Alcide "Yellow" Nunez, the clarinetist-leader, had been in the original nucleus of the ODJB that went to Chicago in 1916. He had also been the one to start the copyright ruckus over *Livery Stable Blues* by appropriating

15. The reader will recognize the basic 3 against 2 patterns we encountered in Chapter 1 in regard to African rhythms. The relationship of Rhoades's drum pattern to the basic meter is strikingly similar to numerous Clap and *Gankogui* patterns discussed by A. M. Jones.

the piece for a Chicago publisher, Roger Graham. By 1917 Nunez had moved on to New York, and in 1919 he recorded some forty sides with the Louisiana Five. One of them, *Yelping Hound Blues,* was almost as big a hit as *Livery Stable Blues,* and the title painfully suggests why. The group was curious in that it had no cornet. As a result it is poorly balanced in texture and range, with Nunez playing in the high register and the other four—trombone (playing mostly bass lines), piano, banjo, and drums—registrally separated several octaves below. Nunez's playing comes straight out of the parade-band tradition of New Orleans, and as such his recordings[16] have a certain authentic charm. He plays what appears to be all that he was capable of playing: the high, shrill melodic lead that he learned from New Orleans bands. But even though Nunez was the only possible melodic carrier in the instrumentation of the Louisiana Five, his playing shows some signs of a desire to vary the melody in final choruses. It is not improvisation, but merely an embellishment technique—filling in the melodic contours with eighth-note obbligatos and the like. His playing seems to reflect exactly the kind of distinction between "embellishment" and "improvisation" to which Buster Bailey referred when he said that in Memphis in 1917 and 1918 he "wouldn't have known what they meant by improvisation. But embellishment was a phrase I understood. And that was what they were doing in New Orleans—embellishment."[17]

A slightly later competitor was the Original Memphis Five. Undercutting the recording fees of the ODJB, they recorded over one hundred sides in 1922 alone, under a variety of names and record labels. Their recordings of this period show clearly how the ODJB's big success with *Margie* in 1920 seduced all similar groups away from jazz toward commercial dance or slapstick music. As such the Memphis Five, despite the inclusion in its personnel of cornetist Phil Napoleon, trombonist Miff Mole, and pianist Frank Signorelli, was rhythmically stiff and played a semi-arranged music that was far removed from New Orleans polyphony. But in their early days—before dozens of similar groups sprang up all over the Eastern seaboard—they

16. One of them is reissued on Columbia C3L 30, side 1, track 2. Their last and best recording, *Slow and Easy* (made in December 1919), introduced the young cornetist Leo McConville, later one of the regulars in the Red Nichols groups.
17. Shapiro and Hentoff, p. 78.

combined the vestiges of James Europe's influence with the pseudo-polyphony of the ODJB. Their 1921 recordings of *Shake It and Break It* and *Aunt Hagar's Children,* both big hits of the year, are representative examples of their spirited approach.[18]

The group most often compared to the ODJB was the New Orleans Rhythm Kings (NORK). Although they were influenced by the ODJB in their formative period, the NORK, with their three "horn" men from New Orleans, Paul Mares (cornet), Leon Rappolo (clarinet), and George Brunies (trombone), were keenly aware of Negro jazz. Compared with the ODJB, the Rhythm Kings played a better brand of jazz, and Leon Rappolo was considered the best white New Orleans musician. They not only really improvised, but they had a different attitude, a humility toward jazz. Whereas La Rocca would deny the Negro musical heritage of New Orleans, Paul Mares proudly claimed that he tried to emulate King Oliver's tone and style.[19]

The point has been made about the NORK that they were at least as important for whom they influenced as for what they actually played. In fact, they were the earliest and most authentic link between the Negro New Orleans ensemble tradition (as epitomized by King Oliver's Creole Jazz Band) and a host of white imitators, including Bix Beiderbecke, the so-called Austin High School Gang, and the whole proliferation of Chicago-style jazz. Though the Rhythm Kings were uneven and lacked an esthetic direction of their own, they were enthusiastic admirers of the best of the New Orleans-via-South Side Chicago tradition. They understood its concept and were among the first to imitate it well. Within this concept they were not particularly inventive or creative, but they at least knew the distinction between real improvised jazz and its codified novelty aberrations, and they defended the former fiercely.

We have seen how one of the NORK recording dates was enlivened by the presence of Jelly Roll Morton. Under his influence, the results were more focused stylistically, more relaxed rhythmically, and more imaginative structurally. But even on their own, as the regular group

18. I am certain that this particular recording of *Aunt Hagar's Children* was one of several jazz records Darius Milhaud took back with him to Paris in 1922. It was as a result of his encounter with jazz during his visit to America (to be guest conductor of the Philadelphia Orchestra) that Milhaud composed his famous jazz-influenced masterpiece, *La Création du Monde.*
19. Shapiro and Hentoff, p. 123.

at Chicago's Friar Inn, they often captured much of the rhythmic flow and polyphonic freedom of New Orleans jazz. Their repertoire consisted of ODJB pieces and some of Morton's compositions, many of which they recorded, starting in 1922, for the Gennett label. In essence they attempted to be a kind of reduced version of King Oliver's Creole Jazz Band, and occasionally they achieved this modest goal. On such titles as *Tin Roof Blues, Sweet Lovin' Man,* Artie Matthews's popular 1915 ragtime piece *Weary Blues,* and Spencer Williams's equally popular *Shimmeshawabble,* they capture the feel and gently rocking swing of New Orleans ensemble authentically, if not consistently. If a record like *Sweet Lovin' Man* had been better recorded, it would certainly be more highly evaluated. On the thin-sounding acoustical Gennett recordings the drive of Paul Mares's trumpet and Leon Rappolo's lyrical clarinet are all but suppressed. Rappolo's breaks and George Brunies's trombone breaks are well timed, with a good, relaxed tone; and the last two ensemble choruses are fine examples of this art. Perhaps their most typical recording, and one that influenced both Bix Beiderbecke and Jimmy McPartland with his Austin High School Gang, is *Tin Roof Blues.* Here one can hear to good advantage the kind of cornet Bix was weaned on, as well as one of Rappolo's most poignant, expressive blues solos.

BIX BEIDERBECKE

The New Orleans Rhythm Kings, as we have mentioned, influenced the greatest white jazz musician of the twenties, Leon Bismarck Beiderbecke (1903-31). Bix, of course, has become a legend, and indeed symbolized the Jazz Age, much as F. Scott Fitzgerald did in the literature of the Jazz Age. But to get beyond the legend, we must look at the recordings he left us and the musical personality they disclose.

Bix's talent was first nurtured by a musical family background that went back through several generations to German ancestors. Despite his musical precociousness and some formal lessons on the piano, Bix did not learn to read music. He was self-taught on the cornet, which, we are told, he started to learn when he was fifteen. He was weaned on ODJB recordings; he picked out La Rocca's trumpet lines and played along with the Victrola. Bix also heard music on the riverboats that came up the Mississippi to his home town, Davenport, Iowa, from Memphis, St. Louis, and New Orleans. There is little doubt that Bix heard Armstrong on one of these riverboats and also a white trumpet player named Emmet Hardy, who unfortunately never recorded. Although age fifteen is late for starting an instrument, Bix's talent for the cornet was so natural that he developed with astonishing rapidity and by 1921, at eighteen, began jobbing around the North Shore Chicago area and listening to the NORK at night downtown. At this time Bix also discovered King Oliver and the maturing work of Armstrong. But to cite these influences is not to deny that Bix contributed his own very distinctive musical qualities. By 1923, when the Wolverines were organized from the nucleus of players with whom Bix had been jobbing, his style was already formed in all of its essentials.

The Wolverines recordings made for Gennett in 1924 are eloquent testimony. Though his beautiful golden tone was to become even richer in subsequent years (and recorded to better advantage), it already stands out as a unique attribute, not equaled even by Armstrong. Bix's tone had a lovely unhurried quality, perfectly centered, with natural breath support and a relaxed vibrato. Here, in fact, Bix showed his independence from Armstrong. Comparing the two, we note the extra daring in Louis's solos, the almost uncontrollable drive, the rhythmic tension—in short, playing in which all technical matters are subservient to the expansion of an instrumental conception, to the exploring of new musical ideas. By comparison Bix was a conservative. His ideas and techniques combined into a perfect equation in that the demands of the former never exceeded the potential of the latter. His sense of time, for example, was an essentially uncomplicated one, seldom leading him to explore, but within its limitations he was almost flawless. He showed a sure attack and a natural feeling for swing. Thus each tone, apart from its rhythmic, melodic, and harmonic relationships, was a thing of beauty: an attack perfectly timed and initiated followed by a pure, mellow cornet timbre.

Bix had a quality extremely rare in early jazz: lyricism. Perhaps he inherited this quality from the romantic strain in his German background; perhaps it reflected the singing tradition of Bix's grandfather's *Männerchor*. But wherever it came from, it was a consistent element in his playing. Indeed, it was linked to his one limitation, an inability to break out of the conservative expressive framework of his style. Bix set his expressive sights much lower than Armstrong. He was content not to explore further; perhaps he was emotionally unable to push beyond his most immediate inclinations. I think we see here an analogy to certain aspects of his personal life of which his biographers and fans have made a mystique. I refer to Bix's somewhat shy and restrained relationship to women, his need for security manifested in joining the Jean Goldkette and Paul Whiteman orchestras, and his vague desires to come to terms with "classical" music. In one way or another these are parallel symptoms of a man who could not let himself go emotionally, a man in whom a conservative discipline acted as a restraining lid or, as George Avakian has put it, "it's like capping a geyser." His tone received both its beauty and its cool reserve from these personality traits. An outburst such as the exuberant rip on *Singin' the Blues,* very common in Armstrong's playing, is rare with Beiderbecke.

The influence of the Original Dixieland Jazz Band on the Wolverines, as sifted through the intermediary influence of the New Orleans Rhythm Kings, appears not only in terms of the material performed—the Wolverines' best titles were ODJB tunes—but also in the manner in which they were performed. Much of the ensemble playing makes direct reference to La Rocca's group. But in contrast to the older ensemble, the Wolverines really improvised. As a result the polyphonic textures are loosened up and more varied, the rhythms swing—frequently in a definite 4/4 beat (*Tiger Rag, Big Boy*).[20] Bix, at twenty-one, is more than equal to the diverse demands of the Wolverines' conception. On *Oh, Baby* his warm tone and easy swing enhance an indifferent tune simply by means of melodic embellishment. On *Jazz Me Blues* there is a real solo at a time when it was still a rarity. *Riverboat Shuffle* shows not only Bix's great lyrical gift, but also his ability to shape the flow of ideas into an economically constructed miniature composition. The musical example (Ex. 2) shows how several ideas (indicated by *X, Y,* and Z) reappear as motivic elements, giving the solo a coolly calculated cohesiveness.

Motive Z, representing a blue note, is not really notatable. It is played the first time with a typical Negroid inflection and flat intonation that places it outside the realm of diatonic notation. The second

20. An excellent illustration for comparison are the ODJB's and Wolverines' recordings of *Toddlin' Blues.*

time, Bix turns the blue note into a glissando traversing a whole tone, perfectly equilibrated across five beats. But in these passages, as well as the related ones at *Y*, we miss the "hot" or "dirty" intonation Armstrong or Oliver would have given these notes. With Bix they are pure and perfectly controlled, their expressiveness drained in favor of pitch and tone control.

Example 2 *Riverboat Shuffle*

Some authorities on Beiderbecke have made much of his penchant for advanced harmonies. It is true that his celebrated piano composition *In a Mist* (1927) uses a chromatic language beyond that of most jazzmen at the time. And the reports of Bix dreamily experimenting between sets with "progressions of discords" (they were really no more than eleventh and thirteenth chords) are probably true. But either this interest in harmonic extensions came after the 1924 Wolverines period or else Bix did not yet dare to put such experiments to use in those ensemble recordings, for the recordings are singularly free of chromatic alterations. They adhere to safe diatonic patterns, beautifully executed to be sure. But there are signs that in 1924 Bix did not yet have his harmonic-melodic language entirely worked out. On *Tia Juana, Royal Garden Blues,* and *Tiger Rag,* he frequently anticipates harmonic changes in an awkward, stiff manner. Here the shape of the ideas did not mesh entirely with the given harmonic structure. But such lapses are rare and are more than outweighed by the rightness of most of his choices, including the unexpected sixth of the chord "leading in" to the last sixteen bars of *Tiger Rag.*

By 1927 he had probed the new harmonic language enough to set it down (with the help of his arranger friend Bill Challis) in his composition *In a Mist.* As an exercise in constantly modulating, unresolved ninth and whole-tone chords, the piece is a rambling, repetitious, popularized version of the kind of chromatic language Debussy and Scriabin had explored nearly two decades earlier. But these composers would not have been Bix's direct sources, or at least not the only ones. At this time Gershwin's *Piano Preludes* and his famous *Piano Concerto,* often performed in an abbreviated version by the Whiteman orchestra, were well known in New York music circles. The sheet music market was glutted with light classics by Cyril Scott, Edward MacDowell, and Eastwood Lane, as well as the compositions of Tin Pan Alley piano stylists like Zez Confrey, Rube Bloom, and Louis Alter. Even closer to Bix's immediate milieu were arrangers like Challis, Ferde Grofé, and Fud Livingston. (The latter, for example, had composed and arranged *Humpty Dumpty* in 1927 for the Frankie Trumbauer orchestra in which Bix played, a piece that featured chromatic progressions imitative of Whiteman's stylings, but otherwise way beyond that of real jazz orchestras, including those of Henderson and Ellington.) Bix was fascinated by the work of these arrangers, and through them he learned about Ravel, Holst, Delius, Debussy, and early Stravinsky. His growing interest in these composers and in symphonic music in general added one more dilemma to the various personal problems crowding in on him toward the end of his life. Fascinated by the music that lay beyond jazz, beginning with the skillful, commercialized music with which Whiteman sought to bridge the two worlds, he was torn between this new fascination and his allegiance to the free, untutored spirit of jazz.[21] To aggravate this dilemma, Bix did not have the theoretical knowledge by which he could sort out the opposing forces pulling at his musical innards. From this area of conflict and others, he turned to escapes such as liquor.

21. Whiteman's role in jazz and popular music is still subject to much controversy and fanciful opining. The hard-core jazz critics dismiss Whiteman summarily as a destructive influence, not only on Bix, but on all of jazz; while the apologists for popular mass culture have seen in Whiteman the great arbiter between jazz and symphonic music. Whiteman was a sociological phenomenon responding to a particular need in the society of his time, the 1920s. As such there are social implications in his career and his music and his influence on American music, the analysis of which go beyond the purview of this book. On purely musical terms, however, the Whiteman orchestra achieved much that was admirable, and there is no question that it was admired (and envied) by many musicians, both black and white. For it was an orchestra that was overflowing with excellent musicians and virtuoso instrumentalists. Its arrangers—Lennie Hayton, Ferde Grofé, and particularly Bill Challis—wrote complex, demanding scores that took everything these musicians could give. It was not jazz, of course—or perhaps only intermittently so. Many of the arrangements were overblown technicolor potpourris, eclectic to the point of even quoting snatches of *Petrushka* and *Tristan und Isolde* (in *Nobody's Sweetheart* and *The Man I Love* respectively). But often enough—to make the point worth making—the arrangements were marvels of orchestrational ingenuity. They were designed to make people listen to music, not to dance. The arrangers made full use of the coloristic variety of Whiteman's basic instrumentation of nineteen or twenty players, augmented by from four to seven strings. The reedmen, particularly the great Chester Hazlett—who played the clarinet solo in the first performance of Gershwin's *Rhapsody in Blue* in the 1924 Aeolian Hall concert—Frank Trumbauer, and Charles Strickfadden were all superb doublers on different instruments. The resultant performances were often more than merely slick. Excellent intonation, perfect balances, and clean attacks do not necessarily equate with superficiality. There is in the best Whiteman performances a feeling and a personal sound as unique in its way as Ellington's or Basie's. It was just not based on a jazz conception. For this we cannot automatically condemn it. At their best, Whiteman's musicians played with a richness and bounce that has its own validity (as in *Changes, 'Taint So Honey, Sweet Sue*). And many of their performances are fascinating musical period pieces, at least as significant in their way as many a mediocre jazz performance which happens to possess the proper pedigree.

Bix's fascination with large orchestrations and arranging techniques did not come upon him suddenly in 1927. Even in the Wolverines days, the recordings of *Copenhagen, Tiger Rag,* and *Royal Garden Blues* disclose advanced arranged riff-ensembles (also beautifully performed) that anticipate Redman's arrangements for Henderson of *Copenhagen* and *Sugar Foot Stomp,*[22] and even some of Morton's Red Hot Peppers records. Despite a small instrumentation, the Wolverines' recording of *Copenhagen* reveals some parallels to the Redman arrangement recorded half a year *after* the Wolverines' version. Similarly the spirit and drive and the integration of solo, arranged ensemble, and collectively improvised ensemble in *Tiger Rag* anticipate Morton so closely that one wonders if both Redman and Morton did not acquire a few ideas from the Wolverines' recordings. In any event, the 4/4 beat and swing of the arranged ensemble after Bix's stiff solo chorus in *Tiger Rag* is amazing in its own right, regardless of historic precedence.

Beiderbecke had an artistic consistency and integrity that never left him, even as he became more and more surrounded by commercial bands and arrangements. His many recordings with various Trumbauer aggregations and Whiteman attest to this: he was never less than remarkable, especially as seen against his surroundings. Very often he was superb, as in his great solo on *Clarinet Marmalade,* the spirited interplay with Adrian Rollini's bass saxophone on *At the Jazz Band Ball,* or his extraordinary attack and bright, joyous tone on *Sorry.* Occasionally there are even, inexplicably, moments of real discovery, as in the middle of his solo chorus on *Sorry,* when Bix plays an "asymmetrical" between-the-beats phrase as naturally as if he had done it every day for years (Ex. 3). But his crowning achievements were the superbly timed, relaxed, mellifluous solos on *Singin' the Blues* and

Example 3 *Sorry*

I'm Coming Virginia. Here is the essential Bix, unspectacular, poignant, with a touch of reserve and sadness shining through.

22. See Chapter 6.

This raises a final point of conjecture. Beiderbecke's career was too short and too checkered to permit a complete view of his work. The period between March 1925 and early 1927 is not represented on recordings at all, and, of course, nothing remains of the hundreds of jam sessions he is said to have played as an antidote to life with the Whiteman band. His premature death precipitated a legend enlivened by accounts of his heroic exploits on the cornet. But even on the basis of his recordings alone, Bix deserves to be more than a legend fashioned out of the extra-musical syndromes of the Jazz Age. He deserves to be called one of the truly great jazz musicians of all time.[23]

CLARINETISTS

The first generation of leading jazz clarinetists came inevitably from New Orleans. The marching band tradition, as we have seen, was highly developed there, and the innumerable bands that found more or less regular employment in the almost daily parades, the holiday concerts, and the funeral processions required a host of clarinet players. Then too, as the smaller groups developed featuring the classic front-line of clarinet-cornet-trombone, the clarinet remained a leading instrument. It was the only high register instrument capable of competing dynamically with the cornet—we need only imagine the weak sound of a flute or oboe in an outdoor concert—and it provided the all-important descant or obbligato possibilities in the early ensemble style of New Orleans.

23. Bix radiated an enormous influence on a large circle of white musicians. The most important of these were the Austin High School Gang of Chicago, with among others Jimmy McPartland (cornet), Bud Freeman (tenor saxophone), Frank Teschemacher (clarinet), Eddie Condon (banjo), Gene Krupa (drums); and the entire circle of Red Nichols, the Dorsey brothers, Phil Napoleon, and Miff Mole. Combined, these musicians made over a thousand recordings in the late 1920s, most of them well played, occasionally even ingeniously contrived. But ultimately they remain in the realm of the commercial performances geared to a thriving mass market requiring a consumer's product. The Wall Street crash ended all that. In so far as a few notable examples of Chicago-style jazz—the term usually applied to the above-mentioned players—survived beyond the 1920s, they will be dealt with in volume two of this work. The interested reader is referred to the appropriate chapters in *Jazzmen,* edited by Ramsey and Smith, in Samuel B. Charters and Leonard Kunstadt, *Jazz: A History of the New York Scene* (Garden City, N.Y.: Doubleday & Company, 1962).

The clarinetists were often the prima donnas of the bands, second only to a few outstanding cornet players. Moreover, within the Creole musical tradition of New Orleans, as early as 1900 a number of outstanding clarinetists had developed, men like the Tio family, Alphonse Picou, and George Baquet, who together influenced or taught almost every clarinet player of the two succeeding generations. Picou was a particular hero since it was he who was featured in the famous Tuxedo Brass Band in the most famous of all early clarinet solos, the high-register obbligato adapted from the piccolo part in the popular march *High Society*.

Out of this milieu developed the three greatest clarinetists of the New Orleans tradition: Sidney Bechet, Johnny Dodds, and Jimmy Noone, and other New Orleanians like Barney Bigard, Omer Simeon, Edmond Hall, Albert Nicholas, Larry Shields, and Leon Rappolo, who all contributed significantly to the clarinet's role in jazz.

"There is an extraordinary clarinet virtuoso who is, so it seems, the first of his race to have composed perfectly formed blues on the clarinet. I wish to set down the name of this artist of genius; as for myself, I shall never forget it. . . ." Those astonishingly perceptive words were written in 1918 in the Swiss music periodical *Revue Romande* by a thirty-five-year-old conductor named Ernest Ansermet, who the year before had conducted the world première of Stravinsky's *Histoire du Soldat*. Ansermet was speaking about Sidney Bechet, who was on a European tour with the Southern Syncopated Orchestra led by Will Marion Cook (see Chapter 6).

Bechet had been playing clarinet since 1903, when he was six years old. He subsequently studied with Baquet, and by the time he was twenty-one had played with almost every major musical organization in New Orleans, alongside Oliver, Bunk Johnson, Freddie Keppard, Buddy Petit, and Tony Jackson, as well as the composer Clarence Williams. His association with the latter was to lead to Bechet's first recording dates in 1923 and 1924 with Williams's Blue Five in New York. By that time Bechet had switched more or less permanently to soprano saxophone, an instrument for which he had a remarkable affinity. Though technically speaking then a saxophone player, Bechet nevertheless belongs in a discussion of clarinetists because he played the soprano saxophone with a technique and style very much out of the New Orleans clarinet tradition. The reed player traditionally thinks of the soprano saxophone as a cousin to the clarinet. This may explain why Bechet had almost no influence on saxophone players in the twenties, except Johnny Hodges of Duke Ellington's band. To appreciate the gulf between the mellifluous soprano playing of Bechet and the playing of other alto and tenor saxophonists in the twenties, one need only recall the stiff slap-tongue playing of Coleman Hawkins or of the Chicago player Stump Evans.

Bechet must have turned to the soprano sax because of its wider, mellower tone and its greater ease of blowing as compared with the clarinet. From his music we can deduce that the somewhat shrill, often thin upper-register sound of the New Orleans clarinet disturbed Bechet. Nor did the clarinet, because of the break in register peculiar to its acoustical properties, allow him to weave as easily the kind of roaming melodic lines he was so fond of. In other words, there is an exact corollary between the kind of music Bechet heard in his mind's ear and his ultimate choice of the soprano saxophone.

There is every reason to believe that this conception of playing was firmly set by the time Ansermet heard Bechet. Certainly this is indicated in his first recordings four years later by the sovereign authority with which Bechet states this style. This authority can be heard on any number of the Clarence Williams Blue Five dates, but perhaps the most striking, yet typical examples occur on James P. Johnson's tune, *Old Fashioned Love* (Ex. 4). The passage is an obbligato embellishment to two statements of the melody, first by trombonist Charlie Irvis and later by trumpeter Thomas Morris. In a way, Bechet's orna-

Example 4 *Old Fashioned Love*

mental garlands unify and enliven the brass players' drab theme statements, and even though Bechet is acoustically in the background, our attention is drawn irresistibly to him. The example shows Bechet's characteristic addiction to decorative, almost rococo, contours stated in free rhythms seemingly disassociated from the prevailing beat. Even his on-the-beat playing seems unconstrained, seems to float above the beat and only occasionally to coincide with it; it is the quintessence of melodic blues. Significantly, as loose and free as Bechet's rhythmic language is, it swings in a way that most players of the period could not yet manage. It is also obvious that no contemporary clarinetist had the digital fluency exhibited on these 1923 recordings. Another example of Bechet's rhythmic inventiveness occurs on the 1923 *New Orleans Hop Scop Blues* (Ex. 5):

Example 5 *New Orleans Hop Scop Blues*

Here, as opposed to Example 4, the playing is not background decoration, but foreground solo. It shows that Bechet, when the occasion demanded it, could deliver a tightly constructed chorus. The excerpt also represents the final chorus of the piece, which would normally have been a collectively improvised ensemble. Bechet not only dared to end with a solo (in 1923!) but realized that such a solo would have to constitute a climax comparable to a final ensemble effect. His solution here was the dramatic accumulation of tension by means of varied repetitions of a short motive (a).

The other striking characteristic of Bechet's playing was the fast, intense throat vibrato. Thus, even a single note snipped out of a solo could be recognized immediately as Bechet's. Again, unorthodox though it is, his vibrato is the logical corollary to his basically ornate style. His elegant arpeggio lines would sound strange indeed if they were interspersed by long vibrato-less tones. It is as if the intense vibrato, paced approximately in sixteenth-note vibrations (in a slow or moderate tempo), is but the sustained alternative to the sixteenth-note arpeggios.

Bechet is one of the supreme melodists in jazz. He had a natural gift for creating long melodies, developed unquestionably out of the blues in a conception much more vocal than that of any other reed player, except again perhaps Hodges. He dramatized the melodic content with subsidiary decorations, almost in the manner of seventeenth- and eighteenth-century ornamental techniques. But unlike many players with a bent for the decorative, Bechet's melodic lines had an inevitability that marks the master. His precociousness in this regard developed consistently and flowered on his 1939 Blue Note recordings. By that time the full force of his improvisational abilities could be exercised because jazz had advanced to the point where the necessity for stating or embellishing themes was no longer as pronounced as in its early days.

Bechet was never the powerful influence he perhaps should have been. In a sense he was inimitable; that is to say, his tone and the elegance of his style were so personal that, unless adopted by a personality equally strong, they could only be imitated outright. Then too, Bechet was from the start a bit of an outsider. As a creative melodist, he had *in essence* a soloist's conception even before Armstrong did, at a time when the New Orleans musicians of Bechet's generation were still trying, with varying success, to preserve the New Orleans ensemble tradition. Finally Bechet spent most of his life in Paris, and he was not involved with the mainstream of jazz developments in the late twenties and thirties. His fame spread when he returned to the United States briefly in the late thirties and also as a result of his celebrated marriage and his being the most illustrious American jazz exile in France after World War II. But by then, of course, jazz fashions had changed, and Bechet's rediscovery was part of a broad revival movement initiated in the late thirties.

Johnny Dodds (1892-1940) occupies a middle position stylistically in the Bechet-Dodds-Noone triumvirate. In many ways he represents the bridge between Bechet's older and (despite its highly personal elements) pure New Orleans conception and the more rhythmically and harmonically "advanced" Chicago style of Noone. Dodds had a bit of both general approaches in his playing, and his middle position manifests itself in the fact that there are really several kinds of Doddses. I believe also that the unevenness of his playing was largely a result of the pulls embodied in these basically opposing trends.

Dodds's inconsistency has made him a difficult subject for jazz historians; and it has led to extravagant statements for and against him. The French writer and composer, André Hodeir, dismissed Dodds on the basis of a handful of recordings which happened not to represent his best work. Other writers have said flatly that Dodds was not only the greatest of the New Orleans clarinetists, but, by extension, of all jazz. The truth lies somewhere between these two extremes.

Dodds had neither the dramatic musical personality of Bechet nor the technical consistency of Noone. He was seldom spectacular. As a musician thoroughly grounded in the New Orleans ensemble tradition, he was not—or so he thought—meant to be spectacular. His work with Armstrong shows how difficult it was at times for him to adjust to the new demands of Armstrong's conception, especially its rhythmic side. We tend to forget that Armstrong's musical "revolution," as positive as its effect was on jazz as a whole, often had a destructive influence on other players, and at the very least demanded psychological and stylistic adjustments which took time to make. Dodds was often caught on the horns of this dilemma.

Dodds was at his best in the ensemble context, although in later years (the late twenties) he frequently played short solos of considerable conciseness and authority. Dodds at his best was conventional; he never held any surprises. He was never superlatively inventive in the way Armstrong, Hines, or Bechet were, but he generally fulfilled the expected. This is not to say that Dodds's playing was merely routine; he had much too much personality for that. But he was not a visionary and not a composer either in the formal sense of Morton or in the creative-performer sense of Armstrong.

One of the problems with Dodds is that, as I have implied, there are really several Doddses. He had, for example, several tonal qualities. Not only was the register break in his playing very pronounced, so that two consecutive passages, one in the low chalumeau register, another in the bright high register, would seem to emanate from two different clarinets; but also he had a variety of basic sonorities, ranging from a lithe, pure, fluent tone to a rather aggressive, biting, edgy quality. It is not always clear to what extent these divergencies are the result of planning, or of reed problems, or indeed of acoustical conditions. At its best (as on the 1929 *Heah Me Talkin'*, on the 1926 *Too Tight Blues* with the New Orleans Wanderers, and on *Flat Foot* from the same year) Dodds's tone was well-centered, with a slightly edgy perimeter that imparted a sizzle to the tone, making it project brilliantly. At such times his playing had a virility and slashing attack that must have been truly exciting when he was heard in person. At other times Dodds could produce a sweet (though not the accepted commercial "sweet") and yearning tone (as on *Jackass Blues,* 1926, with Lovie Austin's Blues Serenaders). He could go beyond this to a yelping, whining style (as on *Lonesome Blues,* a 1925 Ida Cox recording), and he was not beyond parodying the white novelty clarinet players (as on *Weatherbird Rag* with Oliver's Creole Jazz Band). Although he used it rarely, Dodds was also capable of playing perfectly controlled flutter-tongue solos (as on *Rampart Street Blues,* 1925, with Austin).

Dodds rarely covered the clarinet's entire range in a given solo, although he frequently was called upon, especially in Oliver's ensemble-based band, to perform in a variety of functions and, therefore, registers. But that would be generally in successive or disjunct choruses. The register break bothered him, and he realized that the two different sonoric qualities he thus produced presented a problem in continuity.[24] How pronounced this problem was can be heard in his final chorus on *Weary City,* made in 1928 with his so-called Washboard Band (Ex. 6).

Example 6 *Weary City*

For the first ten and a half bars (not counting the anacrusis) Dodds plays with a reedy, slightly raspy, cloudy chalumeau tone. Suddenly

24. It is lamentable that Dodds, given this tonal ambivalence, did not stumble on the concept of playing a duet with himself, delineating two lines, alternatingly, in the two separate registers.

at the point marked ↓ in the example, a new, clearer sound appears, as if a veil had been lifted. This solo also shows Dodds's fine sense of motive construction. Although his solos often tend to ramble, for he was not known primarily for building choruses concisely and constructively, the example shows that he was capable of doing so. For a twelve-bar solo that does not go beyond an octave for eleven bars and is not a mere riff line, it is a well-balanced effort, mixing the expected judiciously with the unexpected.

One of Dodds's very best sides, *Bull Fiddle Blues* was made with his Washboard Band in July 1928. The musicians on the date were all old New Orleans émigrés to Chicago and, except for Natty Dominique, had all played together years earlier with King Oliver. With Johnny's brother Baby Dodds on washboard the group recaptured some of the true balmy New Orleans feeling. The one exception is Lil Hardin Armstrong with a rushing ragtime solo that is completely out of context. Dodds plays in his best ensemble style and contributes a well-shaped, well-timed stop-time chorus.[25]

Dodds was first and foremost a blues player. In the sense that this was a limitation, it was preordained by his limited harmonic ear. He heard everything in strictly diatonic terms, and the only dissonance he allowed to creep in was that of the bent blue note, all, of course, well within the classic blues tradition. A good example of both the diatonic and blue-noted approach occurs in his low-register solo on *Brown Bottom Bess* recorded in 1926 under the Chicago Footwarmers name (Ex. 7). The flatted blue thirds and sevenths are marked by ×. It should be noted that the *a* flats in measures one, two, nine, and ten are played against a sustained *a* natural, a half tone higher in the low register of the trumpet. The two pitches, rubbing against each other in such proximity, unequivocally set up the blues character of this solo.

25. *Bull Fiddle Blues* is also notable for Bill Johnson's bass solo, probably the first full-fledged pizzicato bass solo on records. Johnson (b. 1872), an important figure in early New Orleans jazz, was Jelly Roll Morton's brother-in-law, and had been the organizer successively of Keppard's Original Creole Band and a King Oliver group, with both of which he made extensive tours as far west as California before settling down in Chicago in the early 1920s. He is reputed to have played the bass pizzicato as early as 1911 and influenced all the younger New Orleans bass players, including Pops Foster, Wellman Braud, and John Lindsay. On *Bull Fiddle Blues* he not only plays a fine "walking" solo, but in general drives the band with an easy swing, throwing in little double-time and syncopated figures. (See also footnote 20 in Chapter 7.)

Example 7 *Brown Bottom Bess*

Among the many things that make a man a blues player are his tone and his vibrato. Dodds's vibrato was one of the most unusual in jazz, and it gave his style a peculiar dark intensity, as if the weight of all his people's problems and ills were concentrated into it. It was a vibrato that did not intersect the central pitch area above and below (as in the case of Bechet, for example); it hung below the center pitch. Graphically it could be presented as in Example 8. Vibrato entails

Example 8

Dodds's vibrato

Bechet's vibrato

pitch variation, and in most cases it consists of alternatingly pushing the pitch slightly above and below the core pitch, in such a way that the intended intonation of the note is not crucially impaired. This type of vibrato is represented by Bechet's in the figure above. Dodds's vibrato never rose above the main pitch, but vacillated from that central position to a lower one. While it stopped short of producing a flat intonation, it did give his sustained tones a darker, heavier quality. It is hard to say how this curious circumstance came about. Musicians are often hard put themselves to analyze whether a certain technical idiosyncrasy had a physiological origin which influenced the ear to accept it, or whether, conversely, the ear heard it that way and intuitively, unconsciously influenced the physical constituents—in this case the embouchure—to produce the desired result. In any event, his peculiar vibrato was part and parcel of Dodds's tone and his feeling for the blues, and when all is said and done it may be the most striking personal ingredient of his style.

Hodeir's complaint that Dodds had a poor sense of rhythm can not be substantiated. Dodds did not, of course, swing like Armstrong or, for that matter, his colleague Jimmy Noone, but that is not yet the same as saying that Dodds's time was weak. In dozens of fine breaks he proves otherwise—within the older rhythmic conception, of course. Armstrong floundered, too, on a number of his breaks and solos, and Dodds's average, based on several hundred recordings over a lifetime, is high enough.

In that pivotal year 1929, when so much in jazz ended and so much else started, Dodds began to fall victim to the encroachment of more demanding solo styles and the concomitant decrease in ensemble playing. Like so many of the musicians in this chapter, Johnny Dodds was soon forgotten, and his particular contributions to jazz of the twenties went unused by his successors. Moreover, the revival movement which might have brought Dodds back to active musical life came too late by a few years. After a final group of unsuccessful record dates in 1938, at the height of the Swing Era, Dodds died in 1940, having spent the last six years of his life as a taxi driver.

Bechet had been lauded by Ansermet. Nearly ten years later, another French-speaking musician was to find words of almost equal praise for another clarinet player, Jimmy Noone. The French musician was Maurice Ravel, and his experiences in listening to jazz in Chicago were to affect crucially his next works, *Bolero* and his two piano concertos. Noone in his time was undoubtedly as impressive to an outsider as Bechet had been earlier, and he was about equally advanced in relation to his contemporaries. Noone represented the next post–New Orleans generation of clarinet-playing, providing the link between the older style and the Swing Era clarinet of Benny Goodman, influencing as well men like Barney Bigard, Buster Bailey, Omer Simeon, and Frank Teschemacher. Although Noone was born in New Orleans (in 1895) and studied with Lorenzo Tio, Jr., and Bechet (the latter two years Noone's junior, but evidently more precocious), he moved to Chicago in 1918. By the time King Oliver came to Chicago, Noone was well established, and subsequently played with both Oliver's Creole Jazz Band (briefly) and Doc Cook's big Dreamland orchestra (extensively).

Noone's earliest recordings made with Oliver in 1923 and Doc Cook in 1924 show him to be already an adept clarinetist in either an ensemble or solo context. His playing is already superbly controlled in respect to tone, rhythm, and musical ideas. Whether in the two former categories his studies with the "classical" clarinetist Franz Schoepp (with whom Benny Goodman and Buster Bailey also studied) benefited him is hard to determine at this late date, but I tend to think that the "classical" discipline helped him as it had helped James P. Johnson. It accounts to some extent for the unusual clarity and ease of his playing.

Consider Noone's solo on *Camp Meeting Blues* (with Oliver in 1923). The control of his intonation, the precise way in which he colors the melodic thirds slightly flat, and the controlled manner in which his rhythms are stated without sounding stiff or "legitimate" are marks of a unique talent. This solo also is beautifully constructed in an utterly simple manner. The undulating thirds are repeated four times, leading to a rising phrase topped in a miniature climax by the last phrase, which starts at the highest pitch level in the entire chorus and descends to the starting point. It is linear compositional structure distilled to its simplest, purest—and strongest—form, with an exposition, a development, and a climax all represented in miniature form (see Ex. 9). The initial undulating eighth-note figure is repeated three more

Example 9 *Camp Meeting Blues*—Structure

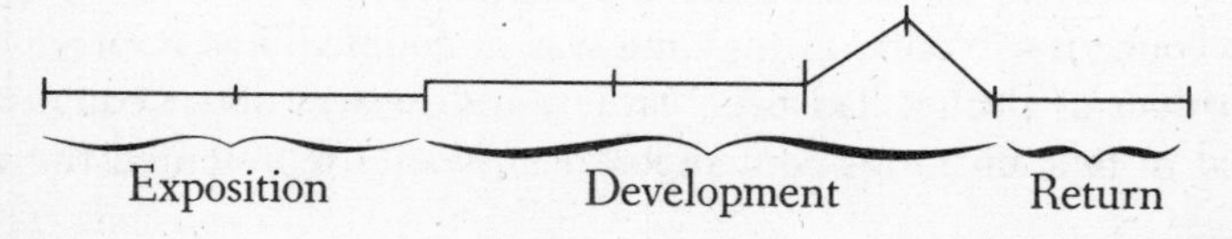

times. On what would have been the fifth time, the figure turns into a climbing eighth-note phrase, reaching its climax on the tenth bar of the chorus and descending again to the tonic. The break immediately following is unusual for its rhythmic timing, which is not the result of rushing. The anticipated *e* flat and g are part of a planned syncopation pattern, one very rarely heard in early jazz (Ex.10). The entire per-

Example 10 *Camp Meeting Blues*—Break

formance shows to what extent Benny Goodman learned from Noone, and whole phrases and the special inflection Noone's tone and legato give them can be heard to this day in Goodman's playing.

Noone learned very early to fill in his breaks and linking phrases with arpeggio figures. But unlike Bechet's arpeggio passages, Noone's never became an integral part of the stylistic melodic fabric; they always remained secondary. His break on Oliver's *London Café Blues* (Ex. 11) is a fine example, and shows the kind of fluency Dodds, for example, did not have.

Example 11 *London Café Blues*

In the early twenties Noone sometimes shaped his phrases in even eighth notes that were excessively stiff. This is a vestige of the pure New Orleans ensemble style, and all the New Orleans clarinet players of that period frequently fell prey to this rhythmic tendency (as in the case of Noone on *London Café Blues* with Oliver and even as late as *Here Comes the Hot Tamale Man,* recorded in 1926 by Cookie's Gingersnaps). But by 1927 and 1928 when his famous Apex Club Orchestra began to be recorded, Noone articulated a thoroughly advanced rhythmic inflection. It fluctuated, depending on the tempo, between swinging eighths (at very fast tempos) and lazy, relaxed triplets (on slow tempos)—a rhythmic conception still in use in the bop period and modern jazz three decades later. In essence, Noone had the same catalyst relationship to Dodds and some of the slightly older New Orleans clarinetists as Waller had to James P. Johnson.

There are any number of examples on the Apex Club Orchestra recordings that illustrate Noone's advanced approach. But perhaps none tells the story more simply and effectively than the manner with which Noone plays the three-note figure ♩♩𝅗𝅥 in *Tight Like This*. The attack, the relaxed but precise tapering of the note, the feeling of over-all phrasing connecting the three notes—in other words the way they flow into each other musically though they are not slurred but semi-staccato—all these subtleties could be equaled at that time by only one man, Armstrong (from whom Noone undoubtedly learned much).

How Noone could use the full range of the clarinet can be heard in his playing on *Four or Five Times* (1928) or the May Alix vocal of *My Daddy Rocks Me* (1929). The former title also shows how well Noone and his alto saxophone player Joe Poston had worked out the problem of fitting the saxophone into improvised ensembles. The ease with which Poston and Noone intertwine their melodic lines or, if demanded, stay out of each other's way, is just short of miraculous.

Noone's Apex Club Orchestra had Earl Hines as pianist, and it was from this group that Armstrong borrowed Hines for the 1928 Hot Five dates. Hines was as unique on his instrument as Noone was on his, and it was inevitable that sooner or later competition or the quest for greater individualism led to their parting company. Hines fulfilled his leader ambitions and went on to form one of the great bands of the thirties. But Noone was at heart an ensemble player, despite his enormous solo capabilities, and he remained at the Apex Club, replacing Hines with pianists who obviously worshipped Hines: at first Zinky Cohn, and later the unjustifiably neglected Clarence Browning. Noone's band of the early and middle thirties made some concessions to the Swing Era and the incoming Moten and Basie styles. But in essence he continued with the original format, still intertwining duets with the alto saxophone (now Eddie Pollack) and relishing Browning's Hines re-creations. He eventually became a part of the revival movement, playing with Kid Ory out in San Francisco in the early forties. It was in 1944, shortly after that band had been engaged by Orson Welles to appear on radio with him, that Noone died, just short of his forty-ninth year.

BRASS PLAYERS

Among the brass players of the 1920s, Louis Armstrong was, of course, the King, succeeding Joe "King" Oliver. By the end of the decade, there was not a trumpet or trombone player who had not been affected in a small or large way by Armstrong's innovations. And yet there were a number of musicians who, though they absorbed Armstrong's influence thoroughly, managed to add something or preserve something of their own. Many of these men, like Bubber Miley and "Tricky Sam" Nanton (whose work will be discussed in Chapter 7), Rex Stewart, Bobby Stark, Joe Smith, Benny Morton, and Charlie Green, became the prominent sidemen of the big bands. Some of them died early, and some barely survived the advent of the thirties and the Depression. Of those not discussed in connection with Henderson and Ellington, three important brass players of the twenties remain to be mentioned: Johnny Dunn, and Jabbo Smith, trumpets; and Jimmy Harrison, trombone.

Harrison led a somewhat erratic life, wandering from one band to another in the late twenties, and died prematurely in 1931. Although he was extremely gifted, his work was uneven and, I think, in its totality it has been overpraised. At his best, Harrison translated Armstrong's solo concept and innovations in rhythm and swing into trombone language. In turn he influenced other trombonists like Dicky Wells, J. C. Higginbotham, Jack Teagarden, Lawrence Brown, and Tommy Dorsey.

In the technical ease with which he handled his instrument, Harrison can be considered the first "modern" trombonist. There were others, like Miff Mole or Snub Moseley, who were even more obviously virtuosic, but their virtuosity remained something slightly apart from their style. Harrison's technical agility was the essence of his style, and in his best work, technique and content were inseparable. As an occasional member of Fletcher Henderson's orchestra, Harrison contributed many short solos, not I think as good as those of his colleagues Benny Morton and Claude Jones, but nevertheless far above average in quality. He was particularly adept at well-placed breaks, especially at above-medium tempos. His high-register solo on the

1928 *King Porter Stomp* is typical of his work with the Henderson band.

Actually Harrison played his best solos for two other bands, Charlie Johnson's Paradise Band in 1928 and Benny Carter's Chocolate Dandies of 1930, one of the first "all-star" bands ever assembled (although it was not called that). Harrison's solos on Charlie Johnson's *Walk That Thing* and *The Boy in the Boat* clearly reveal what used to be called a hot trombone in the thirties and forties. His tone had a hard, unsentimental edge; his attack was sharp and blistering; his slurs crackled in an exciting, inimitable way. On longer notes (especially phrase-ending ones) he adopted from Armstrong the latter's technique of vibrating or "shaking" the tone, what André Hodeir has aptly termed the "terminal vibrato.[26] With his ease in the high register, Harrison was one of the first to expand the range of jazz trombone solos to nearly three octaves.

On *Dee Blues* and *Bugle Call Rag* with the Chocolate Dandies, Harrison plays his two most perfect solos. The one on *Dee Blues* consists of only one chorus of twelve-bar blues, but is so simple and concisely constructed, so clean and relaxed rhythmically, that one is forced to make comparisons with trombonists of at least two decades later. Particularly in the first four bars, Harrison caught hold of a relaxed swing which until then only Armstrong had achieved. His lead-in notes to the solo are only four repeated b flats, but their pure tone and swing can only be described as sublime. The more agitated response (in the second bar) to the four note "call" makes a perfect two-part phrase structure, one of those fleeting moments in which a jazz musician transcends himself and his instrument.

Johnny Dunn and Jabbo Smith are two trumpet players often neglected in jazz histories because they neither appeared with the famous big bands of their time, nor did they record widely as individual soloists. Yet both men were very highly regarded in their day. Dunn, although Memphis-born, was probably the first trumpet player of real importance to dominate the New York scene. Moreover, he brought

26. André Hodeir, *Jazz: Its Evolution and Essence,* tr. David Noakes (New York: Grove Press, 1956), pp. 67-8. See also Chapter 3 of this book, on Louis Armstrong.

blues trumpet playing, particularly King Oliver's wah-wah technique, to New York as early as 1920.

Today Dunn's recordings are hard to obtain, and he has languished in unjustified neglect. But from 1920 to 1923 he was not only a leading musician and entertainer, but was also involved in the initiation of the blues craze as a member of Perry Bradford's Jazz Hounds band that accompanied Mamie Smith on *Crazy Blues,* the record that started it all. On this side and others, like *Don't Care Blues* or the instrumental version of *That Thing Called Love* (1920), Dunn and the band play in a stiff, even eighth-note style that sounds like a cross between the ODJB and Jim Europe's World War I music—certainly still strong influences in New York in 1920. But already in Dunn's breaks, a device for which he had a particular aptitude, we can hear his lean, hard tone and clean attack, very akin to the playing of the concert band cornet soloists of the day. But perhaps his most notable quality was self-assurance to an astonishing degree. His playing had about it a feeling of inevitability that defied competition until Armstrong came to town in 1924.[27] At this point Dunn's recording activity declined sharply, his simple, concise comparatively stiff style being ultimately no match for Armstrong's profounder and more elaborate approach. (Armstrong, incidentally, was the same age as Dunn.) But he remained a very individual player even after Armstrong's ascendancy. His best recordings, made in 1928 as Johnny Dunn and His Band, show his style to good advantage; a brilliant tone, great ease of execution, considerable versatility with mutes and, within a more conservative rhythmic conception, great inventiveness.

Sergeant Dunn's Bugle Call Blues is particularly interesting. This was the piece with which Dunn made a big hit when he first came to New York with W. C. Handy's band in 1918. The 1928 recording shows the arranging influence of Jelly Roll Morton, who happened to play piano on the date. After a bugle call introduction, Dunn is featured in an eight-bar solo accompanied only by the hi-hat cymbals of Mort Perry, no other "rhythm." Succeeding trombone and trumpet breaks have interjections—in typical Morton fashion—by banjo and piano respectively (no drums). Dunn's playing is cocksure, suave,

27. Dunn markedly influenced Ellington's great trumpet player, Bubber Miley (see Chapter 7).

and varied, including a humorous wah-wah break. The final chorus, a collective ensemble, is interesting because Dunn's lead trumpet breaks unexpectedly into broad quarter-note triplets, a rhythm still rarely used at the time. These are immediately followed by a wild tuba break (by Harry Hull) in eighth-note triplets.

Dunn went to Europe late in 1928 and eventually settled in Holland, where he died in 1938.

Jabbo Smith, born in Georgia in 1908, is still living today in Milwaukee, an employee of a national car-rental company. In his day as a trumpet player in New York and Chicago he was considered in some respects Armstrong's only rival. In fact, his virtuosity and (for its time) unique technical facility prompted the Brunswick record company to record Jabbo for some six months in an attempt to compete with Armstrong's bestselling records. Brunswick's attempt failed—Jabbo's records sold poorly; but we are, as a result, able to hear at least a concentrated sampling of his work, albeit from a short and early period of his jazz career.

Jabbo was an alumnus of the famous Jenkins Orphanage Band of Charleston, South Carolina, a musical aggregation that produced many notable jazz talents in its day. At sixteen (in 1924) Jabbo ran away from the orphanage and began working professionally in Philadelphia. In late 1925, he joined Charlie Johnson's Paradise Band (he was not in the band at the same time as Jimmy Harrison) and stayed there three years. As a nineteen-year-old veteran of the band business, Jabbo left the Johnson group to join the pit band of *Keep Shufflin'*, during which period he recorded four sides with Fats Waller and James P. Johnson's Louisiana Sugar Babes which will be discussed later in this chapter. When the show broke up, Jabbo moved to Chicago, where at the request of the Brunswick Company, he formed his Rhythm Aces, a five-man group with which he recorded twenty sides from January to August 1929. On all of these, Jabbo's extraordinary virtuosity, relentless energy, and exemplary musicianship can be heard. He was above all an astonishingly consistent player and musician—a musician's musician, which I am sure is the reason Jabbo Smith was never a great public success. Every one of the arts is full of examples of great technicians and intelligent artists who do not quite catch on because their work is too advanced or sophisticated technically, while at the same time they lack just enough of the personality quotient which is so necessary to communicate with a broad public.

Jabbo's solos with the Louisiana Sugar Babes, with Duke Ellington (he substituted for Miley on the Okeh version of *Black and Tan Fantasy*), with the guitarist Ikey Robinson, and with his own Rhythm Aces all reveal, in addition to his consistency, an exceptional talent for fantasy. His playing is always dramatic and unconventional; making a dull record seems to have been impossible for him. He had a vivid imagination and evidently, by virtue of a natural embouchure and an excellent technical foundation, could realize anything that came to his mind. His endurance and range were formidable, and I believe that he must have outclassed Armstrong in these respects in 1929. His Rhythm Aces recordings are full of high *c*'s, *d* flat's, and a few *d*'s and even one *e* flat, all played with absolute assurance and intonational accuracy.

Jabbo evidently worshipped Armstrong. He imitated many of the latter's most famous solos (particularly *West End Blues*). But occasionally he carried these ideas one degree further in range or in technical skill. Jabbo was also a remarkable singer, sporting at least three different vocal styles, one of which was modeled after Armstrong, raspy voice, scat vocals, and all.

On two of his best sides, *Sleepy Time Blues* and *Sweet and Low Blues,* his various talents pass in review. The long vocal on the former side is handled so easily that we tend to forget how hard it is to sing one of these instrumentally conceived vocal solos, and how rare these still were in the twenties. This one, like most of his vocals, features in addition to many virtuosic phrase turns an octave jump into the falsetto range, and some moments are closely related to yodeling techniques. *Sleepy Time Blues* also proves that Jabbo was not all technique. His opening chorus is full of deliciously sliding blue-note phrases, always with a certain elegance and suavity.

The excerpt from *Sweet and Low Blues* should give the reader an idea of Jabbo's extraordinary facility (Ex. 12). It follows a chorus in which he and clarinetist Omer Simeon, fresh from working with Morton's Red Hot Peppers, engage in a trumpet-clarinet duet. It is astounding for the fact that Jabbo plays in the same range and as fast as the clarinet; it is a real duet, marvelously handled by both players.

Example 12 *Sweet and Low Blues*

(The tremolos at the points marked × were played as fast valve tremolos between alternate fingerings.)

Example 13 shows once again Jabbo's spectacular way with a break, and also his "modern" ear. This stop-time break (from *Till Times Get Better*) is almost worthy of a Roy Eldridge or Dizzy Gillespie.

Example 13 *Till Times Get Better*

After his one big bid for fame, Jabbo Smith gradually retired from the centers of musical activity. He jobbed around Milwaukee and Chicago for years, and eventually formed a small band in Milwaukee. He has as a result been passed over by jazz writers.

HARLEM PIANISTS

Like Jelly Roll Morton, James P. Johnson was at the peak of his career during a period which coincided with the beginnings of jazz as a distinct musical form and with the beginnings of recordings. The solo piano style Johnson brought to its finest flowering was made obsolete by orchestral developments in jazz, and as a result, like Morton, Johnson was soon neglected by musicians and public alike.[28] But *un*like Morton, James P. was able to leave his mark on a succession of pianists that constitute the elite of the jazz piano tradition: Fats Waller, Willie "The Lion" Smith, Count Basie, Duke Ellington, Art Tatum, and on all the way to Thelonious Monk.

Johnson's musical antecedents, of course, were ragtime, and like Morton, James P. transformed that earlier, composed-written style into jazz by the infusion of blues, by the introduction of a more swinging rhythmic conception, and, lastly, through the concept of improvisation. These achievements are considerable enough, but they were projected

28. *Jazzmen*, edited by Ramsey and Smith, fails to mention Johnson once in its more than three hundred pages.

in terms of a sure-fire pianistic technique that surpassed that of all his predecessors. Thus by 1920 James P. was the undisputed leader of the Harlem piano school.

Johnson was born in 1891 in New Brunswick, New Jersey. One of the clues to Johnson's remarkably clear technique can be found in his early musical training, which was directed by his mother and an Italian music teacher, both of whom gave him a solid grounding in "classical" piano techniques. Later, as a young and ambitious teenager, James P. augmented this training by listening to and emulating the leading "classical" pianists of his day, de Pachmann, Rachmaninoff, and Hofmann. At the same time he was absorbing the stomp and rag styles of three slightly older players, Luckey Roberts, Eubie Blake, and a pianist known as Abba Labba. Very little is known about Abba Labba's specific musical capacities, except James P.'s statement that he "had a left hand like a walking beam"; while Blake, who is still alive at this writing, was probably the leading exponent of the ragtime piano style that developed somewhat independently of the Midwestern branch all along the Eastern seaboard as far south as Charleston, with headquarters in Baltimore. As early as 1910 Blake was famous for being able to transpose pieces into all keys, an unheard-of feat in those days. A good idea of Blake's prodigious technique and feel for a varied, chromatic continuity can be gained from his own composition *Sounds of Africa,* which he recorded in 1921.[29]

During the years that James Reese Europe was the rage of New

29. The three-part piece traverses three basic key areas, B flat minor, D flat, and G flat major, all with five and six flats. Within each strain there is a great deal of rhythmic variety in both the melodic right hand and the striding left hand. As a result one feels none of the monotony one often experiences today in listening to early piano recordings, especially those on the more mechanical piano rolls (even some of Johnson's). Of the many interesting rhythmic ideas Blake exploits, perhaps the most unusual (seen in the context of 1921) is the syncopated ragtime stand-by 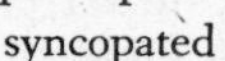 or 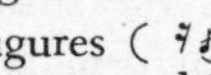 , occasionally shifted over one sixteenth and rephrased: 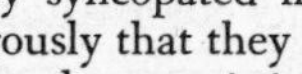 . The shift is an extremely simple one, but it alters the original syncopated proto-figure into a non-syncopated one. This is counterbalanced by many syncopated figures (, or), which are frequently accented so vigorously that they seem to shift the beat. Blake's recording is also worth our attention because it is an excellent example of piano music caught in the transition between ragtime and jazz. In this instance we can savor the rhythmic inflections better than on many Johnson recordings, because Blake's was not done on piano roll, but on one of the Emerson Company's superior recordings.

York Society, James P. was working out his style in places like the Jungle, a rough neighborhood in the west sixties in New York—ironically just west of where Lincoln Center for the Performing Arts now stands. Here James P. associated with the stevedores and longshoremen who frequented the Hell's Kitchen dives, having come up from the Carolinas; and it is from them that he learned the blues, a form of music barely known in New York at the time. As in the case of Morton, the assimilation of the blues in Johnson's style was an important integrative element in the transition from ragtime to jazz. At the same time Johnson was adding to his style "classical" pianistic precision—correct fingerings, well-balanced chords, digital virtuosity.

By 1917 he was the new leader of the Harlem pianists, but he was also pursuing his interests in semi-classical and classical composition and in all manner of show music, working out orchestrations with various units associated with the Clef Club, a Harlem musician's organization founded by James Europe. Johnson evidently performed anywhere and everywhere, in dives, rent parties, or respectable society restaurants, alone or with existing ensembles and groups, or accompanying blues singers like Bessie Smith on recordings. In 1920 and 1921 he played with James Europe's Hell Fighters Band, and soon thereafter collaborated in a number of successful Negro musicals on Broadway. His interest in opera, first inspired by hearing Scott Joplin's ragtime opera *Tremonisha,* eventually led to the writing of an "opera" in collaboration with Langston Hughes, *De Organizer*. Similarly, by the late twenties James P. was beginning to compose symphonic poems and symphonies using basic Negro musical traditions that emulated roughly Liszt's approach in his Hungarian rhapsodies. (James P.'s "serious" work, the least successful of his many interests, will be discussed in the second volume of this work.)

Only a man of extraordinary vitality and talent could have pursued so many goals, all the while resisting the tempting pressures of commercial music. One is surprised to find that, in Ross Russell's words, "the slender threads in the disorganized pattern [of James P.'s life] came to acquire lasting form and color after the rest of the picture had blurred off."[30] James P. Johnson's greatest contribution was to recast the rhythms of ragtime into a more swinging, steadier jazz beat. To implement this he had a steady, rocking left hand providing a reli-

30. "James P. Johnson," by Ross Russell in *The Art of Jazz,* ed. Martin T. Williams (New York: Oxford University Press, 1959), p. 54.

able rhythmic substructure. But even at its "stridingest," his left hand added a flow and forward movement that none of the earlier players had, except Morton. Perhaps this came from the influence of the blues, an essentially vocal music, vocalized even when played on instruments. The point is that the pure ragtime tradition was essentially a piano tradition. As such it could deal easily with vertical, harmonic ideas and a more mechanical, percussive, and rigid application of rhythms than the blues could. But by superimposing the vocal, linear feeling of the blues on the piano, James P. made an important break with the past and changed the piano into an expressive instrument. It is likely that he also heard this same flowing expressivity in a great deal of the "classical" piano playing of the day. One need only refer to recordings by Paderewski, for example, who played with a sentimentalized *rubato* style that was flowing and essentially vocal in conception, even when the music did not call for it.

Even in Johnson's earliest recording, *Harlem Strut,* made on the Black Swan label in early 1921, one can hear the new flow of the music. To be sure, it is tenuous here, because the composition itself was more 2/4 ragtime than 4/4 jazz, more formal and virtuosic than emotionally expressive. But the smoothness of the right-hand runs, the more relaxed flow of the left hand—in other words, the whole "horizontalization" of the music—represented at the time a new direction in jazz piano.

This direction became even clearer on Johnson's first two sides for the Okeh label later the same year, *Keep Off the Grass* and his famous "test" piece on which so many younger pianists, such as Fats Waller and Duke Ellington, cut their pianistic teeth, *Carolina Shout*. Both performances clearly reveal a conscious effort to swing, the sixteenth- and eighth-note subdivisions of the beat filling in rather than merely dividing the beat. Each tiny rhythmic component serves as a link in a longer linear chain.

And yet one must not jump to the conclusion, as many writers have, that Johnson was a great melodist. I have purposely used the word *linear* rather than *melodic*. His compositions and recordings all make clear that he was more involved with rhythmic delineation than with melodic "content." Here again he breaks with the Missouri ragtime tradition, which was essentially more melodic, thematic in conception. With his strong, striding left hand, Johnson focused his attention on the rhythmicization of melodic ideas, often suppressing the latter element to the point of extinction. Many of his "melodies" are essentially rhythmic figures that happen to have pitches attached to them. But rather than being merely destructive, this approach provided the necessary transition to jazz.

It is worth noting that at least as early as these 1921 sides Johnson was striving for a greater rhythmic-metric variety than earlier ragtime had allowed, or for that matter, than his foremost disciple Fats Waller permitted in his playing. Both *Keep Off the Grass* and *Carolina Shout* are full of ternary patterns superimposed on the basic 4/4 beat, all intended to loosen up the vertical structure and to free it from the unremitting binary phrase divisions.[31] A particularly interesting example occurs in the last eight bars (not counting the coda) of *Keep Off the Grass.* The eight bars are divided into a 2+2+4 pattern, but in both two-bar segments the left and right hands articulate two different sub-patterns in ternary units. The right hand divides the phrases into beat patterns of 3+3+2, while the left hand accompanies in 3+2+3. In the succeeding two bars the roles are reversed. A purely rhythmic distillation (no pitches are given) can be seen in Example 14:

Example 14 *Keep Off the Grass*

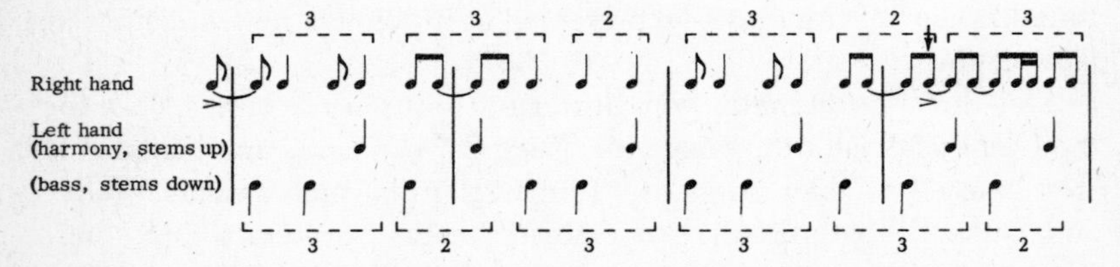

(Points marked ↓ represent syncopated anticipation; they do not alter the basic ternary pattern.)

A variant of this shifting-beat technique is used in the beginning of *Carolina Shout* when, in the ninth to sixteenth bars, the right hand repeats the first eight bars almost exactly, while the left hand strides in a shifting 3+3+2 beat pattern (which it did not do in bars one through eight).

31. Rudi Blesh and Harriet Janis in their book *They All Played Ragtime* (New York: Alfred A. Knopf, 1950) ascribe the convention of the "broken bass" pattern to Abba Labba (p. 194).

Carolina Shout also contains in the third strain James P.'s keyboard version of a "shout," in turn the Negro's extemporized and intensified elaboration of European-American hymn tunes. It is at the same time a call-and-response chorus in the old preacher-to-congregation relationship. In its full-voiced brass-like chords it is a close relative to the famous last chorus of Morton's *King Porter Stomp*.

James P.'s other important break with the ragtime tradition came in his embodiment of improvisation within a broad compositional frame of reference. This can be heard by comparing the different versions of pieces he recorded twice, like *Carolina Shout* and *Harlem Strut*. In both cases, the basic thematic material is varied and embellished in different ways. Johnson was famous in his day for the seemingly inexhaustible fertility of his imagination, which enabled him to produce variation upon variation on the same theme. This technique was exploited particularly at rent parties or cutting contests, where the leading "ticklers" competed with each other in battles of skill and inventiveness. Unfortunately, the time limitations of ten-inch discs and piano rolls restricted the recording pianist to but a few sample variations.

Johnson's improvisational talent can be savored in one of his most perfect realizations, *Worried and Lonesome Blues,* made in 1923. It shows how he was able to combine his imaginative variations with a clear sense of continuity and compositional form. The choruses are twelve-bar blues structures except for the first one of sixteen bars, and each features different thematic material, which is treated almost in the manner of the "classical" variation form or of classical ragtime. The first sixteen bars are stated entirely in triplet eighth-notes in parallel sixths in the right hand; the second chorus (the first of the blues choruses) presents a more varied thematic idea in which both hands participate melodically in alternating call-and-response fashion; the third chorus changes texture drastically with a single-note triplet-eighth run in the high register accompanied by walking tenths in the left hand; the next chorus again takes up the ideas of chorus two, but varies them considerably to constitute almost a new chorus, while the fifth chorus returns to full middle- and low-register chords in a sort of updated boogie-woogie style. Now Johnson launches into what was clearly going to be the final hard-rocking out-chorus, with brass-like riffs and strong walking basses. But James P.'s fingers got tangled up several times, and he decided to try that chorus again. The second time he was more successful, and then a modulatory tag-ending completes the recording. The following full pattern emerges (Ex. 15):

Example 15 *Worried and Lonesome Blues*

	A	*B*	*C*	*B*[1]	*C*	*C* Coda
Continuity	unvaried	varied	unvaried	varied	unvaried	— unvaried
Texture	light	rich	light	rich	rich	— light
Register (of r.h.)	middle-high	full range	high	full range	full range	— varied
Dynamic	*mp*	*f*	*p*	*f*	*ff*	— *mp*

The *C* chorus starts out as if it will be a melodic variant of the initial *B* phrase, but it veers off on its own triplet course. It also contains a delightful *e* natural (over an E flat harmonic area) anticipating C major, where the "wrong note" of course belongs, by two beats. But the melodic shape and inevitability of Johnson's musical idea at this moment is so strong that it makes the "error" sound correct.

A different formal procedure is followed in *Scouting Around* (1923), a blues progression which modulates for the second half to the dominant as if it were a bi-thematic ragtime piece. Here the partitioning of the twelve-bar blues into four-plus-eight-bar phrases with the four-bar segment in the manner of a high-register arabesque-like break, is maintained for the first half of the piece (five choruses). Successive breaks are variants of the original one, demarcating a clear transformation of a melodic idea into a harmonic variant thereof. Example 16 shows the scheme of this gradual progression. Note how the break in chorus 4 has the effect almost of clusters.

Example 16 *Scouting Around*—Breaks

(The fifth chorus returns to a melodic grace-note variant of choruses 1 and 2.)

Scouting Around also has a fine example of shifting stride patterns in the left hand, maintained so stubbornly that the beat seems to have been "turned around" at times (Ex. 17):

Example 17 *Scouting Around*—Stride Piano

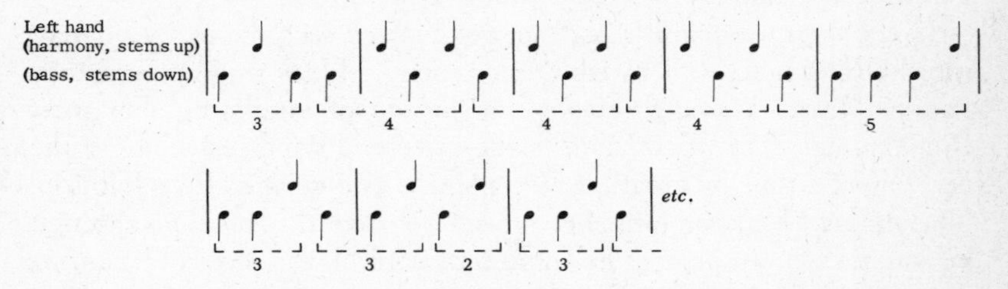

One of the devices Johnson used to introduce more swing into his left hand was the so-called broken tenth. Although probably originated many years earlier by a small-handed pianist who could not reach a tenth, Johnson used it as early as *Carolina Shout* to fill in and "kick off" the beat, exactly in the manner in which the same idea is used by drummers for the same rhythmic effect (encircled notes—Ex. 18A and B)

Example 18 *Carolina Shout*

Because James P. Johnson brought an awareness of earthy Southern blues to Harlem piano, his blues accompaniments for Bessie Smith are obviously of great interest. They show that as much as Johnson may have absorbed the blues and as important as they may have been in shaping his style, there is still a huge expressive gulf between Bessie's singing and Johnson's playing. Perhaps it is unrealistic to expect any pianist to have translated the unique expressivity of Bessie Smith's singing into pianistic terms, at least at that time. Bessie was almost beyond emulation in her day, either by singers or instrumentalists, and only a Louis Armstrong, a Charlie Green, or a Joe Smith could occasionally match her in flexibility and emotional depth. Moreover, we shall see in the section on Bessie Smith how non-blues pianists like Fletcher Henderson and Fred Longshaw provided superb contrasting accompaniments for Bessie (non-blues as distinguished from blues pianists like Lemuel Fowler and Jimmy Yancey).

In the twenties pianists had not yet evolved techniques for emulating the blue notes and variable intonation of blues singing, and they had not learned how to create the *illusion* of emulating that most fundamental element common to the voice and wind instruments, the carrying of a tone by breath. Later, pianists as diverse as Pete Johnson, Thelonious Monk, or John Lewis were to solve this problem through a combination of touch, attack, and tone control, as "classical" pianists, of course, had done already all through the nineteenth century. But in the twenties, particularly in the highly rhythmic, partly percussive Harlem piano tradition, a technique of floating the tone, as it were, had not yet been worked out.

Johnson's playing for Bessie Smith, even on the revered *Backwater Blues*, also leaves the nagging impression that his interests in commercial music and a "classical" repertoire closer to semi- or light classics had left its imprint on his playing. One might say that he played his blues very much the way he would play a show or pop tune. His playing with Bessie often seems heavy-handed and rhythmically stiff—at least in comparison with Bessie Smith's remarkable naturalness of phrasing. The difference between Bessie and Johnson can be best analyzed on their most successful collaboration, *Backwater Blues*. The classic three-line stanza format of the twelve-bar blues more or less predetermines a segmentalization of the structure which alternates two bars of voice with two bars of instrumental response. Bessie's singing is all of a piece, and the two-bar interruptions are bridged perfectly by her. She is able to carry the textual and musical thread of each line over into the next one across Johnson's two-bar answer. By contrast, not always but frequently enough to matter, Johnson plays one kind of idea beneath Bessie's singing and another for the solo responses.[32] There is a notable shifting of stylistic and rhythmic gears at such

32. The fact that these responses are often attempts to echo descriptively the meaning of Bessie's words is not necessarily a justification for the dual approach I have pointed out.

points. In the strictly accompanimental segments Johnson is relaxed and frequently complements Bessie beautifully, as for example under the lines "When it thunders and lightnin' and the wind begin to blow." But in the sixth chorus ("Backwater Blues done cause' me to pack my things and go") Johnson's dichotomous approach is disturbing. Much the same problem arises in *Preachin' Blues,* although here again Johnson occasionally underlines Bessie's words felicitously, as in the low-register chromatic figures underneath the words "Moanin' Blues, holler them blues."

Nevertheless, Johnson's blues accompaniments do meet Bessie more than halfway, and were in fact more than mere accompaniments: they resulted in real duets by two remarkable jazz artists. Johnson seems to have been aware of the progressive encroachment of popular songs and Tin Pan Alley material upon jazz, and indeed upon his own playing. In self-defense he tried to separate the more commercial elements from the purer jazz style. Around 1930 he began to refer to some of his recordings as "commercial" or "modernistic," implying a conscious attempt to stay in the running against the commercially more successful or younger advanced players. His 1930 recordings of pieces like *What Is This Thing Called Love?* and *You've Got To Be Modernistic* are examples of such compromises. Johnson's problem was, of course, that of all sensitive and honest musicians: the compromises he was prepared to make in the direction of commercial music were minimal and certainly insufficient to satisfy the demands of that market. As a result, without Johnson ever quite understanding it, both areas, the commercial and jazz, began to pass him by. In silent despair he concentrated fairly exclusively on his interests in "classical" music, working on his symphonies and tone poems. But these too were not really what he imagined them to be, and the few performances that took place did not—and could not—lead to success. Like so many jazz artists Johnson had become the victim of advancing, changing tastes.

His disciple, Fats Waller, represents a different aspect of the same problem. An enormously facile pianist with an irrepressible spirit, wit, and humor, a composer of a number of songs that have become standards (*Honeysuckle Rose,* for example), Waller was able to survive for a while in a way that his more "serious" mentor and teacher could not. Actually Waller also entertained "serious" aspirations, but he suppressed these under a veneer of extraordinary showmanship and conviviality. He recorded voluminously, mostly in the thirties, and on even his most commercial sides, his extraordinary pianistic skill and innate feeling for jazz never disappear.

Johnson and Waller colaborated once in 1928, teaming up at two keyboards in the musical *Keep Shufflin'*. Out of this collaboration came a curious, very effective, and little known record date with Waller on organ and Johnson on piano. To complete the personnel Waller engaged two musicians also in the show—Garvin Bushell on clarinet, alto saxophone, and bassoon and the great trumpeter Jabbo Smith, whose work has been previously discussed in this chapter. They recorded under the name Louisiana Sugar Babes. It is evident that the four musicians felt very much at home in the material they recorded, all taken from the show *Keep Shufflin'*. *Willow Tree,* a Waller composition, is one of his most haunting and catchy tunes.[33] Although one might have misgivings about the group's strange instrumentation, the inherent problems were beautifully solved. The organ and piano never collide; Waller and Johnson ingeniously complement each other, effortlessly producing a rich, yet somehow transparent, sonority. Johnson plays in his best filigree manner against Waller's sustained organ backgrounds. The two "horn" men come in on the bridges of the thirty-two-bar song, Jabbo elegant and suave, Bushell with a creamy alto sound or a playful Goodmanish clarinet. In *Sippi,* a sentimental ballad of the day by Creamer and Johnson, Bushell's jerky bassoon solo, the antithesis of swing, is completely out of context—the one flaw in the four sides. But *Sippi* is saved by Jabbo Smith, whose playing one would describe as spectacular if it were not so astonishingly effortless and fluent. His last chorus is a superb example of Jabbo's modern sense of form. Ignoring the eight-bar subdivisions of the tune, he constructs new lines with a facility that anticipates the Dizzy Gillespie of the middle 1940s. On *Thou Swell* what starts out sounding like skating-rink organ music—of a high order, to be sure—is enlivened further by another perky, unorthodox Jabbo Smith solo and touches of James P.'s striding accompaniments.

Waller's role was that of a transitional figure linking James P. to

33. A short, compressed snatch of this tune found its way into Waller's *Whiteman Stomp,* recorded by Fletcher Henderson.

the "modern" pianists of the late thirties, like Teddy Wilson and Art Tatum. His real service lay in taking the still somewhat disjunct elements of Johnson's style and unifying them into a single, cohesive jazz conception in which ragtime was still discernible underneath the surface as a source, but no longer overtly active as a separate formative element. In this, Waller, despite Johnson's influence, moved much closer to the pure jazz direction Hines had by then also evolved out of Armstrong's influence.

In these respects Waller and Johnson occupy places similar to those of Mozart and his predecessors like the Bach sons and Telemann. To state it somewhat simply, the latter took the disparate elements of the vestiges of Johann Sebastian Bach's contrapuntal conceptions and the new embryonic symphonic style, consolidating them into a more "modern" style which then, in turn, Mozart could bring to its zenith. The cohesion of Waller's style is evident on his very earliest recordings, like the remarkably fluent *Mama's Got the Blues,* a 1923 piano roll. There is a direct correlation between Waller's full two-handed technique, the integrative ideas that no longer separate right and left hand the way Johnson's approach essentially still did, the greater harmonic sophistication, and finally the greater ability to swing consistently. Johnson, of course, as already pointed out, made registral separation a conscious function of structural-compositional delineation, and to the extent that Waller fused such procedures into a cohesive whole, his approach was eclectic compared to Johnson's. But then Waller was also less of a composer, or more accurately, a composer more of tunes than of compositions, and foremost an indefatigable performer.

Like Johnson, Waller was ultimately unable to reconcile the conflicts in his musical personality: a natural gift for effortless improvisation in a jazz conception (to a large extent of his own creation), the opposing pull toward commercial and show-business success, and finally his unswerving respect and love for "classical" music. Deep down the latter undermined his convictions about his professional career as a pianist-singer-clown, and the clowning was in turn an attempt to conceal his inner confusion. It is ironic that his teacher, Johnson, was to outlive the pupil and recognize—perhaps only dimly—that they both had been plagued by the same enigma, that of a new music with a "suspect" heritage and the stigma of a "popular art" trying to integrate into a larger over-all musical society.

BESSIE SMITH

In the hierarchy of jazz royalty, Bessie Smith was called "the Empress of the Blues." Probably the greatest "classic blues" singer, she certainly deserved the title not only because she was pre-eminent in the field but also because she was the first great professional urban-blues singer,[34] and therefore the first important *jazz* singer.

In order to appreciate Bessie Smith's artistry one must realize two things. The blues before her time (and the time of her teacher Ma Rainey) was a vast field encompassing a wide range of folk material—work songs, field hollers, spirituals, and shouts—mostly sung by everyday people, workers, sharecroppers, and itinerant beggars. Secondly, the blues was originally an area quite separate from ragtime and from early jazz. Individual composers like W. C. Handy began to write out and publish blues in the beginning of the second decade of the century, while others like Jelly Roll Morton consciously fused the spirit and harmonic elements of the blues with other types of Negro music. But the blues and early jazz met mostly in the vaudeville-minstrel shows and carnivals around the turn of the century, and here a part of the classic blues tradition was worked out by professional singer-entertainers, of which the first important one was Gertrude Malissa Nix Rainey, known as Ma Rainey. The more or less specified eight-, twelve-, or sixteen-bar forms began to crystallize, as these singers, in competition with vaudeville acts of dancing girls, freaks and midgets, actors and "medicine men," sang their plaintive commentaries on

34. Actually, Bessie Smith was far from being the first to record vocal blues. That distinction falls to Mamie Smith (no relation). Though Mamie was more of a show and ballad singer than a blues singer, she delivered her songs with a reckless abandon and a wide-open shouting style that was worlds removed from the whimpering balladeers of the day. Through the indefatigable efforts of Perry Bradford, Mamie recorded *Crazy Blues,* a Bradford song (not really a blues), in November 1920, and to everyone's surprise the record was a great success. It sold 75,000 copies in the first month and over a million in the first half-year. In the succeeding months, Mamie recorded prolifically for the Okeh company, backed by Perry's band, to which he had added Johnny Dunn, New York's star trumpeter. As their success continued, other record companies followed suit with the hope of matching Mamie's good fortune. Within months, the jazz craze, initiated by the ODJB, was replaced by the blues craze.

unrequited love and transformed everyday travails into song and poetry.

The development of the blues into a distinct musical form and idiom took many decades. It is easy to see in retrospect that the emergence of a number of great blues singers, the crystallization of the blues conception, and the advent of blues recordings—all in the early twenties—are not merely coincidental. In consort they represented an inevitable development, whose crowning achievement was the artistry of Bessie Smith. She was the "Empress" because no one could equal her in the control of her rich, full voice and in the dramatically intense manner with which she projected her material. She communicated with her people in a way that made their personal identification with her inevitable. But beyond that more than any other singer, she set the blues tradition in terms of style and quality. She not only gave a special musical aura to this tradition but her own singing and the accompaniments of the many great jazz artists who assisted her in her recordings placed it firmly in the broader jazz tradition.

Nothing even remotely related to blues seems to have been recorded before 1920. It is particularly disappointing that Ma Rainey did not record early in her career, which began at the turn of the century when she was fourteen. It would be fascinating to trace through her own artistic maturing the way that vocal blues became the more sophisticated, professional, urbanized blues, whose development Ma Rainey's career undoubtedly parallels. When she did record in the mid-twenties, she was certainly not the first blues singer to do so, and by then she was nearly forty, presumably no longer in her prime.

If we assume that her 1923-29 recordings reveal in essence the stage to which her blues singing had developed already ten years earlier, then this singing represented a more formalized and disciplined approach than that of her contemporaries, the simpler country blues singers. The latter usually had a very limited repertoire, sometimes one or two blues riffs to which they applied an endless series of variants depending on demand, regional problems and characteristics, and the like. The blues has always been an improvised music, but for many of the earliest blues singers the term improvisation would have to be narrowed considerably, for what they sang and played was repetitious thematically and nearly memorized.

Ma Rainey was undoubtedly one of the first singers to broaden both the melodic and the textual content of the blues. But still, compared to Bessie Smith, her repertoire remains limited. Her vocal lines are frequently identical or virtually so, regardless of the subject matter or title of the individual song. Her subjects are less varied, too, than Bessie's, and she was rarely able to build, either in text or music, the complete compositional forms and narrative continuity in which Bessie excelled.

But what Bessie undoubtedly acquired from her teacher during many years of apprenticeship with the Rainey's Rabbit Foot Minstrels was an ear for the broad, tragic quality of voice that differentiated the true blues singers from the more "popular" ballad stylists of the day, who occasionally sang blues. Although Bessie was to enrich the moans and finely controlled microtonal nuances of the blue notes with an even greater expressive range, Ma Rainey had developed their essential quality by the time Bessie came to her as a teenager. The tragic, heavy quality of Ma Rainey's voice can be heard to good advantage on a number of her recordings, particularly the 1925 *Cell Bound Blues.* Ma Rainey's recordings expose clearly what is intrinsic to the blues: not a "cultured" vocal delivery, but an individual vocal expressiveness, where word, meaning, and sound are all one. The beauty of the blues, as sung by Ma Rainey or Bessie, is that it is at once as natural as everyday speech and yet an individualized artistic expression.

The essentially musical aspects of blues singing, as opposed to its textual elements, can best be measured by the quality of the musical accompaniments. Here Bessie was the more fortunate of the two. Often Ma Rainey received brilliant support on her recordings, as, for example, the superb teamwork of her Georgia Jazz Band, featuring Howard Scott (trumpet), Buster Bailey (clarinet), and Charlie Green (trombone)[35] from the Fletcher Henderson band on *Jealous Hearted Blues.* But at other times, the deadly repetitions of phrases by the unknown saxophone player on *Rough and Tumble Blues* and other Ma Rainey 1926 records point up how much the blues depend not merely on having a good singer but on a sensitive, imaginative ensemble conception. When that fails, even the best singer will sound, and in fact be, boxed in by the instrumental background.

35. It is almost miraculous how Scott and Bailey, very often stiff and uncomfortable with Henderson, flourish in the looser, freer spirit of these blues accompaniments.

John Hammond's often quoted 1937 statement on Bessie Smith, "I'm not sure that her art did not reach beyond the limits of the term jazz," is another way of saying that Bessie's singing represented the ultimate fusion of technical perfection with a profound depth of expression that "penetrated"—to complete Hammond's thought—"the inner recesses of the listener." Much has been written about Bessie's depth of expression—a quality canonized by her premature, tragic death—but little has been written about her technical perfection. What, in a musician's terms, made Bessie Smith such a superior singer? Again it is a combination of elements: a remarkable ear for and control of intonation, in all its subtlest functions; a perfectly centered, naturally produced voice (in her prime); an extreme sensitivity to word meaning and the sensory, almost physical, feeling of a word; and, related to this, superb diction and what singers call projection. She was certainly the first singer on jazz records to value diction, not for itself, but as a vehicle for conveying emotional states. Most of Bessie's rivals, including Ma Rainey, sang with a slurry pronunciation, vocally oriented to be sure. But the miracle of Bessie was that her careful diction was never achieved at the expense of musical flow or swing. I believe that much of her great commercial success was based on the fact that her audience really could understand every word and thus identify with her, especially in her many narrative "representational" blues.

Perhaps even more remarkable was her pitch control. She handled this with such ease and naturalness that one is apt to take it for granted. Bessie's fine microtonal shadings, the various "flatnesses" with which she could color a pitch in relation to a particular word or vowel, the way she could move into the center of a pitch with a short, beautifully executed scoop or "fall" out of it with a little moaning slide; or the way she could hit a note square in the middle—these are all part of a personal, masterful technique of great subtlety, despite the frequently boisterous mood or language. I am not saying that she knew these things in the learned "conservatory" sense, but simply that she knew how to do them at will, by whatever combination of instincts, musicality, and physical equipment she possessed.

Unlike instrumentalists, singers have an extra burden to cope with: they must delineate words. For the singer vowels carry the pitch, while opening and closing consonants (if any) or glottal attacks specify the attack and decay pattern of a note. Here again Bessie Smith instinctively used these acoustical "components" in a musical way that almost defies analysis. Because she was never overtly spectacular in her vocal delivery, seemingly effortless style being the key to her art, we are apt to overlook the unique way in which she used consonants or glottal attacks to help delineate rhythmic ideas, to inflect them in a *jazz* manner—in short to *swing*.

These things, too, had to be learned and worked out; they did not appear ready-made overnight. How she learned and progressed can be heard by comparing her earliest recordings with those of her full maturity, 1925 to 1927. On her recording debut, *Downhearted Blues,* made on February 16, 1923, we hear a somewhat shaky, nervous Bessie. Frank Walker and the Columbia recording engineers were not satisfied until she had made five takes, not counting the never-released takes of another tune. The country girl from Tennessee must have been affected by nerves and fright at suddenly finding herself competing with a dozen famous singers at the height of the blues craze. In addition, Bessie on this recording debut was not permitted to sing those numbers with which she felt most at ease, but instead some current hits previously recorded by singers Sara Martin and Alberta Hunter. But despite the debilitating tension, the bedrock of Bessie's talent shines through, and the unequivocal emotional thrust is already there.

It did not take long for Bessie to recover from this relatively shaky start. Soaring record sales, if nothing else, would have told her that she had something unique. By the end of her first year of recording, she had things firmly under control, vocally and emotionally, and was moreover recording material more indigenous to her style and conception. There followed more than half a dozen years of consistent recording activity in which, despite vicissitudes of her personal life, the level of her artistry is rarely less than superb. She maintained a standard of perfection that few jazz artists have matched or equaled.

On her debut record Bessie sang fairly straight. This may have been attributable to her nervousness that day, or it may have been the unconscious influence of the name singers against whom she was competing. It may also be that the vocal, melismatic embellishments that appear on her subsequent records were really acquired during her first year of recording and artistic security. Whatever the case may be, certain personal phrasing and inflective characteristics soon began to appear. Their immediate effect was to liberate the vocal lines melodically and rhythmically, at the same time dramatizing the texts and thereby subtly projecting an over-all continuity from stanza to stanza. On *Downhearted Blues* Bessie's individual text lines still appear disconnected. The separate "two-bar blocks" do not as yet link together into a single compositional-narrative entity. In subsequent records she learned to control and project this technique with infallibility.

As early as *Jailhouse Blues* (September 1923) we can hear the embellishment traits that form the essence of Bessie's style. In the first line (after the scene-setting introduction), "Thirty days in jail with my back turned to the wall," the importance of the words in the sentence determines the degree of embellishment each receives. Almost every word is emphasized by an upward scoop or slide, but each one differently. The words "thirty," "jail," and "wall"—the three main words of the sentence—are also those most modified by slides. "Thirty" starts with a relatively fast upward slur from approximately *e* flat to g flat.[36] "Days" slides more slowly from the blue flat third to the major third, g. The next word, "in," is a slightly flat g, in preparation for a large major-third upward scoop on "jail": the most important word, *ergo* the strongest embellishment.

These four elements are now reused, but with different words, of course, and in a different sequence: a flat g for "with," and *e* flat for "my," a minor-third slide on "back" (similar to "thirty"), and a longer g flat to g slur on the word "turned." In the sense that "with my" is similar to "in jail"—the only difference being that the final return to g on "jail" is not consummated on "my"—we have here a reshuffling of four degrees of slides from the initial order of 1, 2, 3, 4 to 3, 4, 1, 2. The next two words, "to the," transitional and less important, are appropriately unembellished *g's*, rhythmically short and connective.

So far all embellishments have been upward slides. Now, on "wall" Bessie uses one of her other frequently employed ornamental devices, a double slide which at first descends and then ascends to a final pitch. Here, in *Jailhouse Blues,* because Bessie is heading for the tonic, the approximate sliding pitches are  (Bessie used two other variants of this embellishment. Another one, also on the tonic, was

36. The piece is in the key of E flat. All pitches are approximate, since Bessie moves fairly freely within the microtonal subdivisions of the scale.

, a quick downward dip to the sixth of the chord and up again. It is used, for example, on the word "wall" in the repeat of the first line of *Jailhouse Blues.* But her most frequently used double-note ornament was reserved for the third of the chord  .

This latter ornament appears with great consistency starting around 1925, and can be heard on any number of recordings: *Reckless Blues, Sobbin' Hearted Blues, Cold in Hand Blues,* and many others.)

On the word "wall" in the repeat line, we encounter another of Bessie's favorite devices, a phrase-ending "drop-off" or "fall-off." It is usually associated with the tonic and drops quickly to the sixth of the scale  . But occasionally she did similar "drop-offs" on the third and even on the fifth of the key, as in *Cold in Hand Blues,* where the "fall-off" drops to the flat third  .

Two further phrase idiosyncrasies appear in *Jailhouse Blues.* The one is a variant of the "drop-off," longer and more pitch-inflected. We hear it here on the word "turned," an interpolated phrase repeating the last half of the first line as a fill-in. (This two-bar "fill-in" would normally have been an instrumental response to the singer's first line, but since *Jailhouse Blues* was accompanied only by a pianist, Clarence Williams, Bessie occasionally decided to fill in the two bars herself.) On the word "turned" she sings 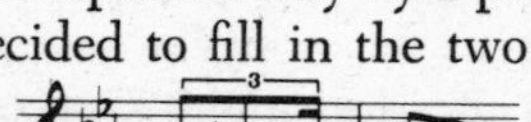 , thus turning the word into a blues moan. Here, although the pitches are still connected by slides, they are nevertheless more articulated than in her other ornaments so that an actual melodic motive emerges.

Bessie also had a unique ability to break phrases into unexpected segments and to breathe at such phrase interruptions without in the slightest impairing over-all continuity, textual or melodic. In the repeat of the "Thirty days" line, Bessie breathes twice at unexpected places: between the words "my" and "back" for a real break in the phrase; then again between "turned" and "to the wall," a smaller interruption. The reason for these breath breaks is the previously mentioned interpolated half-phrase, "turned to the wall," which prevented her from going to the end of the second repeat line without breathing. Thus the over-all partitioning of both lines is as follows (’ is an incidental breath mark, V is a more pronounced interruption):

> Thirty days in jail ’ with my back turned ’ to the wall ’
> Turned V to the wall ×
> Thirty days in jail with my V back turned ’ to the wall.

Note that in the one place where one might have expected a breath, marked × , Bessie goes right on, bridging the natural division of the sentence.

One could cite hundreds of such examples in which word and melodic patterns are broken up in unexpected and often asymmetrical ways. It should suffice to cite one more, the fourth chorus of *Cold in Hand Blues* (not counting the opening verse). Note the breath interruptions here too, the first time after the word "myself," the second time *in the middle of the word,* yet without the slightest loss of continuity (Ex. 19). (The "jiving" chattering trumpet responses are by Louis Armstrong.)

Example 19 *Cold in Hand Blues*

Bessie Smith enjoyed the collaboration of a host of remarkable accompanists and jazz soloists. This was the result to a large extent of the influence of her recording director and part-time manager, Frank Walker, and other musical advisers like Clarence Williams and Fletcher Henderson. We are told that Bessie in her heyday was not eager to share the limelight with other stars, vocal or instrumental. Although she had a few favorites, like trumpeter Joe Smith and trombonist Charlie Green, she seems to have known or cared little about the famous jazz soloists of her day. She is said to have initially disapproved the choice of Louis Armstrong, and agreed to it only reluctantly. Despite this fact, some of Bessie's and Louis's collaborations are memorable jazz.

In a ten-year recording career Bessie was accompanied by half a dozen pianists, about two dozen duo or trio combinations, many of them out of the Fletcher Henderson circle, and three or four larger ensembles, notably Henderson's Six (really seven players), as well as one or two vocal groups in 1929 and 1930. These accompaniments, given their variety and the constant change of personnel, are of a consistently high level. Furthermore, in almost every instance Bessie and her collaborators fashion a unique sound world, each one different from any of the others, each one effective and integrated, each one a little tone poem.

I suppose we can expect arguments about which of these accompaniments is the best for as long as Bessie's records are part of our listening heritage. It depends partly on one's point of view, whether one wants to have the voice unequivocally featured or whether one wants to hear it in an ensemble context, whether one is going to look for social protest or for purely musical evaluations in her recordings.

In the first category, the solo piano accompaniments, Bessie had some superb collaborators. Of these, James P. Johnson and Fletcher Henderson are usually singled out, commensurate with their reputation in jazz. But two other superior accompanists, Fred Longshaw and Porter Grainger, knew Bessie's ways with a song perfectly, particularly Longshaw, and had that rare ability of the true accompanist to stay out of the way of the singer but to fill in with a linking phrase or an appropriate response when required. The work of these men is easily overlooked because they were never spectacular, nor were they meant to be. They were well-disciplined, solid musicians performing with ease in a very difficult (because secondary) role.

Fletcher Henderson, like many of the musicians who assisted Bessie, was obviously inspired by her and under this influence made his best recordings as a pianist—the same can be said of clarinetist Buster Bailey. On *Jazzbo Brown from Memphis Town* and *Gin House Blues* (1926) both men contribute beautifully integrated accompaniments. Curiously, Fletcher Henderson's spry and bouncy rhythmic style and his bright, clear tone are the perfect foil for the heavier, thicker sonority of Bessie's voice. Likewise, Bailey weaves some exceedingly beautiful obbligatos in and out between voice and piano. Both sides, one a joyously swinging romp about a legendary Memphis clarinet player, the other a poignant-to-the-point-of-pain blues, alluding to Bessie's own addiction to gin, are fine examples of her sensitivity to words and her use of consonants and syllabic articulation in order to swing. *Gin House Blues* is also fascinating for the way in which its repeated arching two-bar vocal lines combine fierce intensity and resignation. Each phrase is initiated with a raspy, pain-wracked, pleading quality, and in turn each phrase subsides to the tonic with a bitter-sweet simplicity and resignation. Though the pattern is repeated in essence throughout the record, it is so perfectly controlled that one never tires of it.

Among the various duo and trio accompaniments the most famous are those with Louis Armstrong, Joe Smith, and Charlie Green, often including some of the above-named pianists. Each soloist was distinctive and yet each became in his own way an extension of Bessie's voice. In terms of purely sonoric identification, Joe Smith and Charlie Green were undoubtedly the closest to her of the many "horn" players that accompanied her. Joe Smith's turmpet had the lovely, open, rich quality of Bessie at her most relaxed self, while the match between Green's trombone moans and raspy tone and Bessie's harder, more bitter effusions is sometimes uncanny. On *Lost Your Head Blues* and *Young Woman's Blues* (both 1926), Joe's tone, speed of vibrato, and carefully controlled pitch range provide a perfect matching continuity to Bessie's voice. On *Young Woman's Blues* Smith also shows a huge, almost trombone-sized tone and provides utterly relaxed rococo ornaments.

Charlie Green recorded constantly with Bessie, and on no recordings can he be heard to better advantage. His range of expression ran the gamut from rough humor to salacious sexual imagery. For example, in *Trombone Cholly* (1927) Green and Bessie match rasp for rasp in ribald humor. In *Empty Bed Blues,* Green's growly, grinding trombone perfectly underscores Bessie's various sexual metaphors. Green is heard in a more subtle, more accompanimental role in the superb *Nashville Woman's Blues,* with its wry, worldly-wise, insinuating plunger-and-growl commentaries.

Green's many excellent performances with Bessie have tended to obscure one of the three other trombonists to record with her, Joe Williams. Very close to Green in style, Williams had an extra touch of tension and nastiness in his tone that suited perfectly Bessie's 1928 blues about *Me and My Gin.*

Louis Armstrong cut nine sides with Bessie, all of them, as might be expected, above average. Aside from their intrinsic merits (and slight demerits), the sides with Armstrong had immense importance for Bessie's artistic development. The first five sides recorded on January 24, 1925, reveal the two artists as yet not fully adjusted to each other, their two strong personalities not yet enmeshed stylistically. Armstrong too frequently leans toward cloying sentimentality, perhaps misinterpreting or failing to understand the genuinely sad, yet somehow objective, tone of Bessie's blues.

This lack of empathy is particularly disturbing on *You've Been a Good Ole Wagon,* where Armstrong definitely comes off second best.[37] Bessie, in typical fashion, strips this vaudeville standard of its intended folksy, "back home" humor, and turns it into a serious, poignant blues. Armstrong completely ignores the tears and memories of pain that Bessie injects into the song, so directly and subtly below the surface that they are implied more than explicit. He "jives" away in what were probably intended to be humorous asides, skating blithely across the surface of the material. Only after several choruses does Armstrong realize what Bessie's intentions with the song were, and he withdraws half-embarrassedly, never quite finding Bessie's groove. His bland and silly wah-wah mutterings are like a dash of cold water on Bessie's

37. The Bessie Smith–Louis Armstrong collaborations have always been assessed somewhat uncritically, due to Armstrong's formidable position in jazz history. Paul Oliver's generally excellent monograph *Bessie Smith,* Kings of Jazz series (New York: A. S. Barnes & Co., 1961), also suffers from this.

words, "This man has taught me more about lovin' than you will ever know."

On *St. Louis Blues* Armstrong seems more respectful of Bessie; it was their first cautious try at recording together, and perhaps a mutual respect for W. C. Handy's classic and Fred Longshaw's quaint harmonium imitations of a country church organ combined to produce a more restrained atmosphere. (Incidentally, this recording is a perfect illustration of the point Duke Ellington once made, that jazz need not swing in order to be jazz. Bessie's and Louis's *St. Louis Blues* does not swing in the finger-snapping sense, yet it is unquestionably jazz.)

May 26, 1925, found the two in the recording studio again, along with Longshaw (now on piano) and "Big" Green on trombone. The change in Bessie is surprising and profound. The creamy smooth voice of her early recordings (including the previous date with Armstrong) is gone. In its stead we have a harder, more biting quality, with a raspy undertone, especially on attacks, that I suspect Bessie heard first in Armstrong's singing. The other new element that appears on these 1925 sides is an appreciably greater sense of swing, again the influence undoubtedly of Armstrong. Both elements were to remain irrevocably embedded in Bessie's singing, and in turn produced the first complete jazz singer.

For his part, Armstrong was also much more attuned to Bessie on the four May sides. The additional voice of Green automatically produced an ensemble situation, rather than the earlier duo. Taken purely for their musical value these four sides—*Careless Love Blues, Nashville Woman's Blues, I Ain't Gonna Play No Second Fiddle,* and *J. C. Holmes Blues*—seem to me the epitome of Bessie's recording activity. They swing, they are magnificently improvised ensemble records, and they present Bessie in full vocal control and maturity.[38]

Careless Love, which Bessie herself calls a "song of hate," is turned into an impassioned, bitter diatribe. The performance warms up a little slowly, but the final chorus fairly blazes, with Bessie setting the initial words "Love, oh love, oh careless love" in a searing, sliding, moaning chain of blue notes. *I Ain't Gonna Play No Second Fiddle,*

38. They also suggest how indebted Ella Fitzgerald, one of the great singers of our day, is to Bessie for much of her style and vocal quality. During many a phrase on these 1925 Bessie Smith recordings we are impelled to think ahead to Ella.

features an interpolated repeated phrase (on VI and II)—a sort of extended stop-time break—which through repetition accumulates an astonishing intensity. In *Nashville Woman's Blues* Bessie's expansive phrasing and rich tone seem to be beyond metric or rhythmic confinement. Her vocal lines float in a manner that sounds improvised, but probably was not. (Contrary to lay opinion, successive takes of her recordings frequently show that she had a well-defined idea of what she was going to do on each tune. Like a great actress, she created the illusion of total improvisation, even though every move may have been in some manner prepared and studied.) The two horns of Armstrong and Green offer sensitively placed counterlines and responses, with Longshaw providing strong harmonic backing.

J. C. Holmes Blues is one of Bessie's most remarkable records. Its beautiful melody is set in the key of F, which in turn makes her reach for a high *d* in the seventh bar of each of ist simple eight-bar stanzas. The strain her voice acquires on this arching phrase is beautiful and exciting, the excitement one experiences when an obstacle is successfully overcome. Armstrong and Green, in mutes this time, weave a dense, polyphonic, highly ornamental background in an advanced New Orleans style, while Longshaw stays in solid-moving quarter notes, providing rhythm and harmony. The layer of florid passage work in the horns between the broad outlines of Bessie's singing and Longshaw's piano is one of the ensemble triumphs of 1920s jazz.

Many jazz enthusiasts have brushed aside Robert Robbins's violin playing on several 1924 Bessie Smith recordings on the assumption that the violin never has really found a proper place in jazz, and its use constituted an error of judgment on Bessie's part. Without at the moment going into the question of the violin's role in jazz, I feel that Robbins's playing is most appropriate and effective. It has been aptly described as an "alley fiddle" style, and Paul Oliver points out rightly that in fourteen months of recording Robbins's style came "closer to the folk tradition" from which Bessie had come "than the work of any musician whom Bessie had employed to date."[39] Robbins is at his best on *Ticket Agent, Ease Your Window Down.* His "dirty," sliding double-stops in the second blues chorus (not counting the verse) are a fine compliment to Bessie's pleading blues. So are his double-time

39. Paul Oliver, pp. 26-7.

backgrounds in the next three choruses (marred only by pianist Irving Johns's rushing the tempos). On *Sorrowful Blues,* Robbins is joined by the guitarist Harry Reser. With a piano-less background—just guitar and violin—this blues sounds like a dusty country blues, and the record was undoubtedly intended for the back-home market down South.

Bessie recorded three duets with her closest rival, Clara Smith. Though unrelated, Clara's career parallels Bessie's in some ways—same year of birth, same year of recording debut, and an obscure death only two years apart. Moreover, their voices and styles were so similar that they were often hard to tell apart. Clara recorded much less than Bessie—only a dozen sides—and as a consequence she has been overshadowed in jazz histories and criticism by Bessie. Clara's voice was a shade lighter and brighter than Bessie's. Hers lacked the tragic, weighted quality of Bessie's voice, but she had her own captivating timbre, intense and insinuating. Her singing was also rhythmically more regular than Bessie's, and she was not quite the latter's equal in projecting a blues narrative. Her choice of material was often weak (for example, *How'm I Doin',* 1926). In Clara's earlier records she frequently used a cracking, sobbing voice on important words, a device used in hillbilly and country singing. She also featured a slide used by the popular ballad and vaudeville singers of the day which was foreign to the blues. One can hear this on *I Never Miss the Sunshine* (1923), especially on the last line. In later recordings, such as the 1926 date with Lemuel Fowler, this trait is gone.

Clara loved extremely slow tempos (quarter note at 66, for example), and in her early records she and her accompanist Fletcher Henderson were not always equal to sustaining them. But on her finest recordings she was very close to Bessie's equal. Even on the early (1923) *Awful Moanin' Blues* certain words and sustained notes sound exactly like Bessie: the vibrato and the inflection are the same; only the timbre is a trifle lighter in color. The sustained moans in her second and fourth chorus are particularly beautiful. On the 1926 *Whip It to a Jelly* she is even freer, and much that has been said about Bessie's phrasing and inflection could be applied to this recording.

The first duet date with Clara and Bessie in 1923 was a failure. Both women for some reason sang in a stiff, inhibited manner. Perhaps it was the material; both songs are not only extremely poor in melodic invention, but both are alike. The deadly slow tempo did not help, nor did the contrived format in which Clara "improvises" answers to Bessie's straight rendition of the song. Curiously too, the similarity of their voices, range, and enunciation on *I'm Goin' Back to My Used To Be* detracts from the intended duet nature of the performance.

On *My Man's Blues* (1925) both women are more relaxed. They switch to an eight-bar blues so that each can have half a stanza. As both women argue over the same man, finally agreeing to share him, Clara Smith seems to have the upper hand, outsinging Bessie in a magnificent strong, shouting style. In the two interpolated spoken "hokum" routines we hear the two Smiths' natural voices, coming truly alive for those of us who never heard them in person.

Bessie was master of many moods and of most of the material she attempted to sing. Occasionally, especially after her peak years, the material got the better of her. Such is the case in *There'll Be a Hot Time in the Old Town Tonight* and *Alexander's Ragtime Band;* she does comparatively well, but her renditions of these old-time hits never reach the standard of her more personalized classic blues. Her consummate artistry prevented her from falling on her face musically, but such material was far removed from her real life and must have seemed rather abstract. Nevertheless, the famous standard *After You've Gone* (recorded on the same day, March 2, 1927) is as good an example of what makes a jazz singer, as opposed to a pop singer, as one can find. She virtually recomposes the tune and makes it very much her own and very much a blues.

Rarely did Bessie misjudge in the matter of repetition, and we have seen how she was capable of the subtlest variations in timbre and pitch. But on *Send Me to the 'Lectric Chair* (also 1927) she sings the word "Judge" the same way more than a dozen times, and the repetition becomes painful—indeed, one of her few errors of judgment.

Bessie Smith was a big, powerful woman, and she put a great deal of physical intensity and sheer spirit into her singing. In later years, when her voice was worn out by excessive drinking, sometimes there was *only* spirit, as on the 1930 *New Orleans Hop Scop Blues* or *Black Mountain Blues.* But her 1933 comeback recording of *Take Me for a Buggy Ride,* with the "modernist" backing of Frankie Newton (trumpet), Jack Teagarden (trombone), Chu Berry (tenor saxophone), Billy Taylor (bass), among others, is sung with tremendous drive, especially in the two stop-time choruses. Here her voice has a hard edge to it, showing obvious signs of wear and tear.

In 1929 in two sides with James P. Johnson's piano as solo accompaniment, *He's Got Me Goin'* and *Blue Spirit Blues,* however, Bessie shows how she could control the coloring of her voice to suit subject matter. In the former title, her voice is rich and full in her usual manner, in keeping with the meaning of the song and Johnson's happily romping piano (in my opinion Johnson's best accompaniment for Bessie). On the other side, recorded two months later, she sings of hell, and of fire-and-brimstone visions worthy of a Hieronymus Bosch. Appropriately her voice is hard, narrow, and uncompromising.

Bessie's material in later years became increasingly autobiographical, thus inflicting on herself a sort of public self-punishment. Since her voice was no longer entirely reliable, and her record sales were consequently dropping severely by 1929, the beginning of the Depression, the sad finale of her life was in one way or another inevitable. Her tragic early death was perhaps a less painful exit than a long decline into oblivion. For Bessie Smith was one of the great tragic figures, not only of jazz, but of her period, and she more than any other expressed the hopes and sorrows of her generation of jazz musicians. If that were all, we would have reason enough to eulogize her. But Bessie Smith was a supreme artist, and as such her art transcends the particulars of life that informed that art.

6

The Big Bands

In the popular view of jazz history, its development is capsulized into three major geographic locations and correlated chronological periods. New Orleans is given the first two decades of our century, Chicago gets the twenties, while the thirties and thereafter are associated with New York. Like most popular views, it is one not entirely without a basis of truth; it is merely an over-simplification of what is in reality an exceedingly complex pattern of social and musical cross-references within a surprisingly broad geographic area. In tracing and attempting to understand this pattern, especially as it begins to emerge more clearly in the twenties, the music historian is easily overwhelmed by the staggering amount of available data, be it recordings or verbal and written documentation.

As jazz expands in the 1920s, it becomes increasingly difficult to sort out the many strands of direct or indirect influences, of concurrent or successive developments, and of regional musical-social characteristics. Indeed, the latter area is still one of the more controversial aspects of jazz research. At one level, it is self-evident that the sudden wide dissemination of recordings (and radio) broke down regional differences. A musician in Kansas City did not have to travel to Chicago or New York to know what was being played in those cities. He could hear it on records, and he could be influenced by what he heard (if he was so inclined). At the same time, and at another level of creativity, the burgeoning recording industry, with its potential for reaching an unprecedentedly large market and, in turn, a potential for economic betterment, induced even musicians from outlying areas to compete for a corner of the market. The less gifted did so by imitating the leaders and innovators. The talented developed in their own directions and hoped they would be recorded. And as a result, what had originally been a unique amalgam of numerous influences accidentally situated in one city, namely, New Orleans, now radiated out across the rest of the nation, filtered and modified by local or regional traditions, or—more importantly—reshaped and redirected by individual innovators. By the end of the twenties this process of proliferation was well under way, and its main vehicle had become the "big band."

For people not conversant with jazz, it is always difficult to realize that certain ideas or concepts that are taken for granted in "classical" music had to be rediscovered, as it were, by jazz and reinterpreted in jazz terms. The twenties were especially rich in such discoveries, and that decade abounds with "firsts" which musicians came upon in one way or another, singly or—as is so often the case in the arts—simultaneously with others, yet independently. It may therefore surprise some readers that the larger orchestral ensemble, that is, the big band, as a jazz institution had also to be invented and developed.

In the early decades of jazz, the average ensemble consisted of five or six players, usually the front-line trinity of clarinet, trumpet, and trombone, with piano, drums, and bass added. Larger aggregations did exist, and among these one would have to single out the brass bands in New Orleans and those orchestras that played for polite society dances, ensembles which frequently had a violinist as leader or an extra saxophone or two. But it must be pointed out that many of these slightly larger groups were only peripherally related to jazz. Among the groups at the center of the development of jazz, King Oliver's Creole Jazz Band consisted initially of seven players; the basic instrumentation of Morton's Red Hot Peppers vacillated between seven and eight players; and Louis Armstrong recorded for years with his Hot Five and Hot Seven before becoming permanently involved with the big band. But even these ensembles were considered "enlarged," compared to the more typical five-man groups, like the Original Dixieland Jazz Band, the New Orleans Rhythm Kings, the Louisiana Five, and so forth.

The reasons for the smaller-sized ensembles are inherent in the heterophonic structuring of the music they played. If we are talking about a basically improvised music, polyphonically organized, it is obvious that the musical result could be better controlled with five players than with ten, unless unusual safeguards were imposed. It can be stated another way: once the orchestras grew in size, the polyphonic conception of jazz was inevitably seriously threatened. By the mid- and late thirties, at the height of the Swing Era, when the fourteen-man big band had become a jazz institution, the music it played featured almost exclusively block chords, homophonic section writing, and parallel voicings. This constituted a drastic swing of the pendulum, and to this day it has never swung back fully to re-embrace polyphony in the large-ensemble context.

Back in the twenties, the road leading to a significant orchestral conception in jazz was just in its blueprint stages. Yet even in this formative period, a fork in the road becomes discernible, pointing in two divergent stylistic directions which were to mark the course of jazz for several decades. It will be the business of this chapter to trace the spread of jazz via big bands, and the not unrelated split in stylistic conceptions between the Eastern, mostly New York–based orchestras and their Southwestern, Kansas City–oriented counterparts.

Hsio Wen Shih, the architect and writer on jazz, in a brilliant essay has pointed out most of the social and musical background leading to these expansionary changes.[1] It will suffice to restate them in outline. First, there was a new breed of jazz musician entering the field. He belonged to a younger generation, born around 1900, and was likely to be well educated, perhaps even a college graduate, partly brought up in the North, and capable of going on to one of the professions: in other words, a member of the rising Negro middle class. These men were often schooled musicians, and, unlike most of their New Orleans forebears who regarded music as an avocation, they saw jazz as a profession, and one, moreover, with potential financial rewards. The extravagant way in which some jazz musicians, Negroes included, lived in the late twenties indicates that they were correct in these socio-economic assumptions.

This new breed was typified by Fletcher Henderson (with a degree in chemistry), Don Redman (a conservatory graduate), Duke Ellington, Coleman Hawkins, Buster Bailey, and Walter Page, all with

1. Nat Hentoff and Albert McCarthy, eds., *Jazz* (New York, Rinehart & Company, 1959), pp. 173-87.

some degree of musical education. Many others could read music or had enough formal background to pick it up if needed, and they, quite naturally, wanted to put their newly-oriented talents to use. Still others came to jazz, as pointed out previously, from a variety of popular music traditions—the brass bands, the vaudeville circuits, the strictly dance bands—bringing other disciplines to jazz. They in turn picked up jazz much as white dance bands, like those of Paul Whiteman and Jean Goldkette, turned to jazz: as an addition to the repertory—just as one might add polkas to the band's library.[2] A process of cross-fertilization thus began between the reading, non-improvising, instrumentally schooled musician, and his less literate, though not necessarily less gifted, counterpart—an early and subtle form of Third Stream.

A second factor in the expansion of jazz was the spread of radio and recordings that started in the mid-twenties and hit its full stride late in the decade. This in turn produced a vastly enlarged listening audience, which had to be supplied constantly with newer and more varied fare. Whereas the New Orleans musicians had been essentially conservative in their musical tastes, the younger men in the twenties were willing and technically equipped to experiment with new forms and new instrumentations. The new communications media afforded them excellent opportunities to disseminate these new attitudes, at the same time assuaging the public's voracious appetite for new forms of entertainment.

These new musicians enlarged jazz repertory by taking up the thirty-two-bar popular-song form, with its inherent possibilities for greater harmonic sophistication, which had been standardized only a short time before. In the process of absorbing this new material, some of it very tawdry indeed, jazz proved that it was capable of incorporating outside influences without losing its essence. As a result, jazz (and its new generation of protagonists) proved itself capable of evolution.

NEW YORK

New York was in the 1920s, as it is now, the musical center of the world. The most important publishing houses, recording companies,

2. See the section on George Morrison, Chapter 2, and Appendix.

and other business activity involved with music were located there or nearby. The city irresistibly attracted musicians in all fields and styles. Sooner or later everyone in the music field, regardless of where his first successes were scored, had to come to New York for ultimate recognition. And so too, the new popular music styles and dances that developed during World War I and in the immediate post-war period made their way to New York. This period, of course, coincides with the emergence of jazz on a national scale.

Previous chapters that concentrated on two major jazz figures in Chicago, Armstrong and Morton, may have given the impression that *all* important jazz activity in the twenties centered there. This was true to a considerable extent; but, nevertheless, by 1920 New York was the scene of developments which, we can now see in retrospect, proved crucial steps in the eventual course of jazz. New York played an increasingly important role during the twenties in terms of musical activity and economic potentiality. This development reached its peak in 1928 and 1929, when, significantly, both Armstrong and Morton moved permanently from Chicago to New York.

In New York, Fletcher Henderson's orchestra was for many years the most influential jazz organization. Under Henderson's leadership, but more importantly, through the arranging abilities of Don Redman, the orchestra successfully developed a formula for employing a larger ensemble in an essentially homophonic style that could incorporate a true jazz solo.

Henderson came to New York from Cuthbert, Georgia, and Atlanta University in 1920, working as a song-plugger, house pianist, arranger, leader, and recording-date organizer for the Black Swan Record Company. During the height of the blues craze in the early twenties, he provided accompaniments for blues singers as well as for popular singers like Ethel Waters, and he used a small complement of New York musicians for this purpose. These men were all in their earliest twenties, musicians who jobbed around Harlem in various night spots, occasionally participating in recording dates. They took an integral part in the mounting excitement over jazz, or more accurately, the jazz-derived popular and novelty music that most people took for jazz in those days.

Before we analyze the role the Fletcher Henderson orchestra played in the burgeoning New York jazz scene, we must place it in its musical setting. As in New Orleans, as we have seen, many of the musicians who became associated with jazz history in New York did not play jazz at all. Though exceptional men like Morton brought together ragtime and the blues in an embryonic amalgam we can properly call jazz, most of the musicians in the immediate pre-war period were still playing one of the vast number of popular styles developing at that time, ranging from pure ragtime, through its various adulterated and sweetened sub-forms, all the way to semi-"classical," European-based operetta music. In those years, jazz was but one of these many competing directions in music.

Although every shade of the popular musical styles, *including* New Orleans jazz, was at one time or another available in New York, the music that dominated the decade prior to the arrival of men like Henderson and Ellington was that of a Negro musician by the name of James Reese Europe.[3] Europe's fame rested largely upon his association with the popular ballroom dance team of Irene and Vernon Castle, for whom he provided the music. Out of their collaboration came the foxtrot and many other popular steps that had a major part in initiating the Jazz Age. James Europe's music developed out of ragtime, and was at first performed by large orchestras containing enormous sections of mandolins, banjos, and violins. By the time Europe became associated with the Castles' *thés dansants,* he had reduced this to a more manageable size, basically six- or seven-piece groups, consisting of two violins, cornet, and clarinet playing the melody in bald unison, while a piano, one or several mandolins (or banjo-mandolins), trombone, string bass, and drums provided a thin, tinny rhythmic accompaniment. A cello was also used for the quieter interludes in some of the pieces.

Europe recorded in 1913 and 1914 with his Society Orchestra. It is difficult today to glean the essence of these twelve-inch discs through the primitive recording techniques. But after several listenings and with a little musical imagination, one can recapture the extraordinary direct, naïve excitement of this music. It is hard to imagine that any

3. For the fascinating story of this musician, the reader is referred to Samuel B. Charters and Leonard Kunstadt, *Jazz: A History of the New York Scene* (Garden City, N. Y.: Doubleday and Company, 1962).

music of the period could have been more viscerally stimulating, and one begins to understand Europe's phenomenal success. This music was relentlessly rhythmic and, for all its repetitiousness, somehow not monotonous. It must have been electrifying to dance to. Though it was referred to as "syncopated music" (and Europe's various groups were officially called "syncopated orchestras"), there is considerably less syncopation in these performances than one might expect. The pieces were usually in lively 2/4 tempos (usually around ♩ = 140) with melodies that can best be described as simplified, smoothed-out ragtime tunes. The melody was not only doubled in all the melodic instruments, but rhythmically paralleled by the snare drum; longer durations in the melody were simply filled out by a roll. The pieces, some of them composed by Europe, consisted of half a dozen melodic strains, which were repeated until the leader felt that the dancers were near exhaustion. The approaching end would be signaled in an unequivocal manner: a sudden rise in the dynamic level at the beginning of the final strain and an appreciable emphasis of the rhythm section, especially the drums. And here in these final bars often occur slight touches of syncopation not found in the melody. For example the drummer might play: 2/4 ♫ ♫♬ | ♫ ♪ | ♬♬ | ♫ ♪ ‖ , while the banjos shifted gears in a steady barrage of sixteenth notes. And the final two or three bars were always played *accelerando*.

This procedure is followed with relentless exuberance on *Down Home Rag* and *Too Much Mustard*. In these 2/4-tempo pieces the eighth note is really the beat (♩ = 280), and since the tunes consisted mostly of sixteenth notes, one can appreciate the murderous pace of these performances, which went on for a good four or five minutes at a time.

Castle House Rag has a more varied form. Its first strain in fast sixteenth notes vacillates ambiguously between C minor and C major. The second section is a contrasting quieter interlude, featuring the violin and cello in a more polite salon style, still in the fast tempo, however—simply without the sixteenths. The third section features the cornet of Cricket Smith in typical orchestral ragtime. For its climax the piece ends with a machine-gun-like snare drum stop-time solo by the drummer, Buddy Gilmore.

If we compare Europe's Society Orchestra recordings with other popular records of the day, the reasons for his phenomenal success become evident. The music had a rough excitement and rhythmic momentum that simply carried its audience along physically. Europe, in fact, accomplished what other orchestras failed to do: playing ragtime pieces in orchestration as fast as the piano players did. If one listens to the white concert bands of Patrick Conway, Arthur Pryor, and the Victor Military Band—all three were big sellers on the Victor Record label between 1911 and 1918—one can effectively gauge the difference. The Victor Band's recording of *Too Much Mustard* (1913) is much cleaner in execution than Europe's version. It is pleasant, and also unexciting, proper, and stiff. The comparison is similar on the 1915 *Memphis Blues*, of which Europe's Three Hundred and Sixty-ninth U. S. Infantry Hell Fighters Band, an all-Negro outfit, made a noisily exuberant recording in 1919 in France. The breaks in the second strain on the Victor Band recording are laughably polite, whereas in the Hell Fighters version the breaks are wildly impetuous, including a trombone break which must be the first swinging jazz break on records. The difference lay primarily in the rhythmic orientation. The white concert bands could take a ragtime or early jazz piece and make it stiff and polite. Europe could take a polite salon piece and make it swing—in a rudimentary sort of way. That this was not accidental but a conscious approach on Europe's part is proven by the fact that his Hell Fighters could also play a straight march piece (like *How Ya Goin' to Keep Them Down on the Farm*) with clean intonation and execution. The Hell Fighters Band was a large aggregation of about fifty musicians. In a real sense this was the first big band. Naturally the pieces had to be arranged. To hear a whole clarinet section take a clamorous break, as on *That's Got 'Em* or *Clarinet Marmalade*, is to recapture, I am sure, some of the wild abandon of the early New Orleans marching bands.

In summary, James Europe was the most important transitional figure in the pre-history of jazz on the East Coast. We have already seen (in Chapter 5) how his unison melodies gave way to New Orleans polyphony with the Original Dixieland Jazz Band and Earl Fuller's Band. By 1917, the jazz craze was in full swing, and pieces like Arthur Pryor's big hit, *Coon Band Contest*, could no longer be played in the straightforward concert-band manner that had been popular for nearly a decade. It had to be jazzed up and polyphonically restated (as in Earl Fuller's recording of the same piece) and eventually retired to make way for a new jazz repertory. In some ways Europe was to orchestral jazz the same kind of catalyst Jelly Roll Morton was for piano music. Both added new rhythmic dimensions to ragtime and prepared the way for the full emergence of jazz. Had Europe lived, he might have gone on to make the counterpart to Morton's Red Hot Peppers.

The extent of Europe's popularity and the hold he had on the New York musical scene can be measured in part by the negligible influence exerted at the same time by visiting New Orleans players. For example, in 1915, Freddie Keppard's Creole Band appeared in New York. The fact that they appeared as part of a vaudeville act can not be used to explain why the Creole Band failed to make a significant impact, since two years later an equally vaudevillian ensemble, the Original Dixieland Jazz Band, took New York by storm. It may be that Keppard's New Orleans music, though loaded with comedy and novelty routines, was too strange for "sophisticated" New York ears. There was no blues tradition in New York at this time, and one can well imagine that the rather loose, blues-y intonation of Keppard's band was rejected as merely crude ineptitude. By the same token, the expressiveness of the New Orleans style was perhaps too intense to be appreciated. It had to await attenuation at the hands of the ODJB and other white New Orleans groups before jazz could make a lasting impression on New York's musical life.

That impact came in January 1917 when the ODJB opened at one of the Reisenweber restaurants on Columbus Circle, and made history.[4] This was an era of frantic transition for jazz. What had been called, accurately or not, "syncopated music," was now being dubbed *jazz* or *jass;* or possibly both categories were involved, as in the case of James Europe's Clef Club Orchestra, which was billed as a jazz band but called the "Fifty Joy Whooping Sultans of High Speed Syncopation." A competing group named itself the "Fifty Merry Moguls of Melody," but its leader, Fred Bryan, was dubbed the "Jazz Sousa;" while Tim Brymn, Europe's successor in the military band field, had a group called "The Forty Black Devils Overseas" (see Appendix on George Morrison).

4. See Chapter 5.

At this point the picture indeed becomes very confused. The various leaders of stylistic factions invoked esthetic-musical grounds on which to attack their competitors, when in fact they were merely jealous of each other's ambitions and successes. In 1919, while the ODJB were safely away on a one-and-a-half-year engagement in London, various Chicago colleagues, notably the banjoist Bert Kelly and the trombonist Tom Brown, tried to cash in on the success of "jass" by claiming that they had invented the name or invented the music, or both. In the meantime, the New York jazz bands of that year—like Earl Fuller's, the Louisiana Five, the New Orleans Jazz Band—were more often than not playing a vulgar, corny "novelty" music, compared to which the ODJB could only be termed refined and pure New Orleans.

In another corner, James Europe, who many years earlier had had ambitions to become a "serious" musician, but who had in the intervening years succumbed to great commercial success, was now himself attacked by another segment of the Negro musical community. This was the faction led by Will Marion Cook, who, for the sake of these intramural feuds, was not averse to calling himself a "serious" musician, despite the fact that he was the violinist-leader of a fifty-piece organization called the New York Syncopated Orchestra. He had in earlier years provided the music for Bert Williams's stage shows, and had written several early pop standards (such as *I'm Coming Virginia*). James Europe had added to his fame by forming the aforementioned Hellfighters' Band, which was a sensation in France during the war and in the States upon its return. Cook regarded both Europe's brand of brassy jazz and the novelty bands on Broadway, which claimed to represent the Negro's music from New Orleans, as unworthy reflections upon the dignity of Negro music. He undoubtedly had a point, albeit a small one, since the efforts of Cook and confrères like F. Rosamond Johnson and Harry T. Burleigh, who arranged Negro "spirituals" in romanticized, rose-colored harmonizations, were perhaps in some superficial sense "serious." But they were as inaccurate a reflection of the true dignity of the Negro's music as Liszt's Hungarian folk music was of the gypsy's. Added to the confusion were the religious reformers, who claimed that jazz and the new jazz dances were corrupting "our youth" and were responsible for the "immorality" and "licentiousness sweeping the country."

In the midst of all this wrangling over true jazz and Negro music, a new generation of Negro musicians, unheralded and practically unnoticed, was quietly slipping into New York. They were men like the trumpet player Johnny Dunn, who came to New York with W. C. Handy's orchestra from Memphis; trumpet player Joe Smith and clarinetist Garvin Bushell, both from Ohio; Fletcher Henderson and Wilbur Sweatman; while other men like Bubber Miley, June Clark, and Perry Bradford had either grown up in New York or had already been there for some time before the jazz craze really burst onto the scene. In 1919, most of these musicians were not yet out of their teens. But they were absorbing the many musical currents competing or coexisting in New York. As these men were waiting in the wings, so to speak, the revolution in the American entertainment field was continuing unabated. For one thing, the "slapstick" phase of jazz was going into decline. And in its place, a new craze suddenly erupted which was a long step closer to the heart of Negro music, and unquestionably identifiable with jazz: the blues craze.

Much has been written about the importance of the blues as a generic musical form, as a folk art and folk poetry; and even more has been written about the heyday of blues recordings, its legendary figures, the fortunes that were made and lost. But it has never been emphasized sufficiently that the blues craze, following on the heels of the novelty-jazz fad, served to clarify the distinctions between a deeply felt musical expression of a certain ethnic group and a rather superficial, derived commercial commodity. In the process, the blues craze may even have saved jazz from oblivion. Perhaps King Oliver's Creole Jazz Band of 1923, and the subsequent efforts of Armstrong and Morton, would have saved jazz anyway. But already in 1922, the blues recordings of Mamie Smith and the hundreds of other girls who were keeping the recording studios busy were providing abundant evidence that there was a wide gulf between the blues and its attendant instrumental style, and the tricky slapstick music that was being passed off as New Orleans jazz. At the same time, the blues made quite clear the musical distinctions between it and the commercial world of dance bands with their smoothly insipid saxophones and unimaginative stock arrangements.

A man like Fletcher Henderson may not have been able to articulate these thoughts in 1922, but he was, nevertheless, affected very crucially by this turn of events. For not only did Fletcher and his recording mates support themselves financially by recording accompaniments for blues singers—nearly thirty different blues singers in the early twenties[5]—but he was able to resist the many commercial pressures of his trade. Furthermore, involvement with the blues undoubtedly altered Henderson's musical outlook. His musical background was oriented more toward light "classical" music than toward jazz. He had studied piano with his mother, a "classically"-trained pianist, and the Hendersons were one of those middle-class Negro families who disapproved of jazz and other "low-down" music like the blues.[6] Thus, in recording hundreds of blues over a protracted period, Henderson became more adept in the ways of jazz. And lastly, again through these recordings, Fletcher was able to keep together excellent musicians who, in fact, later formed the nucleus of his first permanent band.

It has been said that, though Fletcher Henderson's impression on jazz was a profound one, he himself did very little overtly to bring this about. Indeed, his life was characterized by a casual unawareness of his role in jazz and its responsibilities. Comparing this to the intense megalomania of a Morton or the tenacious drive of an Armstrong, one wonders how Henderson succeeded in a field so aggressively competitive. Henderson seems to have been one of those fortunate individuals who just happened to be at the right place when destiny beckoned. Jazz in its youthful development had reached precisely that stage where Fletcher's particular talents and musical background could provide the right stimulus. The right musicians were there, as was the place, New York. (One can not imagine the same confluence of circumstances in 1923 in Chicago or New Orleans, for example.) The recording and radio boom were on, so that proper dissemination of his efforts was also assured.

Even the accidental manner in which the Henderson orchestra stumbled into its first long-range club engagement was typical of this casual, circumstantial course. A cellar club on West 44th Street, the

5. See the Bessie Smith section in Chapter 5.
6. The story is told that Ethel Waters, whom Henderson accompanied on a lengthy vaudeville tour late in 1921, was so exasperated by Fletcher's inability to accompany her blues properly that she sat him down in Chicago to listen to some James P. Johnson piano rolls. Also, his parents, who were not happy over his association with a "low-down" blues singer, personally screened the whole enterprise before allowing him to go on tour.

Club Alabam, was auditioning for a band. Fletcher was not very interested, but the musicians who happened to be with him after a morning record date talked him into auditioning. They got the job. I think that the role his men have played in the Henderson band's success has never been emphasized sufficiently, especially in recent attempts to rectify the comparative neglect of Fletcher Henderson in the over-all picture of jazz history. He was not a leader in the sense that Duke Ellington was, or Morton, or even Armstrong. The creative stylistic stimulus did not radiate from him, but rather from his men and most particularly from his chief arranger, Don Redman. Henderson did have a keen sense for hiring a certain kind of talented but disciplined player who fitted into his conception of jazz—neat, clean, well-balanced, and somewhat uninvolved emotionally. But there were several incidents in his career as band leader to indicate that Henderson was not always fully appreciative of his players' abilities and their value to him. In the end this is one of the reasons Henderson did not succeed as consistently as did Ellington or Basie.

In that summer of 1923, the average age of the band's members was twenty-two, and Fletcher was nearly twenty-five. What kind of music were they hearing at that time and what were they after musically?

Aside from the blues singers they all worked with, these musicians had not been immersed in the New Orleans style of playing. The slightly older or more experienced men around New York were playing in the Eastern tradition, one much more geared to better technique and a cleaner, emotionally lighter style. It was a tradition that had absorbed and reshaped the essential characteristics of ragtime, but *without* blending them with the blues as Morton had done. It is no mere accident that Henderson, himself a pianist, and the men in his band, influenced considerably by the instrumental reworking of ragtime, a piano idiom, emulated the clean non-dirty, non-slurry sounds and more precise intonation of a piano. Certainly, except for their accompaniments of blues singers, none of the players were blues players, and these factors were to determine the color and feeling of the band over its entire existence.

In 1922 and 1923, these men were listening to a broad range of musical styles, not always uncritically. There were, for example, the dozens of five-piece groups like the Original Memphis Five (who in 1922 alone recorded well over a hundred sides), or the ODJB, now with a revised personnel and a smoother, more refined style. They could also have been listening to and admiring at least certain aspects of the big white orchestras, like Paul Whiteman's and the California Ramblers. There was not much jazz to admire in the former aggregation, but listeners must have respected the precision work and controlled sound of the four-man saxophone section and some of the specialty effects achieved by the arrangers. Hsio Wen Shih has pointed out that Henderson's original instrumentation was very similar to that of the California Ramblers[7] without their violinist-leader and with a tuba instead of a bass saxophone. The Henderson musicians could also have been listening to the New York- and Baltimore-based pianists, like Luckey Roberts, James P. Johnson, Eubie Blake, and Willie "The Lion" Smith, who were in the vanguard of the Eastern jazz movement by virtue of their harmonic sophistication and increased technical virtuosity.

Henderson and his men would also have been listening to A. J. Piron's New Orleans Orchestra, which was playing in New York in 1922 and 1923. Fletcher's musicians were undoubtedly moved by the relaxed, carefree, yet steady bounce of the Piron band, as well as its gentler, more vocal melodic style. But they probably were not interested in its basically polyphonic ensemble conception, which, with its inflexible assignment of functional roles (and even register), must have sounded repetitious and confining to them.[8] They probably also interpreted the Piron band's relaxed, flowing, and unfrantic feeling

7. During the early 1920s the California Ramblers were a very successful white band, made up mostly of young college graduates. Their slightly jerky, bouncy, carefree music, full of Charleston syncopations, epitomized the early days of the Jazz Age. A successful record of *Copenhagen* prompted Henderson and others to rush in with competitive recordings. (Henderson's will be discussed later in this chapter.) An excellent example of the Ramblers at their best—with smart, perky ensembles and solos—can be heard on Riverside's *History of Classic Jazz,* SDP-11, side 9, track 2. The side, *Sweet Man,* features among others a bass saxophone solo by Adrian Rollini which, in its "modern" conception and well-constructed continuity, anticipates the work of modern jazz musicians like Gerry Mulligan and Pepper Adams by some twenty years.

8. Several Piron recordings made in New York in 1923 and in New Orleans two years later have been reissued in recent years. They are fine examples of the politer branch of the New Orleans style as practiced by the "society orchestras" in the twenties. A subtle influence by white orchestras and their expanded repertory is discernible. They also lack the extraordinary cohesiveness of Oliver's best Chicago recordings, but retain a most important element: the joyous, relaxed feeling that was the essence of New Orleans playing.

as old-fashioned country-style playing. The Eastern players had already developed a much jerkier, more accented, and more nervous style, their tone more brilliant and projecting, but also harsher; and they most certainly must have regarded this as the more up-to-date, "hipper" way of playing.

Henderson and his men probably reacted the same way to King Oliver's first recordings, which created a sensation among musicians in the summer of 1923. But if they were impressed by the juggernaut rhythm of the Creole Jazz Band and its remarkable rhythmic unity, they misinterpreted it, judging by their own first recordings that year. They failed to hear that Oliver's rhythm came from within, that it was a subtle inner energy linked to fluidity of movement, and to the sensitive projection of a vocal conception of tone rather than a purely instrumental one. They heard the 4/4 beats of Oliver's band rather than the singing quality of what happened between those beats. Nevertheless, the fledgling Henderson band launched into its first recordings with a rhythmic drive that was a great improvement over the rather watery, aimless rhythm that had characterized most of their previous blues accompaniments. In a sense, this band was unconsciously rejecting the older, classic New Orleans rhythmic concept in order to create a new one, more suited to a different structure and texture, a rhythmic concept they were to perfect by the early thirties and from which the whole Swing Era evolved.

From its very inception, Don Redman took musical charge of the band. He had been a child prodigy and a conservatory-trained musician who was able to play almost all the conventional instruments and who had already done some arranging for a band from Pittsburgh, Billy Paige's Broadway Syncopators. Since the Henderson band was playing for white patrons, much of their early repertoire consisted of stock arrangements of hit tunes of the day played in a style that imitated to some extent the sound of Whiteman's orchestra and other successful white bands like Sam Lanin's and Guy Lombardo's. But little by little, Redman began to recast the stock arrangements or write original arrangements, not only of standard tunes, but also of Henderson's own compositions.

One of their first records, *Dicty Blues* (August 1923), already shows the new trend in its elementary outlines. Redman's arrangement consists of a mixture of improvised ensembles, solos with (or without) harmonized backgrounds, and a combination of the two where simplified solo-like passages are harmonized and set against even simpler riff figures. In all these combinations, the reed and brass sections are set off against each other, one playing rather static, unmoving harmonies, and the other, more rangy ensemble passages. There is a great deal of orchestrational variety, and Coleman Hawkins's saxophone is given a variety of roles: inside harmony parts, improvised counter melodies, and a solo; at one point he even doubles the tuba, playing a boogie-woogie type of bass line. Then there are brief interjections by chimes, a very "dicty" ("high toned") thing in those days and a device widely used by the more "sophisticated" white bands of the period.

In its rhythmic phrasing, the band placed notes stiffly on the beat, jerky by any standards, and when combined with Hawkins's aggressive slap-tonguing, difficult to take today. The eighth notes are played very much as a dotted eighth–sixteenth pattern (♪. ♬), and there is very little legato playing. It is interesting to note that at the same time (1923) the Oliver and Piron orchestras were playing a more loping, triplet (♩♪) rhythm, while still farther west, the Bennie Moten band was playing even eighth notes in an uncomfortably primitive, stiff manner. These rhythmic-stylistic elements are of great importance for delineating regional characteristics in the early bands.

From this beginning, the Henderson band takes a somewhat erratic path, inevitably vacillating between opposing pulls, catering on the one hand to the tastes of their white dancing audience, trying on the other to deal with new musical problems in an original and honest way. At an early stage (1924) the band gained impetus from the addition of two outstanding soloists, the trombonist Charlie Green and Louis Armstrong.

Henderson really preferred another trumpeter, Joe Smith, and Louis was a second choice, pressed upon him, one suspects, by his musicians after Smith, who had played with several of Fletcher's recording groups from time to time, turned down an offer to join the band permanently. Joe Smith is one of the most interesting trumpet players of the twenties in that he combined a sovereign technical mastery with a sensitivity and lyrical style unknown in those early rowdy days of jazz. Smith was Henderson's ideal, because he had an extraordinarily beautiful sound, a flawlessly clean and graceful delivery, and ease in reading. He could play lead as well as solo. In short, he was the kind of all-around musician Henderson instinctively sought. His many excellent solos with Henderson give ample evidence, at a surprisingly early date in jazz history, that a basically clean (as opposed to "dirty") way of playing was not incompatible with swinging well or playing expressively. We have already mentioned the moving and expressive way he played in accompanying Bessie Smith on many records in the mid-twenties.[9]

When Henderson could not get Joe Smith, he hired Armstrong, for he undoubtedly remembered the day in 1921 when on his Ethel Waters tour he had heard young Louis in New Orleans. He had been impressed by Armstrong then, and, it is said, tried to get him to come to New York. Now in 1924, Louis's reputation was rising fast as the new second-cornet man with the King (Oliver), and he would obviously be a great asset to the ambitions of this band.

However advanced the Henderson band thought it was in 1924, when Louis joined them, it must have become clear that they were still somewhat behind the vanguard. On side after side the band came alive only during Louis's solos, and in the course of time, these solos left an indelible mark on the band's rhythmic swing. Today most people would rate Armstrong and Coleman Hawkins equal (or nearly equal) as jazz soloists. But in 1924 there was a vast difference between Louis and Hawk, as a recording like *Go 'Long Mule* attests. Louis's solo is a real solo in its feeling and melodic freedom. Hawk's brief solos here and elsewhere are more like ensemble parts, or up-and-down delineations of chords. They are not melodies, and their extremely jerky rhythms are difficult to accept today. *Go 'Long Mule* is also an excellent example of the kind of stylistic tug-of-war going on between the material itself (in this case a cakewalk kind of tune that was old-fashioned even in 1924) and the mixture of reactions to it by players in the band. On one level, Armstrong and Redman indulge in "novelty" imitations of a mule (although they really sound more like the neighing of a horse than the braying of a mule). At another level, we find fully arranged trumpet trios in the wah-wah style developed by Henry Busse, Whiteman's popular trumpet player. A little later we have a high-register clarinet duet, which, however, turns out not to be fully written out. Redman plays the tune, stiffly, while Hawkins im-

9. See Bessie Smith section in Chapter 5.

provises a loose two-part harmonization directly below—a practical compromise between a written out and an improvised duo. And almost buried beneath the many disjointed stylistic layers, one finds the kind of musical minutiæ good musicians are always exploring. Underneath Louis's mule-clowning we can hear a tiny little rhythmic experiment going on between Redman and Henderson (Ex. 1) as the clarinet

Example 1 *Go 'long Mule*

Clarinet
Piano

plays an *alla breve* variant of the tune against the rhythm section's Spanish-sounding accompaniment.

Shanghai Shuffle is an obvious attempt to create another *Limehouse Blues*, one of the big hits of 1924. But Redman's sense of economy makes the most out of some unextraordinary ideas. As in all of these early "experimental" recordings, Redman makes a few ideas go very far and thereby achieves a unity of style and form unusual in the jazz of that period. Introductions reappear, sometimes slightly altered, as codas; rhythmic accompanimental patterns are used several times in diverse contexts, as when the initial rhythm (Ex. 2A) is recast underneath Charlie Green's gutty, massive trombone solo into a kind of elaborated stop-time chorus[10] (Ex. 2B). *Shanghai Shuffle* also has the

Example 2 *Shanghai Shuffle*

10. In the ninth to twelfth bars of this chorus Redman, worried about the band losing tempo in the tricky counter-rhythm, pushes the band audibly ahead. Momentarily shaken, the band reunites in the thirteenth bar and surges ahead to regain the lost time.

first recorded use of an oboe in a Negro orchestra, when Redman plays the tune accompanied by two clarinets in thirds.

Copenhagen (October 1924) marks a bigger-than-usual step forward in Redman's work. The lively tempo gave him time within the three-minute limit of the ten-inch disc to exercise his orchestral imagination: the faster the tempo, the more choruses could be fitted onto a record. Moreover, the band had been expanded to eleven men with the addition of clarinetist Buster Bailey.

With the arrival of Louis Armstrong as a featured soloist, Redman had to find the proper stylistic frame for this startling soloist's work. One solution lay in the tempo. For an arranger it is always more difficult to emulate the improvisational freedom of a soloist in a slow tempo than in a fast one; there are obviously many more ways a soloist can fill out a slow beat than a fast one. A bright tempo, in which the rhythmic momentum takes care of itself, was one way of handling, or rather, avoiding the issue. Redman's other solution was based on intuitive recognition of the fact that Louis, who was in a transitional stage at this time, was still close enough to the New Orleans collective ensemble technique to permit a bridge between it and the newer solo-and-section style. *Copenhagen* was Redman's brilliant realization of this intuition.

Despite the fact that much of *Copenhagen* is dissected orchestrationally into four-bar phrases, the performance seems surprisingly uncluttered. This is due to the fact that Redman stressed the contrast between brass and reeds in an unequivocal way (Ex. 3). Brass trios were contrasted with clarinet trios, and the separation of choirs was emphasized by writing parallel sections that contrasted with collective improvisations when the choirs were mixed.

The structural scheme is quite complex and advanced for 1924—even Morton had not yet accomplished anything like it—and shows how, even as a schematic abstraction, contrasts of timbre, texture, and register are fully exploited. No one particular approach is allowed to settle in for very long. As we listen to the record today we are amazed how effortlessly the performance moves between section playing and solo. Only at B^3 is a player, Charlie Green, unable to catch the snappier spirit of the piece. One of the reasons *Copenhagen* sounds so all of a piece is that the performance is tied together by the unswerving, "straight-ahead" approach of the rhythm section; it is as if the whole performance were riding in on a rhythmic assembly line.

Example 3 *Copenhagen*—Scheme

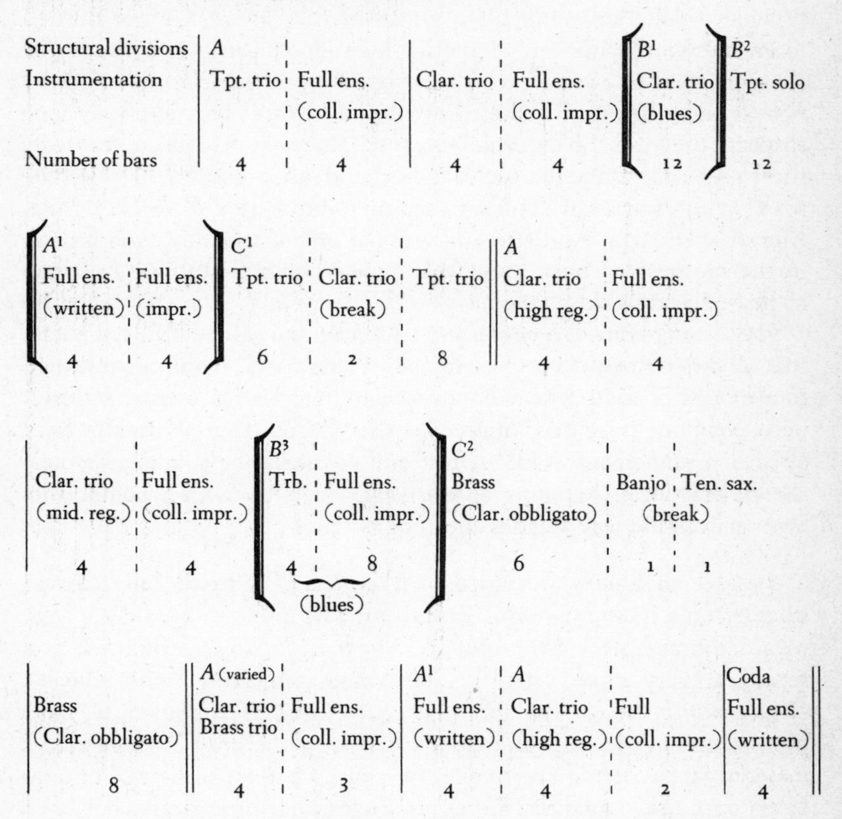

It is interesting to see how Redman begins to break down phrase lengths toward the end of the piece: the one-bar breaks in C^2, and the gradual reduction of the four-bar written ensemble at A^1 to three bars and finally to two bars. At the same time these four-bar segments are juggled into a new sequence by the unexpected reappearance of A^1. In the final four bars Redman turns what at first sounds like another repeat of A^1 into a descending chromatic "tag" that leaves the piece hanging harmonically in mid-air on the tritone of the key.

A word about the clarinet trio as an arranger's device. It has generally been ascribed to Henderson or to Redman. The first assumption is erroneous. The second is true to the extent that Redman, himself a reed man, emphasized and popularized the clarinet trio. It is harder to believe that Redman actually *invented* this device. Garvin Bushell in an interview with Nat Hentoff,[11] mentions playing in a vaudeville show in 1920 or 1921 in which the band had three clarinets. He did not go on to specify whether they played in three-part harmony; one suspects they did. Stock arrangements, moreover, had been featuring three-part saxophone harmonizations; and an orchestra like Whiteman's with its array of doubling reed men, must have used the clarinet trior prior to 1924. And after all, was not one of the most popular acts in the music-show business of that time Wilbur Sweatman's playing of three clarinets simultaneously?

How exceptional *Copenhagen* was, can be gained from the fact that all other late 1924 and early 1925 Henderson recordings returned to a morass of twittering vibratos and unimaginative section writings with pompous interludes and codas that seldom rose above the level of stock arrangements. Only Armstrong seemed to be able to surmount the general level, swinging expansively, freqently with a behind-the-beat feeling that was decades ahead of its time.

Sugar Foot Stomp (recorded in May 1925) is frequently cited as Henderson's most important record, and he himself is said to have regarded it as his favorite. Actually, *Sugar Foot Stomp* strikes me as a record of very mixed quality. The whole association with Oliver's *Dippermouth Blues,* the fact that Armstrong is supposed to have brought the music with him from Chicago, is the kind of "legendary" material jazz writers have frequently pounced upon in lieu of criteria based on musical analysis. Certainly *Sugar Foot Stomp* does not have the cohesiveness of *Copenhagen*. Where in the latter the three techniques employed result in a unified work, in *Sugar Foot Stomp* they do not blend together into a single purpose, and their disparate quality is disconcerting. Redman is responsible for the negative elements, because his additions to the original *Dippermouth Blues* are the weakest links. Louis does exceedingly well with Oliver's old solo, and Redman

11. Nat Hentoff, "Garvin Bushell and New York Jazz in the 1920's," *The Jazz Review,* January 1959, p. 13.

comes up with a smart stop-time device in the middle of it. But the shrill and badly played clarinet-trio choruses and the later sustained "symphonic" sections are out of place next to the solos or semi-improvised passages. The purpose of these sustained sections was, I suppose, to set up a whole-note foil for the succeeding beat and walking bass of the tuba (𝅝 to ♩). But in 1925, the band was not ready to make such quasi-intellectual ideas succeed. Only Kaiser Marshall, the drummer, catches the terrific spirit and swing of Louis's solo; and for a few measures his cymbal back-beats have a flow which anticipates Sidney Catlett, Walter Johnson, and some of the great Kansas City–style drummers.

The succeeding sides made up to Armstrong's departure in October 1925 do not represent any significant steps forward. But Joe Smith had returned once again, and whenever he plays on these records, with his clean, swift, and somewhat clipped style, everything sounds right and of a piece. His articulation and sense of timing are much closer to the band's style than Louis's, whose solos always cause the listener to make an aural shift. Indeed in Armstrong's second solo on *T.N.T.*, he does a flawless imitation of Joe Smith's smoother style. The last part of *T.N.T.* also introduces another idea which we might take for granted after forty years of continual exploitation: a whole chorus or eight-bar phrase played in block chords by the entire band. This six-part wall of sound must have startled the dancers at the Roseland in 1925.

Another young, fresh voice joined the band in early 1926, nineteen-year-old trombonist Benny Morton. His early role (before 1931) with the Henderson band has never been explored, since until recently the trombone playing on the 1926-28 sides was thought to be by either Green or Jimmy Harrison. Actually it is unmistakably Morton. His lithe, modern swinging style and formidable technique were years ahead of other players, even Harrison, and I suspect that he was not really understood or appreciated by Henderson until years later. In bald notation, it is not possible to capture the nonchalant ease and youthful mastery of Morton's playing, but few if any trombone players could at that time have managed passages like the following (in *When Spring Comes Peeping Through*) at a tempo of ♩= 276 (Ex. 4A and B). Besides Armstrong, Morton was the only player to join

Example 4 *When Spring Comes Peeping Through*

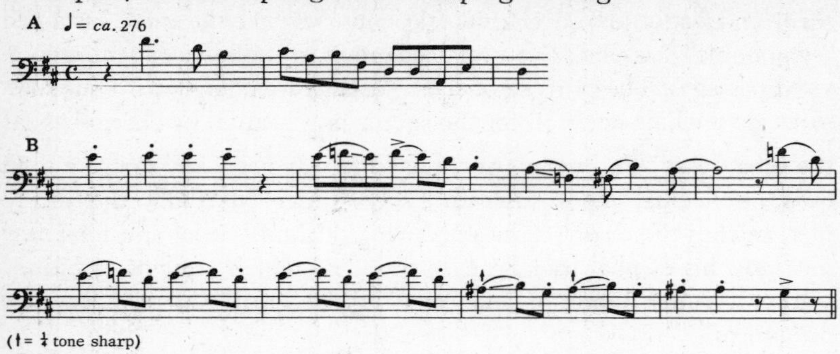

the band who played really swinging syncopations and rhythmic embellishments of the beat, in contrast to the on-the-beat approach of the other members of the band.

From the first seconds of *Stampede* (May 1926), it is clear that there is a new air about the band. Rex Stewart, the replacement for Armstrong, bursts in with a brash, lusty introductory solo that nails down the driving atmosphere of the entire performance. It is significant that now our attention is attracted not to Redman's fancy whole-tone introductions and arranged trios but to the soloists and the new momentum of the band's playing. Hawkins provides a long, well-structured solo melodically fashioned in Armstrong's style. Smith's and Stewart's solos reflect respectively the present and the future of the band's style in contrasting choruses. Even the clarinet trio is better played than usual and features a spectacular break (Ex. 5). The

Example 5 *Stampede*

rhythm is still two-beat in feeling, but it is beginning to have a more horizontal flow in the direction of swing.

By the end of the year 1926 the band could handle a virtuoso arrangement like *Henderson Stomp* as well as any white band, while still retaining the basic jazz feeling. Another fast stomp piece, it was played with robust drive despite its technical and orchestrational intricacies. Redman's writing becomes more full-bodied as he learns to integrate the reeds and brass in separate yet related patterns. It is as if each section presents two aspects of the same idea. He also learns how to keep the instruments moving rhythmically, so that the ensemble passages sound improvised, almost like the work of seven soloists. A special lift is given the performance by Tommy Ladnier's updated New Orleans trumpet, June Cole's tuba, and finally Fats Waller's two-fisted stride piano.[12]

The remaining 1926 sides break no new ground. *The Chant* has a mildly intriguing moment when a banjo solo is superimposed on Waller's organ background—proof that the gimmick-sound was discovered long before the days of modern recording directors. But Redman did not really know what to do with this harmonically interesting piece by Mel Stitzel, as comparison with Jelly Roll Morton's recording from the same period will easily confirm.[13]

Redman and the band fared much better on a number of recordings made in early 1927. Ladnier had developed into a major soloist; Jimmy Harrison, the rising trombone star, had been added to the band; Coleman Hawkins was finding his own voice; and Redman's arrangements were smart as a whip. *Rocky Mountain Blues* (not the same piece as recorded in 1930 by Ellington) shows the capability of the Henderson orchestra at this time. Though it is somewhat over-arranged by Redman, the band takes it all in stride. From a historical point of view, the side's most notable feature is Redman's prophetic ensemble background behind Ladnier's first solo, scored in six-part block chords for three clarinets and three muted brass (Ex. 6).

Example 6 *Rocky Mountain Blues*

12. Ladnier had replaced Stewart, who left the band temporarily because he felt he was not ready yet to play with it. Escudero had left for McKinney's Cotton Pickers, and Fats Waller was substituting for Henderson as repayment on a check for a dozen hamburgers Fats had put away at one sitting and then discovered he could not pay for. In those days, the fate of a recording could be decided by such quotidian practicalities!

13. See footnote 40, Chapter 4.

With the clarinets on top the sonority produced is exactly that of the famous Glenn Miller sound of a dozen years later.

In *Tozo* an ensemble passage of considerable rhythmic interest seems to initiate a flurry of Redman experiments with ternary rhythms (3/4 and 3/8). Brass and clarinet chords alternate in a 3/4 pattern, above the 4/4 of the banjo, and 2/2 of the tuba (Ex. 7).[14]

Example 7 *Tozo*

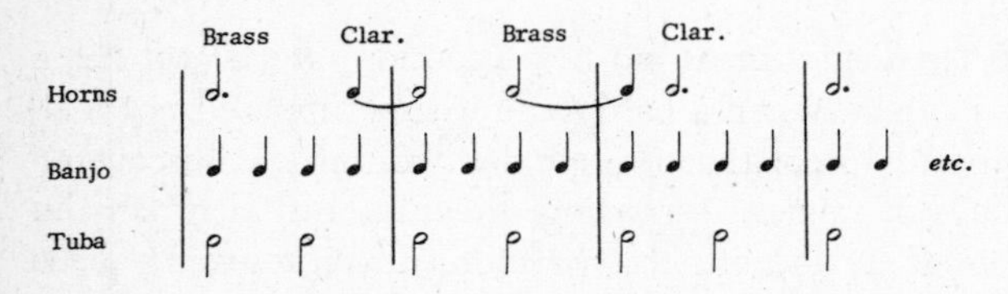

Similarly rhythmic experimentation occurs in *Whiteman Stomp,* a Fats Waller composition arranged by Redman on commission from Whiteman. It is so brashly intricate that, it is said, even the Whiteman orchestra could not play it at first. At a tempo of about ♩ = 240, it has many pompous, over-arranged "look-Ma-no-hands" moments, but one must respect Redman's ingenious way with a variety of 3/8 and 3/4 figures (all in the 4/4 jazz meter, of course), as in Example 8A, B, and C, as well as in Kaiser Marshall's hi-hat cymbal figures. A combination of 5/4 and 2/4 patterns is also tried:

Example 8 *Whiteman Stomp*

At this point a drastic change in the life of the Henderson orchestra took place. Don Redman left in March 1927 to become co-leader of a Detroit band, McKinney's Cotton Pickers. Redman would not be

14. Again, it reminds us of the Clap and *Gankogui* patterns of Chapter 1, only written in "long" notation.

hard to replace as an alto saxophonist, but as architect of the band's style he was virtually irreplaceable. This was borne out by a host of recordings from this period in which Henderson tried out a number of arrangers, including reputedly even Duke Ellington.[15] They are uniformly mediocre, starting with Ken McComber's *Have It Ready* and including such pieces as *Variety Stomp* and *St. Louis Blues,* which I believe are not Redman arrangements, as usually credited, but by Mel Stitzel or merely stock arrangements. The band began to flounder and returned to early mannerisms, such as the saccharine Joe Smith solo on Will Marion Cook's old tune *I'm Coming Virginia.*

In this period also falls the Henderson band's encounter with the music of the ODJB. Within a four-month period they recorded *Fidgety Feet, Clarinet Marmalade* (with the appropriate squealing clarinet by Bailey), *Sensation,* and *Livery Stable Blues,* as well as *Wang Wang Blues* by one of the ODJB's musical heirs, Gus Mueller. Though the band tried hard and the records sold well, the material was wrong and their efforts sounded forced.

The blow dealt to the orchestra by Redman's departure was compounded by the fact that Henderson unaccountably lost interest in the band. An automobile accident in the summer of 1928 made matters worse as Henderson became increasingly listless and bemused, especially in regard to the orchestra's business affairs. Between November 1927 and October 1930, the Henderson orchestra, although considered the most prominent group in the country, made only about a dozen recordings. The discipline, musical as well as personal, deteriorated badly. An example of the former can be heard on the two recordings of *Hop Off,* one of Redman's last efforts for the band, and a good one. As recorded for Columbia in November 1927, it is an exciting, finely shaded piece in an early riff-style, with fine confident solos by Ladnier, Harrison, and Hawkins. (In fact, Hawkins's final four-bar break makes it plain that he is about to become the band's major soloist.) By the time *Hop Off* was recorded a second time for the Paramount label in early 1928, it had deteriorated so much that it is hardly recognizable as a Henderson recording.

During this period Henderson continued to rely on a host of white arrangers for the more "commercial" dance-band numbers he needed

15. *St. Louis Shuffle,* first recorded on March 23, 1927, has frequently been listed as being arranged by Ellington. But listening to the record makes this hard to believe, even by Ellington's not yet matured 1927 standards.

at the Roseland. He also tried what are known as "head arrangements," arrangements worked out collectively by the band but not written out, and even began to arrange some of the pieces himself. None of these methods produced anything up to the previous level. The head arrangements, as well as Henderson's all had one serious fault in common: they petered out in the final chorus. The sense of form and structure Redman had tried to bring to the band was beyond their vision. Time after time a recording starts off well enough but midway begins to run out of ideas. The tempos are generally too slow and the performances ponderous. What swing the band had acquired now had disappeared, and the loss was aggravated by the fact that the tuba player, June Cole, had to leave for half a year, during which time the bass parts were played by Don Pasquall on bass saxophone in a dated, clumsy slap-tongue style.

A few sides still show vestiges of the spirit and momentum developed during the Redman era. *King Porter Stomp,* Jelly Roll Morton's old standard, which was yet to play an important role in Henderson's life, belongs to this category. Although the tempo taken by Henderson is too slow, and makes the performance lurch along erratically, the band manages to pull itself together for the final classic call-and-response riff-chorus, which through Fletcher's 1932 recording and its remake by Goodman in 1935 was to become the single most influential ensemble idea in the entire Swing Era.

With the exception of *King Porter Stomp,* very few of these 1928 sides were able to recapture any of the earlier momentum. A good idea may crop up, but it is immediately crushed by a polka-like clarinet trio (as on *D-Natural Blues*) that might have come from Lawrence Welk; or the partial success of a final chorus is wiped out by a horrifyingly sentimental "blue seventh" ending in the best Lombardo tradition. Other sides, like *Oh, Baby* and *I'm Feeling Devilish,* have a Dixieland feeling which only dodges the real musical issues. In the end the sides are notable at best for occasional details like Bobby Stark's brief but spectacular trumpet solo on *Easy Money,* and Kaiser Marshall's smart, inventive cymbal work, particularly on *Easy Money* and *Come On Baby*.

It was during this period of indecision and uncertainty that a number of New York bands began to threaten the Henderson orchestra's pre-eminence. Foremost among these was Duke Ellington's orchestra, whose development is analyzed in Chapter 7. Three other bands—Charlie Johnson's Paradise Band, The Missourians, and McKinney's Cotton Pickers—seemed even more of a threat, although developments were to show that their success was short-lived.

It is not easy to assess McKinney's Cotton Pickers accurately on the basis only of their recordings, for we are told that the band never really recorded as well as it sounded in person. Older musicians testify to the high quality of the orchestra, but it is possible that they may be talking about externals of performance, the kind of details of execution musicians are often impressed by. Certainly the band was brimming over with good musicians, and its two arrangers, John Nesbitt and Don Redman, were the elite of the field. Nonetheless, the recordings, while above average in quality, did not add any new dimension to orchestral jazz. Paradoxically, the best sides were made not with the Detroit personnel—that city being the band's home base—but in New York with the nucleus of Fletcher's band.

In its use of arrangers' devices and instrumental techniques the band was undoubtedly in the vanguard. The rich, well-balanced block-chord ensembles of *Peggy*, the ensemble trumpet shakes on *Rocky Road*, the 4/4 "walking" tuba and rhythmically complex unison lines on *Peggy*, the advanced voicings, the over-all precision—these were all touches in which the band excelled. There are good solos by alto saxophonist Benny Carter and by Rex Stewart, some delightful piano backgrounds by Fats Waller in the latter manner of Count Basie (as on *The Way I Feel Tonight*), and moments like Billy Taylor's magnificent tuba contra *d* flat at the end of *Miss Hannah*, surely the lowest pitch on any jazz record before or since.

Despite these moments the band leaves an over-all impression of being emotionally uninvolved. More often than not it seems to be trying to emulate the precision and versatility of Whiteman's orchestra, and there are frequent lapses in taste. The McKinney's Cotton Pickers, a high-powered and well-financed orchestra, may have looked like a good thing to musicians in the late 1920s. History has proven that it did not have the staying power of Ellington's and Basie's organizations.

Charlie Johnson's Paradise Band in its time was regarded by many as highly as Duke Ellington's. In a sense the band, located at Small's

Paradise, a Harlem night club, was Duke's closest competitor, for he also provided show music and jungle tableaux for the white patrons from downtown. Through Johnson's band passed a host of fine musicians; Jimmy Harrison,[16] Jabbo Smith, Benny Carter, trumpeter Sidney de Paris, tuba players Cyrus St. Clair and Billy Taylor, and the remarkable band drummer George Stafford. Yet while Ellington was able to thrive in this milieu, Johnson's band did not survive. It did not have the necessary precision and arranger's skills to compete with the likes of Henderson or McKinney's Cotton Pickers, nor did it have a leader with the creative talents and discipline of an Ellington. Much of the band's playing was ragged (for example, the trumpet duet on *Hot Tempered Blues*) or lack-luster (*Harlem Drag* and *Hot Bones and Rice*). The band aspired to emulate Redman's arranging devices, but usually could not carry them off. An exception is a rather well-executed saxophone ensemble chorus on *The Charleston Is the Best Dance After All,* as arranged and led by Benny Carter. The soloists reacted diversely to the band. Some like Harrison and Sidney de Paris (in his superb talking plunger solos on *Boy in the Boat*) reacted well. On the other hand, Jabbo Smith's playing with the band is not on a level with his own Rhythm Aces recordings.

Actually, Johnson's band was at its best when it could indulge in free-wheeling collective improvisations, unhampered by compositional disciplines or other considerations. There exist several such examples in the band's recorded work, the most exciting of which are the last two choruses of *Hot Tempered Blues*. Here the band swings and rocks in a manner way ahead of its time, especially in the final climactic, collectively improvised chorus. In its all-out abandon, it stops just this side of cacophony, a triumph of the art of ensemble improvisation.

The Missourians were another band that took New York by storm in the mid-twenties. Originally from St. Louis, they were the band at Harlem's Cotton Club until Ellington took over that spot late in 1927. The Missourians later (1931) became the nucleus of Cab Calloway's orchestra, once again ensconced at the Cotton Club. They recorded a dozen sides in 1929 and early 1930 which show the orchestra as an unsophisticated ensemble in the manner of Moten's mid-twenties bands. Like most Mid- and Southwestern bands, the Missourians had

16. His work with Johnson is discussed in the Brass Players Section in Chapter 5.

a rough, brash style that a four-year stay in New York had not done much to curb. The band's style was still close to ragtime, with an indefatigable, punchy two-beat rhythm that had at least the virtue of being very danceable. An indication of the band's limitations can be seen in the fact that, despite exotic names like *Ozark Mountain Blues, Market Street Stomp,* and *Stopping the Traffic,* five of the twelve recorded numbers are all *Tiger Rag.* In these numbers the band was at its best and displayed an elemental, fiery drive that probably no other band in New York could match—or probably wanted to. For the Missourians were a band that worked primarily in clichés. Still, as driven by Leroy Maxey's drums, with Lamar Wright's boisterous trumpet solos and George Scott's madcap clarinet embellishments and the band's over-all intensity, the Missourians must have given Henderson and Ellington many an uneasy night.

Fresh new bands were also springing up, full of young, eager talent. For example, 1929 saw the emergence of two bands that were to figure prominently in the 1930s, Andy Kirk's Twelve Clouds of Joy (out of Kansas City) and Chick Webb's orchestra, originally called The Jungle Band. (Both groups will be discussed in the second volume of this book.) For the moment, however, it will suffice to point out that Webb's young band was much respected by both Ellington and Henderson; and well it might be, for it was bursting with new, young talent. Apart from the extraordinary gifts and irrepressible spirit of its drummer-leader, the band had a crop of "modern" players like Jimmy Harrison, trumpeters Ward Pinkett and Edwin Swayzee, saxophonists Louis Jordan and Elmer Williams, the fine pianist Don Kirkpatrick and bassist John Trueheart. Their 1929 recording of *Dog Bottom* gives an excellent account of the kind of fresh ideas, stunningly performed, the band offered.

Crucial changes in personnel occurred in Fletcher's band during the lean years 1928 and 1929. Relations between Henderson and his men deteriorated badly, and there were a whole series of firings and voluntary departures. Both trombonists Harrison and Morton left; so did June Cole and Kaiser Marshall (Henderson's oldest friend) after one of Fletcher's worst escapades in mismanagement. The banjoist Charlie Dixon also left, and was replaced by Clarence Holiday, Billie Holiday's father. Cootie Williams passed through the band briefly, only to be snatched up by Ellington, but not without leaving at least one excellent growl solo (on *Raisin' the Roof*).

At age twenty-two, Benny Carter, a versatile reed player and arranger, joined the band. Inexperienced, with no real orchestral conception of his own, and tending to overemphasize the reeds at the expense of the brass, he was hardly a replacement for Redman. Neither he nor Henderson sufficiently understood how to establish an internal relationship between improvised solo and written ensemble. As a result almost all of their arrangements in this two-year period reveal a structural flaw that has plagued jazz to this day: too much reliance on a string of short solos, sandwiched in between brief ensemble interludes and modulations.[17] Unless soloists are supreme artists, they are not likely to produce at a level comparable to the needs of a really structured performance, whether improvised, arranged, or composed. Nor is there any guarantee that such solos, given the individualism of most jazz improvisers, will have any element unifying them. If the solos are, in addition, of the short variety espoused by Henderson and Carter, neither they nor the interspersed ensemble passages can create a meaningful single conception. One is cancelled out by the other. The danger of this procedure is obvious today; but in 1929 it took a visionary like Ellington to see it.

Nonetheless, Carter provides some direction for the band, and being a talented young man, his arrangements show a marked rate of improvement. By the end of 1930 the orchestra is on the upswing again. It is a new orchestra, of course. Of the old members, only Hawkins, Bobby Stark, and Rex Stewart have stayed on. Harrison returns briefly, but the trombonists are now Claude Jones, who played an advanced style, and Benny Morton, who returned to the band early in 1931. Perhaps the most important changes are in the rhythm section: Walter Johnson, a drummer whose excellence and historical importance have been underestimated by jazz historians; and John Kirby, during whose tenure in the Henderson band the tuba gave way—finally—to the pizzicato string bass.

The new confidence of the orchestra is reflected on its first dates

17. Whereas Redman generally allowed only three or four solos, the list during the 1928-29 Carter period often swells to ten or eleven separate solos (with no increase in the total duration of the pieces, of course).

after the reorganization in 1930. Carter contributes several arrangements that hit the mark, again foreshadowing the swing style of years later. Gershwin's *Somebody Loves Me* and *Keep a Song in Your Soul* mark the rhythm section's conversion to a 4/4 beat, with Kirby's bass walking lightly. It is curious how the rhythm section swings on the former tune in a way that the "horns" can not yet manage. Two months later, however, in *Keep a Song in Your Soul,* the basic rhythmic orientation has been worked out. There is much to admire about this exceptional performance, for here we find the final key to the "Henderson style" in its first unequivocal assertion. Carter obviously has found the long-sought-after solution for making a section swing: the answer lay in syncopation. Soloists like Armstrong, and the more "modern" players in the band like Jones and Morton, had already instinctively understood that the key to rhythmic freedom lay in a syncopation based on a four-to-the-bar beat—not on the two-beat bar, in other words. Once the player could detach himself from explicitly stating the four beats and thus get "inside" the beats a vast field of rhythmic emancipation lay ahead. Perhaps soloists had to wait until the rhythm sections could handle the 4/4 beat.[18] When the soloists were relieved of the burden of stating the 4/4 beat, they could go on to more important things: melodic statements or, in fact, rhythmic counterstatements of their own.

Carter, in *Keep a Song in Your Soul,* applied this principle to section writing and fashioned one of the great arrangements in the Henderson book. If we take the tune of this song and treat it as a hypothetical musical example (without Fats Waller's lyrics), we can show how such a phrase played by a jazz ensemble changed through the years. In 1923 it would have been played as follows:

By 1927 or 1928, it might have loosened up into:

18. It may not occur to everyone how all these factors are related to practical, technical matters. We know that the tuba lasted as long as it did in jazz because of the inadequacy of early recording techniques in picking up the sound of a strong bass. This in turn, I believe, contributed substantially to the perpetuation of the two-beat style, because it is impossible breathwise for a tuba continually to pump out four beats to the bar, especially at fast tempos or for an entire band session.

But in Carter's arrangement the phrase is shaken altogether loose from its four-beat moorings, as follows:

or later on the same side in full sections with trumpet lead in the following variations (Ex. 9A, B, C):

Example 9 *Keep a Song in Your Soul*—Band Variations

Keep a Song in Your Soul also contains three remarkable solos—remarkable in themselves but even more so for the time they were made: Claude Jones's very "modern" beat-freed trombone solo (and behind him some subtle and exciting cymbal work by Johnson); then Carter's alto saxophone solo in which he manages to swing well despite the basic arpeggio format; and, perhaps the most startling of the three, Stark's brief trumpet solo on the bridge of the last chorus (Ex. 10).

Example 10 *Keep a Song in Your Soul*—Trumpet Solo

Again its notation does not tell the whole story, particularly in the first few bars, which, here in 1930, sound *exactly* like the Dizzy Gillespie of ten to fifteen years later. It must be heard to be believed. Lastly we must take note of the tonal splendor of Joe Smith's lead trumpet, high *d*'s and all. With Kirby's deep bass and Smith's big-toned lead, the eight-part harmonies gain a dimension not heard before in jazz.

These late 1930 dates also contain an interesting flag-waver version of the old 1906 standard *Chinatown, My Chinatown,* arranged by John Nesbitt, arranger and trumpeter for McKinney's Cotton Pickers. Set at the terrific speed of ♩ = *ca.* 290, it was the kind of virtuoso display piece all big bands developed in the early thirties. This piece set the tone and standard for all the flag-wavers that followed. Fast saxophone ensemble runs, snappy brass riffs, hot lightning-fast eighth-note solos, and a relentlessly charging rhythm section (playing 768 beats in the short three minutes)—these were the main ingredients, and every respectable big band in the thirties had to have one of these pieces around for the "cutting contests" with other bands.

In March 1931, the Henderson orchestra re-recorded its success of six years earlier, *Sugar Foot Stomp*. Although it was originally arranged by Redman, Henderson now claimed it as his own. In point of fact, it is essentially Redman's, except that the original twelve choruses (at ♩ = *ca.* 212) have now been expanded (at ♩ = *ca.* 276) to sixteen, and their sequence slightly rearranged. As can be seen by

Example 11 *Sugar Foot Stomp*

A) 1925 Version

A	*A*¹	*B*	*A*²	*C*	*D*	*E*	*D*	*E*
Saxes	Tpts.	Cl. trio	Trb.	Tpt.	Sust. ens.	Full ens. (4 beats)	Sust. ens.	Full ens. (4 beats)
1	1	2	1	3	1	1	1	1

B) 1931 Version

A	*A*¹	*B*	*A*²	*C*	*D*	*D*	*C*¹	*A*³	*E*
Saxes	Tpts.	Cl. trio	Trb.	Tpt.	Sust. ens.	Sust. ens.	Trb.	Ten. sax.	Full ens. (2 beats)
1	1	2	1	3	1	1	3	2	1

(In both versions *B* is an eight-bar phrase, all others are twelve-bar blues.)

comparing the two schema (Ex. 11), only the last half of the piece has been readjusted. To attack the source of the problem, the band-sustained ensemble of *D* is overlaid in the new version by a sparkling Henderson piano solo. *D* is directly repeated instead of alternating with *E*. Oliver's original solo, including the break, is now heard not in the trumpet, but in a high-register trombone. It is played brilliantly by Morton, and in the process the stop-time break is recast into a 3/4 pattern:

Morton finishes off with a four-bar lip trill and a couple of admirable flourishes (Ex. 12), undoubtedly trying to top Jones's earlier leaping solo (A^2). Two choruses by Hawkins are inserted now, and the side

Example 12 *Sugar Foot Stomp*—Trombone Solo

ends with the riff patterns of *E,* curiously, though, *not* in 4/4 but in 2/2.

Three other sides were made on that same day. One of these, the old ODJB vehicle *Clarinet Marmalade,* is a very uneven affair. Despite Johnson's deft brush work first on the snare drum and later on the cymbals and good improvisations by Morton, Stewart, and Hawkins, the side suffers from stiff, routine ensembles, and an out-of-tune clarinet solo by Carter's replacement, Russell Procope.

The two other sides are composed and arranged by Fletcher's brother, Horace. When encountered chronologically in the band's development, they provide a surprise, for they introduce several new elements that have had a far-reaching effect on big-band history. These sides are difficult to assess dispassionately because, rather interesting in themselves, they were the kind of composition and arrangement that presented a sure-fire formula for other, less gifted arrangers. As such, the formula was worked to death in hundreds of Swing Era bands, only to peter out gradually in the world of rhythm and blues and early rock and roll in the 1940s and 1950s.

The formula consisted of three primary elements: (1) a steady four-to-the-bar "chomp-chomp" beat, unvaried and relentless in all four rhythm instruments; (2) simple riffs whose melodic contours could fit any one of the three major steps (I, IV, V); and (3) the gradually receding "fade-out" ending, preferably with bent blue notes in the guitar. Out of this formula Glenn Miller made a career, and many other bands, Negro and white, failed in the same ambition, but not for lack of trying.

Hot and Anxious presents this formula in its essence. Already in the second chorus we hear a riff theme which became famous as Glenn Miller's *In the Mood*. Hawkins contributes a "dirty" clarinet solo (one of his rare clarinet appearances), but the side is not distinguished for its solos. Its interest lay in the new kind of swing feeling it presented. It was more illusion than real, but musicians felt comfortable in its "groove." It made no extraordinary demands on either player or listener, an obvious formula for wide success.

Now another fallow period followed during which Henderson fell back on two-beat stock arrangements which were simply "opened up" to accommodate an occasional solo. These were difficult days for the men in the band, but in December 1932 they created a brilliant "head arrangement" of *King Porter Stomp*. Again, as in the re-recording of *Sugar Foot Stomp,* the brighter tempo of the new version helps immensely, as does the smoothly swinging, well-co-ordinated four-beat rhythm section. Everything jells into a single unified concept, and one is hardly aware of any demarcation between solo and ensemble. The format is more or less the same as in the 1928 version, with Stark repeating and embellishing upon his opening statement. Sandy Williams, one of two new trombonists in the band, takes over Harrison's old spot, while Hawkins plays one of his most magnificent solos to date in place of Buster Bailey's old chorus. Rex Stewart is in Joe Smith's old slot, ending on a high *f,* while the other new trombonist, J. C. Higginbotham, winds up the solos, in the process working over a chromatic "lick":

which had occupied Hawkins off and on for quite a few years (ever since 1926 in *Stampede*), and which Red Allen was to appropriate in the next recording of *King Porter Stomp* (1933).

Hawkins's solo is worth a closer look. Here this late-blooming artist comes into his own with a bold conception that was to be his mark for decades (Ex. 13).

Example 13 *New King Porter Stomp*—Hawkins's Solo

In subsequent recordings made in December 1932 and August 1933, the Henderson band becomes all Hawkins, and it is no surprise that the British Broadcasting Corporation, upon hearing these recordings, offered Hawkins a year's contract to work in London. He left Henderson and stayed in Europe until 1939.

This was a severe blow to Henderson. Hawkins had been with him since the pre-band blues recording days, in all over ten years. But instead of firing the whole band as he had threatened to do in his deep depression, he hired Lester Young, then in Count Basie's band out in Kansas City. It was a daring move, but the band, used to Hawkins's big, lusty tone, rejected Young's cooler, airier tenor sound. Young beat a hasty retreat back to the Basie band,[19] and the only musician who could actually fill Hawkins's shoes in similar style, Ben Webster, was engaged.

With the dozen sides cut for Decca in September 1934, we come to the end of the road for Henderson's orchestra. We may admire these recordings for their marvelously light, finger-snapping swing, for some of Webster's and Red Allen's solos, and perhaps even for what they mean to anyone brought up during or immediately after the Swing Era. But beyond these attractions we recognize that the band's beat has become polite; in a few years many white orchestras would take it further down the road and turn it into the "businessman's bounce." We realize also that the nearly flawless ensemble passages have become an aural façade. Controlled, emotionally worn, drained of content, they sacrifice melodic interest to the idea of swing, and in the process spin a subtly constricting harmonic web around the soloists.

As the New Orleans style had passed on soon after its finest flowering, so swing—in a historic pattern—atrophied not long after reaching its zenith, starved from a lack of stylistic and structural nourishment. Henderson, directly or indirectly, was responsible for the growth of this style. But fortunately, it contained another, even more fertile line of development.

THE SOUTHWEST

The vast Southwest was at first largely ignored as a source for jazz. But the research of Franklin Driggs and others in the last ten years has unearthed a body of information which makes possible a more balanced picture of the early decades of jazz. The erstwhile neglect of the Southwest on the part of historians and critics has in turn led in recent years to theories questioning the priority of New Orleans in jazz history. With the typical exaggeration of jazz enthusiasts, factions have formed, declaring themselves either pro–New Orleans or pro–Kansas City. In the balance, however, the primacy of New Orleans has remained unassailable. The controversy has served to establish a more comprehensive view of the various strands that led to the emergence of jazz as a distinct musical language.

19. Lester Young never recorded with Henderson.

THE SOUTHWEST

Important cities in the development of jazz.

The neglect of the Southwestern tradition was due not so much to regional prejudices as to what we might call geographical circumstances. The numerous Southwestern jazz groups, large and small, ranging from small "territory" bands to the large city-based orchestras, were overlooked by the recording companies operating out of New York and, to a lesser degree, Chicago. Occasionally an adventurous recording scout would come upon one of these bands, or one of the orchestras would venture to the big cities. But these were exceptions. The point is that these Southwestern orchestras provided much of the musical entertainment for the region, and in the process developed a self-sufficiency which in turn reflected itself in regional stylistic characteristics.

Although the earliest forms of proto-jazz were known in the Southwest—musicians like Jelly Roll Morton and Freddie Keppard had toured there—local interest in the new music did not become intense until the second decade of the century. Some writers have linked this late start with the closing of Storyville in New Orleans in 1917. Hundreds of musicians were forced to look for work elsewhere, and obviously the Southwest, being nearby, was a vast potential area. And yet, the evidence seems to show that most of the better New Orleans musicians either worked their way up to Chicago or simply remained in New Orleans.

I think a more plausible explanation for the delayed emergence of jazz in the Southwest, particularly Kansas and Missouri, is that this area had an indigenous popular music of its own, and an important one: ragtime. The great centers of ragtime were Sedalia, Carthage, St.

SOUTHWEST JAZZ BANDS

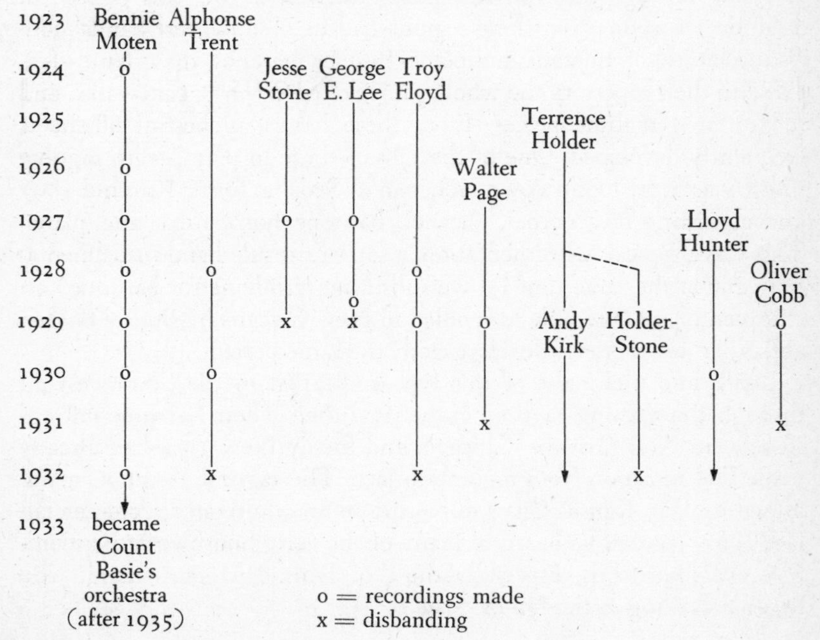

Louis, Joplin, and Kansas City. Although the golden age of ragtime occurred between 1904 and 1907, pianists and brass bands playing ragtime pieces remained popular in the Southwest through the early twenties. Moreover, a second peak of ragtime activity in Missouri and Kansas revolved around James Scott, Charles L. Johnson, and a new generation of composers like Joseph Lamb and Rob Hampton, the latter from Little Rock, Arkansas. All these composers had many ragtime hits (published by John Stark in St. Louis and Sedalia) throughout the middle and late teens, and their music was widely performed in that territory. James Scott, in fact, moved to Kansas City in 1914 and established himself as a teacher, an organist, and an arranger and musical director for the Panama Theater. One can assume that his influence in all three capacities—none of them related directly to jazz—was more than passing.

The Southwest was second only to the Midwest in its passion for concert bands, the most famous of which were Sousa's and Pryor's, the latter specializing in band versions of cakewalk and ragtime pieces. Similarly, minstrel-show bands, like that of W. C. Handy, were still traveling through the Midwest and Southwest during this period. In addition, every town in these regions had its own concert bands, consisting mostly of amateur musicians. Besides marches, these bands featured in their repertory the whole gamut of coon songs, cakewalks, and orchestrated ragtime pieces. From these bands, orchestral off-shoots frequently developed. One of the first of these to play Negro ragtime music was Scott Joplin's own orchestra in Sedalia, formed around 1897 and consisting of a cornet, clarinet, baritone horn, tuba, and piano. This was a typical instrumentation, a sort of capsule band instrumentation, and at the same time (if we substitute trombone for baritone) an embryonic jazz ensemble as typified in New Orleans by Buddy Bolden and other jazz pioneers during exactly the same period.

Bands and orchestras of this type continued in the Southwest all through the waning ragtime craze, at a time when instrumental ensembles in New Orleans, Chicago, and finally New York had already made the transition from ragtime to jazz. The ragtime tradition maintained itself in Kansas City (to be sure in an adulterated, commercialized form), as can be heard in many of the early Southwestern recordings available to us, especially those of Bennie Moten's band, who began recording in the fall of 1923.

Moten, born in 1894, was a ragtime pianist (although he had also played baritone in a brass band as a teenager) who had studied piano with two teachers who were in turn pupils of Scott Joplin. His first jobs, in 1918, were leading a trio consisting of himself, a drummer, and a vocalist. This group expanded to a quintet later; their repertory obviously consisted of ragtime pieces and the sweet popular songs of Tin Pan Alley after World War I. Other Kansas City musicians, like Jesse Stone, George and Julia Lee, and the great Alphonse Trent from Fort Smith, Arkansas, were trained in the ragtime or "novelty" tradition; and like most musicians during this transitional period, they played any variety of popular styles from "sweet" through "novelty" to ragtime, depending on public demand. How tenaciously ragtime survived in Kansas City can be gleaned from a 1925 Moten recording like *Twelfth Street Rag,* which features a lengthy ragtime piano solo by Moten, and shows how pure ragtime was converted into the orchestral medium, even at that late a date.

But New Orleans musicians had drifted through Kansas City and other Southwestern cities from time to time, and eventually jazz in its more advanced form began to take hold in the area. By 1923 Bennie Moten had the most popular band in Kansas City, increasing its size to six players. His first recordings are only of historical interest today. The first two recorded titles, *Elephant Wobble* and *Crawdad Blues,* give a fair indication of the kind of material the band played at this time. In both recordings we hear a New Orleans instrumentation of three front-line "horns"—clarinet, trumpet, trombone—and a three-piece rhythm section, with no tuba. Both sides are rhythmically stiff beyond belief, completely removed from the embryonic sense of swing we can hear at the same time in King Oliver, Piron, or even groups like the ODJB or Louisiana Five. Moten's band at this time played with a plodding, on-the-beat, even-eighth-note rhythm that was not even good ragtime. All the recordings from this early period follow the same format and sequence of ensembles and solos. Woodie Walder's "novelty" clarinet solos appear with monotonous regularity at exactly the same place on each performance, regardless, incidentally, of whether it was a rag piece, a pop song, or a blues. Also a great deal of space is given over to corny minstrel-type banjo solos. Judging by the virtually exact repetitions of choruses, the band was obviously interpolating "solos" into written-out (or stock) arrangements, almost all in the key of B flat. The best player in the group was Lamar Wright, a trumpeter from Texas, who was to become one of the principal members in Cab Calloway's orchestra of the thirties. He showed a marked King Oliver influence in these early recordings. The beat of the band, unvaried and heavy, emphasized the 4/4 meter, contrasting with the many two-beat bands of the period and with the much more sophisticated, lighter, more flowing 4/4 of the best New Orleans orchestras.

It is significant that, out of some twenty sides the Moten band recorded for Okeh in 1923 and 1924, half are blues. By 1923 the Okeh company, having started the blues craze with Mamie Smith, was looking for more blues material to feed the booming market and to compete with Paramount and Columbia. In addition, perhaps more significantly, the blues had always had strong roots in the Southwest, for many of the best-known early itinerant blues singers were born and raised in Texas, Oklahoma, and Arkansas. This is not to contradict my earlier statement that ragtime retained a hold on popular music in this region beyond that of other areas. Blues, as sung or performed on crude instruments, were performed by single singers or musicians, the singers most often accompanying themselves, but occasionally teaming up with another musician. Before the 1920's the blues existed at a separate social-cultural-musical level from that occupied by orchestras playing in hotels or dance halls. Once the blues had broken through into the middle-class urban realm, however, the larger Southwestern orchestras quickly adopted the form and used it more consistently than bands anywhere else. Audiences throughout the region insisted on a large diet of blues, and out of this earthier, deeper feeling in the music developed a way of playing jazz which was eventually to supercede the New Orleans, Chicago, and New York styles.

A simple, often "crude" blues playing can be heard on many of the early Moten sides, banjo solos and novelty clarinet squealings notwithstanding. In fact, pieces like *Eighteenth Street Blues* (or *Strut*) are a fascinating mixture of the pure New Orleans ensemble style and the more heavily accented, blues-drenched feeling typical of the Southwest. In these blues numbers, with their simple I-IV-V harmonic progressions, riffs were developed with increasing frequency and skill, until this, too, in the later Moten and Basie bands, became a fundamental jazz orchestral technique. Indeed many of the 1924 Moten sides feature "solos" which are hardly more than riff statements with slight variations.

Part of the band's repertory consisted of popular songs of the day, and here we can note a striking difference in style and even technical skill. What minimal rhythmic flexibility (at least for our ears today) the band displayed in blues numbers disappears entirely in these songs, intonation deteriorates, and wrong notes begin to crop up. It is as if the band did not really want to play this kind of material.

By 1924 the Moten orchestra had increased to a personnel of eight by adding a tuba and the Kansas City saxophone player (and later leader) Harlan Leonard. When the band recorded again at the end of 1926, it had moved over to Victor, recording now at Camden, New Jersey—in itself a great triumph for a Southwestern band—and it had grown to ten pieces, only two less than Fletcher Henderson's orchestra of that period.

The band's playing was by now much more cohesive in its ensembles, and the solos began to take on a degree of stylistic unity. The most important addition to the personnel was the trumpet player Ed Lewis, later a stalwart in the Basie orchestra. Lewis, then still in his late teens, had obviously listened to Joe Smith, Henderson's off-and-on star trumpeter. He was also listening to Louis Armstrong and represented a new generation, or at least a newer orientation, within the Moten band. Lewis's influence, especially on trombonist Thamon Hayes, can be felt throughout such 1926 sides as *Kansas City Shuffle*. Hayes's playing had always been on the comically primitive side. But by 1926, there is a new drive and "hot" spirit in his solos. La Forest Dent, playing alto and baritone saxophone, was added, filling out the reed section to three, and providing another solo voice to counteract Woodie Walder's still persisting novelty and wah-wah clarinet solos. As a result of these changes and the band's increasing stature in the Southwest, the playing gradually became more sophisticated. Influenced by hearing recordings and broadcasts of Fletcher Henderson, as well as other Eastern bands, Moten responded to the growing competitive spirit both within his own territory and outside of it by exploring more interesting formal schemes and creating a more polished level of ensemble and solo playing. The performances still did not have the elegance and structural cohesion of Jelly Roll Morton's recordings of the period, or even of Henderson's best. But on the other hand each piece now unfolded with at least a modicum of development and direction, in contrast to the formally flat string of repetitious ensembles and solos of the earlier records.

Inevitably, vestiges remained. The final ensemble chorus of *Kansas City Shuffle* is a nearly exact recapitulation of the opening chorus, and the New Orleans spirit still hovers about these ensembles. Embryonic steps toward a more varied instrumentation occasionally appear, such as the clarinet and tenor saxophone duet on *Midnight Mama* or the saxophone trio on *Missouri Wobble*. In terms of musical content these are still quite ordinary, but they represent an almost childish groping for a more varied format and expression. In *Yazoo Blues* other new influences assert themselves, such as the hymn-like final chorus, which Moten might have heard either on Morton or Henderson records (like the latter's *Sugar Foot Stomp*), or as in the twelve-bar structure broken up into four bars of quasi-stop-time solo, followed by eight bars of ensemble.

The recordings of this period are manifestly excellent dance music, and one can readily understand why Moten's band, with its rocking beat, was the most popular in the territory. With each new recording date—the next was in June 1927—the influence and increasing sophistication of jazz bands around the country make themselves felt on the Moten band. One can hear Moten energetically trying to catch up with Eastern orchestras like Henderson's. And in his own backyard there was also developing competition from Alphonse Trent's remarkable organization, and others like Troy Floyd's in San Antonio, Terrence Holder's in Dallas, and the orchestra of Jesse Stone, the Don Redman of the Southwest, who roamed Missouri and Kansas while avoiding Kansas City itself.

New elements continued to crop up in Moten's recordings. The ensembles from 1927 have a rhythmic base that constitutes a more rocking version of New Orleans collective ensemble, and in the last ensemble chorus of *Moten Stomp* the typically cohesive polyphony of New Orleans ensembles has been replaced by a much more Armstrong-oriented individualism of lines. Curiously, the band now played less blues material, obviously trying to appeal to a wider (more white) audience, and as a result the riff technique of the earlier blues sides is also suspended. A new instrumentational sophistication is developing. In *Dear Heart* we hear a sequence involving a harmonically "advanced" interlude for piano and two muted trumpets, followed by a chorus for clarinet trio—Redman's device had now penetrated the Southwest—which in turn is interrupted by a banjo break in whole-tone chords. *Twelfth Street Rag* sports two fancy chordal pyramids, a drum break, unison saxophone lines and fancy modulations (as opposed to the inflexibly monochromatic early sides).

New Tulsa Blues draws heavily for its earthy rocking beat on the boogie-woogie piano style that was spreading like wildfire throughout the Southwest. In the lively *Pass Out Lightly,* a minor-key "jungle mood" sequence (probably inspired by Ellington's *Black and Tan Fantasy,* which had just been released as a record), alternates with two chase choruses, one for two trumpets, the other for tenor and baritone saxophones. The trumpet chorus finds Ed Lewis and Paul Webster dividing the eight-bar phrase structure into interesting overlapping patterns (Ex. 14):

Example 14 *Pass Out Lightly*

A) 1—1—1—1—2—2 B) 1—3—2—2 C) 1—3—1—3 D) 1—3—4 (duet)

(Numbers represent bars.)

Clearly Moten is assembling his style—his "bag," as today's jazz parlance has it—piece by piece. In the process the old and new often fail to blend. In *Ding Dong Blues,* they rub awkwardly against each other as two old-fashioned interludes, straight out of vaudeville pit-band stock arrangements, vie with a new-style vocal trio (one of the first recorded by a Negro band) and with Ed Lewis's modern solo and Willie McWashington's hip Charleston cymbal. Even on *Moten Stomp,* the strongest piece in the 1927 group of recordings, an out-of-place banjo solo still shows past influence.

By late 1928, the Moten band finally shook off the lingering ragtime influences. *Get Low Down* is symptomatic of the change. Moten's opening "raggy" piano is interrupted by a "hokum routine" in which Ed Lewis admonishes Bennie to "stop that ragtime. Let's get real low down." This is followed by some scat singing over a "low down" boogie-woogie piano. The record is otherwise undistinguished, stringing together a series of uneven and unrelated solos. It does, however, serve to introduce to recordings the very advanced (by 1928 standards) and remarkably full-toned baritone saxophone of Jack

Washington, another Kansas City–born player, then barely seventeen years old. His tonal and dynamic control in this solo, especially on low *d*'s, reveals a precociously mature musician who, a decade later, was to be the anchor man in Count Basie's saxophone section.

In *Just Rite,* a driving Ed Lewis number, more complex saxophone ensemble backgrounds give a new fluidity to the band's rocking beat. At the same time, trumpeter Paul Webster, temporarily in the Moten band and one of the first high-note lead men, added a new brilliance to the out-chorus ensembles and, coupled with Vernon Page's deep, full-toned tuba, an expanded pitch range.

This set of 1928 recordings also includes several over-arranged numbers, laden with clichés from Tin Pan Alley and the vaudeville-movie pit orchestras (*Slow Motion, Tough Breaks,* etc.). Obviously the effect of the new communications media was not always salutary. The temptation always existed to resort to formulas and devices used by the commercially most successful orchestras, many of them not even jazz groups in a strict sense. But even apart from these temptations, by 1927 and 1928 through the spread of recordings and radio and the influence of Henderson, Ellington, and other bands, big-band styles were becoming increasingly standardized, nationalized as it were, and in the process causing regional characteristics to disappear.

As long as Moten could come up with the splendid, vigorous collective ensembles of *Kansas City Breakdown,* the best of the 1928 records, his orchestra's future was not materially endangered, even though he had powerful competition in his own territory. Jesse Stone's Blues Serenaders, the Alphonse Trent, T. Holder, and Troy Floyd bands, as well as Walter Page's Oklahoma-based Blue Devils aggregation—all were thriving and flourishing. The few recordings these orchestras made—many of them still rare items—provide us with little more than a glimpse of the abundance of musical talent circulating the area in the late twenties. (See the chart on page 281.)

After losing Bennie Moten's band to Victor in 1926, the Okeh company scouted the Southwest for a suitable replacement. In 1927 it recorded Stone's Blues Serenaders on four sides, two of which are available today on reissues. They are extraordinary sides, and they dramatically highlight the difference between Southwestern and Eastern orchestras. On neither of the two reissued sides, *Boot to Boot* and

Starvation Blues, can one hear any new devices or technical innovations. But the feeling with which the band interprets the two Stone originals is unlike anything one could hear in other areas of the country at that time. The improvised ensembles are as beautifully structured as those of Oliver's Creole Jazz Band. And yet recorded barely four years after the latter's Gennett sides, they embodied a spirit and musical feeling which was at once radically new and thoroughly indigenous to the Southwest. The difference is clearly the blues. The utter freedom and relaxation of the phrasing (one is tempted to characterize it as controlled abandon), the melodic lines richly spiced with blue notes, the earthy, almost rough rhythmic feeling—all exemplify a vocally oriented instrumental style that could only emanate from the blues. In its liberal use of blue notes, including the flatted fifth (used, to be sure, melodically, not harmonically), the Stone band expressed the tragic spirit of the blues in a manner that even Moten, who reflected more a white urban culture than Stone's rural touring territory, never achieved. In fact, in 1927 jazz could as yet offer very little that matched the depth of feeling Stone's orchestra purveyed. It was as if the band were made up of instrumental Bessie Smiths. Oddly enough, this expressivity was achieved in terms of (or perhaps despite) written-out arrangements, and very advanced, sophisticated ones at that. For Jesse Stone was a well-trained musician, a composer and arranger; and Franklin Driggs was told that even solos were frequently written out by Stone for his men.[20]

The most remarkable characteristic of the band was the quality of its tone. Its brass men played with a firm, expansive sound. Albert Hinton was their featured trumpeter and, probably because of his fame, the brass as a section and as soloists were heavily prominent, thus giving the band as a whole an essentially robust, brassy color. Moreover, as in Ellington's orchestra, each of the three brass players were soloists in their own right and varied considerably in tone and style. Hinton had a high range that was said to surpass that of Armstrong. He could also bend blue notes into long, expressive moans and wails. In addition, as in the final exciting chorus of *Starvation Blues,* he provided descant lines with a vibrato so intense as almost to constitute a "shake." Beneath Hinton, the other trumpeter, Slick Jackson, and the trombonist, Druie Bess, weave contrapuntal lines so well

20. Hentoff and McCarthy, p. 199.

integrated and varied that one is led to believe they may have been sketched out by Stone. They are truly melodic lines, rather than harmonic inner parts slightly embellished with melodic turns. The combination of Bess, with his rough attack and strong rhythmic drive, Jackson's open horn intoning the theme, and Hinton's plunger mute produced a balanced three-part brass polyphony that I believe no other band had achieved by then (Ex. 15).

Example 15 *Starvation Blues*—Final Chorus

(Saxophone parts are not included.)

The same qualities manifest themselves in *Boot to Boot,* Stone's version of the classic *Tiger Rag* changes. Again one must admire the wondrous melodic independence of the six "horns" and Pete Hassel's aggressively brassy tuba, in contrast to the more rounded-off, French horn sound developed by many tuba players. Bess's punchy trombone solo has a style and technical fluency that only Snub Mosely and Miff Mole had attained by 1927.

It is lamentable that from the thirties through the early fifties the jazz historians' preoccupation with New Orleans and Chicago jazz led to the total neglect of as remarkable a band as Stone's Blues Serenaders. But Stone was not Moten's only competitor. In San Antonio Troy Floyd led a nine-piece band that lacked the fullness and exuberance of Stone's but featured a simpler, largely arranged style. Its star musician was the New Orleans trumpeter Don Albert, who had an unusually clear-toned, concise approach to the blues. Combining the best of Redman's arranging style with a blues feeling, the Floyd band was very successful in San Antonio until about 1932, when it fell victim to the Depression.

We must judge Floyd's band by the only evidence available today, four sides recorded on the Okeh label in 1928 and 1929. Both pieces, *Shadowland Blues* and *Dreamland Blues,* were recorded in two parts, that is, on both sides of a ten-inch disc. Thus they are six-minute pieces, both slow blues, a loosely constructed forerunner of an extended piece like Ellington's *Diminuendo and Crescendo in Blue. Shadowland,* recorded in 1928, is the lesser of the two performances. It has a soprano saxophone solo by Siki Collins (uninfluenced, it might be added, by Bechet) and an unusual blues vocal by a baritone named Kellough Jefferson, who either was trained in "classical" vocal technique or emulated it. But far too much of the two 1928 sides is taken up by Benny Long's trombone. It is clumsy, crude, gutbucket trombone playing, very close to caricature.

Dreamland I and II features the luminous trumpet tone of Don Albert, a well-constructed solo by the young tenorman Herschel Evans (later with Basie), and some beautiful collectively improvised ensemble choruses. Evans, another Texan, was just twenty when he recorded with Floyd. He represented a much newer melodic and rhythmic conception. If we have read in various jazz histories how Evans was supposed to have been influenced by Hawkins, we may be surprised to find him playing a tenor very much *un*like, and in advance of, the Hawkins of 1929. It is a more fluent, more melodic, and blues-tinged approach, perhaps more elegant, too. To appreciate fully Evans's originality, one has to think away the "choonk-chink" rhythm of the tuba and banjo. Their straight up-and-down rhythms are contrary to the kind of horizontal conception Evans is playing.

The collective ensembles are of special nostalgic interest. They have a haunting, langorous beauty that only Morton and some of the New Orleans bands like Sam Morgan's could achieve. The secret of this beauty in the instance of Floyd lies mainly in the tempo, a slow ♩ = *ca.* 100. Another obvious factor is that these collective ensembles were *not* written. In fact, as played, they are not notatable; and, conversely, if they had been notated by some miracle, they could not have been read and then played in such a relaxed and utterly loose-limbed manner.

The chorus in question occurs three times. Being improvised, the three versions could not be exactly the same. On the other hand, in 1929 one would not normally have expected the subtle differences, really like variations, that the Floyd band achieves here. The first ensemble chorus is played by a high clarinet, two trumpets, trombone, and two saxophones, all instruments improvising except the first trumpet (which is playing the main blues melody). The other two ensemble choruses—one at the beginning of side two, the other directly after Evans's solo—are both for three brass, the first with two saxophones and the second with three saxophones, with the saxophone ensembles head-arranged in *different* versions. Thus what we have here is the classic New Orleans ensemble translated into the full-blooded Texas blues idiom and updated harmonically and instrumentationally.

The basis of jazz rhythm, as opposed to that of "classical" music, is an embellishment, an anticipation, delay, or other ornamentation of the beat. In essence, jazz inflection rotates around a central axis, the beat. It is obvious that the slower the tempo, the more variations in this embellishing process are possible and the more rhythmic splinter-divisions of the beat become available. Thus it is probable that, given six players, all six will decorate that beat in subtly differentiated configurations. If these six are then improvising simultaneously, we are apt to get a vertical rhythmic aggregate of great complexity and beauty. Since this complexity is achieved intuitively, by reflex, so to speak, the result is also completely natural, and in turn brings together two opposites, simplicity and complexity, in the highest form of artistic expression. Such is the case with the *Dreamland* ensembles.

As I have implied, the example from Floyd's *Dreamland II* is not strictly notatable, or the notation would be so complex as to be unreadable. The rhythmic subtleties one may feel in a slow blues tempo are essentially beyond our notation system. But even this approximation (Ex. 16) will give a small idea of the polyrhythms involved here, and how in essence this is the same polyrhythmic character African music has, as transmitted through racial memory into jazz.

The two bands that gave Moten his biggest competition were Alphonse Trent's and Walter Page's Blue Devils. The latter was an ambitious group that had an erratic, short-lived career. At one time or another it contained some of the best players of the region: altoist Buster Smith, trombonist and arranger Eddie Durham, trumpeter

Example 16 *Dreamland II*—Ensemble Chorus

Oran "Hot Lips" Page, trombonist Dan Minor, drummer Alvin Burroughs, and later, in 1928, singer Jimmy Rushing as well as Count Basie. Formed in 1926 in Oklahoma City, the Blue Devils roamed the surrounding territory as far north as Joplin, Missouri, Emporia, Kansas, and Omaha, Nebraska. In various battles between bands Page is reported to have "cut" both Jesse Stone and George Lee out of that entire territory, but Page's ambition was to do battle with the mightiest, Moten. The latter avoided a confrontation as long as possible. But an encounter finally did take place in 1928, and on that occasion Page is reputed to have "wiped out" the Moten band. Moten's natural reaction to this challenge was to try to buy up and take over the Blue Devils intact. When that failed, Moten started raiding Page, taking Basie and Durham early in 1929. Rushing and Hot Lips Page also left when a series of bad bookings endangered the future of the band.

The Blue Devils were a spunky outfit who would take on all comers, including even white sweet bands like those of Vincent Lopez and Lawrence Welk. They never met with Trent in an open contest, since Trent was mostly in the East during the late twenties and early thirties.

The Blue Devils recorded only once, in November 1929, at a time when the best of its personnel were still together. These recordings are of great historical importance, quite apart from their musical merits, since much of the personnel of the Blue Devils sparked the Moten band of the early thirties, which in turn became the nucleus of the Basie band. Of perhaps even greater significance is Buster Smith's presence in the Blue Devils band, he being the main musical influence on young Charlie Parker in the mid- and late thirties.

Blue Devil Blues is not strictly speaking a blues, but a rather simplistic, old-fashioned minor-key piece. Nor has it any great interest as an arrangement; the Blue Devils were not an arranger's orchestra, but a collection of performers who preferred head arrangements with simple backgrounds, often riffed, and solos as their basic musical diet. It worked because they were sympathetic to each other and mined the same stylistic lode. Their outstanding soloists were Hot Lips Page, Buster Smith, Rushing, and Basie, but when the Blue Devils recorded, Basie had already left to join Moten.[21] Hot Lips Page and Buster Smith were twenty-one-year-old youngsters, but the main elements of their styles were already well set. Page had been strongly influenced by the Armstrong of *West End Blues*. His opening solo on *Blue Devil Blues* has great rhythmic freedom and seems to be an almost bar-less music, stemming directly from the blues. He produces a remarkably cohesive solo built on two ideas, both constantly varied. The quality of this achievement must be measured against the fact that for the

21. The discographies have for many years listed Basie as the pianist on the Blue Devils recording date. This is definitely not the case, as comparison of Basie's youthful style on Moten records of the period with the piano playing on the Blue Devils records demonstrates. Apart from a distinct difference in style, Basie has a much sprightlier rhythmic drive, a much more vigorous attack and touch than the Blue Devils pianist, who was probably Willie Lewis, Walter Page's old friend from the Billy King road band, with whom Page had toured the T.O.B.A. (Theatre Owners and Bookers Association) circuit in the early twenties.

sixteen bars of this introductory solo the harmonic background remains unwaveringly locked in C minor. Yet Page turns this harmonic constriction to advantage, as he builds over it a solo that is in effect a miniature composition.

This recording does not start with a theme or state a tune. It is a themeless piece, at least as the term *theme* is applied in composition. Page's opening solo is simply a free improvisation in C minor, and even Rushing's blues vocal is improvised in what was by that time a long-established vocal tradition. Rushing's two choruses are superb. Today when we have lived with Rushing's singing for several decades —primarily through his years with Basie—it is somehow startling to hear in his recording debut the fully matured voice and style we know from the later periods. Page's muted trumpet behind Rushing is in the classic ornamental blues style, perfectly filling in and responding to the voice. Buster Smith's chorus on clarinet is not altogether successful. It is occasionally out of tune (as is Page's opening solo), and while Buster strives for some new ideas, he does not quite realize them. Barely audible but very worth straining for is Ruben Lynch's guitar "comping" in very advanced chords, four to the bar, behind Smith's clarinet. The side ends rather inconclusively with dull, arranged riff harmonies under a meandering piano solo. In a sense the whole performance has neither a beginning nor an ending; but Hot Lips Page's opening solo is a workable substitute for a beginning.

Squabblin' shows clearly how concrete the Southwestern tradition had become by 1929, and how different in spirit and direction this was from a band like Ellington's, for example. Hot Lips Page and Buster Smith are the main soloists, the latter on both alto and clarinet. Walter Page, after playing tuba on *Blue Devil Blues,* now switches to string bass and later to baritone saxophone, and plays all three instruments astoundingly well. Indeed the rhythmic flow of his pizzicato bass gives the whole band's performance its special flavor. The bass's ♩ 𝄾 ♪♩ 𝄽 rhythm in the first chorus creates a new rhythmic mobility. The full chorus for rhythm section (the third chorus on the record) was used frequently by guitarist Freddie Green and Page in future years with the Basie band, but we do not expect to hear it as early as 1929. Here again Lynch is years ahead of his time in his chording and chromatic voice-leading, as is the short lead-in figure to the bridge by pianist Lewis (Ex. 17).

Example 17 *Squabblin'*

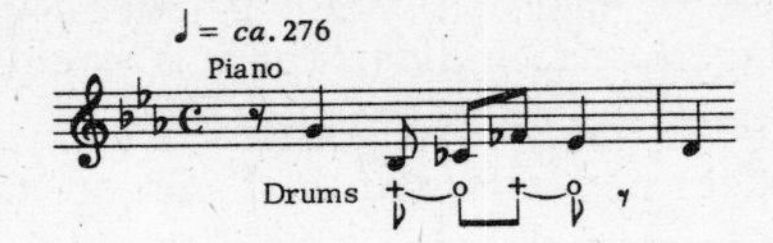

Equally remarkable is eighteen-year-old Burroughs's sharp cymbal work. Not only is it dynamically shaded and integrated into this quietly stealthy rhythm chorus, but the placing of variants and extensions of the following syncopated figure 𝄽 𝄾 ♪♪♩ 𝄾 (half open hi-hat cymbal) would be hard to surpass.

Though Page is playing a two-beat bass line, the four beats of the guitar, Burroughs's flowing cymbal work, and the relaxed propulsion of Page's bass all combine to make a fluid, swinging beat that became the recognizable rhythmic trademark of the Kansas City style.

The two Pages turn in excellent "modern" solos on trumpet and baritone saxophone, the latter with remarkable ease for that time. Walter Page also produces a nice pizzicato bass break, rare in those days of tuba playing. We can only fault him on the clarinet's chorus, where he fumbles and forgets to go to the bridge.

Buster Smith's solos are also advanced for their time, not as free and relaxed as Hot Lips Page's but still syncopated enough to generate considerable swing. His alto solos are especially fascinating because the tone, with its sinewy fullness and slight edginess, was clearly emulated by Parker.

George Lee's band was probably Moten's closest geographical rival. In the mid-twenties, Lee had as loyal a following as Moten, but the latter's Victor contract put him ahead. Moten tried to raid Lee's band in 1929 to get the fine tenorman and arranger Budd Johnson. Unsuccessful in this effort, Moten then raided Page's Blue Devils, as we have seen; but this is evidence of the esteem Lee was held in by his biggest rival.

Lee made his first record in 1927 for an obscure Negro-owned company run by a local politician and by a clarinetist. Of poor technical quality, the record reveals through the noisy surface a nine-piece band playing head arrangements with short solos and a firm rocking beat. The best soloists in the band were trombonist Thurston "Sox" Maupins and Lee's sister Julia on piano, both playing in a style and rhythmic conception in advance of the rest of the band. *Merritt Stomp* closes with an unusual tag-ending VI^7 chord, and *Down Home Syncopatin' Blues* has a blues chorus split into twos for trombone, tenor, alto, and cornet and its final four bars are collectively improvised with a clarinet lead. Like some of Jelly Roll Morton's arrangements in format, the similarity stops there, as the two-bar contributions and the over-all rhythmic feeling are far removed from Morton's superior level.

Lee recorded again in 1929. By this time Jesse Stone had been hired as arranger, and Budd Johnson and Clarence Taylor on alto had come into the band. *Ruff Scufflin'* shows to what extent the band had learned to deal with Stone's written arrangements by way of the Redman influence. The syncopations in the ensemble, the brass and reed exchanges are handled well, and at the end a six-bar coda is played by a trio of cornet and two saxophones, accompanied only by cymbal beats (Ex. 18). *St. James Infirmary* includes a virile George Lee vocal

Example 18 *Ruff Scufflin'*—Coda

and a "modern" solo by Taylor that has thirty-second-note arpeggios (at ♩ = 120), still very unusual in the late twenties.

In some ways the most advanced and idolized band of the Southwest was Alphonse Trent's. Any number of musicians who heard the band have testified to its unique excellence. The comments of Budd Johnson, himself a first-rate, highly respected musician, are typical: "Let me tell you about Trent; that was the greatest band I'd ever heard! They used to thrill me. They were gods back in the twenties, just like Basie was later, only many years ahead of him. . . . They worked nothing but the biggest and finest hotels in the South.—We used to idolize those guys. . . . You have no idea just how fabulous that band was! They were years ahead of their time."[22]

22. Franklin S. Driggs, "Budd Johnson, an Ageless Jazzman," *The Jazz Review,* November 1960, p. 6.

The Trent story is as fabulous a one as the Roaring Twenties has to offer. After jobbing around Arkansas and Oklahoma, Trent took over most of a small territory band called Gene Crooke's Synco Six around 1923. Some time later the famed Adolphus Hotel in Dallas, then the Southwest's most glamorous hotel, offered the Trent orchestra a two-week job in its second ballroom. Trent stayed a year and a half, a spectacular success under any circumstances, but absolutely unheard of for a Negro orchestra in the South, playing in the top white hotel. The Trent band broadcast over a local Dallas radio station, and became the most famous and richest in the entire Southwest and Midwest. The men all dressed in silk shirts and drove around in Cadillac touring cars, since they made the unheard-of salary (in those days) of $150 a week. Though they were lionized by musicians and public alike, though they played the most elegant college proms and governor's inaugural balls and toured all over the South and Midwest, the big Eastern record companies evidently were not aware of them. Trent was not recorded until 1928, and then only by the small Gennett company, with a limited distribution; as a result, Trent's eight recorded sides are rare collector's items today.

By 1928, Trent had enlarged his orchestra to twelve (the size of Henderson's), picking up violinist Stuff Smith in Lexington, Kentucky, tenorman Hayes Pillars from Arkansas, and trumpeter Peanuts Holland from Buffalo on his various cross-country tours. The different style of this orchestra is immediately apparent on their first record date, October 11, 1928. It played with more polish than any other Negro orchestra including Henderson's, and also featured remarkable soloists. The material it played was also out of the ordinary, as can be seen in the first two recorded titles, *Nightmare* and *Black and Blue Rhapsody*. The former is in genre closer to the kind of show or revue pieces Ellington was working with at the Cotton Club than to the tunes played for social dancing in the West. *Nightmare* was a composition with a specified form and certain melodic, harmonic ideas which had to be played in a particular arrangement and manner. *Black and Blue Rhapsody,* although more a dance number, still retained many compositional or arranged sections not associated with conventional dance repertoire. Both pieces were in the key of D flat, which involved *b* double flats in *Nightmare,* and the *Rhapsody* modulates frequently and abruptly. All this the band took completely in stride. They were obviously a well-rehearsed band, and although Trent was not an outstanding pianist himself, he must have had a clear conception of how he wanted the band to sound and how to rehearse to get that sound. Obviously, also, the big white bands of Whiteman and Lombardo were in some respects a model and Henderson and Redman were also influential. Unfortunately it is no longer possible to trace the exact cross-references precisely and chronologically. Since Trent did not record in 1926 and 1927, but was already broadcasting from Dallas, it is entirely possible that Trent exerted a much greater influence on others, perhaps even Henderson, than we might realize. For the Trent recordings of 1928 show that the band was no fledgling organization but had a firmly established style, a sound, a remarkable polish—all qualities one does not acquire overnight.

Actually it may have had too much polish, been too concerned with arranged ensembles that consequently tended to smother the soloists. In this respect, it foreshadowed the inherent weaknesses of the big-band swing style of a decade later. But one can readily understand how musicians revered this polish and perfection that no other Negro band had achieved to such an extent at that time.

Both Gennett sides feature two soloists, violinist Stuff Smith and trumpeter Peanuts Holland. Both players' styles were fully set, although both were still in their teens, a phenomenon we encounter often in the Southwest, where musicians tended to begin professional life at the age of fourteen or fifteen. The band's fine ensemble balance is evident in the four-bar bridge in *Nightmare* (the two diminished chords). Here the four-man saxophone section and the four brass blend into a single sound, leaving Stuff Smith to improvise freely against them. Gene Crooke, the highly-regarded banjoist, with a good sound and a rock-like beat, is also prominent.

Rhapsody shows how completely Trent's men had absorbed the Redman lessons in arranging, particularly in using the instruments as choirs. Trumpet trios and saxophone quartets abound, very cleanly played, no matter how "far out" the modulation or the technical demands. The saxophone section was really extraordinary in its polish. One can hear this above all in the remarkable balance and rhythmic unity in the sixteenth-note saxophone backgrounds in the second section of the piece (starting after the upward-rising unison passages); and later in the two saxes in octaves, alto and tenor. The intonation here must be heard to be believed. The side also marks the first appearance on records of the amazingly gifted trombonist, Snub Mosely, whose formidable technique clearly forecasts the lightning-fast trombones of the Bop Era. Here Mosely saunters in blithely on a high *e* flat, toying with rapid cascading figures as if they were child's play.

Trent's recording of the 1918 Turner Layton classic *After You've Gone* was made in March 1930. It again shows the band's remarkable ease with arranged ensembles set in unusual keys. Starting in C with Peanuts Holland's trumpet solo and a vocal, the piece modulates to D flat for the customary doubling of the beat, then moves to a brilliant B natural for the final full-ensemble chorus. Holland and Snub Mosely are the only soloists. Both players, though original in their styles, were also maddeningly elusive. It was as if they did not quite dare to project their unconventional ideas, and Mosely's solos often contain more silences than sound. Between the sudden spurts and flashes of oblique ideas one is forced to imagine the rest, left unstated, but implied. In the end that is what separates players like Holland

Example 19 *After You've Gone*—Holland Solo

and Mosely from someone like Armstrong or trombonist Dicky Wells: the latter stated their ideas fully, unequivocally, and with complete authority.

A glimpse of Holland's perky, slithery style can be gathered from the musical example (Ex. 19). Incidentally, the *a* naturals Holland plays against the F minor chords in bars two and ten hardly appear as errors in this context. At fast tempos in those days, players—even the best of them—frequently failed to adjust basic patterns to "minor" chromatic shifts in the chord changes; and curiously, at a relatively fast tempo, the ear does not perceive these theoretical errors as serious ear-shattering flaws.

The rhythm section, including tuba, plays in four beats except for the middle section where it plays the customary long meter (making in effect forty bars out of the original twenty). For a block-chord chorus in B natural and in 1930, the final section swings amazingly well—in fact as if it were in B flat and in the mid-thirties Swing Era.

These then are the bands which were competing with Moten for the public's attention. As can be seen, some of the bands discussed (and even some of the ones who were never recorded) had a loyal following and a considerable reputation among musicians. But the one advantage Moten had was a recording contract with Victor. So that even Trent, whom many musicians regarded more highly than Moten (at least in the late twenties, prior to the great 1932 Moten band), did not enjoy the over-all public reputation of Moten. To have landed a Victor contract was a big feather in one's cap, a factor which Moten, who was an even better businessman than a pianist, evidently knew how to exploit.

We have seen that Moten was capable of raiding or buying up entire orchestras. One can therefore assume that he also appropriated, wherever possible, musical ideas worked out by other bands. We left Moten's discography in late 1928, when other Southwestern bands began to record and Moten lost his virtual monopoly of the local recording market. From this point on, major personnel and stylistic revisions caused the orchestra to develop rapidly, acquiring a national reputation and eventually the undisputed top position in the Midwest and Southwest.

In 1929 the Moten band traveled twice to Chicago to record and produced about twenty sides. They reveal how completely the other Southwestern bands, not to mention Ellington and other Eastern orchestras, had outstripped Moten. On these 1929 records the band is trapped in its conservative pose. Evidently Moten, attempting to hold onto his dance and record audience, was trying to appeal to a wide middle-class public with a rough, slightly old-fashioned beat. Even the efforts of the three major soloists—Ed Lewis, Harlan Leonard, and Jack Washington—are canceled out by the monotonous "oom-pah" of the band. This is a pity, because Washington in particular was developing into a first-rate soloist, comparable only to young Harry Carney in Ellington's orchestra. The only new elements in these 1929 sides are irrelevant and musically regressive ones: the increased imitation of the Lombardo saxophone sound in section work, and the addition of accordion solos by Buster Moten (Bennie's brother).

In some minor ways the October 1929 sides are an improvement over the previous July dates. Basie had come in as pianist, and we can hear him work out his early style, vacillating somewhat erratically between two influences, Waller and Hines. The solos tend to ramble or fall into pianistic clichés,[23] although they also reveal the young Basie's potential talent and budding originality of style. Eddie Durham too had joined, doubling on trombone and solo guitar. His solos are also somewhat unformed, but they certainly reveal the advanced harmonic and rhythmic thinking of a man who was to become an important arranger in the Kansas City style, and as such are beyond the stylistic frame of reference set by the Moten band at that time. In *Small Black*, the band tries to achieve a more advanced sense of swing, but all it produces is something Martin Williams has aptly described as "peppy rather than really swinging." *Jones' Law Blues* is of some interest because of its close similarity to *Blue Devil Blues*, recorded only a fortnight after the Moten date. One can only speculate on who influenced whom, as both bands could have had their pieces in the repertory for some time. In any case, they both have the same basic format, same key, same tempo, same relation of a C minor introduction to a succeeding E flat blues, etc., with Moten's version expanded slightly.

A year later, October 1930, Jimmy Rushing and Hot Lips Page had joined Moten, the former mainly as a balladeer and only occasion-

23. This is especially true in his extended solo on *Small Black*, constructed from *several* masters, in the recent RCA Victor "Vintage Series" reissues.

ally as a singer of blues, the latter as third trumpet. But, above all, an arranger was beginning to reshape the band's destiny: Eddie Durham. Judging by the 1930 sides, Durham's first inclination was to emulate the Henderson-Redman-Carter style very closely. Many of their ideas now appear consistently, as in *Oh, Eddie* and *Somebody Stole My Gal*. The beat is beginning to flow more in the direction of a 4/4 concept. This is especially true of *When I'm Alone* and *My Gal*, transitional pieces for the band, now clearly headed toward the marvelous swing of the 1932 *Toby, Moten Swing*, and *Prince of Wales. That Too, Do* is a slow blues, which incorporates Rushing singing *Sent for You Yesterday* in the same style as the later famous Basie recording. The rather curious background behind Rushing is performed by piano, drums, rhythm banjo and improvised commentaries by Durham on guitar and brother Buster Moten on accordion. The recording is also notable for a well-realized "preaching" chorus, with Ed Lewis as the trumpeter-preacher and Rushing and the rest of the band as the congregation, in the familiar call-and-response pattern.

In late 1930 the Henderson band had retaken the national lead, after a fallow period, with arrangements like *Keep a Song in Your Soul* and *Chinatown, My Chinatown*. Benny Carter was now the arranger everyone followed, and Moten, while on tour in the East in early 1931, bought some forty arrangements by Carter and Horace Henderson from the Henderson library. The addition of Walter Page on bass, the arranger and clarinetist Eddie Barefield, and Ben Webster on tenor caused further drastic stylistic changes, and when Moten recorded in Camden, New Jersey, on December 13, 1932, the band sounded brand new.

The Wall Street crash was beginning to take its toll of the music business. The whole big-band business was in a state of economic flux. There were now hundreds of large and small bands, all competing for the dwindling financial market. Many of them collapsed in the early thirties, sometimes because of a lack of bookings or because of dishonest agents. Other bands lost their star personnel and were unable to survive in the highly competitive field. Some were fortunate in finding equal or better replacements. Still other orchestras fled to Europe for a while, as did Ellington in 1932. And curiously, some bands survived the Depression reasonably well, while others like Andy Kirk's Twelve Clouds of Joy, the Jimmie Lunceford band, and a number of Southwestern orchestras actually began life during the early Depression years.

When Moten went on his 1931 Eastern tour, he must have sensed that some drastic changes were called for. Everywhere he went, he encountered bands who had copied the Henderson-Redman-Carter formula and, with the help of a few local soloists, mostly younger men with a modern approach, were holding their own very well. Moreover, before Moten left on tour, he had suffered a disastrous defeat in Kansas City in a giant battle involving six different orchestras. With younger bands breathing down his neck, Moten's conservative style was a millstone. The forty new arrangements were a businessman's quick answer to a vexing problem.

It is difficult today to comprehend how many excellent orchestras there were. Most of them never recorded, some few recorded a handful of sides on lesser labels, issuing only a few hundred pressings. If they are known at all, it is only to record collectors. A clear index of this fact is that the Delaunay discography of 1948[24] lists almost none of these territory bands that recorded. As a result, for many jazz historians these bands have never existed. And yet they were highly active—they had to be to survive—had a loyal local following, were often admired by other visiting traveling bands, and contributed significantly to the rapid stylistic developments then affecting jazz. In view of this neglect in the jazz books, it might be well to examine the efforts of a few of the more representative orchestras that happened to record.

In Omaha and the surrounding territory Lloyd Hunter's Serenaders became successful around 1927 and in 1930 linked up professionally with the New York singer Victoria Spivey. Under her directorship the band toured widely, getting as far East as Boston, but not to New York. Their June 1931 recording of *Sensational Mood,* a composition by Henri Woode and one of the band's alto players, Noble Floyd, gives us a good impression of the high caliber of their soloists and of the sharp section work and rhythmic drive.

The personnel on the recording has not been exactly established,

24. Charles Delaunay, *New Hot Discography: The Standard Directory of Recorded Jazz,* ed. Walter E. Schaap and George Avakian (New York: Criterion, 1948).

but even if it were, knowledge of the player's identity would not alter the quality of the solos. The band was obviously familiar with McKinney's Cotton Pickers, Henderson, and Ellington. *Sensational Mood* is a flag-waver, taken at a good clip (♩ = *ca.* 290). The introduction, in the manner of a late twenties night-club production number, puts one on notice immediately that the band means business. It is the kind of music Lunceford was to parlay into a national hit with his famous *White Heat* in 1934. The introduction, using 3/8 (♩.) and 3/4 (𝅗𝅥.) brass figures over the fast 4/4, leads directly into an arranged ensemble recalling the brass's 3/8 figures of the introduction. A series of brief solos follows, all of which are of the quality one might expect from one of the big Eastern bands, but not from a band whose very name is unknown in the jazz books, at least prior to the sixties. These solos are not original, to be sure, based as they are on the work of soloists from one of the above-mentioned bands: John Stark, Benny Carter, Benny Morton, Rex Stewart. But they imitate that model inventively and with a fine sense of swing. In the first group of solos is one for trumpet in what used to be called the "freak" style espoused by Rex Stewart.[25] The later arranged ensembles set off the reeds and brass in superimposed 3/4 and 5/4 patterns in the best Redman tradition. All of this is done with considerable ease and polish, and the band had obviously absorbed well the rhythmic innovations of Armstrong via Redman's band conception.

Another band that roamed the northern fringe of the Mid- and Southwest was Grant Moore's, more or less headquartered in Milwaukee. Similar in character to Hunter's band, Moore also worked out of the Redman-Carter conception, sporting in addition a respectable collection of soloists. Moore recorded two titles in June 1931, the lively *Dixieland One-Step* and *Mama Don't Allow*. The former begins with a brash introduction set in a bugle-call style. Interestingly, its basic material is derived from a two-note figure ♩ ♩ in the first strain of the old ODJB hit; and this figure returns in variations, diminutions, and augmentations from time to time, finally providing the building ma-

25. The "freak style," most often applied to Rex Stewart's trumpet playing, refers to a highly personal and unorthodox manner of using a variety of mutes (particularly the plunger) in combination with various half or three-quarter valve positions which drastically alter the tone of the trumpet or cornet.

Example 20 *Dixieland One-Step*—Final Chorus and Coda

Stems up = brass Stems down = saxes
(In Example 20 only the top of each four-part [brass] or three-part [saxes] chord is indicated. x is the introductory figure mentioned in the text.)

terials for the extended coda. In fact, the arrangement, probably fashioned by the pianist J. Norman Abron, is quite ingenious, especially in the unique way in which the final ensemble chorus is spun out imperceptibly into the coda (Ex. 20). The perfect transition shows an arranger of considerable originality.

In the introduction, the reed and brass choirs are set apart in block chords in contrary motion, an idea still rarely used in jazz in 1931. Later on there is a two-bar tenor break, in which we hear swinging eighth notes in a manner that became common only with bop. Two unison figures occur in the arrangement, one in octaves for alto and tenor, the other for the full band, again a very unusual device in those days (Ex. 21).

Example 21 *Dixieland One-Step*—Passage in Unison

(The rhythm section accompanies this passage by playing only afterbeats on the second and fourth counts.)

But perhaps the finest moment is Bob Russell's leaping trumpet break (Ex. 22).

Example 22 *Dixieland One-Step*—Russell Trumpet Break

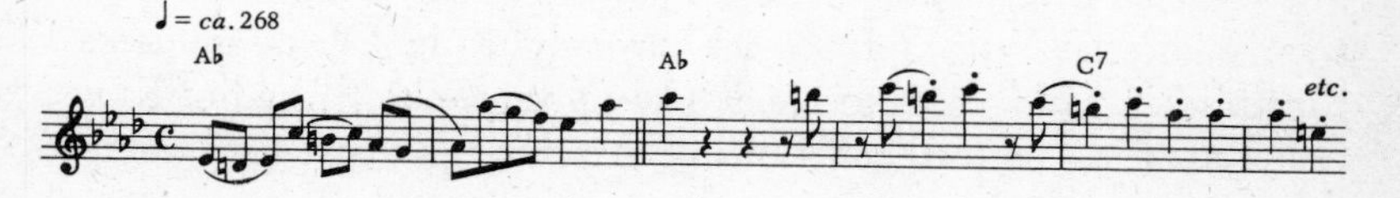

The Moore band's other side, *Mama Don't Allow,* although mainly a vocal-novelty number (sung by the whole band), is still full of enterprising ensembles, sprightly unison figures, and a series of bass drum "bombs," several years before Jo Jones and Kenny Clarke were to explore this latter device. The greatest surprise, however, is the final ensemble chorus statement (Ex. 23), a riff melody very close to the theme of *Moten's Swing*.

Example 23 *Mama Don't Allow*—Final Chorus

In Cincinnati and the territory southeast of Chicago we find Zack Whyte. Besides novelty and suggestive vocals, the band could deliver a poignant *West End Blues* (without Armstrong's spectacular introduction, of course), work over the current popular hits with a friendly, bouncing beat, or—for the rough river trade in the Ohio valley—stomp with a heavy rocking style. As recorded, the band produced a dark, full sound, dominated by a tuba player who not only had a tremendous tone but could play a moaning blues chorus (as on the 1929 recording of *West End Blues*) far beyond the expressive capacities of most other tuba players. Unfortunately, the band did not record in 1933-34 when it had Sy Oliver as an arranger and players like Eddie Barefield, trombonist Vic Dickenson, and the unsung trumpet talent Henry Savage.

St. Louis was one of the first cities to come under the influence of New Orleans musicians on their way up north to Chicago. It had also had a long-standing tradition in brass-band playing, with many German-born teachers giving young St. Louisans a solid technical foundation; and, of course, there was also the venerable ragtime piano tradition. St. Louis was a stopover for all bands crisscrossing the Midwest and Southwest, and as a result its musical life was a rich and varied one. But above all it was a blues trumpet player's town. Within this special area, orchestras ranged from the strongly King Oliver–influenced Creath's Jazz-O-Maniacs to bands like Oliver Cobb's Rhythm Kings. Cobb could do perfect imitations of Armstrong's vocal and trumpet styles both, as on his 1929 recording of *Hot Stuff*. There was also Dewey Jackson, a fine blues-playing trumpeter, who had worked with Creath as well as with the Mississippi riverboat king Fate Marable. In general in the late twenties and early thirties St. Louis clung to the more conservative traditions, its proximity to both New Orleans and Chicago preventing it from developing its own indigenous style.

Further southeast in Atlanta there were a number of good local bands. Atlanta, as the New York of the South, also had several important theaters where traveling musicians performed, particularly the blues singers like Ma Rainey, Bessie Smith, and Mamie Smith. As a consequence, good musicians were constantly coming through Atlanta. In the mid-twenties the pianist Eddie Heywood, Sr., was one of the most respected musicians there. Judging by a 1926 recording, *Trombone Moanin' Blues,* Heywood was able to gather together a number of remarkable players. (The personnel is unknown.) Though the beat of the rhythm section, with a slap-tongue bass saxophone as bass, was at once steady and stiff, the three "horn" men of this six-piece band played a good blues chorus. The trumpet player, for example, makes one think of Bubber Miley at his Ellington best with a very similar tone, a comparable versatility with the mute, and a naturally free conception of rhythm. (Ex. 24).

Example 24 *Trombone Moanin' Blues*—Trumpet Solo

(Open and closed muting effects are not indicated in the example.)

The clarinet is a really whiny blues clarinet in the Dodds tradition, while the "moanin'" trombone could be Charlie Green. Heywood himself appears not to have been a jazz pianist strictly speaking, for he displayed an eclectic mixture of boogie-woogie piano, ragtime, and semi-classics. The final chorus has the clarinet and bass saxophone improvising in arpeggiated vestiges of New Orleans style, while the two brass intone a simple wailing blues riff (Ex. 25), an unusual en-

Example 25 *Trombone Moanin' Blues*—Final Chorus

counter between the worlds of New Orleans and Redman.

A few years later, in 1929, the pianist J. Neal Montgomery recorded two sides, *Auburn Stomp* and *Atlanta Lowdown*. Another blues band, its style was a mixture of many conceptions. Alongside

Redman-type reed and brass ensembles, one could hear a proficient trumpet player caught halfway between Oliver and Armstrong, clarinet runs à la Buster Bailey, raspy Armstrong scat-vocals, Montgomery's Waller-style piano, and strangely harmonized "vamps" like the following (Ex. 26):

Example 26 *Auburn Stomp*—Vamp

The list of bands could be extended, although the foregoing brief regional survey should suffice to show that many respectable, and sometimes even startingly good, bands had mushroomed all over the country by the end of the twenties. Wherever a band toured, it was likely to meet a proud local group ready to do battle. And so there developed a fertile training ground where young musicians could learn—go to the jazz school, as it were—a condition which unhappily has not existed for over a decade now.

On that aforementioned December day in Camden in 1932, the Moten band not only cut ten sides which can only be described in superlatives, but inaugurated a conception of orchestral jazz distinct from that of Henderson and the Eastern axis, a conception moreover which was to bypass the inherent stylistic hazards of the Swing Era and provide at least one of the routes leading to modern jazz and bop.

Musicians who played in the Moten band on that date recall that their tour had been a financial disaster, and they reached Camden broke and hungry. Hearing the exuberant abandon and joyousness of these recordings, one would never guess such conditions. On most of the sides, the band swings with inspired control; the structural balance between ensemble and solo is masterful; and the occasional raggedness of the section work hardly detracts from the over-all expression of virile lyricism.

The two main arrangers, Eddie Barefield and Eddie Durham, contributed strongly, but their arrangements came to life in the hands of the major soloists—Hot Lips Page, Ben Webster, Basie—and the extraordinary rhythm section. Even the written ensembles are played with the kind of inner involvement we associate with solos. To isolate the contributions each member made is therefore almost irrelevant, since no single effort uniquely informs the end product. The Moten band here defined a new interpretation of the word "collective."

Several of the sides have musical ideas or devices in common. Perhaps the most consistently thrilling of these are the brass and reed riff choruses that end the fast pieces *Toby, Blue Room, Prince of Wales, Lafayette*. The Henderson heritage of these riffs is undeniable, and yet they have been extended into a rhythmic realm that gives them another dimension, as in the way each successive riff chorus builds upon its predecessor, in *Toby* for instance (Ex. 27). The same idea

Example 27 *Toby*—Riff Choruses

(The two-bar phrases are repeated in typical eight-bar riff patterns.)

recurs in *Blue Room,* slightly disjoined now, and in a slower tempo (Ex. 28). In the *Prince of Wales* the saxophone figure has been

Example 28 *Blue Room*—Riff Pattern

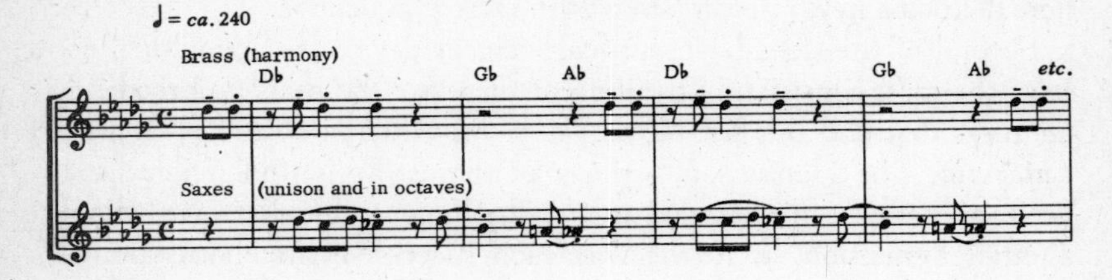

turned into a descending scale pattern (Ex. 29). Another time, on

Example 29 *Prince of Wales*—Riff Pattern

Moten's Swing, we find it in ascending position (Ex. 30).

It is remarkable how the brass ensembles and riffs gradually take over in *Blue Room,* imperceptibly absorbing the solos (and the original theme). The Richard Rodgers theme is never simply stated; it is elaborated immediately, and the bridge (the *B* section in the $A\ A^1\ B\ A^2$ thirty-two-bar structure) is differentiated only orchestrationally, another device consistently employed by Durham and Barefield. The

Example 30 *Moten's Swing*—Riff Pattern

next chorus features Hot Lips Page with a simple sustained saxophone background and Basie's high chime chords. But now as Webster solos, the brass begin a long process of gradual rhythmic and dynamic intensification. The *A* backgrounds are half notes; but already in A^2, they have been tightened up into shorter syncopated durations . In the next chorus, under Barefield's clarinet (he plays very poorly on this side), the spurting brass figures gradually transform elaborations of the tune into pure riff patterns; that is, melody is turned into rhythm. Again the bridge subdivision is delineated by means of orchestration, this time a combination of trombones and saxophones. The next chorus (see Ex. 27 above) continues riffing, with McWashington's noticeably stronger cymbal backbeats a new element. In the final chorus, even the bridge trumpet solo becomes a riff, and the piece rides out on the final ensemble almost in the nature of a coda.

I suppose the biggest surprise for those who have only heard Count Basie in the familiar epigrammatic piano style he favored with his own band will be the revelation of Basie as a powerful two-handed pianist, a technical virtuoso in the best tradition of James P. Johnson, Waller, and Hines. Basie's abilities here can be sampled on *Toby* (at a breakneck speed of ♩ = *ca.* 340) and on his specialty number *Prince of Wales.* In this piece the joyous spirit with which the band lights into the chorus after Hot Lips Page's solo (Ex. 31), and the long four-bar moaning brass lead-in to the final chorus (before Basie's "dramatic" coda) are also unforgettable!

Both Hot Lips Page and Ben Webster are marvelously consistent on these sides, with Page playing in a carefree floating-above-the-bar-

Example 31 *Prince of Wales*—Riff Chorus

lines manner that represented already an extension of Armstrong's rhythmic ideas. In *Moten Swing* Page is no longer playing "changes" but is harmonically freed to produce pure melodic essence. In this respect he reflects a modern approach his colleague Webster had not yet achieved, partly because in those days a tenor saxophone always felt obliged to play many notes. Page's best solos reflect a minimum of activity with a maximum of expression, a lesson Lester Young was to extend several years later. A good example of Page's artistry in this context is his solo on *New Orleans,* an improvisation in essence as mature as his much later recording of *Gee, Baby, Ain't I Good to You.*

These sides also showed clearly that hot swinging jazz need not be played loud. There are a dozen moments here where the band swings at low dynamic levels. The relaxation implied in this kind of controlled playing—control and relaxation are not incompatible—was possible only in relation to the rhythmic conception this magnificent rhythm section had evolved. Here we are truly in the world of the Basie band of later years. One marvels at the unity of Walter Page's walking bass and McWashington's drums. Basie's stride piano, still discernible, is becoming absorbed and, so to speak, horizontalized by the flowing 4/4 of the guitar, drums, and bass. One marvels too at the speed with which this development occurred; only a year or two earlier, the beat was still stiffly vertical. The difference was due not only to Walter Page, but, as I have implied earlier in this book, to the fact that the string bass had replaced the tuba. The 4/4 flow of Page's bass on *Toby* or *Prince of Wales* is unthinkable on tuba.

These recordings produced a rhythmic revolution comparable to Armstrong's earlier one. They spelled the doom of all earlier rhythm-section techniques. They also contained the seeds for a process of total liberation for each of the four rhythm instruments, a process that was to reach another conceptual plateau ten years later in the beginnings of the Bop Era.

We have seen how Moten's band developed from a rough novelty-*cum*-ragtime band to one of the great orchestras of jazz. Although the band was to collapse with the death of Moten in 1935, it survived fairly intact—certainly stylistically—under Basie's subsequent leadership. In this chapter we have seen how somewhat gropingly and erratically Moten's band accumulated its language bit by bit. In a somewhat different environment and exploring quite a different kind of talent, Duke Ellington was traveling a similar path in New York, the subject of the next chapter.

7

The Ellington Style:

Its Origins and Early Development *

Duke Ellington is one of America's great composers. At this writing his extraordinary creativity seems undiminished. In looking back over more than forty years of his career, we can only marvel at the consistency with which Ellington and his orchestra have sustained a level of inspiration comparable in its way to that of the major "classical" composers of our century. By the end of the period covered in this book—the early 1930s—most of Ellington's major works lay still in the future. (They will be discussed in a subsequent volume of this study.) The basic elements of his style, however, were fully developed by this time; and in the great period that followed, Duke and his orchestra largely polished and refined the techniques developed in the decade before. It is now time for us to examine how this unique musical style came into existence and to look at its early flowering in the recordings made in the late 1920s and early 1930s.

Ellington was born in 1899 in Washington, D. C. He began playing professionally in his home town while still a precocious teen-age ragtime pianist. In the late years of World War I, Washington was a beehive of musical activity, with bands playing for dancing and all kinds of social and political functions. Ellington had already played

* This chapter, first printed in a somewhat different form in Nat Hentoff and Albert McCarthy, eds., *Jazz* (New York: Rinehart & Company, 1959), is reprinted here by permission of Holt, Rinehart & Winston, Inc.

piano with some of the more famous orchestras, and by 1919 he was in turn supplying small bands for dances and parties. It was on these jobs that he first began to play with saxophonist Otto "Toby" Hardwick and drummer Sonny Greer, both of whom would later become fixtures in his New York–based orchestra. It is of the utmost importance to our consideration of Ellington's development to note that most, if not all, of the Washington orchestras were more or less commercial groups, generally led by well-known ragtime pianists but otherwise consisting primarily of reading or "legitimate" musicians,[1] since the "best gigs in town" were for society and embassy affairs. However, some of the smaller, rougher outfits undoubtedly played more rags and more of what was then becoming known as jazz instead of the usual waltzes and tangos.

In 1922 Duke and his Washington friends Hardwick and Greer came to New York to join Wilbur Sweatman, who led a large orchestra playing production-type theater dates and acts, although some of its music was recognizable as jazz. Over the next two years there were lean periods in New York working sporadically with the Sweatman and Elmer Snowden bands. There was also a chance to write the music for an ill-fated Broadway musical show, *Chocolate Kiddies of 1924*[2]—the first of a number of Ellington forays into musical comedy, all of them unsuccessful, at least financially. In between, despite a few retreats to Washington, the Washingtonians, as Duke's own group called itself, played at jam sessions, house hops, rent parties, and an assortment of odd jobs, enough to develop a small repertoire of their own. Finally, in 1924, Ellington took over the Snowden band, by then enlarged to six members. By this time Duke's little band found steady engagement at the Hollywood Club, at Forty-ninth Street and Broadway, soon to be renamed the Kentucky Club.

We have seen (in Chapters 5 and 6) how jazz developed in the East, and in New York in particular, in a different way than it did in New Orleans and the Southwest. Eastern jazz was a functional music, geared specifically to social dancing and theater shows, and much of

1. See Barry Ulanov, *Duke Ellington* (New York: Creative Age Press, 1946), pp. 15-17, for details about Ellington's Washington activity.
2. Although this show never reached Broadway, it enjoyed an extremely successful two-year run in Berlin, where the score was played by the Sam Wooding orchestra.

its drive and inspiration seemed to originate in Baltimore and Washington and was based largely on ragtime. Bands in the region attempted to capitalize on the ragtime and fox trot craze by embodying in their arrangements the spirit, if not the style, of the leading ragtime pianists. Indeed, when Ellington first settled in New York, he came under the influence of Willie "The Lion" Smith and James P. Johnson, whose *Carolina Shout* he had memorized from a piano roll while he was still in Washington. The influence of this Harlem piano style marked all of Ellington's early orchestral work. As late as 1927 there exist examples in the Ellington orchestra repertoire of fairly literal transcriptions of Duke's piano playing (*Washington Wobble,* for example). Jelly Roll Morton, by contrast, did not make orchestrations that were mere transpositions of a given piece from one instrument, the piano, to several others but made orchestrations, reworked to fit the requirements of the instruments for which he was writing. Ellington's "pianistic" approach would, however, have far-reaching consequences in relation to the voicing of his orchestra, as we will see later.

In April 1926, Ellington's band, still styled the Washingtonians and now augmented by Bubber Miley and Charlie Irvis, recorded two sides for Gennett.[3] Primarily a race record company, Gennett wanted blues and got *You've Got Those "Wanna Go Back Again" Blues* and *If You Can't Hold the Man You Love,* which strictly speaking, were not blues at all but fairly catchy blues-ish tunes. The band consisted at the time of Bubber Miley (trumpet), Otto Hardwick (alto and baritone sax), Charlie Irvis (trombone), Sonny Greer (drums), Fred Guy

3. The most complete Ellington discography is Benny H. Aasland, *The "Wax Works" of Duke Ellington* (Stockholm: Foliotryck, 1954). While Duke's band made two acoustical records, *Trombone Blues* and *I'm Gonna Hang Around My Sugar,* late in 1925 (according to Aasland), they are inconsequential items that sound like any number of other bands of the period, and are certainly not in the same class with what the Fletcher Henderson band was doing then. Both Ellington sides are typical numbers for dancing, with little "Charleston" touches and many of the syncopated clichés of the time. The personnel, I would guess, consists of Hardwick on alto, Prince Robinson on clarinet and tenor (with a fair tenor solo on the second side), Charlie Irvis on trombone, Ellington on piano, and Fred Guy on guitar. The trumpet and tuba are less individual and thus harder to identify.

(banjo, Bass Edwards (tuba), and Duke on piano. For the record date Duke enlarged the band to twelve men, adding Jimmy Harrison on second trombone and vocal; Don Redman, George Thomas, and Prince Robinson (reeds); Leroy Rutledge and Harry Cooper (trumpets), the latter substituting for Miley. Harrison was just starting his brilliant, short-lived career, while Cooper had played briefly with Bennie Moten. Redman, of course, was beginning to exert considerable influence as an arranger. And yet, though studded with these budding names, the two sides are no more than partial attempts at imitating the King Oliver Creole Jazz Band, with which Gennett had had great success three years before. *If You Can't Hold the Man You Love,* for example, has a trumpet duet (Ex. 1) in the manner of Oliver and

Example 1 *If You Can't Hold the Man You Love*

Armstrong, although it lacks their stylistic grace and precision. It also has a similar full-band collective-ensemble sound on the out-chorus—but again, with almost none of the sensitivity of the Creole Band, and with rather less of a beat.

If one searches for embryonic Ellington elements, the pickings are very lean indeed, but there is at times the characteristic separation of the reeds and brass which marks the entire early Ellington period. There is also, in *You've Got Those "Wanna Go Back Again" Blues,* the first of the nostalgic train-whistle imitations[4] which were to creep into Ellington's work from time to time; and there is in *If You Can't*

4. By 1926 this was a well-established tradition among the orchestras that played the so-called symphonic jazz. Entire train rides were depicted musically, evidently with considerable realism. Ellington's own efforts in this genre, of course, culminated in the virtuosic 1934 recording of *Daybreak Express.*

Hold the Man You Love, a characteristic harmonic progression which —although in this case neither by Ellington nor altogether new—he was to use continuously in ensuing years: B^{b}–G^{b7}–B^{b}–B^{b7}. *You've Got Those "Wanna Go Back Again" Blues* also features Hardwick on baritone and some rather good-natured Irvis trombone, with only a touch of growl (on one note). But on the whole, these initial sides sound more like some of the white bands of the period than like the bands of Jelly Roll Morton and King Oliver.

Animal Crackers and *Li'l Farina,* recorded two months later, with Miley back and only Charlie Johnson (trumpet) and Prince Robinson (tenor and clarinet) added to the original personnel, already have a shade more distinction, although the tunes themselves are rather undistinguished, typical music-hall material. While on the one hand these records prove that Duke's piano was at the time a very sloppy, helter-skelter sort of party piano, and that he and certain other members of the band had a tendency to rush tempos, they also reveal much clearer (possibly better-prepared) ensemble work and, most important of all, a first-rate Miley solo.

Much has been written about Miley's plunger and growl technique. This is understandable, but it has tended to obscure the fact that Miley's solos are highly original from the standpoint of the *actual notes* played. Notice in *Animal Crackers* the daring intervals of his opening two measures, and later on in the twenty-fifth bar of his solo the *d* flat (flatted fifth!) and *b* flat (minor third against the major third *b* natural in the accompaniment) (Ex. 2A and 2B). Miley uses the growl or plunger with great restraint in this solo. It is unfortunate that he pushes the tempo too hard, but it does give that part of the performance a kind of headlong, devil-may-care feeling, which, it seems to me,

Example 2 *Animal Crackers*

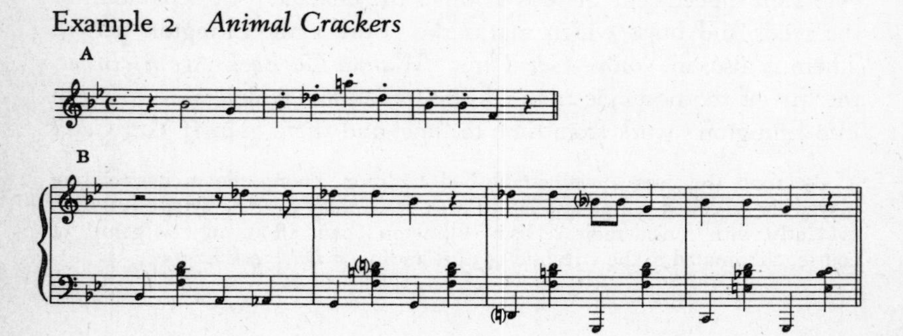

is less annoying than the more characterless remainder of the record.[5] *Animal Crackers,* the less steady of the two records rhythmically—by coincidence both pieces are in the same tempo—fluctuates between ensemble passages that drag and solos that rush. Indeed rhythmic unanimity and collective swing were not a strong point of the Ellington organization[6] until bassist Jimmy Blanton joined the band in 1939.

The next two recorded sides present us for the first time (except for *Li'l Farina*) with Ellington the composer; both tunes are his. *Rainy Nights* has that already-mentioned chord progression in the first three measures. It also contains a full chorus each by Irvis and Miley, both of which are paraphrase improvisations.[7] Irvis's solo is expansive, big-toned, basically simple, and at times quite tender. Behind both solos the rhythm section plays chords on the second and fourth beat of each bar, leaving the first and third empty, which gives the whole section a slightly halting, suspended feeling. (Since the playing of the band in those years was more the result of collective thinking than of anything written down, it would be rash simply to ascribe the idea solely to Ellington). The record ends on a ninth chord, a device that had become "hip" in the middle 1920s, after seventh-chord endings had begun to pale with much overuse.

Choo-Choo, taken as a whole, is the best of these six earliest sides. It is an Ellington tune with a lovely set of chords on which Miley, again sticking close to the melody, fashions a disarmingly simple "paraphrase" solo with little touches here and there of playfulness and nostalgia, and a very discreet use of the plunger and growl (Ex. 3). *Choo-Choo,* as might be expected, ends with the inevitable train whistle, manipulated by Greer.

5. The *a* natural in bar two of Miley's solo could have been accidental. It is possible that Miley tried for the sixth of the chord (*g*) and overshot the mark, since on a trumpet the fingerings for g also give you an *a*. The history of jazz improvisation on brass instruments is full of such chance moments, often with very fortunate results.
6. One of the most solid players rhythmically in the early Ellington days was Bass Edwards, the tuba player (1926), who had not only a remarkably expressive tone but a strong pungent beat. Unfortunately he is heard to good advantage only on four or five sides, some of which, like *Immigration Blues* and *The Creeper,* are very hard to obtain.
7. I am using this term in the sense that André Hodeir has applied to it, namely a type of improvisation based primarily on embellishment or ornamentation of the original melodic line.

Example 3 *Choo-Choo*

(The diagonal lines through the stems of some notes indicate the use of the growl.)

Summing up these first recordings, we find rather ordinary material, a modicum of organization, one lovely tune, and two fine Miley solos. Although the Ellington historian is apt to look with a kindly eye on these early efforts and find little glimpses of future developments, they certainly do not stand up in comparison to such contemporary masterpieces of both orchestration and formal structure as Jelly Roll Morton's *Black Bottom Stomp* or King Oliver's recording of *Froggie Moore.*

Of course Ellington was only twenty-seven, while both Morton and Oliver were just turning forty and in their prime. This accounts, certainly, for part of the difference in quality. But there were also fundamental differences in musical backgrounds. Some of the older musicians, who were maturing in the early 1920s, verify the impression that the Negro music of the South (from Texas to the Carolinas) was slow in reaching New York, and generally reached it indirectly, via Chicago and St. Louis. Furthermore, there seems to have been a greater effort on the part of Northeastern Negroes to assimilate with the whites, especially in the field of music.

One result was that in the early 1920s there were several large orchestras, like Wilbur Sweatman's and Sam Wooding's,[8] that played what was then called "symphonic jazz." In an interesting process of cross-fertilization, these orchestras at first tried to emulate the big white organizations (Whiteman, Hickman, etc.); while, in turn, by the middle and late 1920s the big white orchestras reciprocated by trying to capture the more Negroid strain which began to infiltrate the Eastern bands with the spread of the New Orleans style (notably through Oliver and Armstrong). Moreover, many colored bands of the time had two kinds of music in their repertoire, one for Harlem (uptown) and another for Broadway (downtown). If a rough generalization can be made, one can say that the New York bands, small and large, were showy, "dicty" outfits that catered primarily to white audiences and were slow to shake off the trappings of ragtime and equally slow to adopt elements from the New Orleans style. Paradoxically, such elements were effectively incorporated only after the New Orleans tradition was in decline.[9]

8. Wooding's orchestra was one of the best of the mid-twenties. With the almost unbelievable popularity of jazz in Europe, a number of New York bands were assembled to make European tours. One of these was Sam Wooding's. Its personnel included Tommy Ladnier, trombonist Herb Fleming, Garvin Bushell (on reeds), and a remarkable tuba player named John Warren. Their tour took them all over Europe from Spain to Russia, and they recorded in 1925 in Berlin. Unfortunately the recordings, though excellently played, do not give a fair idea of the band's real potential, for their tour was as part of the revue *Chocolate Kiddies*. The music was typically "sophisticated" revue music, a hodge-podge of "symphonic" introductions and modulations, interspersed with the big tunes from the show and an occasional improvised solo. In a sense they were Harlem's answer to Paul Whiteman. *Break Away* and *My Sin* (both with vocal trios) are typical examples.

There is very little question that Ernst Krenek, whose *Jonny Spielt Auf* was the first opera to use "jazz" elements and became the greatest international operatic success of the 1920s, heard Sam Wooding's orchestra in Berlin. In any event, Krenek's conception of jazz is very close to that offered by the Wooding orchestra in Berlin.

9. See the New York section of Chapter 6 for examples.

The interesting question is how were Ellington and his men, all of whom were very much part of this Eastern tradition, able to transcend it in the late 1920s and early 1930s and create a unique kind of big band jazz. Bubber Miley was largely responsible for the initial steps through his introduction of a rougher sound into the band. Ellington himself is quite clear about Bubber's inffuence: "Bubber used to growl all night long, playing gutbucket on his horn. That was when we decided to forget all about the sweet music."[10] Miley heard King Oliver in Chicago and Johnny Dunn in New York and began to use the growl and the plunger. He in turn helped teach the same techniques to the band's trombonists—Charlie Irvis and his replacement in late 1926, Joe "Tricky Sam" Nanton—who were also influenced by a now forgotten St. Louis trombonist, Jonas Walker, reputed to be the first to apply New Orleans "freak" sounds to his instrument. It was Miley and Nanton who developed the band's famous "jungle" effects through their use of the growl and plunger.

Actually Miley's influence extended far beyond these effects. He was not only the band's most significant soloist but actually wrote, alone or with Ellington, many of the compositions in the band's book between 1927 and 1929. Although the extent of Miley's contribution has not yet been accurately assessed, there seems little doubt that those compositions that bear Bubber's name along with Ellington's were primarily created by Miley. These include the three most important works of the period—recorded in late 1926 and early 1927—*East St. Louis Toodle-Oo, Black and Tan Fantasy,* and *Creole Love Call.*[11]

Miley also had a marvelous melodic gift, one inextricably linked to his growl and plunger technique. As with any great performer or composer, pitch and color derive *simultaneously* from the initial inspiration. In separating these elements here, it is only to point out that Miley's enormous contribution to pure classic melody in jazz has been

10. Nat Shapiro and Nat Hentoff, eds., *Hear Me Talkin' to Ya* (New York, Rinehart & Company, 1955).

11. In the one-year period November 1926 to December 1927, only four of the seventeen pieces recorded were written by song writers outside the band, while five of the remaining numbers, including those named above, were by Miley. Ellington, in turn, created six pieces, and Otto Hardwick, two. Actually some of Ellington's numbers might well belong more properly to other members of the band, as it was common practice—and, indeed, still is today—for the leader of a band to take full credit for works created by the band and written by members of it.

unfortunately neglected up to this point.[12] The theme of *East St. Louis Toodle-Oo* shows Miley at his melodic best. The melodic line is so disarmingly simple that, except for the use of the mute and growl, it would sound like pure folk song; and it may well be, as Roger Pryor Dodge points out, that this thematic material was "common musical knowledge" at the time. It is the striking way the melody is accompanied that most engages our attention, though, for underneath Miley's trumpet, Ellington (I presume) has arranged a moaning, sustaining passage for the saxophones and tuba that provides both framework and contrast to Miley's line (Ex. 4).

Example 4 *East St. Louis Toodle-Oo*—Accompaniment to Miley's Solo

Here we find a dramatic example of what has been called the "Ellington effect."[13] It is evident from what has been said above that Miley deserves much credit for this quality, at least in its early manifestations, although it is usually attributed exclusively to Ellington. As in Example 4, such an effect may often have been a joint creation of Duke and his men. There is no doubt that Duke had the opportunity to promote or discourage these stylistic developments. It is a mark of his talent and vision as a leader that in these early days of his band, while he was learning to use the materials he had in hand, he let his musicians lead the way in forming the band's style. It is evident both from the recordings and also from the statements of contemporary musicians that Ellington was very dependent upon his players at this stage, and that *they* knew it. It is to Duke's credit that he fostered a fierce pride and communal attitude in his band so that it took preced-

12. To my knowledge, only Roger Pryor Dodge has tried to show that Miley's importance goes beyond the fashioning of extravagant, bizarre muted effects: "Bubber Miley" in *Jazz Monthly,* IV (May 1958), 2.

13. An accurate term coined by Billy Strayhorn, Duke's alter-ego and fellow arranger for a quarter of a century after 1940.

ence over the individual contributions and feelings of its members. Through the collaboration of his musicians, Ellington would learn to use the remarkable aggregation of sounds the band contained in a more purely compositional manner.

Ellington made many recordings of *East St. Louis Toodle-Oo* for various record companies, and when compared, these records give us an interesting insight into the Ellington approach, in as much as they span a period of thirteen months. The Vocalion and Brunswick versions, made four months apart, are practically identical in quality and format. In contrast to the better-known Brunswick version, the earlier Vocalion has a slighter livelier tempo and features the rich tone of Bass Edwards.[14] The Brunswick and Columbia versions were recorded eight days apart, and although not identical, are still very similar in form and musical content. The latter is in general a bit more subdued, mainly because of differences in studio and recording equipment. The tempo is slightly faster on the Brunswick master, and Wellman Braud's tuba has less punch than Edwards's on the Columbia version. There is a great similarity between Hardwick's and Jackson's clarinet solos on Brunswick and Columbia respectively, and, except for individual flaws in each version, Nanton's slightly stiff but good-natured solo is also the same, which indicates that once the "improvisations" were set, they remained unchanged for a certain period.

The later Victor version, however, shows some major revisions. The form has changed (Ex. 5); so have the solos and their sequence. Most important of all, the weakest part of the earlier versions, namely the trite polka-like phrase in the reeds, arranged by Ellington (the first part of B^2), has been eliminated. This was done by converting the arranged ensemble of B^2 into a Harry Carney baritone improvisation, inserted between Miley's theme and Nanton's trombone solo to contrast a reed instrument with the two brass. The clarinet solo, which

14. At the time Vocalion was a subsidiary of Columbia; and since Columbia re-recorded the Ellington band in *East St. Louis Toodle-Oo* four months later, I suppose the parent company intended the new version to supersede the earlier one; this would explain why the two Vocalion sides (the first recording of *Birmingham Breakdown* is on the B side) were never reissued. The Vocalion *East St. Louis Toodle-Oo* version is therefore practically unobtainable.

Example 5 *East St. Louis Toodle-Oo*—Form

Vocalion & Brunswick & Columbia	*Intro.*	*A*	*B*	*A*[1]	*B*[1]	*B*[2]	*A*
		32	18	16	18	8 + 10	8
		(Miley)	(Nanton)	(Clar.)	(Brass)	(Reeds-full ensemble)	(Miley)
Victor	*Intro.*	*A*	*B*	*B*[1]	*A*[1]	*B*[2]	*A*
		32	18	18	16	18	8
		(Miley)	(Carney)	(Nanton)	(Clar.)	(Brass)	(Miley)

(The small numbers qualifying the letters indicate variations of the material. The other numbers indicate the number of bars.)

was in the high register in the earlier versions, has become a growly low-register solo. Unfortunately, though the format is improved, except for Miley the performance is poorer. The tempo is slower and drags, the intonation and balance are quite miserable, and Braud's bowed bass is cumbersome and too lugubrious for the occasion. Even Carney, still a bit green (he was only seventeen at that time), is excessively reedy in tone, and his loping, on-the-beat rhythm is a little dated. Miley has taken some of the humor out of the bridge of his theme by slurring one phrase formerly tongued, but his final eight bars have become more aggressive and dirtier in the use of the growl.

Whereas most bands of the period ended each number with full ensemble (sometimes collectively improvised), Ellington—or Miley—chose to end quietly with a short reprise of the theme, a pattern Ellington was to develop thoroughly in the next decade. This recapitulation really saves *East St. Louis Toodle-Oo* from complete deterioration after the tawdry ensemble passages. And it seems to me that the importance of this ending lies not so much in the fact that a felicitous choice was made, but that such a choice was *possible*. It was possible because *East St. Louis* was not a collection of thirty-two- twelve-bar "take your turn" solos, nor was it a totally improvised ensemble piece, but in its faltering way a *composition;* it had a two-part (*A* and *B*) form and a thematic statement that made such a recapitulation both logical and pleasing.

Basically the same points could be made about the other two Miley-Ellington masterpieces of the period, *Black and Tan Fantasy* and *Creole Love Call*. The former gives further evidence of the difference in artistic levels at that time between Miley and Ellington. The piece consists of Miley's twelve-bar theme based on the classic blues progression,[15] three choruses on the same (two by Miley, one by Nanton), an arranged ensemble passage, a twelve-bar Ellington piano solo, and finally a recapitulation with the famous tagged-on Chopin *Funeral March* ending. Of these segments only two can be attributed to Ellington, and they are not only the weakest by far but are quite out of character with the rest of the record. Whereas Miley's theme, his solos —and to a lesser degree Nanton's—again reflect an unadorned pure classicism, Ellington's two contributions derive from the world of slick trying-to-be-modern show music.

Fortunately in *Creole Love Call*—famous for being Adelaide Hall's first attempt at an instrumentalized, wordless vocal—Ellington's role was limited strictly to orchestrating. The melancholy simplicity (again, blues chords) is unadulterated, though the ensemble parts cannot compare with Miley's or Rudy Jackson's radiantly singing New Orleans–styled solos.

A comparison of the three 1927 recordings of *Black and Tan Fantasy* again shows that over a seven-month span the "improvised" solos changed very little. Even when Jabbo Smith substitutes for Miley on the Okeh version, the over-all shape and tenor of the trumpet part do not change drastically, though in terms of particulars Jabbo's rich sound and loose way of playing make this performance even more of a fantasy.[16] Miley's solo on the Victor version is one of his most striking recorded performances. It makes brilliant use of the plunger mute and the growl[17]; but it is, to our ears, forty years later, especially startling in its abundant use of the blue notes, notably the flat fifth in the first bar of the second chorus (Ex. 6). It is also a highly dramatic solo, equal to anything achieved up to that time by the New Orleans trumpet men. And perhaps none of them ever achieved the extraor-

15. Roger Pryor Dodge explains that the melody of *Black and Tan Fantasy* is a transmutation of part of a sacred song by Stephen Adams that Bubber's sister used to sing.

16. In a still later (1930) recording of *Black and Tan Fantasy*, Cootie Williams also adheres to the original Miley choruses.

17. Previous mention has been made of Johnny Dunn's influence upon Miley. The latter's solo on *Black and Tan Fantasy* is an excellent case in point. Both the triplet run in measure nine (Ex. 6) and the use of a plunger mute were basic elements of Dunn's style, as can be heard on his 1923 recordings of *Dunn's Cornet Blues* and *You've Never Heard the Blues*.

dinary contrast produced by the intense stillness of the four-bar-long high *b* flat, suddenly erupting, as if unable to contain itself any longer, into a magnificently structured melodic creation.

Example 6 *Black and Tan Fantasy*—Trumpet Solo (Victor, 1927)

Blue Notes: a = minor third
b = flat fifth
c = minor seventh
d = minor ninth
e is a bent tone which goes from a flat octave through the minor seventh to the sixth degree, anticipating the return to B flat.

Miley's great contribution as composer and player toward the emergence of the "Ellington effect," however, was not limited to these particular pieces. He had a hand in the composing of *Blue Bubbles* and *The Blues I Love To Sing* (both 1927), *Black Beauty* (1928), and *Doin' the Voom Voom* and *Goin' to Town* in his last year with Duke

(1929). Miley also left an indelible stamp on the band's style with great solos on some of the above, as well as on *Jubilee Stomp, Yellow Dog Blues,*[18] *Red Hot Band, The Mooche, Rent Party Blues,* and the earlier *Immigration Blues* and *New Orleans Lowdown.* In addition, Miley played hundreds of nightly improvisations at the Cotton Club, forging (with Nanton) the "jungle style" that was the first really distinguishable trademark of the Ellington band.

If Miley was the prime musical inspiration of the early band, Tricky Sam Nanton was its unique voice. Like Miley, he was a master in the use of the growl, the plunger, and wah-wah mutes, and his style had a similar classic simplicity. But where Miley tended to be dapper and smooth, Nanton had a rough-hewn quality that actually encompassed a wider range of expression. Whether plaintive or humorous, his wah-wah muting often took on a distinctly human quality. His open-horn work also extended from the dark and sober to the jaunty or bucolic. But whatever he was expressing, his distinctive vibrato and big tone gave his playing a kind of bursting-at-the-seams intensity and inner beauty that made every Nanton solo a haunting experience. Melodically or harmonically (it comes to the same thing) Nanton was not as advanced as Miley. But this did not prevent him from creating, over a period of twenty years with Ellington, an endless number of beautiful solos, many of them marked by completely original melodic turns (Ex. 7A, B, C), all the more unforgettable because of their simplicity. In fact, Nanton's solo work, in its totality, is unique and perplexing. Here is a player whose solos rarely go much beyond a range of one octave; who has some real limitations instrumentally (com-

Example 7A *Jubilee Stomp*

pared, for instance, to a different kind of virtuoso like Jimmy Harrison); and who, in a sense, plays the same basic idea over and over again—but who, by some magic alchemy, manages to make each solo a new and wondrous experience.

18. Miley's solo is based on the verse, rather unusual in those days.

Example 7B *Yellow Dog Blues*

Example 7C *The Blues I Love To Sing*

In the period with which we are dealing at the moment (1926-1927), the reedmen did not exert as much influence on the "Ellington effect" as these two brassmen. Otto Hardwick, Duke's right-hand man, although a distinctive stylist himself, with an unusual tone and a lithe staccato style, was to influence the Ellington sound not so much directly as *indirectly*, through his influence on clarinetists Johnny Hodges and Harry Carney, which was to be felt a few years later. Rudy Jackson, a fine player in the New Orleans, Bechet-influenced tradition, evidently did not find the Ellington approach to his liking. The malleability and growth which Barney Bigard, Jackson's successor in early 1928, had was not in Jackson's make-up, and Jackson left to play with Noble Sissle and other bands.

But this imbalance between reeds and brass was soon to undergo changes. As Duke's band made a success of its historic Cotton Club engagement, it began to expand and attract new players, such as Bigard and Hodges. Soon Arthur Whetsol returned (after a leave of absence since 1924), replacing Louis Metcalfe on trumpet; and in late 1928 the brass were enlarged to four with the addition of Freddy Jenkins. From now on each player was to be chosen by Ellington for some distinctive or unique quality; and it was in 1927 and 1928—his imagination kindled by Miley and Nanton, and encouraged by the band's success—that Ellington began to have visions of future possibilities in composition and tonal color. From now on *his* ideas were to become, in increasing measure, the dominant factor in the development of the orchestra's output.

As important as the contributions of Miley and the others were, Ellington's influence was, of course, far from negligible. While he affected certain pieces negatively, he also managed occasionally to contribute wonderful little touches, which foreshadowed similar moments in later records (in some cases as much as a dozen years later!) or prophesied whole future developments.

Since the early Ellington records are often passed over in favor of the masterpieces of 1939 to 1942, it might be interesting to point out some of these early signs of things to come. In *Birmingham Breakdown,* an Ellington composition, he uses for the first time phrases not based on either the thirty-two-bar song form or the various blues forms. The main theme, a jaunty twenty-bar phrase, consists simply of a succession of similar two- and four-bar segments. I think this odd assortment of measures came about because the theme really has no melody to speak of. It is simply a rhythmicized chromatic chord progression. As fetching as it is, especially in its initial exposition, with Ellington's sprightly piano obbligato, it is rather static thematically and wears thin after several repetitions. Ellington wisely switched to the twelve-bar blues for the last two (collectively improvised) choruses.[19] In its simple way, *Birmingham Breakdown* broke the ice for the five-bar phrases of *Creole Rhapsody* or the ten- and fourteen-bar lines of *Reminiscin' in Tempo*. These in turn, of course, led eventually to the larger asym-

19. It is significant that twenty-bar structures, however, were not uncommon in ragtime.

metrical formations of *Black, Brown, and Beige* and other extended works.

As was the case with *East St. Louis Toodle-Oo,* the Vocalion and Brunswick versions of *Birmingham Breakdown* are structurally identical. But, except for a badly muffed ending, the earlier performance (Vocalion) is superior. On the whole, the ensembles are better, and Bass Edwards plays a more interesting (and more audible) bass line than Braud. But what really makes the Vocalion recording unique is something that, to my knowledge, never occurs again in an Ellington record—namely, a dual improvisation, in this case by two trumpets, Miley and Metcalfe. Of course, even the New Orleans or Oliver-influenced collective improvisation of the final choruses on both discs was already a rarity by 1926 and 1927. Although one may bemoan the demise of collective improvisation, with its unpredictable excitement, it is obvious that Ellington, had he retained this course, would never have attained his later creative heights.

Immigration Blues, recorded in December 1926, contains one of Miley's greatest solos. Miley makes a highly imaginative simultaneous use of growl and plunger, and he plays his chorus with a penetrating, nasty tone that almost creates the illusion of speech. There is also an interesting organ-like opening section that in places resembles *Dear Old Southland,* a later Ellington recording based on the spiritual *Deep River*. *Immigration Blues* was quite likely based on similar spiritual material, and it turns up again in the middle section of *The Blues I Love To Sing*. Nanton has a touching solo on *Immigration Blues,* and Edwards plays a fervently singing tuba. The reverse side of the record, *The Creeper,* is a spirited piece based in part on *Tiger Rag*. In fact, there is an earlier, rather frantic version of the four-bar break in the brass that we know from Duke's later record of *Tiger Rag,* and which, incidentally, was borrowed from King Oliver's *Snake Rag*. There is again a good Nanton solo and a typical Hardwick one. The record itself is unfortunately a rare collector's item.

In *Hop Head,* an Ellington-Hardwick collaboration, one can hear in embryonic form the arranged brass-ensemble chorus which, with the gradual enlargement of the brass section, became another of the Ellington trademarks. In *The Blues I Love To Sing,* Wellman Braud abandons the usual two-beat bass line to double up in four beats to the bar.[20] And once having heard it, who can forget Nanton's haunting eight-bar phrase, fluff and all, or for that matter this record's perfect evocation of the mood of the 1920s?

On the final choruses of both *Blue Bubbles* and *Red Hot Band,* Ellington again uses the driving brass ensemble in a repeated, riff-like, wailing phrase that makes effective use of the blue minor third. On the orchestral version of *Black Beauty,* one of Ellington's most beautiful compositions,[21] he plays what could be considered his first good piano solo. For once, his playing is fairly clean and unhurried. The disarming charm of the melody, embroidered in a way reminiscent of Willie "The Lion" Smith, contrasts well with Braud's driving, double-time slap-bass interpolations.

Jubilee Stomp (the Victor version, recorded on March 26, 1928, after Bigard and Whetsol had joined the band) is vintage early Ellington. Except for Duke's frantic piano, it has a controlled, driving beat, rare in early Ellingtonia, and contains not only striking solos (especially Miley's puckish sixteen bars) but greatly improved ensemble work. It also has a rare instance of unison saxophone writing. Above all, the performance *builds* through these solos until Whetsol's sure lead-trumpeting takes the band through the final chorus with surging momentum, capped in the final eight measures by Bigard's New Orleans–styled, high-riding obbligato.

In the introduction of *Got Everything But You* and Spencer Williams's *Tishomingo Blues,* Ellington experiments with "modern" harmonies. Through the highly popular piano playing of Zez Confrey, Rube Bloom, and others, it had become "hip" to use chromatically parallel ninth chords (Ex. 8) in introductions and bridges, and indeed to this day Tin Pan Alley sheet-music "piano solos" are filled with these clichés. Both pieces start with these stereotypes. But in the fifth bar of *Tishomingo Blues* we hear for the first time something that, it seems to me, is one of the striking characteristics of Ellington's voice-leading. In the C-ninth chord (Ex. 9), the baritone plays, not—as might

20. In *Washington Wobble* Braud goes one step further and creates a "walking" bass line, the discovery of which is often loosely credited to Walter Page, despite the fact that Page admits his great indebtedness to Braud. (See Walter Page, "About My Life in Music," *The Jazz Review,* I (Nov. 1958), 12. See also the Johnny Dodds section in Chapter 5.

21. In his biography of Ellington, Ulanov asserts that Miley was responsible for the melody (p. 94).

Example 8 *Tishomingo Blues*—Introduction

Example 9

be expected—the root of the chord, but the *b* flat directly below. This may seem a minor point to some, but it is, in fact, one of the two consistent characteristics differentiating Ellington's saxophone section from all others even today. Ellington ingeniously avoids duplication and the wasting of Carney's very personal tone quality by keeping him away from the bass line and giving him important notes within the chord that specifically determine the quality of that chord. It is this seemingly minute detail of voicing which adds that unusual, rich, slightly dark, and at times melancholy flavor to Ellington's saxophone writing.

Another fine moment occurs during Miley's muted solo in *Tishomingo Blues*. Ellington changes the old tried-and-true chord pattern, as in Example 10A, by altering the last chord (Ex. 10B). Miley, building an idea based on gradually enlarged interval skips, muffs the first two, and in stretching for a higher note than the g in bar three, comes up (perhaps accidentally) with a high *b* (see Ex. 10C). Thus Ellington's altered chord and Miley's luck combine to turn what would otherwise have been a routine break into a very special moment.

On this side and its coupling, *Yellow Dog Blues*, Johnny Hodges's saxophone is the new voice that further enriches Ellington's palette. The ragged brass work[22] points up by contrast the unusually clean and solid

22. Nanton obviously had trouble maintaining the beat while turning from the microphone to blend with Whetsol and Miley.

Example 10 *Tishomingo Blues*

(As indicated in the text, Miley muffs the notes in the first two bars of 10C. For the sake of accuracy, I have notated the notes he actually played, whatever his intentions may have been.)

playing of the saxophone section, now dominated by Hodges's rich tone. *Yellow Dog Blues* has Hodges on soprano saxophone, which gives Ellington a chance (as in *Creole Love Call* and countless others) to write a very high reed trio, with Bigard and Carney on clarinets. Aside from the already-mentioned Miley and Nanton solos, the performance, a very good one, contains a minute touch which later became one of the salient features of Duke's piano playing. In the twelfth bar of Miley's solo, Ellington superimposes over the three sustained clarinets a short figure that momentarily clashes with them in a very subtle way (Ex. 11)—the original precursor of a long line of such harmonic clashes, most notably those in *Ko-Ko*.

Example 11

Through this relatively brief examination of only a few of the many recordings Ellington's orchestra made in the 1920s, we have been able to isolate the elements upon which the group's entire musical development was based. First, Ellington's process of writing (or of dictating head arrangements to the band)[23] generally encompassed five distinct kinds of tunes or compositions: (1) numbers for dancing; (2) jungle-style and/or production numbers for the Cotton Club; (3) the "blue" or "mood" pieces; (4) pop tunes (at first written by others, later in increasing measure his own); and (5) pieces which, although written for specific occasions, turned out to be simply abstract "musical compositions." (It should go without saying that these categories were not always consciously developed and that some pieces defy exact categorization and could belong to several groups.) And second, *within* these categories Ellington worked out specific musical ideas—a certain progression, a certain voicing, or a certain scoring—by repeating them in successive arrangements through a process of trial and error until he had found the best solution for the problem. Then he would move on to tackle the next idea or problem.

The second point answers my original question: how did Ellington, at first a musician with a decided leaning toward "show music,"[24] develop into one of America's foremost composers? It was precisely due to the fortuitous circumstance of working five years at the Cotton Club. There, by writing and experimenting with all manner of descriptive production and dance numbers, Ellington's inherent talent and imagination could develop properly. A leader such as Fletcher

23. A fairly informative account of this process is contained in *The Hot Bach* by Richard Boyer, reprinted in Peter Gammond, ed., *Duke Ellington: His Life and Music* (New York: Roy Publishers, 1958), pp. 36-7.

24. To this day Ellington's overriding ambition is to compose a successful jazz musical or jazz "opera."

Henderson who played exclusively for dances would have very little opportunity to experiment with descriptive or abstract, non-functional[25] music; whereas the need for new background music for constantly changing acts at the Cotton Club in a sense *required* Ellington to investigate composition (rather than arranging) as a medium of expression, and fortunately he found in his band imaginative musicians who could help him develop and implement his ideas.

Thus, from early 1928 to 1931, the greater part of his Cotton Club tenure, Ellington's recordings reveal a wide-ranging experimentation and intuitive probing. Except for hints of orchestration or of harmony that he garnered from Will Vodery,[26] the chief arranger for the Ziegfeld Follies, Ellington developed his ideas quite independently *within* his genre, with almost no borrowing from outside his specific field. There are certainly no traces of any influence from "classical" music, except perhaps vague, unconscious ones, which, in any case, had long before infiltrated jazz and popular music. It was in these years that the personalities of his individual musicians and the sonorities of his orchestra became the instrument upon which the Duke learned to play.

His ability to play this instrument could not, and did not, come overnight. Although Ellington made some 160 recordings between mid-1928 and mid-1931, all of them interesting, very few were completely successful artistically. Only one could compare in originality of conception with *Black and Tan Fantasy—Mood Indigo*. The others either were thematically weak, or had poor or indifferent solos, or were too hastily thrown together and badly played; still others had some fine moments, but a bad introduction or an awkward bridge. In some cases mawkish pop-tune material, used in the Cotton Club shows or foisted on Ellington by Irving Mills's business associates, proved too much for the abilities of even these remarkable players.[27] But slowly and relent-

25. I use these latter two words in their broadest meaning, synonymous with non-descriptive or non-representational.

26. From Vodery, Ellington got an indirect knowledge of modern orchestration and harmony as practiced by Ravel, Delius, and other composers, much favored in the twenties, albeit strained through the sieve of Broadway commercialism. The rather widespread notion that Ellington was influenced directly by Ravel and Delius is untenable, since he never heard or was interested in hearing these composers until years later when his own style had long been crystallized.

27. Ellington was not above trying to hit the white market with established "pop" successes. An early instance of this was *Soliloquy* (1927), a Rube Bloom tune which had become a big hit with Whiteman. Ellington tried to

lessly, through a process of continuous reappraisal, of constant polishing and refining, the Duke's musical concepts began to crystallize.

In this welter of pseudo-jungle dance or production numbers—the kind of thing the "tourist," expecting to be transported to the depths of the African jungle, had come to look for at the Cotton Club—certain performances stand out like milestones along the way.

In the "blue" or "mood" category, Ellington in 1928 wrote *Misty Mornin'* and *Awful Sad,* both leading up to the immortal *Mood Indigo* of 1930. The man primarily responsible for that special nostalgia in these pieces was Duke's old Washington friend Arthur Whetsol. His poignant trumpet style and tone quality—probably unique in jazz, then or now—were the perfect melodic vehicle for these three-minute mood vignettes. Duke loved the melancholy, almost sentimental flavor in Whetsol's playing, and in speaking of *Black and Tan Fantasy,* Ellington once remarked that Whetsol's playing of "the funeral march" used to make "great big ole tears" run down people's faces. "That's why I liked Whetsol."[28] In the two earlier pieces Whetsol's blue-colored tone and Bigard's low-register clarinet were still used separately, but in *Mood Indigo* Ellington combines their sounds, adding the even more unique tonal color of Nanton's trombone, thus returning to the classic New Orleans instrumentation but in a totally new concept of sound. As compositions, all three pieces have in common a feature that was to be an important element in the developing Ellington style: a kind of winding chromaticism *not* to be found in the faster dance numbers or stomps. Ellington found instinctively and logically that chromatic melodies and chromatic voice-leading gave these slow pieces just the right touch of sadness and nostalgia. *Awful Sad,* recorded in October 1928, goes furthest in this direction, in its very unusual chord changes and especially in two of its two-bar breaks[29] (Ex. 12A and 12B). The first (in the trumpet) is in a shifting whole-

---

cash in on the success of the tune. Without prior knowledge, however, it is barely recognizable as an Ellington item.

Irving Mills was not only the publisher of Duke Ellington's early compositions, but his manager as well and even sometimes a vocalist on recordings.

28. This writer recalls a sleepless night—after a one-night stand in Quebec—during which Ellington delivered a lengthy and movingly simple eulogy on Whetsol, who died in 1940.

29. These breaks are unfortunately rushed in tempo every time.

Example 12 *Awful Sad*

tone pattern; the second (with Bigard on tenor) momentarily goes quite out of the key (B flat major) into a slightly "atonal" area, only to modulate suddenly to D major.[30]

Misty Mornin', based on somewhat altered blues changes, once again has that characteristic move to the lowered sixth step of the scale (*b* flat to g flat) which we have already encountered so often; and in the fifteenth and sixteenth bars of Whetsol's solo the unique inner voicings that helped to make *Mood Indigo* so special are tried out very briefly (Ex. 13). Such voicings were unorthodox and wrong, according to the textbooks. But Ellington did not know or care about the textbooks. His own piano playing gave him the most immediately acces-

Example 13 *Misty Mornin'*

sible answer to voice-leading problems. Examples 13 and 14 have the kind of parallel motion that a pianist would use, and Ellington simply applied to the orchestra the voice-leadings he used on piano. It must be remembered that Ellington was an almost completely self-taught musician. As such, contrapuntal thinking has always been foreign to

30. The chromaticism of the "blue" pieces became one of the most original contributions to jazz of the maturing Ellington style, leading Duke eventually to bitonal harmonies and to such masterpieces of the genre as *Dusk, Ko-Ko, Moon Mist, Azure,* and *Clothed Woman.*

him; but the parallel blocks of sound he favors so predominantly are handled with such variety and ingenuity that we, as listeners, never notice the lack of occasional contrapuntal relief. To Duke's ears, reacting intuitively, and unfettered by preconceived rules, the effect of this kind of "piano" voicing, though novel, was good (Ex. 14).

Example 14 *Mood Indigo*

In the production- or show-music category, Ellington produced some two dozen numbers, ranging from such bits of dated exotica as *Arabian Lover* or its companion piece, *Japanese Dream* (pentatonic melodies, ominous Chinese gongs and all)[31] to more original pieces, such as *Jungle Jamboree* and *Rocky Mountain Blues*. Although this category was probably the least fruitful for Ellington's development in this period (except for outright pop tunes), it did lead Duke to some different programmatic ideas that otherwise he might never have chanced upon. It produced, among other things, a whole line of heavily stomping four-beat pieces—a genre for which Duke had a special predilection, especially after the success of the prototypes *Black and Tan Fantasy* and *The Mooche*. In *Harlem Flat Blues, Rent Party Blues,* and parts of *Saratoga Swing, Mississippi, Haunted Nights, Jazz Lips, Lazy Duke,* and *Jolly Wog,* Ellington tried to recapture the success of the two earlier medium-tempo stomps. Some of these were also attempts at conscious jungle evocations—pieces like *Jungle Jamboree, Jungle Blues,* or *Jungle Nights in Harlem,* the latter one of the most patently dated pieces in the band's repertoire. It is easy to imagine how such a number complemented the "primitive" murals on the walls of the Cotton Club.

But as we have noted, in almost every piece—whether bad or good—Ellington and his men tried to work out some new sound and new musical idea. *Saratoga Swing,* for instance, was an early, successful

31. Undaunted, the Victor labels continued to read "Hot Dance Orchestra."

attempt to employ a small group within the big band. Played by a septet consisting of Hodges, Bigard, and Cootie Williams, plus the four rhythm instruments, *Saratoga Swing* became the forerunner of many similar small-band recordings, notably the series made in the late 1930s under the leadership of various Ellington sidemen. Two other early septet recordings—among the finest of this period, though unfortunately not as well known as many lesser sides—were *Big House Blues* and *Rocky Mountain Blues.*

Rocky Mountain Blues shows very clearly how Ellington's musical mind was not long satisfied with the tried and true. In this piece, basically founded on the twelve-bar blues progression, Ellington finds a very imaginative alternative for the fourth bar, which should have been a B-flat seventh chord. As can be seen in Example 15, a subtle

Example 15 *Rocky Mountain Blues*

shift of two notes (the expected *b* flat and *d* to *c* flat and *e* flat respectively) results in a wondrously new sound. The three "horns" thus end up in the key of A flat minor, while Braud's double-time walking bass holds on to the basic B flat chord, thus creating a delightful bitonal combination.

Primarily, the jungle pieces offered Duke a more or less legitimate excuse to experiment with "weird" chords and sounds—as, for instance, in *Jungle Blues.* Similarly, *Harlem Flat Blues* gave Nanton his first opportunity to produce a lengthy "talking" solo. He was to return to this idea hundreds of times in his career, but this early fantasy, evoking a not-quite-human language, stands out as one of his best. During this period Ellington also learned to use Nanton's trombone (mostly cup-muted) with two low-register clarinets, a very unusual sound; and when he added a second trombone in the person of valve trombonist Juan Tizol, Duke had not only another color at his disposal but a highly chromatic instrument that could be used interchangeably with the trumpets or reeds as the occasion demanded. An early example of Ellington's use of the chromatic-trombone line can be heard in the final seven-part ensemble of *Jazz Lips* (Ex. 16).

Example 16 *Jazz Lips*

On some of these sides, guitarist Teddy Bunn appeared as soloist. His simple, lean melodic style stood out in contrast to the now-enriched, more and more vertically conceived tonal quality of the band. In *Haunted Nights* the contrast is most apparent. In this piece—an obvious attempt to produce another *Black and Tan Fantasy*—only Bunn's guitar is able to re-create the expressive simplicity of Miley's playing.

By and large, the most successful pieces in terms of jazz came out of the category of music written for dancing. Among these, the best were a whole series of up-tempo stomps, headed by *Old Man Blues* (especially in its first recorded version). Others, almost as good, were *Double Check Stomp, Cotton Club Stomp, Stevedore Stomp, Wall Street Wail, Duke Steps Out, Hot Feet, Ring Dem Bells*—direct descendants of earlier flag-wavers like *The Creeper, Birmingham Breakdown,* and *Jubilee Stomp*. All were very similar in intent and content, and some—like *Double Check Stomp* and *Wall Street Wail*—were even based on the same chord progressions. They were mostly head arrangements, thematically rather noncommittal. But they inspired the major soloists, most notably Carney and Nanton, to create a profusion of fine improvised solos. Interestingly, time and time again in these pieces, Nanton teams up with Braud. The great trombonist seemed to thrive on the near-slap-bass punch of his colleague, and together they produced some of the hottest and most swinging moments on these sides. During this time Bigard seemed to be coming into his own, although he had not yet quite found the liquid quality of later years; more often than not, though, he relied on old New

Orleans clichés that he remembered from numbers like *Tiger Rag.* Also, his time was still rather shaky. Cootie Williams was developing rapidly, especially in the use of the growl and plunger, a role left to him by the departure of Miley. His best solos—*Saratoga Swing, Ring Dem Bells, Echoes of the Jungle,* to name but a few—already show a considerable mastery of this difficult style, at times even glimpses of a more imaginative use of it than Miley's. Hodges was used mainly in flashy, bubbling solos, not yet having discovered the subtly wailing style that was to make him famous in later years. As lead alto he added a tremendous solidity to the reed section; and his solo work, generated by an endless flow of melodic inspiration, was never less than reliable. His playing already had an inevitability about it—not to be confused with predictability—that seemed always to guarantee the right note in the right place. Hodges's solo, for example, on *Syncopated Shuffle*—otherwise a minor record—has this quality, and his solo break at the end is far ahead of its time in its freedom and perfect timing.

The solo capacities of these players were often considerably constrained by the show material and/or arrangements. A series of pieces based on the old standard, *Tiger Rag,* was probably intended to give the musicians a chance at some uninhibited freewheeling improvisation. The most cohesive of these was the two-part *Tiger Rag* itself. The early *Creeper* and *Jubilee Stomp* had been based—in part, at least—on these same familiar chords, and now *Hot and Bothered* and *High Life* were added to the repertoire. All of them were fast, hard-driving numbers, underscored by Braud's indefatigable though occasionally erratic bass. As a staple of the jazz repertoire, *Tiger Rag* had, of course, been done to death by innumerable bands through the years. This poor vehicle, originally popularized by the ODJB, was customarily overloaded with a wide assortment of corny or humorous instrumental effects. The Ellington band's version suddenly changed all that by presenting a staggering array of non-gimmicky, highly individual solos. Even Bigard's chromatic run—under other circumstances a fairly tawdry idea—has in this context a propulsive drive that turns it into a high point of the record.[32] The two players who seemed to feel most at

32. Hearing this record, one also tends to suspect that Juan Tizol was already a member (or perhaps just a guest that day) of the trombone section. I find it fairly hard otherwise to explain the low *b* flat trombone trill just before Freddy Jenkins's famous chorus.

home in these *Tiger Rag* pieces were Bigard, who suddenly found himself transported to a thrice-familiar mold, and Freddy "Posey" Jenkins, whose bent for the flashy, high-stepping solo happily coincided with the obviously ostentatious nature of the pieces. Jenkins's trumpet solo became a regular fixture of the *Tiger Rag* numbers. Not only did he virtually repeat it in *High Life,* but in a later version of *Hot and Bothered,* for the obscure Velvetone label, we find Cootie Williams (according to Aasland's discography, at any rate) playing the same solo. Still later it was arranged for trumpet ensemble.

It was the original *Hot and Bothered* recording, incidentally, made in October 1928 and issued later on English Parlophone, that so excited the British conductor-composer and Ellington enthusiast Constant Lambert. He likened it to the best in Ravel and Stravinsky, which not only seems somewhat exaggerated, but ignores several other Ellington sides that surpass *Hot and Bothered* in terms of both conception and performance. Indeed, the performance leaves something to be desired, a fact which Lambert in his enthusiasm failed to notice. Admittedly, it is emotionally rousing, again due largely to Braud's excitable bass. But the wrong entrances of Miley, vocalist Baby Cox, and Braud, as well as the ragged saxophone ensemble work in the final chorus—which Lambert found so "ingenious"—indicate that the piece was not quite ready to be recorded. Also, Bigard had troubles with his timing, and even Hodges seems less assured than usual. The point is, of course, that a flashy virtuoso piece is very little without flashy virtuoso playing.

It was Lambert, too, I believe, who first compared Ellington to Frederick Delius, which in turn led to a kind of tacitly accepted notion that Ellington had indeed been influenced by the English impressionist. Aside from my point earlier about the *indirect* influence on Duke of certain European composers (footnote 26), I cannot see how the use of lush ninth and eleventh chords or the tendency toward an "impressionist" approach constitute sufficient justification for such a claim. It smacks of over-simplification and the kind of snobbism that implies a piece of jazz music is not very good until it can be equated with some accepted European compositions.

The fact is that Ellington's harmonic language is quite original, and as different from Delius's as Debussy's *Jeux* is from Ravel's *Daphnis and Chloe*—perhaps more so. To cite just two obvious differences,

Delius's harmonic writing in his best works constantly features first, second, and even third inversions of chords. The somewhat suspended feeling thus engendered allows him to drift in endless chains of unresolved modulations. Obviously this is not the case with Ellington, who rarely uses such inversions and whose phrase endings are quite clearly defined by resolutions of whatever has passed before. Furthermore, I do not find Ellington to be entirely the "impressionist" the comparison to Delius implies. True, there are dreamy landscapes like *Dusk* and *Misty Mornin'*, and atmospheric abstractions like *Mood Indigo* and *Moon Mist*. But what about the hundreds of vigorous, earthy, directly *ex*pressed pieces that make up the bulk of the Ellington repertoire?

It is the link to Delius, I believe, that has also fathered the notion that Ellington is a "rhapsodist" and most at ease in the looser form of the rhapsody. This again is only partially true. Ellington may be a rhapsodist in terms of musical expression (even this is debatable); but he certainly is no rhapsodist when it comes to form. In this respect he is a strict *classicist,* perhaps only surpassed by Jelly Roll Morton. And certainly Ellington's forms are more concise and symmetrical than those of any number of nineteenth-century romantic composers. In fact, when compared to the great formal achievements of a Beethoven —or even a Chopin—Ellington's form, in the majority of cases, seems almost hackneyed and naïve in its restraint. This was, of course, already inherent in the principle of linking small twelve- or thirty-two-bar structures into one single larger form. The fact that Ellington was able to infuse these stereotyped forms with such life and—by the late 1930s—such seamless continuity, is one of the measures of his genius as a composer. It is precisely because he is *not* a rhapsodist in the formal sense that Ellington has been largely unsuccessful in the big, extended forms. He is basically a miniaturist and lacks the control and discipline a good "rhapsodist" has—and *must* have—in order to contain his inspiration within a logical form. But the problem of Ellington's large works of the past twenty years will be dealt with in the second volume of this work.

Two oddities from this prolonged "workshop" period are *Oklahoma Stomp* and *Goin' Nuts*. In them the rhythm instruments outnumber the "horns" (Hodges, Cootie, Jenkins, and Nanton). Teddy Bunn on guitar, and a washboard player by the name of Bruce Johnson, were added to the normal four-man rhythm section. *Oklahoma Stomp* is very aptly named, because, with its modern-sounding hard drive, emphasizing the second and fourth beats, it sounds very much like the strong, rocking rhythmic music characteristic of the Southwest. In this respect the record is unique in the Ellington discography. The unusual rhythmic feeling is especially noticeable during Bunn's solos. Here the group sounds like some imaginary, superior multi-guitar hillbilly band from the Ozarks. Unfortunately the side also contains what must be Ellington's worst and most unintelligible piano solo on records.

Hot Feet is another fine record from 1929. After a "jazzy" syncopated opening, designed to get the dancers on the floor, Cootie scat-vocals *à la* Armstrong, answered by Freddy Jenkins in a sort of chase chorus. A two-bar bridge, used later in *Reminiscin' in Tempo,* leads to a Hodges solo, followed by a chorus of some of the above-mentioned blistering Nanton-Braud teamwork. Brass riffs, embellished by some superb three-part saxophone ensembles, lead to one of Ellington's most startling endings: a sudden brass pyramid followed by a major seventh chord on the already often-encountered lowered sixth step of the scale (Ex. 17).

Ring Dem Bells is a similar piece, slightly slower and again with a responding chorus, this time Cootie's vocal answering Hodges. Cootie

Example 17 *Hot Feet*

then solos, with some wonderful "rolling" saxophone figures as accompaniment.[33] Fluent yet bursting with a kind of controlled excitement, these figures are the perfect contrast and complement to Cootie's jabbing solo. As in *Hot Feet,* the final chorus features five-part brass chords, through which one can hear the running saxophone ensem-

33. As I have indicated, a musical idea such as this was subjected to repeated experimentation. First used in *Stevedore Stomp* in early 1929, it was heard again in *Duke Steps Out,* and in 1931 in *It's Glory* and *Echoes of the Jungle.*

bles. These brass figures are an expansion of the riff figures played earlier on the chimes (incidentally, by Charlie Barnet, later a prominent band leader of the Swing Era).

Perhaps the best record of this period (1928 to mid-1931), outside of *Mood Indigo,* is *Old Man Blues,* especially in its first version, recorded by Victor. This date took place in Hollywood, where the band had gone to make a movie called *Check and Double Check* (from which came *Double Check Stomp*). Listening to the results of that session, one gets the impression that the visit had an invigorating effect on the band. Certainly *Old Man Blues* was played with a verve and excitement that many of the previous sides had lacked. Musically, the record revealed for Ellington, to an unprecedented degree, the effectiveness with which a composition—be it head arrangement or an actually written-out piece—could form a framework, a point of departure for the talents of his particular group of soloists.

Earlier pieces like *Black and Tan Fantasy* bore the stamp of one particular musician—Miley, in that case—and we have seen how Bubber's solo talents were to some extent at odds with the prearranged musical framework fashioned by Ellington. One senses the lack of a uniform concept. Through the dominance of one soloist, the collective equilibrium that was such an integral part of jazz was temporarily disturbed; and, thus, the seams of the structure began to show. But here, in *Old Man Blues,* the collective excitement and the feeling that the performance was truly the sum total of all its parts were re-established, and the perfect balance between composition and improvisation was achieved. This achievement is, of course, above all else, Ellington's greatest contribution to the development of jazz. As Francis Newton summarized so brilliantly in the *New Statesman,*[34] Ellington "solved the unbelievably difficult problem of turning a living, shifting and improvised folk-music into *composition* without losing its spontaneity."

The form of *Old Man Blues* (see outline in Ex. 18), though hardly revolutionary, was an excellent example of how the relationship between form and musical content could be solved. That is to say, a way was found to preserve for the musician the freedom inherent in jazz, while the piece in its totality satisfied the demands of organized or pre-determined form. To quote again from the Francis Newton article,

34. October 11, 1958, p. 488.

Ellington produced a music that was "*both* created by the players *and* fully shaped by the composer."

Example 18 *Old Man Blues*—Form

Introductory vamp	*A*	*B* (march)	A^1
8	(16 + 8 + 6)	(4 + 8 + 8)	(16 + 8 + 8)
	(Nanton, with Bigard obbligato)	(Rhythm-Saxes-Tpts.)	(Tpts.-Nanton-Tpts.)

A^2	A^3	*B*	Break	A^4
32	(16 + 14)	6	4	(16 + 8 + 8)
(Carney, with Piano obbligato)	(Hodges-Jenkins)	(Saxes)	(Brass)	(Brass-Nanton-full ensemble with Bigard obbligato)

On *Old Man Blues*, the musicians do not seem to be restricted by such seemingly conflicting demands. As a matter of fact, they were probably unaware of the large form, and therefore not inhibited by it. To them it was just another chorus, which would be good, bad, or indifferent. As it turned out, the solos are of a high caliber, with Bigard—again relying too much on his *Tiger Rag* routines—perhaps the least inspired. Certainly Carney and Nanton are at their best: Carney in a rare rambunctious mood and Nanton in three separate, contrasting solo spots. *Old Man Blues* is also blessed with moments of fortuitous recording balance, as, for example, in the bridge of the first chorus, where Nanton's trombone blends with Bigard's low-register clarinet embellishments in such a way that the two instruments jell perfectly into one sound—almost as if both parts were played by one man. Ellington's excellent background piano behind Carney, and Braud's walking four-to-the-bar bass, are also worthy of mention. Harmonically, too, *Old Man Blues* has its touch of originality. In a four-bar

Example 19 *Old Man Blues*—Break

break before the final chorus, three trumpets and one trombone play a chord (Ex. 19), repeated in syncopation, which is similar to the chord at the end of *Hot Feet,* and once more placed on the lowered sixth step of the scale.[35]

It was during this period of intensive experiment that Ellington began to create, with some consistency, pieces that were not *strictly* functional—pieces that, although perhaps originally geared to some specific function (as background music for a Cotton Club tableau), had a life of their own, *independent* of that functional purpose. These are what was referred to earlier as pure or abstract musical composition. The great 1927 masterpieces, like *Black and Tan Fantasy* and some of Morton's better creations, had already shown that jazz was capable of this. From 1928 to 1931 a number of these compositions make their appearance. They were not merely arrangements or arbitrarily thrown-together chains of choruses but disciplined musical creations which could be judged by standards of musical appreciation and analysis established for centuries in "classical" music, and which by their *character* as much as by their quality distinguished themselves from the other jazz-*Gebrauchsmusik.*

As a matter of fact, it is often only the *character* of a piece which establishes it as this category of composition. For numbers like *Take It Easy, Dicty Glide, Drop Me Off in Harlem,* and even *Creole Rhapsody* are at times of questionable *quality.* On the other hand, high quality and a purely compositional vision do go hand in hand in *Old Man Blues, Rocky Mountain Blues,* and the incomparable *Mood Indigo.*

At any rate, as Ellington's control over his unique medium sharpened, he was able to create more works that assumed an independence apart from their original impetus. It is the one quality that has made them live beyond their time. This compositional element appears more frequently as Ellington's style matured and is represented by such later masterpieces as *Concerto for Cootie, Ko-Ko,* and *Sepia*

35. This chord, a commonplace today, was still daring in jazz at the time of the recording. The other early instance of its use, to my knowledge, occurs in the final chorus of Alphonse Trent's 1930 *I Found a New Baby.* Incidentally, the advanced writing and highly skillful playing of this great Southwestern band raises the intriguing question of whether Trent's and Ellington's paths ever crossed, and whether any influencing occurred. This would seem to be a fascinating subject for research.

Panorama; and, still later, the orchestral suites and stage works, *Jump for Joy* and *Beggar's Holiday*.

Having perfected form on the level of the three-minute, ten-inch record in *Old Man Blues* and *Mood Indigo,* Ellington's restless and by now fully stimulated musical mind next tackled the problem of a larger form. By January 1931, he had created *Creole Rhapsody* in two versions, half a year apart. Comparison of the two versions is revealing in regard to Ellington's methods. I find it difficult to agree with the prevailing opinion that the second (expanded) version (on Victor) is inferior to the first (on Brunswick). I have already said that the piece in general represents a step forward formally. In it Ellington also experimented with, among other things, asymmetrical phrase lengths[36] and a trombone duet (perhaps the first in jazz). But it must be stated that most of the *playing* on the original *Creole Rhapsody* is second-rate. Unlike *Old Man Blues,* the form was rather haphazardly strung together. This, plus the fact that *Creole Rhapsody* was more of an Ellington composition than a collectively created head-arrangement, made the players uncomfortable and rigid. and Ellington's own dated piano interludes (happily changed and cut to a minimum in the second version) disjoint the piece even more. In addition, the disparate compositional material of the original really was not suited to being played at the same tempo throughout. In the half year that elapsed between the two versions, Ellington must have realized this. For in the Victor performance each section is played in different tempos. This is not to say that the composition is thereby improved, but the performance of it certainly is. As a matter of fact, it is obvious that the band had, in the meantime, learned to play the piece. The ensemble work is immeasurably improved, and the tempo changes—then as well as now a rarity in jazz—come off surprisingly well. The solos, too, are better, though not yet remarkable.

Furthermore, almost the entire second side of the first version has been scrapped in the second and replaced by added material in the dreamy, lyrical vein of *Mood Indigo,* making this the first ternary-form piece by Ellington. This new section is treated in loosely variational

36. See an article by this writer on "The Future of Form in Jazz," originally printed in *The Saturday Review of Literature,* and reprinted in *The Saturday Review Treasury* (New York: Simon and Schuster, 1957), p. 561.

form: Arthur Whetsol first states it in his inimitable fashion; it then returns in an incredibly creamy blend of saxophones and muted valve trombone (Tizol); and lastly it is played in a free-tempo version by Bigard and Duke. The three saxophones accompanying Whetsol achieve a sound, in terms of both tone quality and voice-leading, that Ellington only approached in the 1940 color masterpieces, *Warm Valley, Moon Mist,* and *Dusk.*

In the second version of *Creole Rhapsody* the expansion of what was already an extended form proves too much for Ellington; and despite (or more likely, because of) some subtle "borrowing" from Gershwin's *Rhapsody in Blue,* the last minute or so does not hang together too well. Despite this error in judgment, the greater part of the Victor performance must be considered an improvement, and it is certain that in his quiet way Ellington benefited in later compositions from the experience of *Creole Rhapsody.*

With this innovational experiment out of the way, Ellington returned to more conventional areas. In striking contrast to the fifty-odd sides per year in the preceding period, the Ellington orchestra recorded only four other sides in 1931: *Limehouse Blues, Echoes of the Jungle, It's Glory,* and *The Mystery Song.* All four not only represent the peak of this "workshop" period, but are also the beginning of a long period of consolidation and refinement. In these four 1931 sides the basic sound and approach of the great Ellington era of 1940-42 is no longer embryonic. His style had achieved full individuality, needing only the further ripening with which youth mellows into full maturity.

These 1931 sides belong to the "compositional" category. Perhaps the most limited is *It's Glory,* for its dated dance rhythm and slap bass detract from its value as pure composition. But the quality of the writing for the brass and reeds—rich eight-part blended sounds—almost makes us forget that we are listening to what is basically another arranged chorus. Moreover, the record contains two inspired moments. The first occurs in the bridge of the second chorus, where Nanton plays the lead part—with a subtle touch of wah-wah—accompanied by a trio of two low-register clarinets and muted valve trombone,[37] thus

37. Ellington had tried this instrumental combination previously in *Lazy Duke* and *Creole Rhapsody*—further evidence of how he tested his ideas many times in different contexts until he satisfied himself that their full potential had been exhausted.

creating a "blue" sound which must have amazed musicians in 1931, and which still sounds completely fresh and fascinating today. The other fine moment comes in the next chorus, where Ellington once more employs the soft "rolling" saxophone figures behind Cootie Williams's solo.

Ellington's compositional talent had matured so fully by 1931 that he could even transform someone else's composition—a hackneyed standard at that—into a purely Ellingtonian work. Thus, on *Limehouse Blues* we hear sounds that could never be confused with those of any other band of the time. The brass shine with a rich yellow, and the blue combination we just encountered in *It's Glory* is offered once more as contrast. Ellington wisely refrained from any obvious Orientalisms (tinkly pentatonic patterns on the piano, which all other bands used on this tune and which the Duke himself had succumbed to earlier in *Japanese Dream*). Only the dated, vertical two-beat rhythm limits the experience of this record, but this is more than counterbalanced by the flowing horizontal lines of the ensemble passages.

Echoes of the Jungle, presumably written by Cootie Williams, undoubtedly came into being as a production number for the Cotton Club, designed to give the customers their glimpse of darkest Africa. But as the English writer, Charles Fox,[38] has pointed out, it is "paradoxically an extremely sophisticated" piece of music. In its haunting originality, aided by a superb performance, it is the least dated of these sides—indeed, as fresh and timeless today as it was in 1931. Again we marvel at the incredibly rich blend of the brass, this time muted and embellished by Hodges's full-toned alto. Cootie solos twice—first open, with a sensuous urgency; then with the plunger mute, in one of his most imaginative improvisations. And once more we hear the chromatic, rolling saxophone figures behind him—an instrumental combination Ellington seemingly never tired of. The succeeding connecting passage, featuring Bigard in low register, answered by Fred Guy's rustling banjo glissandos, is like the ominous lull before a storm. And in the final three measures Ellington creates a big-band sound and harmony that anticipate the final choruses of *Ko-Ko*.

Without having been present at the Cotton Club in June 1931, one has difficulty in visualizing what tableau or act inspired the sheer magic of the opening of *The Mystery Song*. A perfectly conventional

38. In Gammond, p. 83.

piano introduction suddenly gives way to an inspired sound, one of those moments so unique that it can in no way be duplicated or imitated without remaining pure imitation.[39] The mixture of sustained harmonies, the distant, muted tone color, and Guy's restless, subtly urgent banjo conjure up a haunting sound. Unfortunately Ellington was unable to sustain this level of inspiration beyond the exposition. (This may have had functional reasons related to the particular dance routine.) At any rate, everything that follows this glorious opening is anticlimactic and commonplace. It is a pity that Ellington has never given this bit of inspiration the framework it deserves.

The consolidation of Ellington's style in the early 1930s coincided with a similar coalescence in jazz in general. Very clearly the early 1930s represented the end of an era as well as the beginning of a new one. The first generation of great jazz artists was passing from the scene, at least in terms of providing the innovational stimulus, and a younger generation of players was beginning to take the lead. These younger players, moreover, came from a higher social stratum than their immediate predecessors, a development concomitant to changes in the entire social status of jazz and its relationship to American society. The nation's social climate was experiencing a drastic reorientation precipitated by the Depression. Likewise, jazz was reaching toward new artistic goals and a broader social acceptance. Sobered and matured by the Wall Street crash and the Depression, the hellion audience of the gangster-ridden "jazz age" gave way to an audience characterized by a more personal, deeper involvement with jazz. The speakeasy was replaced by the college campus; and more people saw in jazz a form of *musical* expression, rather than merely a "wild" new form of exotic entertainment. Although jazz was still primarily associated with social dancing, a significant minority of jazz buffs, who regarded jazz as a new art form, was beginning to emerge. The impetus for this development came largely from Europe, where a number of "intellectuals," "critics," and writers began to publish some remarkably knowledgeable articles on jazz, its history and nature.

No wonder, then, that a growing list of jazz musicians—most notably Duke Ellington's orchestra and Coleman Hawkins—left during the early

39. The nagging thought persists, however, that Ellington had heard and was improving upon a very similar brass passage in Whiteman's *Sweet Sue* (1928).

1930s for the seemingly greener pastures of Europe. In a corollary development, indigenous European jazz groups, such as the Hot Club of France, the Spike Hughes Orchestra in London, small groups in Scandinavia and Czechoslovakia, began to spring up all over Europe.

But most importantly, by the early 1930s jazz had developed to the point where it had a history of its own and could point to its own traditions. And so, too, for the first time the cleavage between the advancing "modernists," like Ellington and saxophonist Lester Young, and traditionalists, like the "Chicago-style" players, began to make itself felt.

All these stylistic, social, and economic pressures changed jazz. A new audience called for a new music, smoother in its execution, broader and more sophisticated in its artistic content. The roots of an indigenous American musical form had taken hold, and were now reaching out toward a broader environment. The first flowering period of jazz had passed into history.

Appendix

The following is an edited transcript of the author's interview with George Morrison, violinist and band leader, in Morrison's studio in Denver, in June 1962.

I was born in Fayette, Missouri, a small town one hundred and twenty-five miles southeast of Kansas City, in the year 1891.

My father was a musician. In fact, as far back as you can trace the Morrison family, the men were all fiddlers—in those days instead of violinists they called them fiddlers. There was Uncle Jack and Uncle Alfred and my father, Clark Morrison. He was the king fiddler of the state of Missouri. He played those old time fiddling tunes like "Arkansas Traveler," "Devil's Dream," and "The Fisher's Hornpipe, for square dances. The only thing they knew in those days was square dancing. They didn't play any concert music or anything. They couldn't read a note—never knew what a note looked like—played everything by ear. But they had the natural talent that God blessed them with.

My father died when I was two years of age. In my family there were born fourteen children and, to my knowledge, only eight survived, five boys and three girls. I always wanted to learn to play the violin. I used to crawl under my father's and mother's bed where he would keep his fiddle, and I'd open up the old wooden case and the old flour bag he'd wrap it up in and I'd take the bow and draw the bow across the strings. One day he caught me doing that and spanked me. My mother said, "Don't you spank that boy; some day he will play a better fiddle than you, 'cause he love it." A few years later I began to make my own violins. I was so fond of the violin that I would go out and take a corn stalk and hollow it out. I would take a knife and cut the stalk in four strips, and then I'd get me a little piece of wood and put some cord strings on there. I'd tighten them up myself by driving a little nail up in the head of it, and tighten them up just as tight as I could by hand. I would go out and get me a little stick from a pussy willow tree—and bend it. That would be the bow. Then I'd rub charcoal on the strings and I'd produce a tone. The charcoal took the place of the rosin, to produce a tone on the strings, to make a sound. I was about five years old when I was doing that. Then later, as I grew older, I made my violins out of cigar boxes.

I had my first formal training in music after my sister brought me to Boulder, Colorado. I was 'round ten years of age. But before coming to Colorado we had already formed a string band called the Morrison Brothers String Band. I played the guitar at that time, my brother played the mandolin. My oldest brother played the string bass, and my brother-in-law played the guitar. We played a lot of engagements around Fayette, Missouri. We'd go out serenading the people at night. We'd play for them and they'd throw money down to us, which was a great help to us because we were *very* poor in those days. Occasionally we would get a job playing for the white people, playing square dances. We'd play all night long, starting at six o'clock Saturday night until seven o'clock Sunday morning; and they'd give us a dollar apiece for playing all night long. With that money we could buy maybe a sack of flour, or maybe a sack of corn meal, and molasses. And we survived in that way. It was very hard for us in those early days.

We played the old popular tunes of the day, and we played by ear. We couldn't read a note—never knew what a note looked like. We played things like "After the Ball Is Over" (a waltz), "The Double Eagle," "Silver Threads Among the Gold," and pieces like that. They were popular numbers in those days, what we called two-step numbers. The two-steps were six/eight numbers. We played them more or less straight. We couldn't improvise, we never knew how to improvise. We were lucky to play them straight.

My sister and my brother-in-law moved to Boulder, and after they were there a year they came back to Fayette, Missouri, and brought my brother Lee (who has passed on) and myself to Boulder, because my brother-in-law saw a great field for music up at Boulder. In those days they had no musicians to play up in the mountains—up in the mining towns. So my brother Lee and I got together, practiced up and advertised the Morrison Brothers String Band in Boulder. We started playing our engagements up in the mountains in the mining camps, like Cold Hill, Sunset, Rustle Gulch, and towns like that. We advertised by handing out little handbills, and it wasn't long before we were in great demand. They had no bands up there in those days to supply them with music for dances. As a rule we worked just during weekends. They didn't have any theatres or anything. We'd just play in a little dance hall, or a wooden shack. We'd have to drive up there by horse and buggy, up the mountains, and sometimes the road was so slippery that the old surrey would slide off the road. If it wasn't for the horses, we'd be rolling for six months before we reached the bottom. And those horses knew just how to negotiate those roads. We'd get up there and play all night long. People would come from miles around—from the other little towns, and dance all night long, from seven o'clock until eight the next morning. And this was all year round. For them we played waltzes and two-steps and fox trots. Occasionally we'd even sandwich in a square dance. Like what my father played. Later we became so famous that we began to get work down at Boulder, and then we started to get work up on the hill in the university [the University of Colorado, Boulder], in the fraternities and sororities.

I stayed about twelve years in Boulder before I moved to Denver. I was actually making a living as a musician.

When I first moved to Boulder I was pretty green. I want to tell you about this. On the train from Denver to Boulder (when we first came from Fayette) I saw a mountain for the first time in my life. As we approached Boulder the mountains became more and more plain to me. They looked *so* large, *so* enormous. I said to myself, "What are those things up there?" I didn't even dare ask the conductor. I thought by getting up so close to those mountains, they were gonna fall on me, and I ran like a little boy under the seat and started crying. So the conductor says, "What's the matter, young man?" I said, "Oh, I'm afraid of those things up there, I'm afraid they goin' to fall on me." He says, "Oh, they won't fall on you; those are mountains—they been there for years."

Well, I managed to get to Boulder, and soon I became accustomed to the mountains. In Boulder at first I went to work with my brother in a barbershop, shining shoes. After school we'd shine shoes and clean up the barbershop. As I say, I was just a green little fella, and those barbers would send me all over town lookin' for a left-handed monkey wrench and a meat augur. It was about a week before I caught on to what they were doing.

Another thing they asked me to do was to blow out the electric lights. Now at that time I didn't know what a 'lectric bulb looked like; we used the old coal oil lamps down home in Missouri. Here they had me blowin' my brains, tryin' to blow the light out of an electric bulb. You see, I was just a servant there, and whatever they asked me to do, I'd go and do.

With the money I made working at the barbershop, I bought me a violin, And a case, and a bow. And I started takin' lessons on the violin. My first teacher was Miss Nellie Greenwood, in Boulder; she was a violinist who had finished in some conservatory. I'd go out in the alley behind the barbershop, in the coal bin, and I'd use a lump of coal for my music rack. I'd go out there and practice my Kreutzer Etudes. Then later on, as I progressed on the violin, I went to Professor Howard Reynolds. He was a native of Boulder. He had been sent by his parents to the New England Conservatory, and had graduated from there. To me he was the American Leopold Auer. He still lives in Denver today. He was a great teacher. Although he's now way up in his eighties, he's still turning out pupils. In fact, many of his pupils are violinists here in the Denver Symphony. And his daughter has been playing in Eugene Ormandy's Philadelphia Symphony for years—Vida Reynolds. I studied with Professor Reynolds, I'd say, about twelve years. In fact he loved to teach me so much that he just went all out. He'd give me lessons maybe twice a week or three times a week at seventy-five cents an hour. And after I moved to Denver, he used to come down on the 'lectric train just to give me lessons. He had no other pupils in Denver at that time.

I advanced so rapidly with him that he put me in a contest of all his pupils —forty-two—all violinists. I was his only Negro pupil. This contest was sponsored by some wealthy person in Boulder, and the winner was to be sent to the New England Conservatory in Boston. And I won the first prize.

But in the meantime I was coming down to Denver to attend dances—I had to have a little recreation and pleasure in life. In a little old town like Boulder, we didn't have many Negroes, and so I used to come down to Denver. One night at a certain dance, I met my wife. And that broke up the New England Conservatory! We married in 1911 and I moved to Denver. It was in those years that I started working in the parlor houses, for Mattie Silks, one of the most famous madams. That was around 1913 and 1914, around in there. I played the violin and the guitar. Some people might think that my wife minded my working in the parlor houses. But what mattered was that I was working. My gracious, I was trying to make a living in music any way I could, and when I'd bring that money home, she never refused it. Of course, when we played in the parlor houses, they wanted mostly kind of quiet music. And they didn't want any long pieces. Short, very short, maybe two choruses. And no rest, for us. Their philosophy was to get the customers to buy a drink. They almost never allowed the girls to dance, you know. The music was there for music lovers that wanted to hear some nice numbers and maybe once in a while dance one number. And it was not noisy music. We had no drummers, for example —never—in the houses. Just violin, piano, and guitar. We'd play pieces like "Blue Bell"—that was a waltz. And "Red Wing"—that was a two-step. As a specialty we'd do "Silver Threads Among the Gold" for them, or "Goodbye, My Lady Love," and "Down on the Farm," "Lady Lou," "Call Me Back," and "Just a Dream." All those old numbers. We'd also play pieces like "Darktown Strutters' Ball"—pretty fast and lively. We played that as a jazz number.

I first heard the word jazz way back around 1911. Yes, when I married, that word was coming in then. I remember it well because in 1911 when I first got married and I played for the dances, it was jazz we played. I had a sign on my little Model T Ford with a clef sign and lines and notes and everything, in green and gold and black, and on each side of my car I had a sign on the running board: George Morrison and His Jazz Orchestra. Yes, sir. Right at the time when we got married. Improvised jazz music. I don't mean ragtime pieces like "Maple Leaf Rag" or anything like that. Just taking a tune and jazzing it up by improvising. Like what I did on that *I Know Why* recording—of course that was 1920. But I did that when I first started out with my fiddle.

Anyhow, I heard some people improvise even before I did it. That's where I got the idea. Like Benny Goodman—Benny Goodman's orchestra. Not the Benny Goodman that became famous later; this was a Benny Goodman orchestra here in Denver. He's dead and gone now. He was a violinist and he improvised just like I did on the violin. And we had piano players who improvised on the piano. That's what we did up in those mining towns, too.

But in those days people thought that jazz was a bad music. Parents didn't let their children play jazz. If you played the Dvořák "Humoresque," fine, but if you played "Darktown Strutters' Ball," that was awful. This was very common then. When I first started out in my career, if a white boy picked up an instrument to play, it was a disgrace to his family. For a white boy to beat a drum and play for a living was a disgrace. They'd disown him. They wanted nothing but the colored man to play for them. And now, look at today; they're breaking their necks buying instruments and things for him to become a musician, and want him to make it his career. But personally, I'm just the opposite. I'm glad I never forced my son to become a musician.

Another job I did in those days was to play for the people going to the rodeo in Cheyenne, Wyoming. The largest rodeo in the world is put on there yearly. I have played that job, sponsored by the *Denver Post,* for fifty years. I remember when it started in 1912, we would carry four coaches, and one baggage car, and probably about one hundred and fifty men on the train, all guests of the founders of the *Denver Post*. There were about fifteen girls, and food and drink, and my band, made up of about six or seven pieces in one car. And we played, and the guests would dance with the girls. Then it grew each year. And soon we had one hundred and fifty girls, and we'd have two baggage cars. And that augmented my band to fourteen pieces. And I'd direct both bands, one in each baggage car, going from car to car, playing all the way from Denver to Cheyenne. Now they've discontinued the girls, and it's a stag affair. But our band has remained the same, until today we carry twenty-four coaches and eleven hundred men, all sponsored by the *Denver Post*. And on the way back we play continually until we arrive in Denver. It's called the Million Dollar Trip, and men come from all over the world for this.

It was at that time that I was also studying theory and composition and harmony with Dr. Horace E. Tureman. He used to be the conductor in those days of the Denver Symphony Orchestra. He often said to me, "I regret so much, Morrison, that I can't have you in my symphony. You know, the racial situation." He said, "I'd have you as my concert master if you were a white man." Well, I never felt bad over it. What I was trying to do was to accomplish something and learn something. I thought to myself, "When I learn that, I'll have it, and nobody can take it from me but God, and I'll get recognition somewhere. Some day I'll get recognition." So I just went on studying. We were using the theory books of George W. Chadwick.[1] I also attended the concerts of the Symphony at that time.

In Denver I had played in an orchestra called Emmett Webster's orchestra. Little three-piece group—violin, trumpet, and piano. Emmett Webster played piano. A white fella, Charles Harris, was the cornet player. And I was the violinist. We played for all the dances. We worked for a long time that way,

1. Chadwick was the President of the New England Conservatory.

but when I married and moved to Denver for good, I decided to start out a little band *myself,* also with three pieces: piano, violin and drums. And my first engagement was on the roof garden of the Adams Hotel. That was about 1916.

A few years later, I moved to Chicago, because I wanted to attend the Conservatory there, the Columbia Conservatory of Music. I knew that I had to get some work in order to help pay for the Conservatory. I had no money. So I got a job playing at the Panama Cabaret at Thirty-fourth and State Streets. And I played there with a jazz band. There was also a theatre called the Grand Theatre, where Dave Peyton was the orchestra leader. When Dave Peyton caught me down at the Panama Cabaret, he said, "Young man, I'd like to have you come up and play with me at the Grand Theatre." I said, "Well, I'm working here, Mr. Peyton, I don't see how I can get away. And I'm going to school at the Columbia Conservatory of Music." He said, "Well, I think I can arrange all that." He went to the proprietors of the Panama Cabaret, and persuaded them to let me play the show at the Grand Theatre until ten thirty or a quarter to eleven. When I was through there I ran down to the Panama Cabaret and played there till five o'clock the next morning. I would go to the Conservatory in the afternoon, then sleep a little and then I'd practice the violin. In Chicago I studied under Professor Carl Becker.[2] That was round 'bout 1918.

By the way, I was very fortunate to get some fine points in arranging from Dave Peyton when I was with him in Chicago. He was arranging for the big Follies shows then. He was a tough customer to work for. Man, don't ever make any mistake; he'd curse you out for all he was worth. He was rough!

When I got back from Chicago I started with my three-piece band again—violin, drums and piano. In those early days, we had three prominent white bands, and one was named Benny Goodman—he played the violin—a very fine hot fiddle player. Then there was Joe Mann, and the other one was called Tony Loman, who was an old-timer here. He was older than all of us. Those were my competitors. But it wasn't long before my band grew so great in popularity that everybody wanted my band. I first started out at the Albany Hotel. I played there with my three pieces, first in the Pink Room, and then later the Cathedral Ballroom. We ended up putting in eleven years there—eleven consecutive years. People from all over the city were clamoring for George Morrison. I built up such a reputation that people would pay me fifty dollars just to make my appearance after booking another band there. Just so they could say George Morrison will appear here tonight. And I'd go there and play two or three tunes and I'd go on to the next place and do likewise. My main band was in such demand, we just couldn't take care of all the engagements. Soon I augmented my band to five pieces, saxophone, piano, violin, trombone, and drums. Then later on I added another two saxophones. That made seven. My drummer was Eugene Montgomery; piano player, Jesse Andrews; trombone player was Ed Carwell; saxophone was Ed Kelly, and banjo was Lee Morrison, my brother. And then I put in a string bass, Emilio Gargas, a French Creole.

2. A Chicago-born violin maker and teacher whose instruments were used by many prominent violinists early in the century.

Then I put in another saxophone, and that was Andrew Kirk. Then later on I put still another saxophone, Cuthbert Byrd, and a trumpet, Leo Davis, into my band. All at the Albany Hotel; we were just packing 'em in into the Cathedral Ballroom. You know I also had Jimmie Lunceford in my band. In fact, for a while I had two pianists; Andy Kirk's wife, Mary, was also my pianist. That was before 1920.

We played jazz with that band. Of course, we had been playing jazz with my little three-piece band also. And I was improvising on my violin. The other players played mostly straight, but I improvised. We had no written arrangements. We just played the music. Later when we got up to our seven-, eight-, nine-, and ten-piece band, we had arrangements, of course—simple arrangements. I helped to make the arrangements and all the boys—together—we worked them out. We never wrote them down, just talked about them—what we call head arrangements. Whatever riffs came to mind we'd work out right here in this room. The other players too, like the trombone player, they'd occasionally take solos on tunes like "Dardanella" and "Royal Garden Blues" and "Ja-da."

You know at that time I was so very fond of the Art Hickman band out at the Fairmont Hotel in San Francisco. He never did come to Denver, but I heard his records. Art Hickman made records just before I did for the Columbia people. In fact, I followed him into New York in 1920.

Around that time some fella here in Denver—I can't think of his name—was so interested in my band that he said, "George, I'm gonna get you to New York with your band. If Art Hickman can go there and play, hell, you can too." So we wrote the Columbia people. They sent a representative out to hear me at the Albany Hotel. This scout heard us and asked us to come to New York. So we got to practicing on our numbers till we had them down perfect. We thought that's what we were gonna record, but when we got to New York we found out different. We record what *they* say, what *they* wanted us to do!!

That's an old, old story. Yes Lord, we were never so disappointed in our lives. And in those days the string bass wouldn't record. Drums wouldn't record; you couldn't hear a drum. And so we had to leave the string bass out, and my drummer had to beat on wood blocks all through, which you can hear on the record, *I Know Why*. The engineer said, "That damn thing can't be heard on a record. Ain't you got a bass tuba, or something?" I said, "No, sir." I never knew that a string bass wouldn't record. Otherwise I'd try to hustle around and get me a tuba player.

Incidentally, if I had one publisher waiting on me after my arrival in New York, I bet you I had fifty, begging me, on their knees, begging me to play their tunes. One of them was Jack Robbins and for some reason the Columbia people said, "We'll take a Jack Robbins tune, 'I Know Why.'" Ted Lewis was recording on the other side. In those days Jack Robbins was just barely eating. If he could find a hot dog he'd grab it and some water and that's be his meal for the day. *Now* think of Jack Robbins—ended up a millionaire. When I was in New York in '45, and I went to his office, he called all of his employees and said, "I want you to know this man right here. This is the man who helped give me my start, George Morrison, whom I'm indebted to greatly." Well, he's so indebted to me he never published any of my numbers.

Did you ever hear of Joe Smith and his orchestra? Well, W. C. Handy and Harry H. Pace had just moved from the south into New York and their offices were in the old Gaiety Theatre building. So while I was there one day, the mailman brought the mail to W. C. Handy. He says, "Morrison, I want to show you just what this business is paying you when you get a hit." Joe Smith had made a record for him, *Yellow Dog Blues*. And there was a check of ten thousand dollars in royalties. That was a lotta money, lotta money in those days —a ten thousand dollar royalty from just the *Yellow Dog Blues* from Joe Smith. And I said, "My Lord sakes alive, I certainly wish that I could get in on a gravy train like that." And he said, "Well, just keep on, you'll make it."

It was at the time I recorded for the Columbia people that Mr. King of the Victor company came over to my hotel up in Harlem and asked me if we would be interested in recording for the Victor company. I said I'd be interested. I don't know how he heard our band, but he heard it. Those people in New York—you know, I don't have to tell you—they're the smartest people in the world. How they do it I do not know. Maybe he heard me up at the Carlton Terrace [Broadway and 100th Street] where I was working. Anyway, Mr. King invited us to Camden, New Jersey, for a tone test. After the test he offered us a contract to record for Victor. He offered us a one hundred thousand dollar contract. The boys went back home to the hotel and we said it can't be true! A hundred thousand dollars! That was on a Friday afternoon. Next day, Saturday, it was raining bullfrogs. The phone rang. "Mr. Morrison?" I said, "Yes?" "This is Mr. McDonald of the Columbia Recording Company. I would like for you to come down to my office right away." And man, I went out in that rain; before I could get down to the subway, I was soaking wet. When I got there, we chatted about the rain. He lit a cigarette and said, "Morrison, we brought you here on a contract, didn't we?" "Yes." "To record solely for the Columbia people." I said, "Yes." He said. "What's this about you going to Camden, New Jersey, yesterday to make a tone test?" Man, I could have gone through a keyhole! I could have gone through the eye of a needle! "Well, what about it, what about it? Speak up!" And I said, "Well, it's true, we did." "Who authorized you? Did we authorize you to do that?" "No, sir." He said, "Well, I want you to know this once and for all. You're not gonna record for no Victor people or no other company long as you're in New York. You're under a contract with us and we're gonna bind you to that contract. I let you go up here and play at the Carlton Terrace to help you, and now you're going over to Camden, New Jersey, to make a tone test for them. By God, if I hear of you making a tone test for any of them you're gonna do more than crawl back to Colorado." He says, "I don't ever want to hear of you recording for another company." And he said, "If you are playing around recording Ill know about it." He knew all about me going to Camden, New Jersey. What do you know about that? *Smart* people! They're wide awake in New York.

Then there was this little fella by the name of Perry Bradford. He came up to my hotel, at the time I was recording. He says, "Morrison, you wanna make some money? I've got a sure bet—sure thing." And I says, "But I ain't got no money." "Well, come on, go with me up here and have breakfast, and we'll talk this matter over." Well, he had two orders of ham and eggs, and I had one order of hot cakes—and he never had a dime. I had to pay for it all. Then he says, "Now, we'll go up here to this place because I got a sure bet. She's a knockout. She's a blues singer—out of this world—and all I need is your orchestra." I said, "My orchestra?" He wouldn't even give me a chance to talk. And he took me up there to this house, and there she was in this old house, and the old lamp light burnin'—in the daytime, now, mind ya. It was simply awful in there—whooo! simply awful. And who was it? Mamie Smith. The first blues singer [to record]. She was up there ironing. Perry said, "Kid, we've got it made! Mr. Morrison here's goin' to finance this thing, and we've got it made. Now I want you to get yourself together. We're going to dress you up." I guess those stockings that she put on must have tickled her to death.

I'd been saving my money before the wife and daughter arrived in New York, and I had all this money way down in my trunk in my room. And so I went and got a hundred and fifty dollars and I bought Mamie a hat—great big old hat, and then I bought her some lingerie, and shoes. I dressed her from the inside out. Everything. I had never heard of that woman—never *seen* her before. Mamie said she was gonna pay me back. She was going to record for Okeh records. I told Perry, "I'm gonna nip this in the bud right now. I'll let you have the money to dress Mamie up, but I can't play for her. Columbia will not let me." "By God," he says, "we gotta do something. We got it made now; got her dressed up. What are we gonna do?" And we went out and got a bunch of white boys and colored boys, had a black and tan orchestra. That's the first recording she made, with white boys and colored boys. And I went with them and helped them with Mamie Smith on her record, and helped her in her singing. And she started to making these records, and it was about three weeks before she called me and told me she wanted to see me. Perry was there, too, and she gave me my hundred and fifty dollars back. Yes, she paid me back. And that's the last I ever had to do with Mamie and Perry Bradford. That was my last dealing with them. But I was responsible for helping her get started.

Naturally I had to tell Mr. King I couldn't record for him. So he said, "Well, Morrison, do you know of a band out west—a good jazz band?" I said, "Yes, I know of someone; he and I studied together, practiced together; he's a white boy and his daddy's in the music department in a school out in Denver. He's a pretty good musician; his name is Paul Whiteman. His father, Wilberforce Whiteman, is in the school system out there." And Mr. King said, "Do you think that I could interest him in coming back here to make records for us?" "Well, you could give it a try." "By God, I'm gonna get on a train and go out there and see him." So he signed Paul Whiteman up and brought him back to New York and gave *him* one hundred thousand dollars. He told him, "Go and get the best there is; we've got to outsell Columbia." Columbia had Art Hickman, and Ted Lewis, and George Morrison. We were all selling jazz records like sixty. And so Paul Whiteman went to Chicago, got this trombone player, that musician, and arrangers, and all the good musicians from all over the country. So it was through me that he got his recording band together. And he knows it today, and he gives me that recognition. I was on television and made this same statement, and I couldn't make it unless it was true. Incidentally, Matty Malneck, his violinist, also graduated from high school right here in Denver. I introduced him to Paul Whiteman when he played here at Lakeside. Paul took him with him that very night. Now Matty lives in Hollywood. Stairway to the stars!

After my recording date, I stayed in New York about nine months, working at the Carlton Terrace. We got our job at the Carlton Terrace through a fellow by the name of Tim Brymn.[3] He was a very popular man, following in the footsteps of James Reese Europe, who had just died. (Unfortunately I never met Jim Europe.) Tim Brymn had a band, not an orchestra, a band called the 70 Black Devils Overseas. Now I had never been in the service, and I didn't know the Hundred and fiftieth Artillery from the Hundred and forty-ninth Infantry. But Carlton Terrace needed a band, so Brymn booked us in there. Aside from leading *his* band, Brymn acted as my booking agent.

Incidentally, when I was at the Carlton Terrace in 1920, I had to play violin solos every night. So one night I played *Tambourin Chinois* by Kreisler. About half an hour after I finished a man came up to me and said, "Young man, you are a very, very talented musician. You play beautifully. Would you accept my card?" I said, "Yes, sir." And when I looked it said, "Fritz Kreisler." I nearly dropped my violin, bow and everything! Perspiration popped out on me just like water down Niagara Falls! I'm telling you, I couldn't play any more that night. Had I known he was in there, I probably wouldn't have been able to play my solo. But he said, "I'd love for you to come see me." I said, "Mr. Kreisler, I'd be very happy to do so." He says, "By the way, do you happen to know Will Vodery?" I had met Will Vodery through W. C. Handy. Vodery was a marvelous musician and arranger. "Yes, I know Mr. Vodery." "Well, have Mr. Vodery bring you over to see me." So Will took me to see him and Mr. Kreisler gave me six lessons, free of charge. He gave me some help on my flying staccato in the Mendelssohn Concerto. He taught me how to get a beautiful, clean-cut pizzicato. He taught me so many valuable things in violin playing. He and I corresponded up until the time he got hurt, when a truck ran into him.

Years later I saw Mr. Kreisler again in Albuquerque, when he gave a concert out at the University of New Mexico. I was playing at the Franciscan Hotel. The manager there didn't believe me that I knew Mr. Kreisler. I told him, "We'll see." And they informed Mr. Kreisler that George Morrison was here to

3. Brymn was initially associated with James Europe and Harlem's first large musical organization, the Clef Club. Later, in 1918, like Europe, Brymn formed an overseas army band. It nearly rivaled Europe's Hellfighters Band in fame and had the distinction of playing for President Woodrow Wilson at the peace conference.

see him. He was getting a shave. I went in there and said, "Pardon me, Mr. Kreisler, I know that you're busy getting your tonsorial work done, but this is George Morrison, the one you gave lessons to in New York with Mr. Will Vodery." "Oh, yes, yes, my dear boy, yes, certainly, certainly. I'll see you, I'll see you when I come in to have dinner." He and his accompanist, Mr. Lamson, asked me to play for him. "My dear boy," he said, "what do you do in music?" I said, "Well, I have an orchestra and I'm playing dance work." "Oh, you're not doing solo work, classical work?" I said, "Well, I'm married and I have two children and I have to make a living." He says, "Well, I can understand that too, son. Well, I'd love to hear you play." I played "Nobody Knows the Trouble I've Seen." When I got through he said, "Why, you play as beautifully as ever." And in the paper the next night it said: "Mr. George Morrison, famous orchestra leader at the Franciscan Hotel, played for Mr. Fritz Kreisler last night, and one master bowed to another master." He asked me to come out to hear him play the Mendelssohn Concerto.

Speaking of Albuquerque reminds me that that's where I first met John Lewis.[4] You see while I lived there in Albuquerque we visited often with his family. Our neighbor who lived behind us was related to Mr. Lewis's family. That was when my daughter was about twelve, and John Lewis was just a little fella.

Speaking about my career here in Denver, I have trained a lot of outstanding musicians such as Andrew Kirk, who worked with me for many years until I encouraged him to go south and take over the T. Holder band. I already mentioned his wife, Mary Kirk. Another musician I trained was Jimmie Lunceford. I trained him right here in this house in rehearsals, when he first started playing engagements with me. And I encouraged him to go on to Tuskegee Institute to finish his musical education. I sent him some of my arrangements when he was organizing his band down there.

Do you know that I once had Jelly Roll Morton in my band? That was after I came back from New York. Of course, he didn't last long. He couldn't stay in one band too long because he was too eccentric and too temperamental, and he was a one-man band himself; he wanted to be everything. I couldn't do anything with him. I did everything to try to control that man, but I couldn't. He was just—he—he—I can't explain it to you, how he was. Oh, but he could stomp the blues out. When he got to pattin' that foot, playing the piano and a cigar in his mouth, man, he was gone—he was gone—he was gone! But I couldn't do nothin' with him. I couldn't keep him long.

Alphonse Trent was also my pianist at one time. He was a wonderful pianist, the best dance-band player that I ever had in my band. That was in '32, out at the Casa Mañana—*after* he had his own band. He had had a *terrific* band. And he was one of the nicest persons that I've ever worked with—so considerate. And you didn't need a bass when he got through pounding that bass line. He was a real orchestra man. He knew his business.

4. Of the Modern Jazz Quartet.

Another famous musician I got to know was Count Basie, who was playing with Bennie Moten's band out here at the Rainbow in Denver. That was in the early thirties. Bennie could not come along because he had to have a throat operation. Well, he went on the table, and sorry to say never recovered from the operation. The boys were here in Denver, Count Basie and Bennie's brother, Buster, who was in charge of the band.

A lot of those boys, like Eddie Durham and Eddie Barefield, got their inspiration from my band when I was on the Pantages circuit in Kansas City. Some of them were going to Lincoln High School, and they were so carried away with my band that they took up music. The inspiration they received was from George Morrison's orchestra.

I founded a place out here called Rockrest with another fellow by the name of Mulvihill, an Irishman. I put in a five-piece band out there, and later augmented it to eleven. We did a tremendous business during prohibition. I had a sign up there, "This place is heated by George Morrison's music"—'cause we never had a stove in it. We'd go all winter long. Between that moonshine and my music, we really kept that place hot. You could just see everybody running out after dancing; here was a bottle under this tire and here was one on top of the car, and here one lying under the hood. People never asked whose bottle it was, just as long as they found the bottle, they'd take a drink, come right back and start to dance—ten cents a dance. I made a lot of money.

Well, in those days we had the Ku Klux Klan out here. They used to meet up on old Table Mountain at Golden, Colorado. Every Tuesday night you'd see them in a line five miles long—cars one right behind the other going up to Table Mountain. One night we had the windows all open while we were playing and here comes a big tall rawboned guy and a little guy—they looked like Mutt and Jeff. They stood right there by that window where we were playing. Suddenly I hear the tall guy say to the little fella, "This is the first goddam place we gonna blow up." And I'm playing my fiddle and listening. The little guy asked, "Why?" "Because its run by a goddam nigger and a Catholic." I heard it! I said to myself, "Anytime a man joins that organization there's something wrong up in the head. And if he's fool enough to join that organization, he is just fool enough to come in here and set a bomb under this place. And I'm not worried about myself, but I don't want him to hurt my fiddle! I think it's moving day for me."

So I pulled out. That's when I went on the Pantages circuit. I got my band together, and Hattie McDaniel and I got our act all worked up, practicing about seven or eight hours a day, every day, and got it down pat. We opened up in Minneapolis, Minnesota, with Hattie McDaniel as the featured entertainer in my act. We were billed as George Morrison, the colored Paul Whiteman, and Hattie McDaniel, the female Bert Williams, because she looked like him. That was in 1924. We played mixed programs on the circuit, including some classics. We opened up with *Pagliacci*[5] behind the curtains—big introduction—then we'd

5. Morrison is referring to the famous aria *"Vesti la giubba"* from Leoncavallo's *I Pagliacci,* an aria very popular in vaudeville for decades.

quiet down, and after we'd finish *Pagliacci*—boom—we'd segue right into "By the Waters of Minnetonka."

On the circuit we played Minneapolis; Tacoma, Washington; Seattle, Portland, San Francisco, Los Angeles, Salt Lake City, Kansas City, and a lot of little towns. I'll never forget in Los Angeles where Mr. Pantages lived. One day he asked me to come and see him. He said, "You know, I've had many a violin player on my circuit, but I never had one do to me what you have done." I said (to myself), "*Now* what have I done?" "I wanted my daughter to be a violinist and I bought her a very fine instrument. She never cared for it, and the violin is sitting out in my home deteriorating. As beautiful as you play, I'm gonna give you that violin. You come with me." And he pressed a button and his chauffeur appeared. I got in that big Cadillac and rode out to his big fine home there in Los Angeles. The violin was up in the corner—strings broken, the hair broken on the bow. It was in deplorable condition. "Mr. Morrison, that violin cost me ten thousand dollars. I'm going to give you this instrument. I want you to keep it in memory of me. I've never heard anyone play so beautiful in my life as you." So Mr. Pantages gave me the violin and he sent me to his son-in-law in Salt Lake City, a Mr. Landau, a violin repairman. "He'll get that violin in shape for you." I've been offered ten thousand dollars three times for it, but I still have it. That's the one I play all the time. It's a Giovanni Paolo Maggini.[6] Philip Rubin, the violin connoisseur, has eaten many a meal in this house trying to get that fiddle.

In 1934 I won first prize on the violin at the Exposition of Chicago in a national audition. Eubie Blake had his band playing at this Exposition, and the great Sidney Bechet was playing with him then. The audition was for violinists, brass and reeds, and vocalists—all kinds of instrumentalists. I had to give concerts all the way to Chicago to help pay my expenses. When I arrived there, it was all week before they got to me, because—you know those Easterners, they think they're the the hottest people in the world; they think there's nothing out west and they just overlooked me. Every morning I'd go down thinking they were gonna give me my audition. I'd stay all day—no audition. At last on Friday they called me. I'd heard all the violin players play by then, so I wasn't worried after hearing them. I played the Seventh Concerto by Vieuxtemps. The wife of Judge George—the first Negro judge in Chicago—was one of the judges. So I got up there, my daughter accompanied me, and I played. When I got through they just applauded, applauded, and applauded. They wouldn't let me go, so I came back and played my *Lullaby* as an encore. They announced the winner! Mr. George Morrison. I was to get fifteen hundred dollars for being winner of the first prize of the violin division. I was so happy! I sent a telegram back home. I'm gonna get fifteen hundred dollars! So what little money I had, I started spending in Chicago. I was down to five dollars, expecting to get this check for fifteen hundred. But they said, "Mr. Morrison, we will mail you your check because our bookkeepers and auditors have to go through certain routines

6. A famous Italian seventeenth-century violin maker, whose instruments are valued almost as highly as Stradivari's and Guarneri's.

and it's impossible for us to pay you now." I says, "My Lord, I need my money; I got to get back to Denver. I've only got five dollars." And the man said, "Well, I'm sorry, but we can't issue any money to you now." And I had to borrow five dollars from A. Raymond Ward, a minister who used to be here in Denver, who was a big man in Chicago. That gave us ten dollars to get home on. And when I got to Denver, I think I had about fifty or seventy-five cents. Here I'm looking for this check to come in every week, and, Mr. Schuller, that check hasn't come in here yet! The check hasn't come in here yet and that was 1934! National Auditions, Incorporated. Those rascals wrote me a letter, saying "we are sorry to inform you we were forced to file bankruptcy" on account of something. And I ain't never got my money.

Speaking of Chicago and other Negro violinists, Eddie South and I went to school together at the Columbia Conservatory. We used to meet on the El. He was a trained musician, and one of the best in the popular field. "Angel of the Violin." Terrific in jazz.

I recommend to every pupil today to go and get all the Bach, all the Haydn, all of the technique that he possibly can get. Whatever you want to resort to then, *after* you get it, that is your business. And if you should resort to popular music, you're gonna be outstanding because you're gonna be able to do things from a technical standpoint that the others can't do. Why was Eddie South such a terrific violinist? Because he had technique. And then when he went over to jazz and playing popular music he could just turn it upside down. What would Heifetz do if Heifetz would turn to nothing but jazz? And Nathan Milstein and Yehudi Menuhin—if they would just devote their time and learn to master the swing of popular music like they did classical? With all the technique that they got, God only knows what they could do!

People that just come around copying from a record of some great jazz technique player, you are gonna find out when you keep listening to them, they have a style, they have a way of playing, but each number's gonna remind you of every other number they play. But when you have a schooled pianist, he's gonna be able to throw in so much technique in so many ways that he won't have to play his pieces the same way. What helped me so greatly in my popular music was the technique that I acquired on my fiddle. And right now, I haven't practiced in thirty-five years—I can't practice on account of my arthritis —but I pick up my fiddle and I go out there and play a dance tune and people are just amazed at me playing it.

Glossary

Note: In addition to the use of roman numerals for the various degrees of the scale, the following signs occur in the musical notations:

o = diminished chord
ø = half-diminished chord (reading upwards, two minor thirds and one major third)
+ = augmented chord
m = minor chord

All other chords not modified by one of the above signs are assumed to be major chords.

ACCELERANDO Speeding up in tempo.

ACOUSTICAL RECORDINGS The early method of recording by which instrumentalists and singers recorded into huge acoustical horns or megaphones. The method became outmoded in the mid-1920s with the advent of *Electrical recordings*.

ADDITIVE METER A concept of musical meter in which large units are built by adding together various groupings of the smallest rhythmic unit in a given context. Compare *Divisive meter*.

ALTERNATE-FINGERING An effect produced on valve or keyed instruments when alternate or "false" fingering is used to produce a note.

ANACRUSIS MEASURE, ANACRUSIS NOTES A term applied to the initial notes or (less commonly) measures beginning on an unaccented or weak beat. Identical with the term "upbeat."

ANTIPHONY A form of musical response, as of one choir answering another; a music characterized by the alternation of two or more different parts.

ARPEGGIO The production of the tones in a chord in rapid succession, i.e. not simultaneously.

ATONALITY Absence of tonality; a music characterized by a method of organization without reference to a key or tonal center, one using the tones of the chromatic scale impartially and autonomously. See *Chromaticism*.

BIMETRIC A term applied to the use of two different meters simultaneously. See *Polymetric*.

BINARY TIME A metric or rhythmic structure characterized by units of two, such as 2/4 or 2/8.

BITONALITY The simultaneous use of two different tonalities or keys.

BLOCK CHORDS Large, many-voiced chords, which usually move in parallel motion.

BLUE NOTE A microtonal variant, usually flatted from the pure intonation of the note. It is associated almost exclusively with the third, fifth, and seventh degrees of the scale. It is freely used in *Blues* and jazz.

BLUES A form of folk music developed by the Negro slaves in the United States during the nineteenth century. Blues were notated, harmonized, and published beginning in the second decade of the twentieth century. The typical blues text has a stanza of three lines, the second of which is a repetition of the first. It usually tells of moods of depression, natural disasters, or the loss of a loved one. As the blues became urbanized, the subject matter became broader, including eventually the evocation of happier moods. In a corollary development, the blues form crystallized into a specific chord and measure pattern. The most common form is the twelve-bar blues set in the following chord progression: I-IV-I-V-I. Eight-bar and sixteen-bar blues are also relatively common. Today blues can refer to a vocal blues song, or simply to the twelve-bar blues structure, the most basic musical form in jazz.

BOMBS Colloquial for strong, off-the-beat accents used by drummers; a device that became very common during the Bop and modern jazz eras, but was not unknown to drummers before that time.

BOOGIE-WOOGIE A "primitive" manner of playing the blues on the piano. It is characterized by a steady, repetitive *ostinato* figure in the left hand or bass.

BOOK The term used to describe the library of a band or combo.

BOP The name given to a period in jazz, and to the music characteristic of that period (*ca.* 1943-53). Also known as Be-bop or (less familiarly) Re-bop.

BREAK A short rhythmic-melodic *Cadenza* interpolated by an instrumentalist (or singer) between ensemble passages.

BRIDGE The name given to the third eight-bar section in a thirty-two-bar song form; i.e. the *B* part of an *A A B A* song form.

BROKEN TENTH The interval of the tenth or a chord spanning this interval played not simultaneously but in rapid succession. Left-hand patterns using a series of broken tenths to fill out a chord progression came into use in the 1920s. They may have been initiated originally by pianists whose hands were not large enough to reach a tenth on the keyboard.

CADENZA An extemporized section in a composition, particularly a concerto, providing a soloist with an opportunity to display his virtuosity.

CAKEWALK A dance developed in the late nineteenth century by American Negroes.

CALL-AND-RESPONSE PATTERN A musical form common to much jazz and African music in which a "call," usually by a solo singer or instrumentalist, is answered by a "response," usually by an ensemble or (in African music) the assembled participants in a ritual; a pattern found in religious ceremonies in which the congregation responds to the "call" of the preacher.

CANON A musical form or technique in which a second (or third, fourth, etc.) part imitates a first part or melodic line. Canonic imitation is frequently used in *Contrapuntal* works.

CANTE HONDO A traditional Andalusian gypsy song; literally "profound song" in Spanish.

CANTOR A singer; in religious music the singer of the "call" in a *Call-and-response* pattern.

CHACONNE Originally a Spanish and Central American dance; later a musical form characterized by a series of variations over a persistent and usually unvaried ground bass.

CHALUMEAU An obsolete forerunner of the clarinet; also, by inference, the lowest register of the clarinet.

CHANGES See *Chord changes.*

CHARLESTON A type of dance, extremely popular in the 1920s, characterized by the subdivision of the 4/4 meter into 3 + 3 + 2 eighth-notes; hence also this particular rhythm or variations thereof.

CHORD CHANGES Another term for a chord progression. In jazz, the term "changes" is commonly used alone, as in "the changes of a tune."

CHORD PROGRESSION A series of successive chords.

CHORUS A musical form in jazz delineating a chord structure or progression which in its totality forms the basis for an improvisation, such as a "blues chorus"; the term is also used by jazz musicians to denote an improvised solo. To play such a solo is to "take a chorus." Also the main body of a popular song, as distinct from the prefatory *Verse*.

CHROMATICISM The use of chromatic intervals and of chords altered by chromatic means. The term "chromatic" in music refers to tones foreign to a given key and to the free utilization of altered notes and the half-steps of the chromatic (12-tone) scale.

CODA A distinct and clearly demarcated closing section, from the Italian word for "tail."

COMPING An abbreviated term synonymous with "accompanying." It is most frequently applied to the harmonic backgrounds of piano or guitar.

CONTRAPUNTAL See *Counterpoint*.

COON SONG A song associated with "coons," a colloquial, somewhat derogatory, and now obsolete term for Negroes. Coon songs developed in the days of minstrel shows through the latter part of the nineteenth century, and survived into the early days of recording. Stylistically they were a vocal relative of piano ragtime.

COUNTERMELODY A secondary melody accompanying a primary voice or musical idea.

COUNTERPOINT Music in several independent yet related parts. See *Polyphony*.

CROSS-ACCENTS See *Cross-rhythms*.

CROSS-RHYTHMS The use of two or more rhythmic patterns in such a manner as to produce counterrhythms or non-simultaneous accentuation; the placing of stressed notes or accents against one another.

CUTTING CONTEST A term for *Jam sessions* or dances at which various bands or—less commonly—individual players try to "cut" each other, i.e. battle for first place.

DEMOCRATIZATION OF RHYTHM The rhythmic and dynamic equalization of the smallest units within a rhythmic pattern or phrase.

DESCANT LINE The term "descant" has had many meanings through the centuries. Here it is used in the sense of an improvised line played in a higher register than the other instruments are playing.

DIATONIC Pertaining to the standard major and minor scales and to the tonality derived from these scales.

DICTY Slang for "elegant," "high-class."

DIODY, DIODIC A term applied to music or a composition in which a melody or top-line is accompanied by a second melody or line in consonant intervals; a two-voiced harmony, as differentiated from *Polyphony*.

DISJUNCT CHORUSES Two separate or disconnected choruses.

DIVISIVE METER A concept of musical meter in which larger units are broken up into small ones, as a 4/4 measure divided into sixteen sixteenths. Compare *Additive meter*.

DOMINANT The fifth degree of the diatonic scale; the triad on the fifth degree.

DOUBLE-STOPS Two notes played simultaneously on one stringed instrument. (The strings are "stopped" by the fingers.)

DOUBLE TIME A term applied to doubling a tempo so that it becomes twice as fast as the original. In a 4/4 meter, the playing of eight eighth-notes as if they constituted two bars of twice-as-fast quarter notes is an example of double time.

ELECTRICAL RECORDINGS A method of recording involving the use of microphones. The sounds are transformed into electrical impulses, amplified, and cut into a grooved pattern on a round disc of wax, acetate, or metal. Compare *Acoustical recordings*.

EMBELLISHMENT Ornamentation.

EMBOUCHURE Originally French, but widely used in English; signifies the shaping and holding of the lips against the mouthpiece in order to produce a musical tone on a wind instrument.

ENHARMONIC An adjective referring to two different notations for the same tone, as, for example, *f* sharp and *g* flat; therefore, the interchangeable spelling of the same note.

EXTENDED FORM IMPROVISATION A loosely defined term denoting an improvisation in which a chord structure involving a minimal harmonic change (i.e. a single chord or two chords) is "extended," or elongated, at will by the improviser.

FERMATA A pause or holding of a note (or chord).

FIELD HOLLER An early primitive forerunner of the *Blues;* a holler or shout used by the Negro slaves as they worked in the fields on the plantations. The field holler was sometimes a secret means of communication among slaves.

FLAG-WAVER A term used to denote a fast, climactic band arrangement or composition. Every well-known band has "flag-wavers," often used in competitions with other bands.

FLAMENCO A style of Andalusian gypsy singing and/or dancing.

FLATTED FIFTH The flat variant of the fifth degree; the interval formed by the lowered fifth degree and the tonic. In the key of C, *g* flat is the flatted fifth (see *Tritone*).

FLUFF A mistake or missed note.

FOURS A term applied to the alternating or trading of four-bar improvisations between instruments or sections.

GEBRAUCHSMUSIK A German term attributed to the composer Paul Hindemith (1895-1963), implying a utilitarian music, more accessible to amateurs and non-professionals. *Gebrauch* means consistent use.

GHOST NOTES Notes more implied than actually played. They are used consistently in jazz on all instruments, but particularly wind instruments, and are most often associated with subsidiary or passing notes.

GIG A job; a professional engagement.

GLISSANDO A sliding effect between two notes, usually with the implication that the entire distance is covered in an ascending or descending slide, as on a trombone or violin.

GROWL A raspy, rough effect used on wind instruments, particularly the brass. It is often used in conjunction with the plunger mute.

GUTBUCKET An earthy or low-down manner of playing.

HEAD ARRANGEMENTS Arrangements improvised or worked out collectively by an entire band or group; usually not written down, but memorized "in the head." Compare *Stock Arrangements.*

HETEROMETRIC A musical structure characterized by total metric and rhythmic independence of the individual parts.

HETEROPHONY A term denoting an even greater harmonic and rhythmic independence of individual parts than in *Polyphony*.

HI-HAT CYMBAL An essential part of a jazz drummer's equipment: two small cymbals that can be struck together by operating a foot pedal.

HOMOPHONY, HOMOPHONIC Music in which a primary melodic line is accompanied by subsidiary harmony parts; the opposite of *Polyphony*. Generally applied to chordal writing in music.

HORIZONTAL RELATIONSHIPS The melodic, or linear, aspects of a musical structure as differentiated from the harmonic, or chordal. Relationships notated and read horizontally, i.e. across the page from left to right, in musical notation. See *Vertical relationships*.

"HORN" In jazz parlance any wind or blown instrument.

HOUSE HOP Synonymous with *Rent party,* the expression developed from the expression "the houses really hopped" at these parties. A later 1930s version was "the joint really jumped."

IMPROVISATION A manner of playing extemporaneously, i.e. without benefit of written music. Improvisation, if it is not absolutely essential to jazz, is considered to be the heart and soul of jazz by most jazz musicians and authorities. It is equatable with composing on the spur of the moment.

INFLECTION In jazz, inflection connotes the entire gamut of individual phrasing idiosyncrasies developed by jazz artists, such as accenting, attacking, holding, bending, flattening of notes, and the manifold combinations thereof. The inflections peculiar to jazz are an essential requisite of *Swing*.

JAM SESSION An informal gathering of musicians, playing on their own time and improvising, often exhaustively, on one or two numbers. Jam sessions began as a spontaneous after-hours diversion for jazz musicians who felt musically constrained during professional engagements. In the late thirties pseudo-jam sessions were organized by entrepreneurs who engaged musicians specifically to "jam." In the 1950s and '60s, jam sessions became a rarity.

JIVE A slang expression denoting glib or foolish talk; the jargon of jazz musicians (now slightly obsolete).

JUNGLE MUSIC A term applied to certain pieces (and a style derived therefrom) by the Duke Ellington band in the late 1920s; named after the jungle-like sounds and imitations particularly of the brass instruments.

KEY CENTER See *Tonic*.

LEAD MAN The top or leading voice in a section, most frequently applied to the first trumpet in a band.

LEADING TONE A note that leads toward another, most commonly the raised seventh degree of the scale.

LICK A short phrase or passage; often with the connotation of a commonly used phrase or a cliché.

MELISMATIC An adjective referring to florid melodic ornamentation.

MELOS A term used to designate the ascending or descending movement of tones, particularly in the ancient Greek modes. Richard Wagner (1813-83) used the term as synonymous with "melody" and, by extension, to designate the musical and intervallic characteristics generated by melody.

METRIC MODULATION A modulation by which a time unit in one tempo is used as a link to a succeeding different tempo. In the metric modulation ♪ = $\overline{♪}^{3}$, if the first tempo is ♩ = 90, the new tempo will be ♩ = 60. (An ♪ in the first tempo equals 180; if an $\overline{♪}^{3}$ = 180, the corresponding quarter note equals 60.)

MICROTONE, MICROTONAL An interval smaller than a half-tone, for example, a quarter-tone or a sixth-tone.

MINSTREL SHOWS A form of entertainment developed in the nineteenth century by Negro entertainers; a forerunner of vaudeville.

MODULATION The process of changing from one key or tonality to another.

MONODY, MONODIC A term applied to music or a composition with but a single voice (or instrumental) part.

NOODLING An expression common among musicians denoting the playing of isolated fast passages or runs, usually done in private practice or during a pause in a rehearsal.

OBBLIGATO An accompanimental or semi-independent melody; an embellishment of a melody.

ORGANUM A voice or instrumental part accompanying a melody or primary line in parallel motion. (See also *Diody*.)

OUT-CHORUS A final chorus; in a band, usually a climactic full-ensemble chorus.

PANTONAL A term, sometimes considered synonymous with "atonal," denoting music in which no single tonality can be inferred.

PASSACAGLIA A dance form similar to the *Chaconne*.

PASSING TONE A non-harmonic note (or notes) between two harmonic notes of successive chords.

PEDAL POINT A sustained note held, usually in the bass, under a series of moving chords or melodic lines.

PEDAL-POINT BREAK A *Break* executed over a harmonic *Pedal point*.

PENTATONIC Consisting of five notes; a five-note scale.

PITCH The identification of a musical tone as determined by the frequency of vibrations of the sound waves. In Western notation pitches are given a letter name from the alphabet and are represented by a particular degree in the musical staff. Pitch is a more precise term for note or musical tone.

PIZZICATO Italian for "plucked," primarily used in connection with string instruments.

PLUNGER A common rubber toilet plunger used as a muting device by trumpet and trombone players.

POLYMETRIC Applied to the use of three or more meters simultaneously.

POLYPHONY A term, from the Greek "many-voiced," denoting a musical structure characterized by the independence of its parts. "Polyphony" can be applied to the simultaneous use of several melodies or contrapuntal lines.

POLYRHYTHM The use of three or more rhythms simultaneously in different parts.

POP TUNES Popular tunes.

QUADRILLE A dance, originally designed for four couples, extremely popular in France and New Orleans during the nineteenth century. The quadrille was set in a 6/8 or 2/4 meter.

QUICK STEP A spirited, lively step or dance, especially one in a quick march tempo.

RACE RECORDINGS A term applied in the 1920s to the recordings made specifically for the Negro market.

RAGTIME A music characterized by syncopated melody over a regularly accented rhythmic accompaniment. In its strictest sense ragtime refers to a music style developed on the piano in the late nineteenth century.

RENT PARTY A term applied to informal parties given in the 1920s and early '30s among the Negro population, at which musicians, primarily pianists, were invited to play. Guests normally paid a small admission or a charge for drinks and food which went toward paying the rent of the hosts. Popular among musicians because for them food and drinks were free.

RIDE CYMBAL A suspended cymbal used since the 1930s to delineate the main "time" patterns of jazz drummers.

RIFF See explanation Chapter 1, pp. 28-30.

RING-SHOUT A song-dance in which dancers move counter-clockwise in a ring, singing in a leader-chorus, i.e. *Call-and-response,* form.

RIP A rapid upward figure on brass instruments, usually produced by tightening the embouchure without using correct fingerings, i.e. playing basically on the harmonic overtone series.

RITARDANDO Slowing up in the tempo.

RONDO An instrumental form alternating two contrasting subjects; in its simplest form: *A B A B A Coda.*

ROOT NOTE The fundamental note upon which a chord is built; often the lowest note of a chord in its primary position.

RUBATO Free in tempo.

SAMBA A Brazilian dance of African origin with a rhythm similar to that of the *Charleston.*

SCAT-SINGING A manner of singing employing nonsense syllables.

SERIAL MUSIC A term applied to a style or school of composition in which pitch organization is based on arranging the twelve notes of the chromatic scale into a particular series or succession, known also as a tone-row or set. This method of composition was first generally applied by Arnold Schoenberg (1874-1951) in the 1920s. In the 1950s the term became associated with an extension of Schoenberg's technique in which other musical elements, such as dynamics, timbre, and rhythm, are also subject to serial procedures, or serialization.

SHAKE An instrumental effect sounding like a trill, but usually encompassing a wider intervallic range. It is produced by literally "shaking" the mouthpiece against the lips in a lateral motion. Generally speaking, valves are not used; the shake therefore uses the tones of the brass instruments' harmonic series.

SHOUT A style of singing the blues in a forceful, "shouting" manner. The term was also applied to instrumentalists who played in a similar manner, such as the "shout pianists" James P. Johnson and Fats Waller.

SIDEMAN A player in a jazz or dance band, as differentiated from the leader.

SPIRITUAL A form of vocal music developed by the Negro slaves in the United States during the nineteenth century. Although originally a quasi-religious folk music, spirituals were notated, harmonized, and published beginning in the early decades of the twentieth century.

STANDARD TUNES, STANDARDS Familiar, well-established popular songs or instrumental compositions, used by jazz musicians as a basis for improvisation.

STOCK ARRANGEMENT A published commercial arrangement, usually simplified and standardized; the term is derived from arrangements that are in stock as opposed to especially written arrangements. Compare *Head Arrangements*.

STOMP A term synonymous with "blues"; it has an extra connotation of a heavy or strongly marked beat.

STOP-TIME A type of discontinuous rhythm used to accompany tap dancers and, by extension, instrumentalists and singers; a typical example of stop-time in jazz is the playing of only the first beat in every two bars.

SUBDOMINANT The fourth degree of the diatonic scale; the triad on the fourth degree.

SWING 1. A rhythmic element and a manner of playing (inflecting) rhythms peculiar to jazz (see Chapter 1, pp. 6-8).

2. A period in the development of jazz (1935-1945) characterized by the emergence and national popularity of "swing" bands; the Swing Era.

SYNCOPATION A temporary shifting or displacement of a regular metrical accent; the emphasis on a weak or unaccented note so as to displace the regular meter.

TAG-ENDING A colloquial expression used by musicians to indicate an added, or "tagged-on," ending to a composition or performance.

TERMINAL VIBRATO A vibrato used at the end of a held tone.

TERNARY TIME A metric or rhythmic structure characterized by units of three, such as 3/4 or 3/8.

TETRACHORD A series of four tones, usually associated with the *Diatonic* scale and whose outer range consists of the interval of the perfect fourth.

THIRD STREAM A term applied in its widest sense to a music or style which combines the essential characteristics and techniques of both jazz and "classical" music.

TIMBRE The tone quality that differentiates one instrument from another; the acoustical properties of an instrument defining its "tone color" (German: *Klangfarbe*).

T.O.B.A. Abbreviation for Theatre Owners Booking Association, an organization that booked Negro attractions, including jazz bands and groups.

TONAL CENTER Identical with *Tonic*.

TONIC The first degree of the scale; the triad on the first degree, and in tonality the key identified with it.

TRIO In marches, scherzos, and minuets, the contrasting central section.

TRITONE The interval of the augmented fourth. In the tempered tuning of the piano, it is identical as well to the flatted fifth.

TRUMPET–PIANO STYLE A style of piano playing associated initially with Earl Hines, imitative of the more melodic (i.e. non-chordal) style of trumpeter Louis Armstrong.

TURNBACK A jazz musicians' term for that part of an improvised chorus during which the chord progression returns to the initial chord of the piece or the tonic. A turnback usually occurs at the last two bars of an eight- or twelve-bar structure. Most jazz musicians have a number of "improvised" turnback phrases at their command for various turnback chord progressions that are standard in jazz tunes.

UNISON Two or more instruments or voices sounding on one pitch; the interval of a perfect prime.

VAMP An accompanimental or transitional chord progression of an indefinite duration, used as a filler until a soloist is ready to start or continue.

VERSE The introductory section of a popular song or ballad, as distinguished from the *Chorus*. The latter consists most commonly of thirty-two bars while the verse may have an irregular number of bars and may be sung or played in a free tempo.

VERTICAL RELATIONSHIPS The harmonic, or chordal, aspects of a musical structure as differentiated from the melodic, or linear. Relationships notated and read vertically, i.e. up and down the page, in musical notation. Also, the rhythmic aspects of a musical structure. For example, a rhythmic simultaneity, i.e. a chord, will appear vertically aligned in musical notation, whereas non-simultaneous rhythmic elements will appear vertically unaligned. (See *Horizontal relationships.*)

VIBRATO The artificial wavering of a note, consisting of slight, rapidly recurring fluctuations of pitch.

VOICE-LEADING A term referring to the manner in which the various voices in a harmonic progression are placed by the arranger or composer or, in a *Head arrangement,* by the individual players. The term is commonly used in all music.

VOICING The particular placing of the voices (notes) of a chord. See also *Voice-leading.*

WALKING BASS A term applied to a pizzicato (plucked) bass line that moves in a steady quarter-note rhythm and in scalar or intervallic patterns not limited to the chord tones; i.e. including *Passing tones.*

"WEAK" NOTES Rhythmically unstressed notes.

A Selected Discography

The following listing includes those longplaying recordings that are considered essential listening in connection with the present volume. A majority of the records listed are available at the time of writing (October 1967). However, record companies frequently drop recordings—particularly reissues—from their catalogues, and there can be no guarantee that records listed here will be available several years hence. Many of the listings—marked with an asterisk—are even now out of print, but are considered worth searching for. As this book goes to press the state of the entire Riverside catalogue remains undecided. Interested readers are referred to specialty jazz record shops.

Unfortunately many of the recordings discussed in this book are not available at all in longplaying reissues, and indeed many of them may never become available in this form. For such records the only source is a number of record collectors scattered around the country who sell "collector's items" for from three to fifty dollars a record. Insofar as such rare 78 rpm recordings have not been reissued on LP, they do not appear on the following list. Since only record titles were used in the text, the interested reader is referred to any of the standard discographies, of which Charles Delaunay's *New Hot Discography* is the most famous.

Records marked * are now out of print.
Records marked † are particularly recommended by the author.

Chapter 1 The Origins

†*African Drums,* Folkways FE 4502
African Music Recorded by Laura C. Boulton, Folkways 8852
†*Anthologie de la Vie Africaine,* Ducretet-Thomson 320C 126-128

Been Here and Gone, Folkways FA 2659
†*The Blues Roll On,* Atlantic 1352
The Birth of Big Band Jazz, Riverside RLP 12-129
Denis-Roosevelt Expedition to the Belgian Congo, General Album G10
The Golden Age of Ragtime, Riverside RLP 12-110
Music from the South, Vol. 1-10, Folkways FP 650-659
Negro Church Music, Atlantic LP 1351
Sounds of the South, Atlantic LP 1346
Note: The Stan Getz excerpt from *Early Autumn* can be heard on *The Three Herds,* Columbia CL-683. The excerpt from *Toby* can be heard on *Count Basie in Kansas City: Bennie Moten's Great Band of 1930-1932,* RCA Victor LPV 514.

Chapter 2 The Beginnings

LOUIS ARMSTRONG:
†*Louis Armstrong: 1923,* Riverside RLP 12-122
†*Young Louis Armstrong,* Riverside RLP 12-101
Sidney Bechet Memorial, Fontana 682 055 TL
†*This Is Bunk Johnson Talking,* American Music 643
King Oliver, Epic LN 3208
ANTHOLOGIES:
†*History of Classic Jazz,* Vol. 4, Riverside SDP 11
†*Jazz,* Vol. 3, Folkways FJ 2803
†*Jazz,* Vol. 11, Folkways FJ 2811
†*Jazz Odyssey,* Vol. 1: The Sound of New Orleans, Columbia C3L 30, Disc 3
†*Jazz Odyssey,* Vol. 2: The Sound of Chicago, Columbia C3L 32, Disc 1, Side 1
New Orleans Horns, London AL 3557
New Orleans Jazz: The Twenties, RBF RF 203 (2 vol.)

Chapter 3 The First Great Soloist

LOUIS ARMSTRONG:
†*Louis Armstrong: 1923,* Riverside RLP 12-122
†*Young Louis Armstrong,* Riverside RLP 12-101
†*The Louis Armstrong Story,* Vol. 1-4, Columbia CL 851-854
Sidney Bechet Memorial, Fontana 682 055 TL
The Perry Bradford Story, PB 101
FLETCHER HENDERSON:
The Birth of Big Band Jazz, Riverside RLP 12-129
†*Fletcher Henderson,* Riverside RLP 1055
†*A Study in Frustration: The Fletcher Henderson Story,* Columbia C4L 19
Jazz Odyssey, Vol. 2: The Sound of Chicago, Columbia C3L 32, Disc 1, Side 1

Chapter 4 The First Great Composer

JELLY ROLL MORTON:

The Incomparable Jelly Roll Morton, Riverside RLP 12-128

†*Jelly Roll Morton and His Red Hot Peppers,* EMI Records, DLP 1071‡

Jelly Roll Morton: Hot Jazz, Pop Jazz, Hokum and Hilarity, RCA Victor LPV 524

Jelly Roll Morton: Stomps and Joys, RCA Victor LPV 508

The King of New Orleans Jazz, Jelly Roll Morton, RCA Victor LPM 1649‡

†*Jelly Roll Morton Classic Piano Solos,* Riverside RLP 12-111

†*Jelly Roll Morton, The Library of Congress Recordings,* Vol. 1-12, Riverside RLP 1001-1012

N.O.R.K., New Orleans Rhythm Kings with Jelly Roll Morton, Riverside RLP 12-102

‡Note: There is considerable duplication between these two records. While the RCA Victor reissue contains titles not on the British EMI reissue, the quality of the latter is far superior to the American reissue, and worth the extra effort in finding it.

ANTHOLOGIES:

The Golden Age of Ragtime, Riverside RLP 12-110

†*History of Classic Jazz,* Vol. 2, Riverside SDP 11

†*Jazz,* Vol. 3, Folkways FJ 2803 (includes Morton's *Mournful Serenade*).

†*Jazz,* Vol. 11, Folkways FJ 2811

Chapter 5 Virtuoso Performers of the Twenties

Sidney Bechet Memorial, Fontana 682 055 TL

BIX BEIDERBECKE:

Bix Beiderbecke and the Wolverines, Riverside RLP 12-123

†*The Bix Beiderbecke Story,* Vol. 1-3, Columbia CL 844-846

The Perry Bradford Story, PB 101

JOHNNY DODDS:

The Immortal Johnny Dodds, Milestone 2002

Johnny Dodds and Kid Ory, Epic LA 16004

Johnny Dodds, New Orleans Clarinet, Riverside RLP 12-104

JAMES P. JOHNSON

James P. Johnson: Rare Solos, Riverside RLP 12-105

Yamekraw, Folkways FJ 2842

MA RAINEY:

The Immortal Ma Rainey, Milestone 2001

Ma Rainey: Classic Blues, Riverside RLP 12-108

†*Young Louis Armstrong,* Riverside RLP 12-101

†*The Bessie Smith Story,* Vol. 1-4, Columbia CL 855-858
†*Jabbo Smith,* Vol. 1-2, Melodeon MLP 7326, 7327

FATS WALLER:
Young Fats Waller, Riverside RLP 12-103
Fats Waller, Fractious Fingering, RCA Victor LPV 537

DIXIELAND AND WHITE JAZZ GROUPS:
**The Original Dixieland Jass* (sic) *Band,* RCA Victor "X" LX 3007
The Original Dixieland Jazz Band, Riverside RLP 156/157
N. O. R. K., New Orleans Rhythm Kings, Riverside RLP 12-102
**Chicago Style Jazz,* Columbia CL 632

BIG BANDS:
A Study in Frustration: The Fletcher Henderson Story, Columbia C4L 19
**Charlie Johnson's Paradise Band,* RCA Victor "X" LVA 3026

ANTHOLOGIES:
†*A History of Jazz: The New York Scene,* RBF RF 3 (includes interesting tracks by the ODJB, Jim Europe, Louisiana Sugar Babes, The Missourians, Mamie Smith, Charlie Johnson, etc.)
†*History of Classic Jazz,* Vol. 3, 4, 6-9, Riverside SDP 11
†*Jazz,* Vol. 2, Folkways FJ 2802
†*Jazz,* Vol. 11, Folkways FJ 2811
†*Jazz Odyssey,* Vol. 1: The Sound of New Orleans, Columbia C3L 30, Discs 1, 2
†*Jazz Odyssey,* Vol. 3: The Sound of Harlem, Columbia C3L 33, Discs 1, 2
**New Orleans Styles,* RCA Victor, "X" LVA 3029
Thesaurus of Classic Jazz, Vol. 1-4, Columbia C4L 18

Chapter 6 The Big Bands

FLETCHER HENDERSON:
**Fletcher Henderson,* Riverside RLP 1055
†*A Study in Frustration: The Fletcher Henderson Story,* Columbia C4L 19
*†*Fletcher Henderson Memorial Album,* Decca DL 6025

BENNIE MOTEN:
Bennie Moten's Kansas City Orchestra, 1923-1924, Historical Recordings, Vol. 9
**Bennie Moten's Kansas City Jazz,* 3 vol., RCA Victor "X" LVA 3004, 3005, 3038
†*Count Basie in Kansas City: Bennie Moten's Great Band of 1930-1932,* RCA Victor LPV 514

DON REDMAN:
McKinney's Cotton Pickers, RCA Victor LPT 24
Don Redman—Master of the Big Band (McKinney's Cotton Pickers), RCA Victor LPV 520

OTHER BANDS:

The Bix Beiderbecke Story, Vol. 3: The Whiteman Days, Columbia CL 846

**Charlie Johnson's Paradise Band*, RCA Victor "X" LVA 3026

The Missourians, French RCA Victor 430.385s

ANTHOLOGIES:

The Birth of Big Band Jazz, Riverside RLP 12-129

†*A History of Jazz: The New York Scene*, RBF RF 3 (includes Jim Europe example)

Jazz, Vol. 8, Folkways FJ 2808 (includes Henderson, Moten, Ellington, McKinney's Cotton Pickers, Luis Russell, Chocolate Dandies)

†*Jazz Odyssey*, Vol 2: The Sound of Chicago, Columbia C3L 32, Disc 3, Side 1

New Orleans Jazz: The Twenties, RBF RF 203 (2 vol.)

The Original Sound of the Twenties, Columbia C3L 35, Discs 1, 2

Rare Bands of the Twenties, Historical Records No. 3 (includes *Nightmare* by Alphonse Trent)

Chapter 7 The Ellington Style: Its Origins and Early Development

The Birth of Big Band Jazz, Riverside RLP 12-129

**The Duke—1926*, London AL 3551

†*Duke Ellington: The Beginning*, Vol. 1: 1926-1928, Decca 9224

**Early Ellington*, Brunswick LP 54007

†*The Ellington Era: 1927-1940*, Vol. 1, Columbia C3L 27; Vol. 2, Columbia C3L 39

Index